FAULT LINES

The Environment in History: International Perspectives

Series Editors: Dolly Jørgensen, *University of Stavanger*; Christof Mauch, *LMU Munich*; Kieko Matteson, *University of Hawai'i at Mānoa* Helmuth Trischler, *Deutsches Museum, Munich*

Volume 1
Civilizing Nature: National Parks in Global Historical Perspective
Edited by Bernhard Gissibl, Sabine Höhler, and Patrick Kupper

Volume 2
Powerless Science? Science and Politics in a Toxic World
Edited by Soraya Boudia and Natalie Jas

Volume 3
Managing the Unknown: Essays on Environmental Ignorance
Edited by Frank Uekötter and Uwe Lübken

Volume 4
Creating Wildnerness: A Transnational History of the Swiss National Park
Patrick Kupper
Translated by Giselle Weiss

Volume 5
Rivers, Memory, and Nation-Building: A History of the Volga and Mississippi Rivers
Dorothy Zeisler-Vralsted

Volume 6
Fault Lines: Earthquakes and Urbanism in Modern Italy
Giacomo Parrinello

Fault Lines
Earthquakes and Urbanism in Modern Italy

Giacomo Parrinello

First published in 2015 by
Berghahn Books
www.berghahnbooks.com

©2015, 2020 Giacomo Parrinello
First paperback edition published in 2020

All rights reserved. Except for the quotation of short passages
for the purposes of criticism and review, no part of this book
may be reproduced in any form or by any means, electronic or
mechanical, including photocopying, recording, or any information
storage and retrieval system now known or to be invented,
without written permission of the publisher.

Library of Congress Cataloging-in-Publication Data

Parrinello, Giacomo.
 Fault lines : earthquakes and urbanism in modern Italy / Giacomo Parrinello.
  pages cm. — (The environment in history : international perspectives ; volume 6)
 Includes bibliographical references and index.
 ISBN 978-1-78238-950-7 (hardback : alk. paper) — ISBN 978-1-78238-951-4 (ebook)
 1. Earthquake resistant design—Italy—Messina. 2. Earthquake resistant design—Italy—Belice River Valley. 3. Earthquake engineering—Italy—Messina. 4. Earthquake engineering—Italy—Belice River Valley. 5. Messina (Italy)—Buildings, structures, etc. 6. Earthquakes—Italy—Messina—History—20th century. 7. Earthquakes—Italy—Belice River Valley—History—20th century. 8. City planning—Italy—Messina. 9. City planning—Italy. I. Title. II. Title: Earthquakes and urbanism in modern Italy.
 TA658.44.P37 2015
 693.8'5209458111—dc23

2015003134

British Library Cataloguing in Publication Data

A catalogue record for this book is available from the British Library

Printed on acid-free paper

ISBN: 978–1–78238–950–7 hardback
ISBN: 978–1–78920–809–2 paperback
ISBN: 978–1–78238–951–4 ebook

To Lilla and Pippo, for all their love

Contents

List of Illustrations ix

Acknowledgments xi

Sites of Disaster Map xiv

Introduction. Can Earthquakes Speak? 1
    The Voice of the Earthquake 2
    A Tale of Two Earthquakes 6
    The Structure of This Book 10

PART I. THE 1908 MESSINA EARTHQUAKE

Chapter 1. The 1908 Messina Earthquake 21
    Earthquake, Tsunami, and Fire 22
    Earthquake Science 30
    Earthquake-Proof Urbanism 36

Chapter 2. Urban Reform 1880–1908 48
    Sanitizing the City 49
    A New Geography of Urban Water 57
    Engineering the City's Environment 65
    To Live Happily and Forget the Quake 70

Chapter 3. The Modern City 1909–1943 84
    The Provisional City (and Its Permanent Consequences) 85
    The Master Plan 91
    The City Developers versus the Hut Dwellers 98
    The New City and Its Darker Sides 104

PART II. THE 1968 BELICE VALLEY EARTHQUAKE

Chapter 4. The 1968 Belice Valley Earthquake 121
    "Like an Atomic Wasteland" 122
    The Disaster of Poverty 128
    Road Maps to Development 133

Chapter 5. Rural Modernity 1933–1967   150
    Reclamation and Redemption   151
    Development Plans   156
    Grassroots Countermeasures   161
    The Many Virtues of Water   166

Chapter 6. Urbanized Countryside 1968–1993   181
    Tents, Barracks, and Committees   182
    The City-Territory   186
    New Towns and Ghost Factories   191
    Rural Urbanism   197

Conclusion. Fault Lines   213
    Tales of Earthquake Urbanism   214
    Fault Lines in a Seismic Country   218
    Hazards, Urbanization, and Nature   222

Bibliography   231

Index   251

Illustrations

FIGURES

Figure 1.1. Refugees waiting to leave Messina, January 1909. Courtesy of the Naval History and Heritage Command.   26

Figure 1.2. Messina in ruins, January 1909. Courtesy of the Naval History and Heritage Command.   28

Figure 1.3. Soil composition in Messina and the distribution of damages as recorded by Mario Baratta. Cartography by Mary Lee Eggart.   33

Figure 2.1. Port of Messina before the earthquake. Courtesy of the University of Michigan Library.   49

Figure 2.2. Messina, second half of the nineteenth century. Courtesy of GBM Edizioni.   51

Figure 2.3. Messina and the planned water intakes for the new aqueduct. Cartography by Mary Lee Eggart.   61

Figure 2.4. Garibaldi Street, Messina, before the earthquake. Courtesy of the University of Michigan Library.   70

Figure 3.1. Extent of destruction. Light grey identifies completely destroyed buildings. Courtesy of Giorgio Stagni.   86

Figure 3.2. A poor woman's attempt to shelter her family in Messina. Courtesy of the Library of Congress, image LC-USZ62-73448.   87

Figure 3.3. Huts in the Mosella encampment, 1912. Courtesy of Bibliothèque Nationale de France.   90

Figure 3.4. Master plan by Luigi Borzì with sewage pipes. Courtesy of Biblioteca Regionale di Messina.   95

Figure 3.5. The state of reconstruction efforts in 1918. Courtesy of Guido Stagni.   101

Figure 3.6. Population in Messina 1861–1931   103

Figure 4.1. Aerial view of Gibellina, January 1968. Courtesy of
Leonardo Mistretta.   124

Figure 4.2. Ruins of Gibellina, January 1968. Courtesy of Leonardo
Mistretta.   126

Figure 4.3. Tent encampment in Santa Ninfa, January 1968. Courtesy
of Leonardo Mistretta.   127

Figure 5.1. Boundaries of the Belice Reclamation District and of
the Local Development Committee organization. Cartography
by Mary Lee Eggart.   169

Figure 5.2. The March for Western Sicily. Picture by Toni Nicolini.
Courtesy of CRAF (Centro di Ricerca e Archiviazione della
Fotografia).   171

Figure 6.1. Baraccamento Gibellina Rampinzeri, 1968. Courtesy
of Dipartimento della Protezione Civile.   184

Figure 6.2. Baraccamento Poggioreale, 1968. Courtesy of
Dipartimento della Protezione Civile.   185

Figure 6.3. Partially or entirely relocated towns. Cartography by
Mary Lee Eggart.   192

Figure 6.4. The Garcia Dam and irrigated lots in a project from 1974.
Cartography by Mary Lee Eggart.   200

Figure 6.5. The construction of the Cretto by Alberto Burri, 1987.
Copyright Osvaldo Amari, used with permission.   203

TABLES

Table 2.1. Overview of Planned Waterworks, 1861–1900   59

Acknowledgments

This book began with an email exchange. Many more emails, conversations, and encounters have followed that first one, in many different countries. All of these exchanges have made me a different person, and I am grateful for that. Discussions with Mariuccia Salvati and Paolo Capuzzo at the Università di Bologna stimulated my curiosity about the earthquakes, from which it all started. The Università di Siena gave me access to a stimulating academic community, and time and money to conduct research in Italy and abroad. Simone Neri Serneri at the Università di Siena and Michèle Dagenais at the Université de Montréal have never ceased to be generous with thoughtful comments and insights, and have supported this project and myself enthusiastically in too many ways to synthesize in one sentence. Colleagues in Siena and Montreal have been untiring partners in many discussions, companions at gourmet dinners, and accomplices for outdoor thermal baths. All of this interaction has made its way into this book.

Fault Lines is the synthesis of a research effort that spans many years. I have had the privilege of presenting pieces of this research in several international venues, from Ghent, Belgium to San Francisco, California. I am grateful to my audiences and co-panelists for enriching discussions and comments. It is also a pleasure to acknowledge the associations, institutes, and grants that funded many of my travels: the European Association for Urban History, the E.V. and Nancy Melosi Travel Grant of the American Society for Environmental History, the European Society for Environmental History, and the Rachel Carson Center for Environment and Society. During that time, I have published some of the materials and arguments that have been infused into this book. I wish to acknowledge these publications in full. I have written about migration in *Global Environment* 9 (2012), 26–49, about the Belice Valley modernist planning in *Planning Perspectives*, 28, no. 4 (2013), 571–93; and in Italian about contested memories of the Belice Valley earthquake in *L'Italia e le sue regioni* (vol. 3, 244–56) published by the *Istituto dell'Enciclopedia Italiana Treccani*.

Several people assisted me throughout the many complications of research in Italian archives and libraries. I wish to express my gratitude to Pina De Simone, Fosca Pizzaroni and the staff of the *Archivio Centrale dello Stato* in Rome, the *Biblioteca Regionale Centrale* and Sara Rabito, director of the *Archi-*

vio Storico del Parlamento Siciliano in Palermo, the Biblioteca Regionale Universitaria in Messina, the Biblioteca Nazionale in Naples, and the Biblioteca Universitaria in Bologna. The generous assistance of Ida Fazio proved crucial in gaining access to the Archivio di Stato di Messina when met with unexpected resistance by the archive director. The trust of Sergio Castenetto allowed me to sift through the Archivio Storico della Protezione Civile in Rome, and the archival knowledge of Flavio Gottardi and the kindness of Giuliana Priore made possible for me to get the best out of it. Alessandro La Grassa unhesitatingly gave me free use of the collection of records, books, interviews held at the Centro Ricerche Economiche e Sociali per il Meridione in Gibellina. Louisiana State University gave me access to a wealth of library resources that has greatly facilitated the final revision of the manuscript. My thanks extend to all those individuals, libraries, and archives for their help in identifying the images included into this book, and to Mary Lee Eggart for the original cartography.

The book that you are holding in your hands would not exist without the generous support of the Rachel Carson Center for Environment and Society, its directors Christof Mauch and Helmut Trischler, its amazing staff, and its outstanding group of fellows and researchers. Thanks to them, I had the opportunity of spending nine months in beautiful Munich in Germany, working full time at the manuscript in the most nurturing, creative, and forward-looking academic environment one could ever dream of. I had the chance to discuss my ideas and my writing on multiple occasions with the superb scholars who I am proud to call my friends, and I have learned a lot from their own projects. If there is something good in this book, then the Rachel Carson Center and its people share responsibility for it.

I wish to thank especially those friends and colleagues who have found time in their busy schedules to read and comment on parts of the manuscript at various stages, at the RCC or elsewhere. In no particular order: Michèle Dagenais, Tom Lekan, Sabine Wilke, John Meyer, Eva Jakobsson, Karen Oslund, Franz-Josef Brüggemeier, Ellen Arnold, Lawrence Culver, Uwe Lübken, and Craig Colten. The two anonymous reviewers were tremendously generous and encouraging. The enthusiasm and support of the indefatigable Christof Mauch as series editor have been invaluable to the realization of this book. He believed in it from the first moment, and has accompanied me through its completion with unshakable trust. The editorial talents, sensitivity, and intelligence of Katie Ritson, Brenda Black, and the editorial team of the Rachel Carson Center enormously improved the quality and clarity of my prose. Berghahn Books has guided the manuscript through the production process with patience and understanding. I could not have wished for a better team. Of course, I am solely responsible for any factual mistakes or false interpretations that may remain.

Life has brought me very far from home, while this book has kept me close to it. I am grateful to my friends, who made my journeys lighter and each one of our encounters memorable. My family has always been there for me: their unflagging love and support is what kept me grounded while moving across the globe. Isabelle has been by my side all along, and for that, I have no words.

Baton Rouge, Louisiana, November 2014

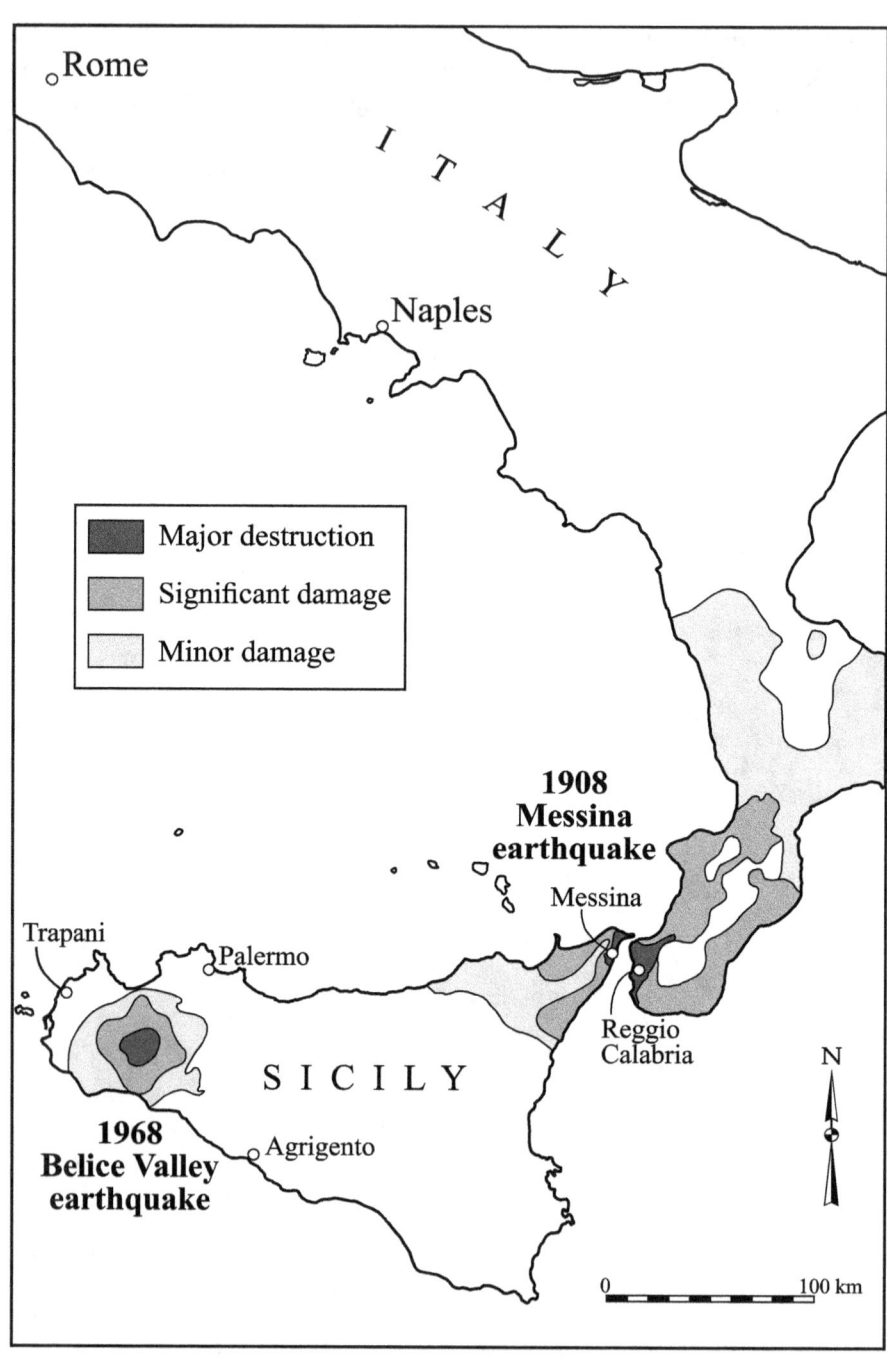

Map of the disaster areas. Cartography by Mary Lee Eggart.

Introduction
Can Earthquakes Speak?

I grew up in the shadow of the earthquake. The city where I was born, Messina, lies in one of the planet's seismic hotspots, and a long time ago, a destructive earthquake wiped it out and killed many of its inhabitants. Strangely enough, I never felt a tremor during the eighteen years I spent there. The earthquake, however, was a constant presence in my life and in the lives of those around me. My parents experienced a strong earthquake before I was born, and one of their favorite tales was about my father reaching out for my mother during that seventies' night. When the story invariably led to my question about the possibility of another one, they recalled the reassuring faith of my grandfather, an engineer, in the virtues of reinforced concrete. The earthquake's influence, apart from that, was all over the city, in the very few traces of historic architecture as well as in the poor shantytowns hidden in too many corners. As our elders taught my friends and me, the beautiful city that Messina had once been was gone forever. The shanties remained as a shadow of the earthquake's misery, almost one hundred years after its tragic visit.

This book tells the story of the earthquake in my city, the 1908 Messina earthquake, and the story of the one that hit the valley of the Belice River, Sicily, exactly sixty years later. These are two of the biggest seismic disasters in the history of modern Italy, and two equally tragic and fascinating stories of destruction and rebirth. In both places, two brand new environments materialized from the ruins of the earthquake. Each of these environments epitomized a pivotal moment in the history of urbanization in Italy—the modernization of historic cities between the nineteenth and the twentieth century and the urbanization of the countryside in the second half of the twentieth century, respectively. These post-quake environments, at the same time, exaggerated the characteristics of those two key moments as in a distorting mirror, due to the exceptional context from which they emerged.

A fundamental curiosity drives this book: Can earthquakes speak,[1] or are they just background noise in the historic landscape? What role do earthquakes play in the history of built environments and of the communities that inhabit them? Are they really drivers of change? What do they actually transform, and how? Can geological fault lines translate into historical ones? Questions like these have a lot to do with my experience with earthquakes and their effects, perhaps even more than the choice of the case studies. Yet these questions, in a sense so personal, may also speak to a broader audience and intersect with questions and curiosities arising from other places, experiences, and contexts, about other fault lines, real and metaphorical. To understand whether earthquakes can speak is, in effect, to tackle the broader question of the role of natural hazards in modern urban environments, and of nonhuman forces and features in history. I will now discuss those issues, and the significance they have for the stories I shall tell you. First, however, let me introduce the main character of this book: the earthquake.

The Voice of the Earthquake

In 1807, the German romantic writer Heinrich von Kleist published a short story titled "Das Erdbeben in Chili" (The Earthquake in Chile). The story narrates fictional events that take place during a real historic occurrence: the earthquake that devastated Santiago, capital of the Spanish Kingdom of Chile, in 1647. So reads the blazing incipit of the story:

> In Santiago, the capital of the kingdom of Chile, at the moment of the great earthquake of 1647 in which many thousands lost their lives, a young Spaniard called Jeronimo Rugera was standing beside one of the pillars in the prison to which he had been committed on a criminal charge, and was about to hang himself.[2]

In this artfully crafted paragraph, Kleist introduces at once the context and the main character, and propels us right into the middle of the action: at the very moment of the earthquake, a man in prison is about to commit suicide. As we discover later, the man was in prison for a love affair that had turned into a major city scandal, and, knowing that his lover and their son were about to be executed, he had decided to kill himself. He had irrevocably made his decision and was about to end his life, when, all of a sudden, the ground started to shake furiously. Suddenly, his will started to crumble together with the prison's wall, and instead of embracing death, he sought to survive by any means possible. The story goes on to recount how Jeronimo Rugera wandered through a devastated Santiago, the reasons for him being in prison, the fortuitous encounter with his lover and their child, and the adventures that lead to a breathtaking finale.

Kleist's story is a brilliant and gripping attempt to articulate a narrative of the earthquake. The earthquake shapes the setting of the story, destroying Santiago and creating a new order of possibilities. It even changes the characters' intentions radically, as in the case of Jerome's suicide attempt. It disrupts social relations and the ruling order, producing both the extreme poles of classless fraternity and brutal mob violence. The earthquake, in sum, speaks resoundingly throughout the entire narrative, becoming its principal, albeit unconventional character. My book, very much like Kleist's short story, is a narrative of the earthquake. The transformative power of the earthquake, however, will be the interrogative of a historical inquiry, rather than the main device of a fictional plot. As we shall see, in history, earthquakes do not necessarily speak the language of change, and often other voices and characters conceal or confound their voice.

Kleist's short story is just another example of the fascination that earthquakes have exerted on human cultures across time and space. Earthquakes have given rise to beautiful and vivid mythologies such as the *Namazu*, Japan's earth-shaker catfish, philosophical meditations by Seneca and Voltaire, among others, and countless scientific theories. Nowadays, the scientific study of earthquakes is deeply entrenched in the theory of plate tectonics. In short, plate tectonics postulates that the Earth's crust is made of giant plates of solid rock, floating on a thick layer of magma. The encounters between these plates are responsible for mountains, volcanism, and earthquakes. Tectonics theory, which was accepted by the global scientific community in the 1960s, is today virtually uncontested.[3]

Earthquakes, however, still represent a frontier of science and a slippery and multiform object of knowledge. This intriguing status is due to several factors. One is, without a doubt, their resistance to visual scrutiny. Paradoxically, even though technology allows us to look into molecules and atoms, into outer space and, to a certain extent, beneath the deep ocean, the earth's crust remains impenetrable. Our ideas about what lies underneath are largely based on evidence from the surface, such as volcanic rocks and seismic wave propagation.[4] This resistance to visual scrutiny mirrors the earthquake's resistance to prediction. Despite all efforts, prediction, which rules most contemporary sciences, does not apply to earthquakes. The study of earthquakes, then, necessarily involves disparate practices and knowledge systems, spanning from archival research and archeology to geology and chemistry. It is structurally transdisciplinary, and therefore difficult to put in one of our reassuring epistemological boxes.[5]

With the significant but isolated exception of historical seismology, historians have rarely investigated earthquakes.[6] This is perhaps due to their contradictory status as historical fact. An earthquake occurs in a precise point in time and space that is more or less precisely mappable. At the same time, each earthquake is also a consequence of plate tectonics, whose encounters and collisions happen on a planetary scale. Despite its very short duration, an earthquake is the point of intersection of a process measurable in hundreds or thousands or even millions of years in the geological history of planet Earth. This meeting of timescales has rendered earthquakes problematic to incorporate into historical narratives. Their exact and unique localization in time and space is incompatible with the project of generalization typical of the discipline of history. On the other hand, the temporality and spatiality of geological processes exceed the span of usual historical accounts.

Despite these difficulties, historians have recently started to turn their attention towards earthquakes. This turn has been part of a general burst of attention in the social sciences and humanities focused on so-called disasters. Pioneering work by human geographers such as Kenneth Hewitt and Pierce Blaikie argued that these events cannot be seen as purely "natural" occurrences, for they are rooted in the economically and socially determined vulnerability of a given population.[7] According to anthropologist Anthony Oliver-Smith, disasters should be seen as "processes" rather than "events," for they are rooted in the long term interplay between the features of a human settlement and society and its biogeophysical environment.[8] Historians have started to follow this path of inquiry. In his historical study of notable modern disasters in the United States of America, Ted Steinberg has stressed how the popular notion of "acts of God" belies the anthropogenic, socially conditioned character of these events and their consequences.[9] Greg Bankoff, in turn, has made the case for analyzing the interactions between hazards and society over a longer time frame, considering various forms of cultural and social adaptation.[10] Notions of adaptation and resilience are very much central to the recent work of historical geographer Craig Colten, who has highlighted the importance of looking into historical patterns of institutional response to and "social memory" of hazardous events.[11]

These perspectives apply compellingly to seismic disasters. Seismic disasters, indeed, are always the product of the historical interplay between geophysical forces and features—the magnitude and duration of an earthquake, but also the composition of the soil, and the characteristics of a built environment and community—and building techniques and materials, but also the social and economic resources of the population.[12] Examinations of historical processes are thus crucial to understand the occurrence and impact of earthquakes. Building on this common insight, literature on earthquakes in history has developed along two interrelated lines that largely reproduce parallel developments in the historical study of other hazardous events.

One significant trend is the investigation into disaster repetition. Typically, these studies recount the evolution of knowledge, institutional practices, and coping strategies related to a succession of hazards in a given time and space. Each single episode from this vantage point assumes its historical significance as part of a series. The responses of communities and institutions and the development of new understanding and practices show the influence of earthquakes on human affairs. This approach underpins the compelling study of earthquake-related knowledge and practices in twentieth-century California by Carl-Henry Geshwind, as well as Gregory Quenet's account of the emergence of the notion of risk in early modern France.[13] Similarly, long-term perspectives on earthquake repetition and societal change underlay Gregory Clancey's informed analysis of the connections been seismic science and national identity in modern Japan and Deborah Coen's transnational account of the transition from sensorial observations to instrumental earthquake science.[14]

The other significant trend consists of analyzing a single earthquake and its consequences. The earthquake, in these studies, is the point of departure: scholarly studies narrate its impact, the opportunities it created, and the transformations it rendered necessary. Depending on the focus of each narrative, the impact, opportunities, and transformations examined may concern culture and politics, economy, or architecture. All these studies, however, consider earthquakes as significant opportunities to investigate features of historical processes, rather than significant moments of historical change in their own right. In a pioneering monograph, Augusto Placanica analyzed the multilayered cultural reverberations of 1783 Calabrian earthquakes, an investigative trend later followed by other scholars of modern Italy.[15] Charles Walker utilized the 1743 Lima earthquake as a window through which to examine colonial relationships in eighteenth-century Chile.[16] Mark Healey, contributing to the emerging scholarship on earthquakes and political change in Latin America, repositioned the origins of Peronism in the aftermath of the 1944 San Juan earthquake in Argentina.[17] Conevery Bolton Valencius has proved the significant environmental, cultural, and social impact of the 1812 New Madrid earthquakes, while exploring the causes of the paradoxical oblivion that followed.[18]

This book belongs decidedly to this second family of studies. It investigates the way earthquakes may be entrenched within historical change, and how the earthquake's voice resounds in the history of built environments and communities. However, there are some significant differences with my approach. When I started researching this project, I assumed that I would focus on the aftermath of the two events, as most existing studies do. Later on, I realized this is not enough. As I will argue throughout this book, earthquakes speak at multiple levels with very different consequences. At some levels, they may speak clearly and unmistakably about rupture. At other levels, the earthquake's voice is the object of mutable and contested translations. Sometimes, then, earthquakes do not speak at all, or their voice fails to reverberate. The historical outcome of an earthquake is a blend of ruptures and continuities, sometimes very evident, sometimes more subtly dispersed in the tapestry of historical facts. Historians should unravel these different threads if they want to let earthquakes speak in their stories. To read the traces of earthquakes in the complex text of historical change, what happened before the earthquakes is just as important as the aftermath. For that reason, this book is not just about what happened after the earthquake. It is a book about how the voice of the earthquake resounds in the history of places. It is about geological fault lines and historical ones.

A Tale of Two Earthquakes

This book looks at the earthquake's role in history with a precise focus, namely the making of urban environments in modern times. The history of modern urbanism has greatly benefitted from the fresh approaches brought about by environmental scholarship. The production of built environments, from the perspective of this environmental history, is never a purely human enterprise. On the contrary, historians of urban infrastructure and pollution, such as Joel Tarr, Martin Melosi, and others, have demonstrated that it involves the (often problematic) mobilization of resources and ecosystems.[19] Environmental historian Bill Cronon, on the other hand, has pointed out how processes of urban growth rest upon the large-scale and often radical transformation of natural sites.[20] In their making, cities have reshaped the ecological features of large regions and have modified hydrological cycles, tamed rivers, and concreted over large areas of soil. Yet their very existence stands upon those same environmental forces and features they seek to harness.[21] Emphasizing this mutuality, Verena Winiwarter and Martin Schmid have claimed that we should see cities as "socio-natural sites," sites where social and natural processes blend almost indistinguishably, rather than sites from which nature has been expelled.[22] Urban environmental scholarship, while stressing the importance of looking at urbanization as environmental transformation, has brought into focus the human side of the process. "Socio-natural" perspectives put forward by recent scholarship invite us to look at the other side of the coin. Sometimes nonhuman forces and features shape cities as much as humans do, and we should regard them as important drivers in the making of urban environments.[23] Earthquakes are one of those forces.

By exploring the role of earthquakes in the making of urban environments, this book aims to strengthen a conception of urbanization as a process of reciprocal, rather than unidirectional, influence between human and nonhuman forces and features. Over the years, a handful of scholars have touched upon the consequences of hazards on cities, maintaining their varied influence on urban developments.[24] Earthquakes are a particularly compelling example of urban hazards. In a few seconds, an earthquake can flatten cities that humans took centuries to build—often the destruction unleashed was increased due to poor choices made by generations of city builders or to unbridled urban developments. Earthquake destruction generally creates opportunities to rethink the features of a settlement and can result in transformative changes that mitigate the risk of future disasters, or even the abandonment and/or relocation of the settlement. Moreover, earthquake destruction can facilitate long-debated improvements by removing the physical, social, and economic obstacles to their realization.[25] An earthquake can also trigger processes that have a profound impact on a settlement, such as migration, new investment, or the redistribution of property and income. Not all of these forms of influence have the same weight, nor are they necessarily all present together. In every case, however, the voice of the earthquake translates into the text of urbanism, just as much as the human voices do.

This book tries to understand this voice—its sound, its translations, and its echoes—in two fascinating histories. The 1908 Messina earthquake was one of the worst seismic disasters in European history. On 28 December, a devastating 7.1 earthquake-tsunami hit the cities of Messina and Reggio Calabria, and dozens of towns and villages on both sides of the strait that divides Sicily from continental Italy. Messina was the most prominent urban center of the region and home to 140,000 residents, and there almost nine buildings out of ten were turned to rubble, killing as much as half of the resident population. The 1968 Belice earthquake was not as deadly, but its physical impact was just as ruinous. Between 14 and 15 January, a series of five increasingly powerful tremors hit a rural region in southwestern Sicily known as the Belice Valley. The towns of Gibellina, Salaparuta, Montevago, and Poggioreale were completely destroyed; ten other towns lost up to 80 percent of their buildings and dozens more registered severe damages. Overall, despite the absence of a prominent urban center in the region, the earthquakes affected a population of some 100,000 inhabitants.

The 1908 Messina earthquake and the 1968 Belice earthquake were two of the most destructive quakes in the history of modern Italy. The story of destruction, however, is not the only similarity they share. After both earthquakes, survivors and authorities rebuilt the devastated settlements in a completely new fashion. To avoid new disasters, Messina's planners and builders followed a new building and planning code and adopted the earthquake-resistant technology of reinforced concrete. In addition, the new Messina had a transformed street pattern designed to improve circulation and networks; it extended over double the original surface area, incorporating former agricultural areas into the urban space. The reconstruction provided the city with a comprehensive sanitation infrastructure. Similarly, after 1968, planners redesigned the Belice Valley as a modern urbanized region. For a combination of geological and economic reasons, the authorities imposed the abandonment of fourteen settlements and relocated the population to new towns. In sharp contrast to the abandoned settlements, the new towns were equipped with suburban-style housing, modern urban infrastructure, and an interconnecting road network that favored car-centered mobility. In both cases, the reconstruction was in fact a radical transformation of the settlements, in line with contemporary ideals about urban modernization and improvement and combined with risk mitigation strategies.

These solutions were the outcome of two exceptional situations. Nevertheless, in many aspects they epitomize two key moments in the history of modern urbanization in Italy. Between 1880 and 1930, most historic cities in Italy underwent profound transformation. In most cases, these transformations went under the banner of *risanamento,* sanitation. City engineers and municipal authorities demolished old walls and neighborhoods, and replaced tortuous labyrinths of medieval alleys with wider and straighter boulevards. They planned and built aqueducts and sewage pipes, power lines, and promoted the construction of railroad stations, tramway lines, and street lighting. Each time, these transformations translated into a substantial revision of the relationship between the urban environment and the ecosystems of larger surrounding areas. The transformation experienced by Messina after the earthquake therefore resonates loudly with contemporary developments in Milan, Rome, Naples, and dozens of other Italian cities, in which the urban environmental configuration of the modern city was replacing the medieval and renaissance city.[26]

Whereas Messina epitomizes the modernization of historic Italian cities, the Belice Valley is representative of another major turning point. The wave of modern urbanism, once it had washed over the historic cities of the peninsula and changed them profoundly, began to lap at the countryside. Anticipated to a certain extent by reclamation policies in the 1920s and 1930s, the modernization of rural areas characterized most of the second half of the twentieth century. Electrification, road networks and cars, aqueducts and sewage works—bit by bit, they arrived in every settlement in the Italian countryside, transforming everyday habits and ecologies irreversibly. Knowledge, practices, and material arrangements that were centuries old disappeared, and the gap between rural and urban life diminished dramatically. This transformation had different drivers in Southern and Northern Italy: sprawling industrial suburbs met coalescing hinterlands in the North, state investments for economic development and civil infrastructure afforded momentum in the South. Everywhere it brought about the end of rural life as a contrast to the city, and the almost ubiquitous affirmation of the urbanized countryside. The transformation of the Belice Valley after the earthquake is a clear example of this widespread process.[27]

Other European and American countries have experienced similar transformations. Albeit with differences in periodization and under different conditions, the biggest European and American cities underwent changes largely comparable to those in Italian cities between 1880 and 1930. The demolition of old medieval neighborhoods and the creation of large boulevards in Paris during the Second Empire are representative of a general trend throughout much of nineteenth-century Europe. The installation of energy and transport networks was a powerful driver of urban transformation as well, and contributed to the global emergence of the modern city. Almost everywhere, the creation of new aqueducts and sewage systems was an important part of this process, with significant environmental and social consequences. In the midst of these processes, cities revised their ecological relationship with the large hinterland in profound ways, forged new hierarchies and powers, and transformed the life of their inhabitants deeply.[28]

The urbanization of the Italian countryside also has equivalents in other countries. An influential view is that which originates from Cronon's study of Chicago, with its notorious claim of the deep interconnection between urban growth of the metropolis and ecological transformation of the countryside.[29] Alongside this insightful perspective, scholars have investigated other dimensions and drivers of urban-rural blending. In urban-industrial regions, metropolitan growth and suburbanization have often resulted in the physical metamorphosis of the countryside, a phenomenon that mass motorization has also contributed to enormously. In many parts of the developed world, the progressive expansion of sanitation, electrification, and motorization to rural settlements has happened even without the presence of big industrial cities. Although the pace, drivers, and effects of this latter process have been far less thoroughly investigated than in larger urban centers, old rural ecologies and settlement patterns have disappeared or shrunk considerably almost everywhere in the developed world during the second half of the twentieth century.[30]

As much as Messina and the Belice Valley can be placed within with these two key phases of modern urbanization, they still stand visibly apart. One can find many examples of sanitation and urban reform between the nineteenth and the twentieth century; but sanitation is generally coupled with the persistence of other forms, structures, and functions from past ages, at least in Europe. In Messina, on the contrary, modernization was realized in a radical rupture with the urban past, a past that was virtually erased from the cityscape. Similarly, one can find many cases of modernization and urbanization of the countryside in the second half of the twentieth century. Even in those cases, however, this transformation merged with the enduring features of a rural past. The intermingling of new and old is evident in many aspects of today's Italian countryside, such as the shape and architecture of rural towns and in patterns of land use, the historical significance of which led environmental historian Mauro Agnoletti to call for the creation of a national register of historical rural landscapes.[31] In post-earthquake Belice Valley, on the other hand, modernization and urbanization were predicated upon the almost complete eradication of the past, and the radical reshaping of settlements and landscape was projected onto an empty canvas. The purpose of this book is to understand how strongly the earthquake's voice spoke in the peculiar urbanism of Messina and the Belice Valley, and how much of their story is, on the contrary, representative of more general processes of urban change.

The Structure of This Book

In order to accomplish the purpose, this book adopts a rather unusual approach that should be considered integral to its methodology. As anticipated, instead of recounting mainly what happened after the two earthquakes, this book incorporates a broader historical view that embraces the pre-earthquake period as much as the aftermath. The tales this book will tell thus start almost thirty years before the earthquakes and end some thirty years after. This, I believe, is one of the most original features of this book's approach, and one that I hope will offer new insights into the ways in which earthquakes are part of the making of modern urban environments. By looking at key elements of urban life before the earthquakes, the changes that followed them can be picked out more clearly, and shown alongside the continuities with the pre-earthquake contexts, debates, and plans.

The structure of the book follows this historical approach. The book consists of two distinct sections: section one is concerned with the story of Messina, and section two recounts the story of the Belice Valley. Each section has a tripartite narrative structure. The first chapter of each section propels us into the middle of the action, recounting the earthquake and its immediate consequences. The following chapters trace the pre-earthquake and the post-earthquake history of the place, building narrative continuity between before and after, through which the earthquake's voice can resonate more clearly. At the end of the two sections, a concluding chapter summarizes both narratives and explores some final ideas.

Chapter 1, the opening of the first section, brings us directly to 28 December 1908, when an earthquake-tsunami devastated Messina, a city of 140,000, killing thousands of people and leaving behind 1 million cubic meters of rubble. The future of the city itself seemed in doubt. Local authorities and other public figures were convinced that the location and site of Messina would guarantee the rebirth of the city and its future prosperity. Earthquake scientists and engineers, on the other hand, stressed that the city was located on a hazard-prone site. If the city was to be rebuilt where it had stood before, adaptation strategies were required. The ultimate solution was a new building and planning code to reduce the vulnerability of the city to future earthquakes. The code would prevent the city from being reconstructed along the same lines as before. But how was the city before?

Chapter 2 answers that question, and moves back to the pre-earthquake decades in Messina. As many cities at that time, late nineteenth-century Messina was entering an age of changes and starting to plan major transformations. Much of these transformations revolved around urban sanitation: the demolition of working class neighborhoods, the creation of new roads, and the installation of a new urban water cycle using comprehensive aqueducts, sewage pipes, and rainwater drainage. On the eve of the earthquake, however, much of the planned urban changes remained unachieved. While issues such as the port renewal and peri-urban reforestation expanded the urban reform debate, minor earthquakes struck the city in 1895, 1905, and 1907. Surprisingly, those earthquakes did not provoke any response by the authorities, despite the persistent memory of past disasters. The lack of effective measures after those earthquakes contributed largely to the extent of destruction in 1908.

Chapter 3 examines how the pre-earthquake agenda interacted with the post-earthquake situation. While the authorities established two huge hut camps on the outskirts of the city, municipal engineer Borzì drew up a master plan for rebuilding. The earthquake building code imposed of necessity a new shape on the city. Borzì took this opportunity to introduce, along with measures to ensure seismic safety, most of the innovations planned before the quake, but on a larger and more ambitious scale. Unprecedented flows of public money, inward migration, and difficulties in clearing the camps of huts, however, scattered many assumptions of the master plan and prevented the realization of some of its features. On the eve of World War II, a new city had materialized, but the new Messina was a paradoxical blend of urban modernity and shantytowns: partly due to pre-earthquake debates and plans, but also largely an outcome of the 1908 earthquake and of its direct and indirect effects.

Chapter 4 introduces the second section and is devoted to the 1968 Belice earthquake. On January 1968, the combination of five increasingly strong earthquakes destroyed fourteen towns and affected a population of 100,000 residents. The earthquake was given extensive coverage by the media, and most commentators deemed the "backwardness" of the region directly responsible for the disaster, singling out the poor housing and economic poverty of its inhabitants in particular. Legislators shared the view that the disaster was linked to underdevelopment, and established special socioeconomic development policies to accompany the rebuilding of the destroyed towns. In addition, they considered the permanent relocation of some of the communities to safer sites. Rebuilding was thus to correspond to a comprehensive redevelopment of the entire area. But what was the true condition of the area before the earthquakes?

Chapter 5 answers that question. Among the poorest and driest areas in Sicily, homeland of the early rural Mafia and a symbol of the "backward" *Mezzogiorno*, after World War I the Belice Valley became the target of a number of special improvement programs. In the late 1920s, under the auspices of advantageous national policies, local landowners created a "Reclamation Consortium," aimed at boosting agriculture by transforming the valley's biogeophysical environment. Before and after World War II, colonization of large estates, agrarian reform, and development funding were brought in, but in the 1950s not much had been accomplished. Faced with mass emigration and failure of improvement schemes, in the early 1960s a network of activists formed local committees for community-based development. Over the years, the committees researched and expounded their own development ideas, and they had just put forward a new comprehensive plan for development when the earthquake hit the valley.

Chapter 6 explains how much of these plans outlived the earthquake. Disregarding the grassroots movement, the authorities entrusted a national institute for social housing with a plan for complete redevelopment of the valley. The planners sought to redevelop the valley into "city-territory:" a network of modern towns that would function as a single urban unit based on an industrial economy. Actual reconstruction work did not go as planned, and despite the fact that urban infrastructure had been created and towns relocated, the absence of industrialization prevented much of the plan from being effective. Unprecedented flows of public money and the completion of a long-awaited reservoir on the Belice River, however, encouraged the growth of a modern agricultural economy. Today's Belice Valley is a landscape of suburban settlements in a deeply transformed but still rural countryside: the paradoxical outcome of pre-1968 plans, post-disaster redevelopment, and a combination of the direct and indirect consequences of the earthquakes.

The concluding chapter wraps up and compares the two narratives, retracing the voices of the earthquakes in the text of continuities, discontinuities, and unintended consequences that underlay the urban development of Messina and the Belice Valley. By placing these histories in the long and dense history of disastrous earthquakes in Italy, I suggest that earthquakes have been a powerful force in urbanization throughout the country. If we broaden our view to take in other countries and continents, the role of earthquakes in the making of modern urban environments is just as significant. From California to Japan, from Chile to Portugal, earthquakes have been a powerful force in transforming urban environments, by stimulating conscious adaptation strategies, facilitating plans for reform, or triggering unexpected social processes. Earthquakes are not exceptional in this regard. Natural hazards are a permanent feature of our world, and our urban environments are the always-provisional outcome of their continuous influence on human intentions, actions, and cultures. Earthquakes can speak. We just need to listen.

Addendum

All authors have some personal ties with their stories, and in the beginning of this introduction, I tried to identify my own. Historians, however, are bound to past facts, and that is the difference between history and other narrative genres. Sources and documents are the currency by which we acknowledge our bond. This book relies upon a number of primary sources from several libraries and archival collections, some unknown or underexploited. I provide a detailed list at the end of this book, but I would like to offer an overview here. The first section on Messina draws in particular on the rich miscellany in the collection of the *Biblioteca Regionale di Messina,* and on archival material from the *Archivio di Stato di Messina* and the *Archivio Centrale dello Stato* in Rome. The second section on the Belice Valley relies on grey literature mainly from the *Biblioteca Regionale di Palermo* and the *Biblioteca del Senato della Repubblica,* and on archival material from the *Archivio Centrale dello Stato* in Rome, the *Archivio Storico del Parlamento Siciliano* in Palermo, the *Archivio Dolci-Barbera* in Gibellina, and the *Archivio Storico della Protezione Civile* in Rome. The second section also makes use of oral testimonies from the collection of the CRESM Gibellina. I use these testimonies only sparsely to integrate information or points of view on the events and processes discussed in the book. These testimonies, and many others that are still awaiting collection, could be used to explore the voice of the earthquake in the survivors' lives—I suspect with extremely interesting results. Such an endeavor, however, falls outside the purpose and scope of this book: I can only hope that the analytical perspective put forward here might stimulate others to undertake it. Finally, this book has benefitted from the wisdom and information of a number of secondary sources in various languages, all conscientiously cited in the relevant notes and in the bibliography. Although I believe I am offering a fresh perspective, I would have found this book much more difficult to write without the work of the many fellow scholars who are as fascinated or as haunted by earthquakes as I am.

Notes

1. This formulation is inspired by Timothy Mitchell, who asked in the first chapter of his book *Rule of Experts,* "Can the mosquito speak?" See Timothy Mitchell, *Rule of Experts: Egypt, Technopolitics, Modernity* (Berkeley, 2002), 19–53. Mitchell was trying

to advance a critique of the human-nature divide and the traditional view of human agency with which this book is largely sympathetic.
2. Heinrich von Kleist, *The Marquise of O—And Other Stories* (Harmondsworth, 1978), 51.
3. Tectonics, however, is not entirely capable of explaining so-called "intraplate earthquakes," of which one of the most notorious case is the New Madrid earthquakes in 1812. See Conevery Bolton Valencius, *The Lost History of the New Madrid Earthquakes* (Chicago, 2013).
4. Kent C. Condie, "Crustal Composition and Recycling," *The Oxford Companion to the Earth*, ed. Paul L. Hancock and Brian J. Skinner (Oxford, 2000), 192–95.
5. On the epistemological status of earthquakes, see Deborah Coen, "Witness to Disaster: Comparative Histories of Earthquake Science and Response," *Science in Context* 25 (2012): 1–15.
6. Historical seismology applies the methods of historical research to the identification of past earthquakes. It has developed as an autonomous branch. Its impact has been much more substantial on seismology and earthquake science at large than on historiography. It is indeed of pivotal importance in determining the seismic risk of a certain area, but is largely underrepresented in history departments. For a state-of-the-art overview of this discipline, see Emanuela Guidoboni and John E. Ebel, *Earthquakes and Tsunamis in the Past: A Guide to Techniques in Historical Seismology* (Cambridge, 2009).
7. Sociologists have studied disasters for several decades, producing a rich literature on the social response to disruptive events. See Havidán Rodriguez, Enrico L. Quarantelli, and Russell R. Dynes, eds., *Handbook of Disaster Research* (New York, 2006). Starting in the 1980s, a more politically and socially aware strain of literature in human geography has shifted attention toward issues of resource access and social and economic inequalities, and introduced notions of risk and vulnerability. See Kenneth Hewitt, ed., *Interpretations of Calamity: From the Viewpoint of Human Ecology* (Boston, 1983); Ben Wisner, Piers Blaikie, Terry Cannon, and Ian Davis, eds. *At Risk: Natural Hazards, People's Vulnerability and Disasters* (London, 2004).
8. Anthony Oliver-Smith, "Theorizing Disasters. Nature, Power, and Culture," in *Catastrophe and Culture: The Anthropology of Disaster*, ed. Susanna Hoffman and Anthony Oliver-Smith (Oxford, 2002).
9. Theodor Steinberg, *Acts of God: The Unnatural History of Natural Disasters in America* (New York, 2006).
10. Greg Bankoff, *Cultures of Disaster: Society and Natural Hazards in the Philippines* (London and New York, 2003). See also Greg Bankoff, "Time is of the Essence: Disasters, Vulnerability, and History," *International Journal of Mass Emergencies and Disasters* 22, no. 3 (2004): 23–42. Along a similar vein, a growing literature has developed in the last decades. A rich collection of case studies from around the globe is in Christof Mauch and Christian Pfister, eds., *Natural Disasters, Cultural Responses: Case Studies toward a Global Environmental History* (Lanham, 2009).
11. Craig E. Colten, *Perilous Place, Powerful Storms: Hurricane Protection in Coastal Louisiana* (Jackson, 2009). Over recent years, the concept of "resilience" has driven most new research on natural hazards and society in geography. See for example Neil W. Adger, "Social and Ecological Resilience: Are They Related?" *Progress in Human Geography* 24 (2000): 347–64.

12. On the specific dimensions attached to earthquake hazards in comparison to other types of hazards, see Wisner et al. *At Risk*, 239–41.
13. Carl H. Geschwind, *California Earthquakes: Science, Risk, and the Politics of Hazard Mitigation* (Baltimore, 2001). Gregory Quenet, *Les tremblements de terre aux XVIIe et XVIIIe siècles: la naissance d'un risque* (Champ Vallon, 2005).
14. Gregory Clancey, *Earthquake Nation: The Cultural Politics of Japanese Seismicity, 1868–1930* (Berkeley, 2006); Deborah Coen, *The Earthquake Observers: Disaster Science from Lisbon to Richter* (Chicago, 2013).
15. Augusto Placanica. *Il filosofo e la catastrofe: un terremoto del Settecento* (Turin, 1985). See John Dickie, John Foot, and Frank M. Snowden, eds., *Disastro! Disasters in Italy Since 1860: Culture, Politics, Society* (New York and Basingstoke, 2002); and John Dickie, *La catastrofe patriottica: il terremoto di Messina* (Rome and Bari, 2008).
16. Charles Walker, *Shaky Colonialism: The 1746 Earthquake-Tsunami in Lima, Peru, and Its Long Aftermath* (Durham, 2008).
17. Mark Healey, *The Ruins of the New Argentina: Peronism and the Remaking of San Juan after the 1944 Earthquake* (Durham, 2011). For the emerging scholarship on Latin American, see Jürgen Buchenau and Lyman L Johnson, eds., *Aftershocks: Earthquakes and Popular Politics in Latin America* (Albuquerque, 2009).
18. Valencius, *The Lost History of the New Madrid Earthquakes*.
19. Martin V. Melosi, *Garbage in the Cities: Refuse, Reform, and the Environment 1880–1980* (College Station and London, 2005). Joel Tarr, *The Search for the Ultimate Sink: Urban Pollution in Historical Perspective* (Akron, 1996). For a European view, see also Dieter Schott, "Resources of the City: Toward a European Urban Environmental History," *Resources of the City: Contribution to an Environmental History of Modern Europe*, ed. Dieter Schott, Bill Luckin, and Geneviève Massard-Guilbaud (Aldershot, 2005).
20. William Cronon, *Nature's Metropolis: Chicago and the Great West* (New York and London, 1991). Studies on the ecological relationship between cities and hinterlands are growing. See for example the contributions collected by Gilles Billen, Josette Garnier, and Sabine Barles, eds., "History of the Urban Environmental Imprint," special issue, *Regional Environmental Change* 12, no. 2 (2012).
21. Craig E. Colten, *An Unnatural Metropolis: Wrestling New Orleans from Nature* (Baton Rouge, 2005).
22. On the concept of the "socio-natural site" in urban environmental history, see Verena Winiwarter, Martin Schmid, and Gert Dressel, "Looking at Half a Millennium of Co-Existence: The Danube in Vienna as a Socio-Natural Site," *Water History* 5, no. 2 (2013): 101–19.
23. Perspectives on cities as sites of interplay and blending of natural and social have dominated urban environmental scholarship from the mid-2000s, in both geography and history. See Bruce Braun, "Environmental Issues: Writing a More-Than-Human Urban Geography," *Progress in Human Geography* 29, no. 5 (2005): 635–50. Nik Heynen, Maria Kaika, and Eric Swigendouw, "Urban Political Ecology: Politicizing the Production of Urban Natures," in *The Nature of Cities: Urban Political Ecology and the Politics of Urban Metabolism*, ed. Nik Heynen, Maria Kaika, and Eric Swigendouw (London and New York, 2006). Simon Gunn and Alaistar Owens, "Nature, Technology and the Modern City: An Introduction," *Cultural Geography*, 13 (2006): 291–96. Matthew

Gandy, "Rethinking Urban Metabolism: Water, Space and the Modern City," *City* 8, no. 3 (2008): 363–79. Martin V. Melosi, "Humans, Cities, and Nature: How Do Cities Fit in the Material World?" *Journal of Urban History* 36, no. 1 (2009): 3–21; Joel A. Tarr, "The City as an Artifact of Technology and the Environment," in *The Illusory Boundary: Environment and Technology in History*, ed. Martin Reuss and Stephen H. Cutcliffe (Charlottesville, 2011), 145–70. See also the introduction to Stéphane Castonguay and Matthew Evenden, eds., *Urban Rivers: Remaking Rivers, Cities, and Space in Europe and North America* (Pittsburgh, 2012), 1–13.

24. One pioneering example is Christine Rosen Meisner, *The Limits of Power: Great Fires and the Process of City Growth in America* (Cambridge, 1986). Another important contribution is the collection by Geneviève Massard-Guilbau, Dieter Schott, and Harold L. Platt, eds., *Cities and Catastrophes: Coping with Emergency in European History / Villes et catastrophes: Réaction face à l'urgence dans l'histoire européenne* (Frankfurt am Main, 2002). More recently another edited volume specifically centered on fires has been published: Greg Bankoff, Uwe Lübken, and Jordan Sand, eds., *Flammable Cities: Urban Conflagration and the Making of the Modern World* (Madison, 2012).

25. Geneviève Massard-Guilbaud, "The Urban Catastrophe: A Challenge to the Social, Economic and Cultural Order of the City," in Massard-Guilbaud, Platt, and Schott, *Cities and Catastrophes*, 9–42. See also Piero Bevilacqua, *Tra natura e storia: ambiente, economie, risorse in Italia* (Rome, 2005): 73–112. See also Giuseppe Giarrizzo, "Lo storico e il terremoto," in *La Sicilia dei terremoti: Lunga durata e dinamiche sociali*, ed. Giuseppe Giarrizzo (Catania, 1996), 439–41.

26. Literature on this is abundant. Guido Zucconi, *La città contesa: dagli ingegneri sanitari agli urbanisti (1885–1942)* (Milan, 1999). Giovanna Vicarelli, *Alle origini della politica sanitaria in Italia: società e salute da Crispi al fascismo* (Bologna, 1997). Simone Neri Serneri, *Incorporare la natura: Storie ambientali del Novecento* (Rome, 2005). Simone Neri Serneri, "The Construction of the Modern City and the Management of Water Resources in Italy, 1880–1920," *Journal of Urban History* 33, no. 5 (2007): 814–15. Annalucia Forti Messina, "L'Italia dell'Ottocento di fronte al colera," *Storia d'Italia, Annali 7: Malattia e Medicina*, ed. Franco Della Peruta (Turin, 1984), 431–94. Roberto Ferretti, "The Formation of a Bureaucratic Group Between Center and Periphery: Engineers and Local Government in Italy from the Liberal Period to Fascism (1861–1939)," In *Municipal Services and Employees in the Modern City: New Historic Approaches*, ed. Michèle Dagenais, Pierre-Yves Saunier, and Irene Maver (Aldershot, 2003), 66–83. Denis Boucquet and Samuel Fettah, eds. *Réseaux techniques et conflits de pouvoir: Les dynamiques historiques des villes contemporaines* (Rome, 2007). Salvatore Adorno and Filippo De Pieri, eds. "Burocrazie tecniche," special issue, *Città e storia* 5 (2011). On Syracuse, see Salvatore Adorno, "Luce e acque: conflitti e risorse nella modernizzazione di una periferia meridionale; Il caso di Siracusa," in Bocquet and Fettah, *Réseaux techniques et conflits*, 103–36. On Naples, see Frank M. Snowden, *Naples in the Time of Cholera, 1884–1911* (Cambridge, 1995). On Rome, Denis Bocquet, *Rome, ville technique (1870–1925): une modernisation conflictuelle de l'espace urbain* (Rome, 2007).

27. Giuseppe De Matteis, "Le trasformazioni territoriali e ambientali," *Storia dell'Italia repubblicana*, vol. 2, *La trasformazione dell'Italia*, part 1, *Politica, economia società*, ed. Francesco Barbagallo (Turin, 1994): 661–709. Giuseppe Gamba, Giuliano Martignetti, "Ambiente e territorio," in *Guida all'Italia Contemporanea 1861–1997*, vol. 1,

Risorse e strutture economiche, ed. Massimo Firpo, Nicola Tranfaglia, and Pier Giorgio Zunino (Milan, 1998), 1–87. Simone Neri Serneri, "Urbanizzazione, territorio e ambiente nell'Italia contemporanea, 1950–1970," *I Frutti di Demetra* 6 (2005): 33–39. Salvatore Adorno and Simone Neri Serneri *Industria, ambiente e territorio: Per una storia delle aree industriali in Italia* (Bologna, 2009). Piero Bevilacqua and Manlio Rossi-Doria, "Lineamenti per una storia delle bonifiche in Italia dal XVIII al XX secolo," in *Le bonifiche in Italia dal '700 ad oggi,* ed. Piero Bevilacqua, Manlio Rossi-Doria (Rome and Bari, 1984), 5–78. Giuseppe Barone, *Mezzogiorno e modernizzazione: Elettricità, irrigazione e bonifica nell'Italia contemporanea* (Turin, 1986). Giuseppe Barone, "Stato e Mezzogiorno: Il primo tempo dell'intervento straordinario (1943–1960)," *Storia dell'Italia repubblicana,* vol. 1, *La costruzione della democrazia,* ed. Francesco Barbagallo (Turin, 1994), 293–409.

28. On urban transformations and the birth of urban planning: Anthony Sutcliffe, *Towards the Planned City: Germany, Britain, the United States, and France, 1780–1914* (New York, 1981). For a more recent account on European cities, see Andrew Lees and Lynn H. Lees, *Cities and the Making of Modern Europe, 1750–1914* (Cambridge and New York, 2007). On the role of environmental infrastructure in urban modernization see: Joel A. Tarr and Gabriel Dupuy, eds., *Technology and the Rise of the Networked City in Europe and America* (Philadelphia, 1988). Martin V. Melosi, *The Sanitary City: Urban Infrastructure in America from Colonial Times to the Present* (Baltimore, 2000). Schott, Luckin, and Massard-Guilbaud, *Resources of the City.* "Cities, Environment and European History," special issue, *Journal of Urban History* 33, no. 5 (2007): 691–847.
29. Cronon, *Nature's Metropolis,* esp. xiii-xv.
30. Claims about the increasingly blurred boundary between the city and country have a long tradition within rural and urban sociology. The issue has been recently revived in urban studies by considering networks and coalescing hinterlands over the last decades. See Edward W. Soja, *Postmetropolis: Critical Studies of Cities and Regions* (Malden, MA, 2000) and Soja, "Beyond Postmetropolis," *Urban Geography* 32, no. 4 (2011): 451–69. Stephen Graham and Simon Marvin, *Splintering Urbanism: Networked Infrastructures, Technological Mobilities and the Urban Condition* (London and New York, 2001). Thomas Sieverts, *Cities without Cities: An Interpretation of the Zwischenstadt* (London and New York, 2003). See also Marc Antrop, "Changing Patterns in the Urbanized Countryside of Western Europe," *Landscape Ecology* 15, (2000): 257–70, and Marc Antrop, "Landscape Change and the Urbanization Process in Europe," *Landscape and Urban Planning* 67 (2004): 9–26. On urbanization in the countryside in environmental history, see Adam Rome, *The Bulldozer in the Countryside: Suburban Sprawl and the Rise of American Environmentalism* (Cambridge, 2001). On historical debates on sprawl and their cultural and political implications, see Robert Bruegmann, *Sprawl: A Compact History* (Chicago, 2005). On modernization and development in French countryside see Sarah B. Pritchard, "'Paris et Le Désert Francais': Urban and Rural Development in Post-World War II France," in *The Nature of Cities,* ed. Andrew C. Isenberg (Rochester, 2006), 175–91. To my knowledge, there are no historical studies that investigate in detail how the structural transformation experienced by major cities translated into small country settlements.
31. Mauro Agnoletti, ed., *Italian Historical Rural Landscapes* (New York and Berlin, 2013).

 PART I

The 1908 Messina Earthquake

 CHAPTER 1

The 1908 Messina Earthquake

In the early morning of 28 December 1908, the ground shook furiously in the Strait of Messina. As a result, Messina, Reggio Calabria, and dozens of other towns and villages were reduced to wasteland. The earthquake took the lives of tens of thousands and left the survivors in complete desolation. This chapter will recount the history of that tremendous disaster, the impact it had on the city of Messina, and the way that humans coped with the immense destruction.

The 1908 earthquake was a global event. As happened after the 1906 San Francisco earthquake, news of the disaster spread around the world, traveling at the speed of the telegraph. In the following weeks, films and pictures of the city circulated worldwide, displaying the horrors and destruction of Messina. Financial aid flowed from the United States and Canada, scientists and earthquake experts arrived from Japan, and members of the Russian and British navies who had participated in the rescue operation were celebrated as national heroes back home. The Sicilian earthquake of course unleashed a reaction in Italy too. Spontaneously formed committees collected donations all across the country, and the state launched an unprecedented aid campaign, inaugurating a new interventionist approach towards earthquake disasters. The transnational and national reception of the disaster, however, paled in comparison with the earthquake's physical impact on the city and its inhabitants. The earthquake caused the collapse of nine out of ten buildings, destroyed the urban infrastructure, and killed and maimed countless people. Most survivors escaped the devastated city after the quake in a true mass exodus, and the army was dispatched to the area. The commander-in-chief declared martial law and ordered the immediate execution of anyone suspected of looting. Soldiers were only able to free a few of those trapped under the ruins, and they buried most of the dead in mass graves. Thousands of corpses rotted under the debris, unseen and unnamed.

A true urban apocalypse seemed underway on the shores of the strait, and the future of Messina seemed in doubt. Practitioners of burgeoning sciences such as geology and engineering made their voice heard in the post-disaster debate: according to their knowledge, Messina was situated on a perilous site, from both a geological and a seismological viewpoint. Yet theirs was not the only interpretation of Messina's site and natural features. From the very first weeks following the quake, a large and heterogeneous coalition of politicians, journalists, and survivors claimed that the city had to be reborn where it had stood for centuries. Their discourse disregarded risk and stressed, on the contrary, the set of natural advantages attached to Messina's site and position, which in their view could guarantee the renaissance of the city and its future prosperity. The confrontation between these two perspectives would ultimately shape some of the most fundamental choices concerning the reconstruction. Messina would rise again where it had stood before, but the adoption of a new building code would mitigate the seismic risk and favor better adaptation to the hazardous site.

Earthquake, Tsunami, and Fire

The Strait of Messina is a complex geological formation and a unique geographical site. A deep underwater valley abruptly cuts the mountain range that crosses Italy from north to south, the Apennines. There, the Italian peninsula ends, and after a few kilometers of sea, the mountains of Sicily commence their rugged track. In this short but deep strait, the cold water of the Ionian Sea encounters the warm water of the Tyrrhenian Sea, generating the terribly strong currents and whirlpools that Homer identified as the mythological monsters Scylla and Charybdis. If one could travel to the bottom of the sea and explore beneath, one would see that in such a spectacular and unique place, other encounters occur. Under the cold water of the strait, floating over the sea of magma that lies underneath the surface of our planet, the Eurasian and the African tectonic plates collide, forming what geologists call a convergent or destructive boundary. The Eurasian and the African plates eventually release their accumulated energy in the form of an earthquake.[1]

In this peculiar place, and despite the recurrent hazards, a city has existed since around 730 BCE. The reasons for such a remarkable persistence are most probably the same ones that convinced a group of Greek citizens from Chalcis to establish a colony there: the unique features of the site. On the Sicilian shore of the strait, a strip of land shaped like a crescent forms a deep-water natural harbor. The Greek colonists called that peninsula ζάγκλον, a sickle, in the Greek transliteration of the indigenous language, and named the city after it. The peninsula faces a coastal plateau and is supplied with water flowing down from the surrounding Peloritani Mountains. Such a well-provided and well-protected site lies in a strategic position: it has a central location in the middle of the Mediterranean between Sicily and Italy, but it is also on the route between southwestern Europe and Greece, Asia Minor, and the Middle East.

For almost three millennia, these conditions meant fortune and prosperity for many of the generations that inhabited the city.[2]

Earthquakes have been a constant presence in the history of human settlements on the Strait of Messina. According to the *Catalogue of Strong Earthquakes in Italy,* the first documented earthquake in Messina occurred in 361 CE.[3] Since then, 54 earthquakes of notable intensity have hit the city—none with a magnitude of less than 4.9. The most recent episode of severe destruction prior to 1908 happened in 1783, during a seismic sequence that devastated the neighboring region of Calabria. In Messina, many buildings crumbled and several thousand inhabitants perished. After those earthquakes, the Kingdom of Naples, under whose authority both Sicily and Calabria were at the time, promoted the introduction of a new building code based on the *casa baraccata* technology, a version of the *gaiola* that Portuguese engineers had developed after the 1755 Lisbon earthquake.[4] The authorities imposed the relocation of some of the most damaged Calabrian towns but promoted the rebuilding of Messina's destroyed neighborhoods along mostly the same lines. After some years, the city regained its former shape, proving its resilience once again.[5]

With the possible exception of the 361 CE event, none of the past seismic disasters in Messina can compare to that in 1908. Not only was the magnitude of the quake unprecedented, but also the extent of the destruction and the impact on the human population. The main tremor occurred on 28 December at 04:21 GMT and had a magnitude of 7.1.[6] Renowned historian and militant socialist Gaetano Salvemini was living in Messina at that time, where he was professor of history at the local university. He was the only member of his family to survive the disaster: his wife and five children died under the rubble. This is how he described the strong tremor:

> I was in bed when I perceived everything moving around me and I heard a sinister sound coming from outside. As I was, dressed only in my shirt, I jumped out of the bed, and quickly I went to the window to see what was going on. I had just time to open it when the house fell in a sort of a vortex, it sank, and everything disappeared in a dense fog, pierced by the sound of an avalanche and cries of people falling and dying. Everything disappeared but the master wall where the window was, and I resisted, hanging from the curtain in a frenzy of desperation. Under me—you have to think that I was on the fourth floor—the ruins had made such a heap that my fall was less harmful than I expected. I was hurt but I survived.[7]

Salvemini's testimony is very similar to numerous other reports and recollections: the details change, but not the core of the narrative. The first and strongest tremor destroyed most buildings. Private houses and public edifices alike crumbled within a few seconds and, since most people were sound asleep, they buried thousands under the ruins. The earthquake, however, did not come alone. In the minutes that followed, the seism caused a tsunami wave.[8] This is the account of Captain Falkenburg, commander of the ferryboat *Calabria*:

> I was directing the maneuver from the deck when, all of a sudden, a dark, prolonged roar that seemed to come from the depth of the sea kept me. Then, before I could pay attention to the strange phenomenon, I felt the *Calabria* sinking with horrific speed, while passengers on the deck and in the cabins of first and second class started screaming. I distinguished clearly two walls of water, illuminated by the lights of the boat, digging an abyss into which the *Calabria* sank. Then, with the same lightning speed, we resurfaced.[9]

The tsunami washed over both sides of the strait for miles, and those who had escaped the crumbling buildings and sought refuge along the seashore perished under water. In Messina, the wave was less strong than on other parts of the coast, yet it probably took many lives and contributed to the destruction of the docks.[10] After the tremor and the tsunami, fires broke out at different points. Although these fires never coalesced into a general conflagration, they sometimes caused the complete ruin of those buildings that, until then, had resisted the tremor. Several fires seemingly kept burning during the following days, and, on 2 January 1909, a reporter wrote that still, in various places in the city, "the fire is burning with the highest flames."[11] By the end of this catastrophic sequence, an immense wasteland had replaced the former city.

The earthquake-tsunami did not affect only Messina. The epicenter of the seism was on the northern side of the strait, and the impact of the earthquake extended across a huge surface, along the coast of northeast Sicily, and above all in southern Calabria. There, it devastated hundreds of towns and villages.[12] The most damaged areas were the most populated ones: Messina and Reggio Calabria. According to a municipal statistical bulletin in the national archives, which seems to be the last official survey available, the city of Messina counted 109,516 inhabitants in 1907; including its hinterland, the population was more than 166,000. Reggio Calabria counted more than 30,000 inhabitants.[13] In both cities, the devastation was complete, and the number of victims was uncountable. Messina, though, was one of the most prominent centers in Southern Italy, and the impact of its destruction was bigger than that of any other settlement in the earthquake area. The large population of the city, then, meant that Messina paid by far the highest human price for the earthquake. Today's estimates vary considerably, due to the lack of reliable data and inconsistency in official records: while some insist on a traditional estimate of 60,000 dead, others claim that 30,000 would be a more accurate figure.[14] To my knowledge, none of the existing estimates seems to have taken into account the figure provided by the aforementioned 1907 statistical bulletin, only that of the 1901 national census. In any case, Messina's victims would account for at least half of the entire number of fatalities in 1908.

The news of the disaster took time to leak out. The morning after the earthquake-tsunami, the national authorities were completely unaware of the disaster. The earthquake and tsunami had damaged, entirely or in part, all transport and communication infrastructure, so the news reaching Rome came only from less affected peripheral areas. The early telegrams to the authorities in Rome, therefore, described a quite reassuring and inaccurate scenario. Those few public officers and soldiers who had survived tried to arrange rescue and sent a request for help, but the first telegraphic communication directly from Messina reached Rome only in the late afternoon of 28 December. For the whole day of 28 December, therefore, no kind of state relief reached the survivors, and preparation for the official rescue operations began only after night had fallen.[15] In the meantime, some assistance came from Russian and British sailors. Their boats were nearby for military exercises, and they noticed the effects of the earthquake-tsunami. While attempting to gather more information on what had happened, they docked in what remained of Messina's port on 29 December and immediately started digging in the ruins for survivors.

State aid reached the strait later in the day of 29 December. At that time, there was no established organization for post-disaster relief, so the national government entrusted the military with the emergency operation and appointed General Francesco Mazza as commander-in-chief. According to his report, when he arrived in Messina the situation was desperate and almost out of control: "The immensity of the disaster had swept away all social restraints … looting began after the dolorous scene of the earthquake and raged for the whole of 28 December and more or less also 29 December, with the participation of vulgar criminals from neighboring villages and of several convicted criminals who had escaped from prisons."[16]

The need for a coordinated aid initiative, and the fear of widespread social disruption fueled by the horrific accounts arriving from the earthquake zone, convinced national authorities to grant General Mazza extraordinary authority and powers. Mazza declared a state of siege, putting 11,000 soldiers under his absolute authority and submitting survivors to martial law. Under the state of siege, any soldier could immediately execute anyone suspected of an illicit act such as looting. Besides restoring public order, the army undertook all those activities considered urgent, such as searching for survivors, burying the dead, protecting property and goods, and assisting the survivors with food, water, and clothes. The organization of efficient medical assistance took much more time, and first aid was initially given on a small number of boats anchored in what was left of the harbor.

As already indicated, the number of casualties is uncertain. Institutional sources during the early days and weeks offer us an imprecise and vague picture. Estimates changed rapidly: the first telegrams announced hundreds of dead, but during the following days the number increased to up to 60,000. A number of corpses remained underneath the ruins and the army buried unidentified corpses in common graves, with no attention paid to keeping statistics on who or how many people were killed. To be sure, it was true carnage. As soon as the news of the earthquake circulated, spontaneous committees formed in almost every Italian city, in a rush of patriotic feeling and national solidarity. As recounted by historian John Dickie, these committees organized all sorts of initiatives to collect food, medicine, clothes, and money and arranged to send groups of volunteers into the disaster area. In response to that movement, the government established a Comitato Centrale di Soccorso (Central Relief Committee) to coordinate donations efficiently and organize all manner of voluntary interventions in the area.[17]

Meanwhile, most survivors left the city for other destinations, escaping from devastation and death (see figure 1.1). On 5 January 1909, the newly established Central Relief Committee sent three telegrams to the local representatives of the government in the main Italian cities. The first telegram was directed to the authorities in the principal port cities, requesting the creation of a systematic register of all survivors arriving by boat. The second was directed to the cities where the largest groups of refugees were already settled,

Figure 1.1. Refugees waiting to leave Messina, January 1909. Courtesy of the Naval History and Heritage Command.

asking local authorities how many people they could still accept. The third telegram, directed to all the main Italian cities, asked for information on how many people they were prepared to shelter.[18] These telegrams illustrate the concern of the public authorities about the unexpected and sudden population movement: all at once, the Italian state had to manage an unknown and unforeseen population of unemployed and homeless citizens.[19]

Nevertheless, as much as the authorities feared the destabilizing effects of migration, the evacuation of the earthquake area was needed to facilitate rescue operations. Thus, rather than preventing the flight of Messina's inhabitants, they tried to control it, gathering information about the identities and profession of the people leaving the disaster area. While the accuracy of this information did not meet the expectations of the central authorities themselves, it offered at least a general overview of the numbers and ultimate destinations of the refugees. The largest community was in Catania, the major urban center on the eastern coast of the island. According to the first survey of the local prefect, more than 20,000 refugees were living in the city a few weeks after the quake. Other substantial refugee communities were in Palermo (11,000), Naples (8,000), and Syracuse (2,600). Due to the attempts of the national government to distribute the people across the national territory, however, smaller groups settled in almost all Italian cities.[20]

According to estimates by historian Luciana Caminiti, population displacement during the first month following the disaster involved no less than 40,000 individuals.[21] The geographical proximity to Messina can easily explain the location of the biggest groups. The chosen cities were the sites of the nearest railroad terminals—such as Catania and Palermo—and/or the nearest ports, such as Naples. These destinations do not reveal a long-term migration strategy, but rather a sudden escape, probably made with the intention of coming back later. Some survivors did attempt international migration. We do not have reliable quantitative data, but we do possess some qualitative evidence: for instance, the Italian ambassador in the United States received a list of potential emigrants who wanted to reach family or friends in Boston, Massachusetts. It was an extremely difficult path to follow. In 1909, U.S. legislation forbade those classified as "assisted" from entering the country. Since most of the survivors had received a monetary allowance from the Italian authorities, the U.S. authorities considered them assisted persons. Therefore, the Italian authorities did not encourage migration to United States.[22]

The exodus from Messina was the direct consequence of a basic fact: the city had become an uninhabitable wasteland. Most houses were in ruins, and due to the prevailing use of stone and brick, debris covered the entire surface of the city, including virtually every road and square. The few structures still standing were unsafe because of the risk of aftershocks. In addition, the earthquake had badly damaged water supply and energy networks. The basic infrastructure that made urban life possible—dwellings, roads, and pipelines—was not in place anymore. Yet the earthquake had not only destroyed the material structure of the city. It had also profoundly affected the fabric of urban social and economic life. The combination of physical destruction, mass death, and the exodus of the survivors shattered the network of institutions, groups, functions, authorities, and activities that make the existence of a city possible. The central state provided the only form of rule and authority through the presence of the army, and no kind of economic or social initiative was possible apart from rescue operations and assistance to injured people.

The physical destruction of the city and the apparent dissolution of the bonds that held urban society together had an immense cultural impact, both in Italy and abroad. A remarkable series of earthquakes had hit various corners of the country in the two decades prior to 1908. In 1883, an earthquake on the island of Ischia had badly damaged the town of Casamicciola and had claimed more than 2,000 deaths. In 1887, another earthquake had stricken the coastal region of Liguria, in northwest Italy, damaging a number of towns and causing almost 650 fatalities. In 1894, 1905, and 1907, several strong earthquakes affected the region of Calabria, causing the ruin of many houses, hundreds of fatalities, and leaving thousands homeless.[23] Nonetheless, in 1908 two entire cities, of which one was one of the most important urban centers of the

Figure 1.2. Messina in ruins, January 1909. Courtesy of the Naval History and Heritage Command.

country, had collapsed overnight, almost all its inhabitants dead or gone, and nothing else remaining but ruins, death, and despair. In the pre–World War epoch, such sudden and immense destruction was a new and shocking experience that clashed violently with nineteenth-century trust in progress and in the bright future of urban-industrial civilization.

To capture and represent the devastation, contemporary witnesses mobilized an elaborate cultural repertoire. Reporters described the terrible stench and the sounds of the dead city, and the scenes of despair witnessed among the survivors, while photographers pictured repeatedly the devastation of once splendid houses and public edifices and the horrors of corpses rotting among the debris.[24] Accounts of the earthquake repeated ceaselessly how it had proved the fragility of men's achievements against the almighty power of Nature:

> Everyone met his death at home, as a snail squashed by a passer-by. It seemed as if the disruptive force, instead of starting from the bowels of the volcanic earth, had come from above, and that the will of a tremendous, wild God had crushed with one fist this fragile and transitory heap of powder that men had called a city. We have seen something similar when a match burns a beehive, when a hoe destroys an ants' nest. Bees fly and buzz with no direction, the silent ants limp frantically while trying to escape. Men behave exactly the same in the face of an invisible power.[25]

Confronted with the "invisible power" of the earthquake, this journalist claims, humans must realize that cities, so often mistaken as a perennial symbol of civilization, are in fact fragile and impermanent. This was the hard lesson of Messina's destruction. The use of cultural metaphors and images highlighting the limitedness of humankind against overwhelming powers is a commonplace after major seismic events. In the aftermath of the 1908 Messina earthquake, though, similar metaphors and images served a further purpose. They conveyed the message that Messina was gone for good. Facing the immense destruction, the sudden depopulation of the area, and the horrors witnessed among the ruins, several intellectuals and journalists pronounced the definitive death of Messina: "the city has to be cleared and demolished," wrote one of them, "every attempt to build it anew would be pointless." The only possible future for Messina, in those people's opinion, was to become a cemetery.[26]

Philosophical meditations on human impermanence and claims about the death of Messina, such as those quoted above, testify to the stark impression the earthquake had made on contemporary observers. Nevertheless, not everyone believed that Messina was a dead city, and after a week or so, those claiming the rebirth of the city became more vocal. This was also due to the slow but visible restoration of a provisional settlement among the ruins, promoted by a group of volunteers led by Giuseppe Micheli, a Catholic member of Parliament from Parma. Those volunteers supported the creation of a camp for the few survivors who had not left the city, which soon became known as "Michelopoli" after Micheli. The newspapers devoted considerable space to the creation of this camp, represented as the embryo of a renewed urban community. Together with Micheli and his volunteers, a small group of civilian officers were involved, such as special commissioner Nicola De Berardinis, who contributed to restoring basic municipal services as far as was possible.[27] In the camp, officers and volunteers organized a form of civic register to keep track of the population, issued a newspaper entitled *Ordini e Notizie,* and activated basic administrative services for the release of official papers and documents. The camp seemed to provide a sense of order after the disruption, giving hope that Messina could rise again even after the tremendous disaster.[28]

As the embryo of an urban community coalesced among the ruins of Messina, several newspapers carried comments from Messina's supporters that recalled the reasons why the authorities could not permit the abandonment of Messina's site, even after such a catastrophe. Among them, unsurprisingly, there were members of the local elites who had survived the disaster, such as Ludovico Fulci, a member of a powerful local family, politician, and member of Parliament.[29] Other prominent politicians such as Vittorio Emanuele Orlando and Francesco Saverio Nitti joined the chorus of those in favor of rebuilding.[30] The position of the city and the exceptional topography of the site were the most repeated arguments. The natural harbor enclosed within the semicircular peninsula and facing an ample coastal plain was extremely well situated for a port city. The strategic location in the middle of the Mediterranean, moreover, was a perfect precondition for a successful commercial economy. The same reasons for the city's prospering for three millennia, in other words, should warrant its rebirth even after the worst devastation of its long history. Messina should rise again, and in the same place where it had always been.

Earthquake Science

Italian and international scientific communities did not agree with these arguments. In 1908, knowledge of earthquakes was incomparably greater than a century earlier. Since the groundbreaking research by Robert Mallet in 1857, which introduced the notion of seismic waves and called for the constant observation of earthquakes, the accumulation of data and research on earthquakes and their causes had been steadily growing. At the turn of the twentieth century, the work promoted in Japan by a group of Western and Japanese scientists had brought about remarkable improvements in the technology for recording seismic shocks, the seismograph. Systematic registration of earthquakes around the globe and the study of particular events such as the 1906 San Francisco earthquakes had allowed some scholars to formulate early theories on fault lines, and research on historical seismology had enabled the first maps of seismic risk in countries such as Japan and Italy to be drawn.[31]

As understanding of the geophysical mechanisms responsible for earthquakes progressed, so did the understanding of the causes of seismic disasters. The notion of seismic waves discussed by Mallet in his 1862 essay on the 1857 Neapolitan earthquake[32] had helped shed light on the role played by different soil compositions in favoring or reducing the propagation of the energy released through earthquakes. This in turn reinforced the acknowledgement that building technologies could reduce the impact of earthquakes. The systematic application of advanced mathematics in engineering had rendered it possible to calculate precisely the amount of energy that a structure could bear and what kind of materials and techniques could increase its resistance. In the wake of these improvements, engineers had developed new technologies, such as reinforced concrete and steel frames, which would prove key to earthquake-resistant buildings.[33]

Italian engineers and scholars contributed to these developments. One of the pioneers of modern seismology was Giuseppe Mercalli, whose research took place from the late nineteenth to the early twentieth century. In 1883, Mercalli published the first seismic map of Italy as an appendix to his volume on volcanism.[34] Based on historical records of past earthquakes, this map arguably inaugurated historical seismology in Italy. One year later, Mercalli published a study on the 1883 Ischia earthquake in which he stressed the strong connections between the composition of the soil, civil engineering, and the extent of the damage.[35] Subsequently, in 1901, he published his seminal study on the assessment of earthquake damages, which introduced the classification system for earthquakes later known as the Mercalli scale.[36] During the last decade of the nineteenth century, geographer Mario Baratta furthered the study of historical seismicity in Italy. In 1901, Baratta published the first comprehensive monograph on the topic, followed later by a detailed cartography.[37] In addition, both Mercalli and Baratta studied the Calabrian earthquakes of 1894, 1905, and 1907 in great detail. In the light of the historical records of past quakes in the region, they drew similar conclusions about the extremely high seismicity of the strait area.[38]

The series of earthquakes that preceded the 1908 event gave Italian scholars and professionals opportunities to advance their understanding of seismicity on Italian territory and experiment with some of the new building technologies. After the 1883 Casamicciola earthquake, the government established a special commission charged with investigating the causes of the seism and proposing methods and strategies for the prevention of future disasters. This commission pointed out the poor quality of civil engineering in Casamicciola as the principal cause of the disaster and advocated that a number of technical standards for earthquake-resistant buildings be applied to the entire island of Ischia.[39] The authorities established similar commissions after the 1887 Ligurian earthquake, and after the 1894, 1905, and 1907 Calabrian earthquakes, promoting the construction of earthquake-resistant buildings in reinforced concrete.[40]

In the aftermath of the 1908 earthquake, this knowledge was intensively mobilized to explain the disaster and, by the same token, to prevent new seismic disasters from occurring. Virtually every institution or professional association even remotely related to natural sciences or engineering conducted enquiries into the earthquake. The result was a remarkable number of publications on the great catastrophe: a recent survey has calculated that more than one hundred publications about the Messina earthquake came out in 1909 alone.[41] Most of these studies and scientific reports drew similar conclusions: the disaster was due to a combination of bad construction techniques and materials, a weak soil composition, and the power of the seismic shock.

Giuseppe Mercalli himself took part in the mobilization of scientists and professionals. He visited the city in April 1909 and disseminated his observations later in a special issue of the bulletin of the Reale Istituto d'Incoraggiamento alle Scienze di Napoli (Royal Neapolitan Institute for the Advancement of Science). In his opinion, the disaster was due to the combined action of the force of the earthquake, the quality of the soil, and building techniques and materials. "While visiting the ruins of Messina," wrote Mercalli, "I noted that the disaster was generally bigger in the city's old neighborhoods than in the new. ... This depended on the greater compactness of the hills' quaternary soil, whereas the soft soil of the plain slid and shifted chaotically." He concluded: "Regardless of the nature of soil, the main cause of the human disaster, that is to say the huge number of victims in the city of Messina, is the construction of poor housing, without any respect to the most elementary rules of earthquake-resistant engineering."[42]

Mario Baratta formulated an identical diagnosis in his much more comprehensive study of the 1908 earthquake, which was commissioned by the Società Geografica Italiana (Italian Geographical Society).[43] Like Mercalli, Baratta pointed out the role played by soil composition. Baratta observed that most of Messina's coastal plain consisted of alluvium, that is, a mixture of diverse types of small rocks and detritus brought by water and accumulated over time. The coastal plain where Messina lay largely corresponded, in fact, to the cones of dejection of the streams flowing down from the Peloritani Mountains. Alluvial soils diffuse seismic waves almost without resistance: the same geological input—an earthquake of undetermined magnitude—would have very different effects on a rocky soil compared to alluvium. That unstable coastal plain created by water's erosive action was the site of the most populated and densely built part of the city, and the one that suffered most of the damages. According

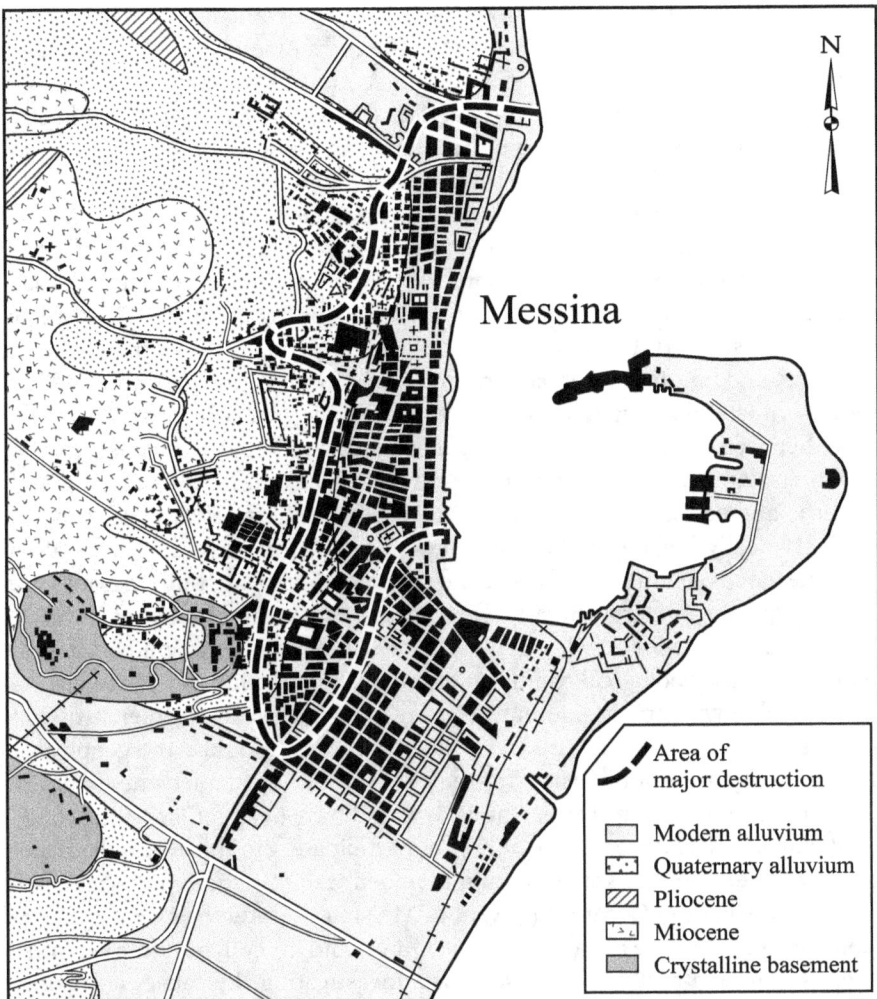

Figure 1.3. Soil composition in Messina and the distribution of damages as recorded by Mario Baratta. Cartography by Mary Lee Eggart.

to Baratta, therefore, the root of the city's fortune and prosperity, i.e., its advantageous coastal location, was also a major risk factor.

Even for Baratta, human intervention played a pivotal role. After the earthquakes in 1783–1784, which seriously affected Messina and most of Calabria, the government of the Kingdom of Naples had promulgated an innovative set of technical standards for the reconstruction of houses and public edifices. As mentioned earlier, this was based on the system that Portuguese engineers introduced in Lisbon after the 1755 earthquake. Buildings had to be provided with an internal structure of completely interconnected wooden beams, i.e., a timber skeleton elastic enough to resist seismic movement. The name of this kind of architecture was *casa baraccata*. The technology had not been explicitly included in the post-1783 city's building code, but the same code explicitly detailed earthquake-resistant construction standards.[44] As Baratta could state during his fieldwork, however, builders rarely adhered to the 1783 code in the first place, and their successors simply forgot about it. In addition, building materials and engineering were poor and inadequate. Builders had often made cement and bricks with sand collected from the seabed or from the beds of urban streams: the same materials that formed the unstable soil of the city. Walls were thin, and beams were generally not strong or big enough for the weight they had to support. Even the roofs were generally too heavy for the rest of the building, and buildings that had originally been built with two or three storeys had to withstand a fourth or even a fifth floor added on years later.

Other factors accounted for the general destruction. The owners of those buildings damaged by the earthquakes of 1894, 1905, and 1907 had made only superficial repairs, without securing the structure effectively. In addition, due to the typically narrow streets and alleys of the historic city, a falling wall, or just one block of stone, could cause the ruin of neighboring buildings and prevent escape. By and large, Baratta's argument was as unambiguous as it was detailed: the destruction of Messina was the result of an interaction between the earthquake, the geological condition of the soil, and the human-made features of the built environment. Humans were responsible for the immense tragedy of Messina as much as nature was. Had they not overlooked the geophysical features and the seismic history of the site, and better adapted the urban environment to seismicity, the earthquake would have been far less disastrous.

Italian scholars were not the only ones participating in this research. Professor Ōmori, eminent seismologist and member of the Japanese Imperial Earthquake Investigation Committee, went to Messina to study the event, as he had done two years before in San Francisco. Ōmori and his collaborators examined the disaster area and met local scientists investigating the causes and consequences of the earthquake. As a result of this fieldwork, Ōmori wrote a scientific report on the Messina disaster, published in the official bulletin of the Imperial Committee. While maintaining his mistaken theory that Messina was now safe, as was every site that had already been hit once by a major earthquake, Ōmori nonetheless specified that those killed in Messina should be regarded "as having fallen victims to seismologically bad construction of houses."[45]

The conviction that the disaster was more the result of human lack of consideration than nature's overwhelming power underlay the work of other scientists and engineers in the aftermath of the earthquake. Accordingly, many of them devoted their time to identifying solutions and strategies to better adapt the urban environment to the geophysical features of a seismic site. On 7 January 1909, the Royal Neapolitan Institute for the Advancement of Science established a special commission for a complete study of the disaster. The goal of this study was not only to understand the 1908 earthquake event but also to find the best technical solutions for safe engineering in seismic areas. In its final report, published before the end of the year, the commission stressed that high seismic risks menaced the whole of Italy, as shown by the sequence of destructive earthquakes that had struck the country in the past two decades, from the 1883 Casamicciola earthquake onwards. The only effective response to prevent similar disasters from occurring again, advised the commission, was the countrywide adoption of a set of technical standards for earthquake-resistant engineering.[46]

Even the Società degli Ingegneri e Architetti Italiani (Society of Italian Architects and Engineers) created a special commission on the 1908 earthquake. That commission focused almost exclusively on earthquake engineering, in line with the principal area of expertise of the association. The commissioners analyzed in great detail technologies for earthquake-resistant engineering throughout the world. These included early skyscrapers with steel frames, whose resistance had been tested two years before in San Francisco, traditional wooden architecture in Japan, and the newly introduced reinforced concrete. The report concluded by rejecting both the U.S. and the Japanese solutions as unfit for Italy, and opted instead for reinforced concrete. The commissioners justified this rejection by stressing the need to adapt technology to the social and cultural features of the country. Concrete could better accommodate the features of Italian architecture due to its adaptability, while still providing the necessary solidity.[47]

Other reports, studies, and analyses that filled the pages of bulletins, journals, and newspapers for months shared similar conclusions. Ideas about science and adaptation to seismicity, however, were not limited to "high" scientific culture. On the contrary, there is evidence of the diffusion of similar patterns of reasoning in popular culture, too. The state archives contain an unusual collection of letters addressed to King Vittorio Emanuele III, to Prime Minister Giovanni Giolitti and the President of the Central Relief Committee. The authors of those letters were people from different social origins and professions—artisans, school teachers, army officers—who put forward their own version of events and their solutions for effective prevention. Sometimes strange and bizarre, sometimes surprisingly clear-sighted, these proposals offer a fascinating cross section of popular opinions about the disaster.[48]

Onorato Arbuffo wrote one such letter on 17 January 1909. Arbuffo introduced himself as a typographer aged 64 from the Ligurian city of Sanremo. According to his understanding, earthquakes such as that which had hit Messina depended on "heat and fire" burning underneath the surface of the earth. For that reason, concluded Arbuffo, the only way to prevent earthquakes from occurring again was to extinguish the heat and fire. Humans could accomplish this by diverting the course of rivers into volcano vents, and thus "putting out or calming down whatever kinds of substances produce all of a sudden such horrible movements in the bowels of the earth."[49]

While Arbuffo wanted to eliminate the cause of the earthquakes themselves, others focused instead on earthquake engineering. On 21 January 1909, Antonio Barreca, who was in Syracuse as a refugee, wrote to the king to illustrate his ideas about the reconstruction of Messina. He acknowledged the unstable quality of Messina's soil, perhaps after having heard or read accounts about scientists' field trips in Messina in the newspapers. Despite the poor soil, he was in favor of rebuilding the city on the same site. This would be sustainable by adopting a technological solution he had conceived to increase buildings' resistance to shocks: "new edifices should be built in iron sheets without foundations, as one usually builds a merchant ship," so that during an earthquake they could shake without collapsing.[50] Many other letters are in much the same vein, and sometimes propose even more elaborate solutions. Italo Siffredi imagined an earthquake-resistant city in which the houses "would stand on foundations of cast-iron pedestals." These houses would be built with bricks made of "seaweed, as one can find along the sea coast, washed in fresh water, then dried and ground; sawdust, dung, and white sand." These seaweed houses would rise "no more than one meter above the ground" and should be "furnished with little spherical bells, extremely sensitive, which will serve as an alarm in case of seismic movements."[51]

This fairy-tale city of little houses, seaweed walls, and bells was destined to remain nothing more than a figment of Siffredi's vivid imagination, as were other bizarre proposals based on astrology, astronomy, electricity, or electromagnetic machines. Their authors were home-based inventors and self-proclaimed geniuses, totally outside the scientific establishment. Nonetheless, they had much more in common with acclaimed geologists and engineers than one would expect. They all shared the conviction that technology could prevent new disasters. The earthquake, to them, was not an unavoidable, deadly fate, but rather a natural event for which the city and its inhabitants should be better prepared. This shared conviction would guide the most fundamental choices concerning the future of the settlement.

Earthquake-Proof Urbanism

Among associations and institutes promoting studies on the earthquake was the Accademia dei Lincei (Lincean Academy), one of the oldest and most prestigious scientific institutions in the country. On 3 January 1909, the academy decided to propose a comprehensive study of the disaster and to request the direct involvement of the national authorities. Accordingly, a few days later the president of the academy, Senator Pietro Blaserna, wrote to Prime Minister Giolitti. Blaserna claimed that the government should undertake a scientific inquiry of its own and base its policies on the findings.[52] The proposed study should investigate "what had really happened on the strait," not by means of theories and abstract speculations, but with "strictly experimental methods." Furthermore, the study should analyze "the best building method" to adopt in a country like Italy that was "exposed to the terrible calamity of earthquakes."[53] Blaserna then nominated himself to lead such an inquiry.

The following day, Giolitti received another letter from the Minister of Agriculture, Francesco Cocco-Ortu, reporting a similar request he had received from the Reale Società Geologica (Royal Geological Society).[54] To my knowledge, these two letters are the only archival traces of lobbying activity by the scientific community aimed at obtaining a state commission to examine the 1908 earthquake event. The close connections between scientists and legislators, however, suggest that lobbying might actually have been much more extensive. The large majority of directors and presidents of those research institutes, scientific societies, and professional associations that were proposing investigations and studies on the disaster were also members of Parliament. The promoter of Giuseppe Mercalli's study of Messina, for instance, was Senator Faina, president of the Commissione parlamentare d'inchiesta sulle condizioni dei contadini nelle provincie meridionali (parliamentary commission of enquiry on the conditions of peasants in Southern Italy). Professor Raffaele Cappelli, president of the Italian Geographical Society and member of Parliament, appointed Mario Baratta. Francesco Saverio Nitti, member of Parliament, influential politician, several times minister, and promoter of a number of groundbreaking laws for Southern Italy, chaired the Special Commission of the Royal Neapolitan Institute for the Advancement of Sciences on the 1908 earthquake.

At any rate, on 9 January 1909, the prime minister replied to Pietro Blaserna, assuring him that the government would reflect attentively on his proposition, "which requires the maximum consideration."[55] As is borne out by subsequent events, this was not an idle statement. On 12 January 1909, Parliament passed the main piece of legislation on the disaster. This law defined almost all the financial and administrative means to provide assistance and recovery, inaugurating a long-term mode of hazard response centered on consistent public spending by the central authorities. The law introduced special taxes to cover the costs of the entire operation, facilitated expropriation procedures, and gave special powers to the government to bypass Parliament for any matter related to the disaster that should need an urgent response. Article 7, furthermore, announced that the reconstruction of all the affected localities should follow a "technical and hygienic" building code, the content of which the authorities would specify later with the support of a special commission of experts to be appointed by the government.[56]

Article 7 deferred the creation of the commission to a decree. When the time came to enact that decision, the government opted for the creation of two commissions, both established on 15 January by means of two distinct decrees. The first commission's official entitlement was "the study and proposition of mandatory building standards for the municipalities struck by the 1908 earthquake or those previous," and included among its members university professors, deputies, and high-ranking officers from the Genio Civile and Genio Militare (Civil and Military Engineering Corps). The president of the commission was Italo Maganzini, also president of the Consiglio Superiore dei Lavori Pubblici (Superior Council of Public Works.) Several commissioners visited the disaster area between 3 and 10 February 1909. Their report noted which types of constructions had withstood the quake: firstly, those few buildings that had followed the building code introduced after the 1783 earthquake; secondly, low houses with deep foundations and built with good materials; thirdly, new infrastructure such as rail bridges. In addition, the commissioners noted that the few houses that were built using reinforced concrete had resisted the earthquake, proving the effectiveness of this new technology. Other commissioners focused solely on written sources, studying the various solutions adopted after past earthquakes in Italy and other countries, from Jamaica to Japan.[57]

In March 1909, after field trips and lengthy discussions, the commission issued a final report, which listed a series of rules the authorities should enforce in the entire disaster area. The commissioners chose not to advise on specific technologies, but rather on standards and features that the builders had to apply to all types of buildings: the maximum heights and number of floors allowed for each building, and the minimum width for streets. On 18 April 1909, only three months after the government had established the commission, a decree introduced a new mandatory building code for the disaster area. The new building code replicated entirely the commission's proposal. Among the provisions of the new code, Article 2 established for each building a mandatory limit of two floors and maximum height of 10 meters from the ground. Article 22 imposed a mandatory minimum width of 10 meters for all streets.[58]

The decree enforced the new building and planning code in the entire disaster area. Neither the commission's report nor the decree, though, gave the final word on the precise locations where the rebuilding would be allowed. For that purpose, the authorities had established a second commission, whose task was precisely "to identify the most adequate areas for the reconstruction of the settlements struck by the earthquake of 1908 or those previous."[59] This commission was the direct result of the letter the president of the Lincean Academy wrote to Prime Minister Giolitti. As he had originally suggested, Blaserna himself was appointed president of that commission. Other members included the directors of the seismic observatories of Catania and Messina, the directors of state research institutes for hydrography and geodynamics, and members of the military and civil geological services. These experts would study the geophysical conditions of the strait area and draw conclusions on seismic risk and reconstruction. The commission started its work in January 1909 and expected to finish by April 1909. Nevertheless, by the end of May 1909 the commission had only produced a brief field report that confirmed what other geologists were repeating: Messina's soil was an unstable alluvium and this had certainly increased the impact of the earthquake on the built environment; furthermore, the whole area was undoubtedly subject to strong seismicity. The report concluded abruptly by stating the necessity of a more detailed investigation.

In the meantime, the situation had changed somewhat since the very first weeks after the earthquake. Michelopoli, the tent camp that volunteers had set up on the outskirts of the ruined city, was growing into a more sizeable, albeit still informal, settlement. Basic commercial and administrative activities had started again, and the special commissioner whom the Minister of Home Affairs had appointed to deal with municipal affairs during the emergency had remitted his mandate to the reconstituted city council.[60] By April 1909, many of those survivors who had left the ruined city in the aftermath were moving back. The unwillingness of local communities to shelter them any longer, along with the strict surveillance and many social limitations attached to their status as refugees, were pushing them back to Messina, and the national authorities eventually approved their return.[61] An urban community was coalescing among the ruins of December 1908, whilst the authorities had not yet made any official decision. Nonetheless, formal authorization was needed in order to begin the reconstruction, and everything depended on the geological commission.

The government petitioned the commissioners repeatedly, asking for a quick conclusion to the research. Already by mid-February 1909, members of the government, including the prime minister himself, had appealed the commission "to undertake its task with the most alacrity," postponing those studies that were not "absolutely urgent." Blaserna answered, invoking the importance of the commission's work for future generations and thus the need for a serious and in-depth study of the strait's geological and seismological conditions that did not sacrifice accuracy for speed.[62] After the promulgation of the new building code in April, appeals became more pressing, and in May 1909, the Ministry of Public Works lamented that, because of the commission's delay, the reconstruction and planning were stalled even where they could have started already.[63] Despite these pressures, the commission finished its report only at the end of June 1909. This report, moreover, although it gave a final assessment of several localities, did not examine the most important one: Messina.[64]

Claiming the area to investigate was too large for the time and the resources at the commission's disposal, Blaserna recruited another expert to report specifically on Messina. This expert was Secondo Franchi, a geologist from the Regio Ufficio Geologico (Royal Geological Bureau). Franchi visited the city in

June 1909. Once again, his conclusions were similar to those of all other studies: Messina stood on top of highly unstable alluvial soil in an area subject to frequent and powerful earthquakes. Yet, in spite of that clear statement, when he came to express his opinion on whether to rebuild Messina on the same site, he assented. Messina, he claimed, had to be reborn in the proximity of the "wonderful harbor which Nature had placed on a main commercial route," obeying the "'inescapable economic and geographic laws" that had permitted a settlement to emerge there in the first place, and prosper for almost three millennia. "With the rigorous application of the technical norms established by the Royal Decree of 18 April 1909," wrote Franchi, "it will be possible to rebuild on the recent alluvium, except for the places where the ground has subsided."[65] The natural advantages provided by the site and location would outweigh the hazards, and the adoption of the recently enacted building code would mitigate the risk of new disasters.

The commission shared that conclusion, and, in the final report, recommended rebuilding Messina alongside the natural harbor, despite the conditions of its soil and the seismicity of the strait. The only necessary condition would be the strict enforcement of the building code and the additional interdiction of construction within 100 meters of the coastline.[66] On 15 July 1909, a royal decree incorporated the commission's conclusion in its entirety. The decree listed the localities where the authorities would allow reconstruction on the condition of strict application of the earthquake building code, and Messina was among them. As mentioned previously, many refugees who had left the city in the aftermath began to return after a few months, and basic administrative and commercial functions had been restored. Thus, in many respects, the final decision of the geological commission and the ensuing royal decree was the result of the recognition of the actual situation in the field. The decree, however, formalized an idea that would underlie the entire reconstruction strategy. The city would rise again by the "sickle" of the harbor where it had always stood. But this time it would become an earthquake-proof urban environment.

Conclusion

The 1908 Messina earthquake was a tremendous catastrophe, the terrible consequences of which make it one of the worst seismic disasters of its time. In 1891, a major earthquake known alternatively as the Mino-Owari or Nobi earthquake severely affected a vast region of inland Japan. In 1906, two cities in the Americas suffered greatly from the consequences of major earthquakes: Valparaiso, Chile, and San Francisco, California. In Nobi, Valparaiso, and San Francisco, the earthquakes and the chain of consequences that were set in motion determined the physical destruction of urban environments. In none of these cases, however, was the number of people killed comparable with the victims of the 1908 Messina earthquake. In both Valparaiso and San Francisco, earthquakes and fires killed around 3,000 people, and in the Nobi region, almost 8,000 people died. In Messina and the entire disaster area, the earthquake provoked an immense massacre, killing tens of thousands of individuals, and leaving hundreds of thousands homeless. The physical infrastructure and social fabric of the city seemed irreversibly destroyed, prompting some to believe that Messina itself was gone forever.

In the period during which these tragic events took place, earthquake science changed remarkably. Understanding of both the causes of earthquakes and of the methods to prevent major damages advanced greatly, laying the basis for today's seismology and earthquake engineering. Nobi, Valparaiso, San Francisco, and Messina were landmarks in this history. In Japan, the Nobi earthquake led, among several things, to the creation of the Imperial Earthquake Investigation Committee and to a revision of the dominant approach in building engineering.[67] In the United States, the San Francisco earthquake led eventually to the recognition of San Andreas Fault as the cause of earthquakes and permanent seismic risk in California.[68] In Chile, as a response to the Valparaiso earthquake, the government established the Seismological Service of Chile.[69] In this pioneering era of seismology, innovations in science and technology circulated globally. Experts in every country, including Italy, were fully aware of what was being done elsewhere, and were often in direct contact with foreign colleagues.[70] The 1908 Messina earthquake was caught into this transnational web of knowledge and expertise, and the response to the disaster was tied to the global advancements in seismology and earthquake engineering.

The 1908 earthquake was also a turning point in Italian earthquake response and practices, starting with the 1909 legislation on earthquake engineering. The introduction of a building code was not new by any means: the authorities of the Kingdom of Naples had introduced a code in the aftermath of the 1783 earthquake, and this kind of building code became common practice after every earthquake on the peninsula from that time on. In 1909, the legislators introduced a building code not only in the disaster area, but also in all regions considered at risk due to their seismic history.[71] The Messina earthquake also fuelled the rise of reinforced concrete. Despite the fact that the 1909 building code did not prescribe any particular technology, the studies produced in the wake of the disaster consecrated reinforced concrete as the most suitable earthquake-resistant technology. Due to its suitability for modern building standards along with its earthquake-resistant properties, reinforced concrete became the protagonist of Italian engineering in the twentieth century.[72] Finally, the 1908 earthquake changed the scientific status of seismology in Italy. The incorporation of earthquake science into national legislation in the aftermath of 1908 was the first step of its gradual institutionalization as a public science. This process, enhanced by subsequent major earthquakes such as the 1915 Marsica earthquake and the 1930 Irpinia earthquake, led eventually to the creation of the Istituto Nazionale Geofisica (National Institute for Geophysics), a national research institute devoted to monitoring and studying seismic phenomena.[73]

Above all, the 1908 earthquake had a profound and immediate impact on Messina's site and settlement, both in terms of its physical characteristics and how it was conceived. The earthquake devastated the city to an unprecedented extent. The terrible destruction and the sudden depopulation of the site prompted many to question the advisability of rebuilding the city *tout court*. The research and findings of dozens of scientists and engineers pointed out some dangerous features of Messina's site and position, namely the lack of stability of its alluvial soil and the persistent seismic activity in the strait area. This would advise against its reconstruction and in favor of the permanent abandonment of the site. However, the argument for rebuilding the city on its former site won out in the end. In the opinion of the principal decision-makers, the "inescapable laws" of geography and economy evoked by Secondo Franchi outweighed the geological risks of the site. Messina's coastal location, the natural harbor, and its strategic position on the strait would "naturally" warrant the rebirth and economic prosperity of Messina, while modern earthquake science and technology would mitigate, if not completely nullify, the impact of future seismic hazards.

The attempt to balance risks and advantages is common to the history of many urban settlements located in hazardous sites. Referring to the case of New Orleans, Ari Kelman recalled a classic distinction between "site" and "situation." The situation of the French colony was extremely advantageous, being at the junction of the Mississippi (North America's most important waterway), the Gulf of Mexico, and the Caribbean Sea, and thus of transatlantic commerce. Its site, however, posed multiple threats related to its watery environment and subtropical climate.[74] The idea that the advantages of the "situation" outweighed the risks of the "site" motivated the pursuit of European settlement in such a place and the search for strategies to mitigate those risks. In 1908, due to the exceptional crisis provoked by the earthquake, survivors, scientists, and political elites openly debated the balance between risks and advantages of Messina's site and location, and the authorities made binding decisions within a matter of months. Advocates of Messina's reconstruction gained support by evoking continuity with the maritime past of the city and the supposed natural advantages of the city's situation and site. The state commission finally embraced the same view. Ironically, the building code that was introduced to ensure continuity would in fact impose a radical modification of the entire urban environment and effect a profound caesura in the history of the city.

The earth's crust has always been in motion. The rocks, the mountains, the ocean's depths are a dynamic and changing environment. Unlike other parts of the nonhuman world, changes in the earth's crust usually happen too slowly for humans to perceive them. Geological change, though, sometimes encounters the short time frame of human events. The 1908 earthquake was one such case. The seismic shock of 28 December originated in the constant collisions between the African plate and the Eurasian plate. This global geological phenomenon had tragic and disruptive consequences for Messina, causing an almost fatal crisis for the city and stimulating a profound revision of the settlement's features. This view, however, does not sum up the impact of the earthquake on the history of the city. To appreciate that impact and its diverse ramifications more deeply, we will now look at how Messina was changing before the earthquake, and the kind of city it became afterwards.

Notes

1. Lorenzo Bonini, Daniela Di Bucci, Giovanni Toscani, Silvio Seno, and Gianluca Valensise, "Reconciling Deep Seismogenic and Shallow Active Faults through Analogue Modelling: The Case of the Messina Strait (Southern Italy)," *Journal of the Geological Society* 168, no. 1 (2011): 191–99; Carlo Doglioni, Marco Ligi, Davide Scrocca, Sabina Bigi, Giovanni Bortoluzzi, Eugenio Carminati, Marco Cuffaro, Filippo D'Oriano, Filippo Muccini, and Federica Riguzzi, "The Tectonic Puzzle of the Messina Area (Southern Italy): Insights from New Seismic Reflection Data," *Scientific Reports* 2 (2012): 970.
2. Amelia I. Gigante, *Le città nella storia d'Italia: Messina* (Rome and Bari, 1980).
3. Emanuela Guidoboni, Graziano Ferrari, Dante Mariotti, Alberto Comastri, Gabriele Tarabusi, Gianluca Valensise, "Earthquake Sequence 00 00 361, Stretto di Messina," *Catalogue of Strong Earthquakes in Italy 461 B.C.–1997 and Mediterranean Area 760 B.C.–1500*, Database, INGV-Istituto Nazionale di Geofisica e Vulcanologia. http://storing.ingv.it/cfti4med/quakes/50056.html. accessed 4 August 2014. Sources on that earthquake, along with the possibility that it might have been an event comparable to the 1908 earthquake, are discussed in Emanuela Guidoboni, Anna Muggia, Alberto Comastri, and Gianluca Valensise,"Ipotesi sul 'predecessore' del terremoto del 1908: Archeologia, storia, geologia," in *Il terremoto e il maremoto del 28 dicembre 1908: Analisi sismologica impatto, prospettive,* ed. Guido Bertolaso, Enzo Boschi, Emanuela Guidoboni, and Gianluca Valensise (Rome and Bologna, 2008), 483–516.
4. Stephen Tobriner, "La Casa Baraccata: Earthquake-Resistant Construction in 18th-Century Calabria," *Journal of the Society of Architectural Historians* 42, no. 2 (1983): 131–38; Rafaela Cardoso, Mario Lopes, and Rita Bento, "Earthquake Resistant Structures of Portuguese Old 'Pombalino' Buildings," *13th World Conference on Earthquake Engineering,* Vancouver, Canada, 1–6 August 2004, Paper no. 918, http://www.iitk.ac.in/nicee/wcee/article/13_918.pdf.
5. Michela D'Angelo and Marcello Saija, "A City and Two Earthquakes: Messina 1783–1908," in *Cities and Catastrophes: Coping with Emergency in European History / Villes*

et catastrophes: Réaction face à l'urgence dans l'histoire européenne, ed. Geneviève Massard-Guilbaud, Dieter Schott and Harold L. Platt, (Frankfurt am Main, 2002), 122–40.

6. To ensure consistency, throughout the book I will adopt the magnitude measuring system used by Guidoboni et al., *Catalogue of Strong Earthquakes*. For details on the methods used to calculate "equivalent magnitude" see Paolo Gasperini and Graziano Ferrari, "Deriving Numerical Estimates from Descriptive Information: The Computation of Earthquake Parameters," *Annali di Geofisica* 43, no. 4 (2000): 729–46, esp. 736–37.
7. Testimony originally published in *L'Avanti*, 8 January 1909, reprinted in *Il terremoto di Messina: Corrispondenze, testimonianze e polemiche giornalistiche*, ed. Francesco Mercadante, (Reggio Calabria, 2006; 1st ed. 1958), 12. All citations taken from Italian sources are my own translations unless otherwise stated.
8. Bertolaso et al., *Il terremoto e il maremoto del 28 dicembre 1908*.
9. Testimony collected by Tommaso Gialansè, "L'alba del 28 dicembre nello stretto di Messina, 19 gennaio," originally published in *Roma*, 22–23 January 1909, reprinted in Mercadante, *Il terremoto*, 33.
10. Giovanni Platania, "Il maremoto dello Stretto di Messina del 28 Dicembre 1908," *Bollettino della Società Sismologica d'Italia*, 13 (1909): 369–458.
11. Antonio Scarfoglio, "Messina in fiamme, 2 gennaio 1909," originally published in *Il Mattino*, 4–5 January 1909, reprinted in Mercadante, *Il terremoto*, 246.
12. See Emanuela Guidoboni, and Dante Mariotti, "Il terremoto e il maremoto del 1908: effetti e parametri sismici," in Bertolaso et al., *Il terremoto e il maremoto del 28 dicembre 1908*, 17–136.
13. Ufficio Statistico Municipale, *Bollettino Statistico del Comune di Messina*, III Trimestre 1907, in box 38, Ministero dell'Interno, Direzione Generale dell'Amministrazione Civile, Terremoto Calabro Siculo [hereafter MI, DGAC, Terremoto calabro-siculo], Archivio Centrale dello Stato [hereafter ACS].
14. Caminiti calculates no more than 30,000 dead: Luciana Caminiti, "Fonti per la ricostruzione della popolazione messinese nel terremoto del 1908," in *La Grande Diaspora: 28 dicembre 1908 la politica dei soccorsi tra carità e bilanci* (Messina, 2009), 249–55. Restifo maintains the validity of the traditional estimate of 60,000 dead: Giuseppe Restifo, "Il vortice demografico dopo la catastrofe: morti e movimenti di popolazione a Messina fra 1908 e 1911," in Bertolaso et al., *Il terremoto e il maremoto del 28 dicembre 1908*, 295–304.
15. Sergio Castenetto, Mirella Sebastiano, and Fosca Pizzaroni, *La gestione dell'emergenza nel terrremoto calabro-siculo del 28 dicembre 1908* (Rome, 2008); Giorgio Boatti, *La terra trema: Messina 28 dicembre 1908; I trenta secondi che cambiarono l'Italia, non gli italiani* (Milan, 2004).
16. *Relazione sull'opera del R. Commissario Straordinario Tenente Generale Mazza nelle regioni sicule colpite dal terremoto del 28 dicembre 1908 (con 5 allegati)*, p. 18, in box 380, folder 4, Presidenza del Consiglio dei Ministri [hereafter PCM] 1909, ACS.
17. John Dickie, *La catastrofe patriottica: il terremoto di Messina* (Rome and Bari, 2009).
18. Telegrams no. 1268, no. 1371, and no. 1373, 5 January 1909, in box 25, folder 10.1.a, Ministero dell'Interno, Comitato Centrale di Soccorso pei danneggiati dal terremoto del 28 dicembre 1908 in Calabria e in Sicilia [hereafter MI CCS 1908], ACS.
19. Caminiti, *La Grande Diaspora*, 134.

20. "Tabella su Movimento profughi per provincia: arrivati e partiti," in box 25, folder 10.1.e, MI CCS 1908, ACS.
21. Caminiti, "Fonti per la ricostruzione," 249–55.
22. We do not have reliable quantitative data, but some qualitative figures about groups of people who wanted to reach family or friends in the United States. See the lists of potential emigrants sent to the Italian Ambassador in the United States in box 25, folder 10.6.8, MI CCS 1908, ACS.
23. Emanuela Guidoboni and Gianluca Valensise, *Il peso economico e sociale dei disastri sismici in Italia negli ultimi 150 anni, 1861–2011* (Bologna, 2011).
24. See for instance the pictures in Giovanna Naldi, ed., *Terremoto calabro-messinese 1908/2008* (Rome, 2008).
25. Giuseppe A. Borgese, "Con la testa riversa e le palme protese," originally published in *Il Mattino*, 1–2 January 1909, reprinted in Mercadante, *Il terremoto*, 4.
26. Goffredo Bellonci, "Messina perduta per sempre," originally published in *Il Giornale d'Italia*, 4 January 1909, reprinted in Mercadante, *Il terremoto*, 98.
27. Nicola De Berardinis, *Relazione letta dal Commissario Straordinario Cav. Avv. Nicola De Berardinis, Consigliere Delegato dalla Prefettura di Messina, letta il 14 febbraio 1909, prima seduta del Consiglio Comunale dopo la catastrofe del 28 dicembre 1908* (Messina, 1909).
28. Luigi Lodi, "L'onorevole Micheli e gli altri," originally published in *La Vita*, 4 February 1909, reprinted in Mercadante, *Il terremoto*, 682–84; A. Salvatore, *Michelopoli* (Messina, 1958).
29. Antonio Scarfoglio, "I Messinesi non vogliono abbandonare la loro città," originally published in *Il Mattino*, 6 January 1909, reprinted in Mercadante, *Il terremoto*, 259.
30. See for instance the interview with Vittorio E. Orlando in Tullio Giordana, "V. E. Orlando: La regina dello stretto risorgerà," originally published in *La Tribuna*, 5 January 1909, reprinted in Mercadante, *Il terremoto*, 478–81; also Francesco Coppola, "La ricchezza perduta e quella che risorgerà nelle cifre e nei commenti dell'onorevole Nitti," originally published in *La Tribuna*, 24 January 1909, reprinted in Mercadante, *Il terremoto*, 720–24.
31. For a history of these early developments, please refer to Carl H. Geschwind, *California Earthquakes* (Baltimore, 2001); Gregory Clancey, *Earthquake Nation* (Berkeley, 2006), and Deborah Coen, *Earthquake Observers* (Chicago, 2013).
32. Robert Mallet, *Great Neapolitan Earthquake of 1857: The First Principles of Observational Seismology* (London, 1862).
33. Robert Reitherman, *Earthquakes and Engineers: An International History* (Reston, VA, 2012), 105–57.
34. Giuseppe Mercalli, *Vulcani e fenomeni vulcanici in Italia* (Milan, 1882).
35. Giuseppe Mercalli, *L' isola d'Ischia ed il terremoto del 28 luglio 1883* (Milan, 1884).
36. Giuseppe Mercalli, *Sulle modificazioni proposte alla scala sismica De Rossi-Forel* (Modena, 1902).
37. Mario Baratta, *I terremoti d'Italia: saggio di storia, geografia e bibliografia sismica italiana* (Turin, 1901); Baratta, "Carta sismica d'Italia," in *Sulle aree sismiche italiane* (Voghera, 1901).
38. Giuseppe Mercalli, *I terremoti della Calabria Meridionale e del Messinese: Saggio di una monografia sismica regionale* (Rome, 1897); Mercalli, *Alcuni risultati ottenuti dallo studio del terremoto calabrese dell'8 settembre 1905* (Napoli, 1906); Mario Baratta, *Il*

grande terremoto calabro dell'8 settembre 1905: Alcune considerazioni sulla distribuzione topografica dei danni (Pisa, 1906); Baratta, *Il nuovo massimo sismico calabrese, 23 ottobre 1907* (Rome, 1907).

39. Commissione per le prescrizioni edilizie dell'isola di Ischia, *Relazione della Commissione per le prescrizioni edilizie dell'isola d'Ischia istituita dal Ministro dei Lavori pubblici dopo il terremoto del luglio 1883* (Rome, 1883).

40. A complete bibliography and detailed analysis of the results of these commissions is in Commissione del R. Istituto di Napoli per la ricerca delle norme edilizie per le regioni sismiche, "Contributo," *Atti del R. Istituto d'Incoraggiamento di Napoli* 6 (1909): iii–xxv. See also Guidoboni and Valensise, *Il peso economico e sociale dei disastri sismici*, 63, 193. On the experimental use of reinforced concrete after 1905 see Crescentino Caveglia, "Pensieri sull'impiego del cemento armato in località soggette a terremoti," *Annali della Società degli Ingegneri e degli Architetti Italiani* 24, no. 6 (1909): 149–54.

41. Massimo Ciacagli, "Cento anni di studi scientifici sul terremoto e maremoto del 1908," in Bertolaso et al., *Il terremoto e il maremoto del 28 dicembre 1908*, 255–70.

42. Giuseppe Mercalli, "Contributo allo studio del terremoto calabro-messinese del 28 dicembre 1908," *Atti del Reale Istituto d'Incoraggiamento di Napoli* 6 (1909): 249.

43. Mario Baratta, *La catastrofe sismica calabro-messinese (28 dicembre 1908): Relazione alla Società Geografica Italiana* (Rome, 1910).

44. See Andrea Gallo, *Relazione data all'illustrissimo Senato di questa città da Andrea Gallo Pubblico Professore di Filosofia e Matematica in questo Real Collegio Carolino* (1784). The document is reproduced in full in Enrico Guidoni and Nicola Aricò, *Cartografia di un terremoto, Messina 1783* (Milan, 1988), 126–31.

45. Fusakichi Omori, "Preliminary Report on the Messina-Reggio Earthquake of Dec. 28, 1908," *Bulletin of the Imperial Earthquake Investigation Committee* 3, no. 1 (1909), quoted in Clancey, *Earthquake Nation*, 172–73. An interview with Ōmori during his visit to Sicily was reported in Istituto di Sociologia di Catania, "Pel risorgimento di Messina: inchiesta dell'Istituto di sociologia di Catania," *La Scienza Sociale* 11, no. 1 (1909): 9–11. In box 43, MI CCS 1908, ACS.

46. Reale Istituto di Incoraggiamento di Napoli, "Contributo del R. Istituto d'Incoraggiamento di Napoli alla ricerca delle norme edilizie per le regioni sismiche," *Atti del Reale Istituto d'Incoraggiamento di Napoli* 6 (1909): iii–xxv.

47. Commissione della Società degli Ingegneri e degli Architetti Italiani, "Norme edilizie per i paesi soggetti a terremoti: Relazione generale," in *Annali della Società degli Ingegneri e degli Architetti Italiani* 24, no. 7 (1909): 177–217.

48. These letters are collected in box 43, folder 3.a, "Mezzi per prevenire i terremoti," MI CCS 1908, ACS.

49. Onorato Arbuffo to King Vittorio Emanuele III, 17 January 1909, in box 43, folder 3.a, "Mezzi per prevenire i terremoti," MI CCS 1908, ACS.

50. Antonio Barreca to King Vittorio Emanuele III, 21 January 1909, in box 43, folder 3.a, "Mezzi per prevenire i terremoti," MI CCS 1908, ACS.

51. Italo Siffredi to King Vittorio Emanuele III, 30 January 1909, in box 43, folder 3.a, "Mezzi per prevenire i terremoti," MI CCS 1908, ACS,

52. Both letters are in box 380, folder 4, PCM 1909, ACS.

53. Pietro Blaserna to Prime Minister Giovanni Giolitti, 6 January 1909, in box 380, folder 4, PCM 1909, ACS.

54. Minister of Agriculture, Industry and Commerce Cocco-Ortu to Giovanni Giolitti, 7 January 1909, in box 43, folder 3.a, MI CCS 1908, ACS.
55. Minutes of the letter of Giovanni Giolitti to Pietro Blaserna, 9 January 1909, in box 380, folder 4, PCM 1909, ACS.
56. Law no. 1, 12 January 1909, *Gazzetta Ufficiale* no. 8, 12 January 1909.
57. Commissione Reale incaricata di studiare e proporre norme edilizie obbligatorie per i comuni colpiti dal terremoto del 28 dicembre 1908 e da altri anteriori, *Relazione* (Rome, 1909).
58. Regio Decreto [RD] no. 193, 18 April 1909, entitled "Portante norme tecniche e igieniche obbligatorie per le riparazioni ricostruzioni e nuove costruzioni degli edifici pubblici e privati nei luoghi colpiti dal terremoto del 28 dicembre 1908 e da altri precedenti elencati nel R.D. 15 aprile 1909 e ne designa i Comuni."
59. Commissione Reale incaricata di designare le zone più adatte per la ricostruzione degli abitati colpiti dal terremoto del 28 dicembre 1908 o da altri precedenti, *Relazione* (Rome, 1909).
60. De Berardinis, *Relazione letta dal Commissario Straordinario* (Messina, 1909).
61. Caminiti, *La Grande Diaspora*, 224-25.
62. Ministero di Agricoltura, Industria, Commercio to Presidente del Consiglio dei Ministri, 13 February 1909, in box 380, folder 4, PCM 1909, ACS.
63. Ministero dei Lavori Pubblici to Presidente del Consiglio dei Ministri, 26 May 1909, in box 380, folder 4, PCM 1909, ACS.
64. Pietro Blaserna, Accademia dei Lincei to Presidente del Consiglio dei Ministri, 29 June 1909, in box 380, folder 4, PCM 1909, ACS.
65. Secondo Franchi, "Il terremoto del 28 dicembre 1908 a Messina in rapporto alla natura del terreno ed alla riedificazione della città," in *Bollettino del R. Comitato Geologico d'Italia* 40, no. 2 (1909): 111-57, here 153-54.
66. Commissione Reale incaricata di designare le zone piu adatte per la ricostruzione, *Relazione*, 43-45.
67. Clancey, *Earthquake Nation*, 160.
68. Geschwind, *California Earthquakes*, 20.
69. Abstract of Edgar G. Kausel, "Chilean National Centennial Report to IASPEI," in *International Handbook of Earthquake & Engineering Seismology*, ed. W. H. K. Lee, H. Kanamori, P. Jennings, C. Kisslinger, vol. 2 (Amsterdam and Boston, 2002), 1315.
70. Reitherman, *Earthquakes and Engineers*, 105-57.
71. Sergio Castenetto and Massimilano Severino, "Dalla prima normativa antisismica del 1909 alle successive modifiche," in Bertolaso et al., *Il terremoto e il maremoto del 28 dicembre 1908*, 425-40.
72. Tullia Iori and Alessandro Marzo Magno, eds., *150 anni di storia del cemento in Italia: Le opere, gli uomini, le imprese* (Rome, 2011) esp. 70-71. See also Amy E. Slaton, *Reinforced Concrete and the Modernization of American Building, 1900-1930* (Baltimore, 2001).
73. Giovanna Calcara, "Breve profilo dell'Istituto Nazionale di Geofisica, 1936-1963," *Quaderni di Geofisica* 36 (2004): 5-21.
74. Ari Kelman, "Boundary Issues: Clarifying New Orleans Murky Edges," *The Journal of American History* 94 (2007): 695-703.

CHAPTER 2

Urban Reform 1880–1908

It is the morning of 27 December 1908. A pair of visitors disembarking from the ferry in Messina would have had to weave their way through the sustained traffic of carriages along the waterfront. A noisy tramway wagon runs along the unbroken line of buildings, and the curve of the street holds the sails and masts of the harbor in a picturesque embrace. Walking to the city center, our visitors cross narrow streets and alleys, overshadowed by five-story buildings and impregnated with the smells of fried food, fish, and excrement. On Garibaldi Street in the center of the city, white curtains protect the entrances of shops of all sorts, and bourgeois inhabitants in suits and hats walk alongside mule-riding peasants, cyclists, and horse-drawn carriages. Monumental edifices and churches, new infrastructure and dilapidated houses alike, dot the lively urban landscape, revealing a rich past, a complicated present, and a promising future. By the following morning, this city will have crumbled, killing many of its inhabitants—including, most probably, our unfortunate visitors.

The pre-earthquake history of Messina is often seen as unrelated to the disaster and its aftermath. There are of course good reasons to make such a case: the earthquake destroyed almost everything, killed many thousands of people, and was followed by an *ex novo* reconstruction. Nonetheless, I argue that without properly considering the history of Messina in the decades that preceded the disaster, our understanding of both the tragic event and the following reconstruction would be largely incomplete. In this chapter, therefore, I will chronicle the history of the city from 1880 to the eve of the seism. As we shall see, the pre-earthquake years set the agenda for the comprehensive urban reform that formed an important basis for the post-disaster reconstruction. Moreover, during this period, the exposure of the urban environment to earthquakes grew considerably, creating the preconditions for the tragedy.

During the three decades preceding 1908, the city witnessed one of the most remarkable periods of growth and transformation in its very long history. From the 1860s, the population rate started rising at a remarkable pace, while the local authorities proposed plans to adapt features of the urban environment to a fast-changing society. The introduction of sanitation discourse and practices in the 1880s produced substantial discontinuity and accelerated the pace of urban reform. It stimulated a new holistic conception of the ur-

Figure 2.1. Port of Messina before the earthquake. Courtesy of the University of Michigan Library.

ban environment and its transformation, and fostered the establishment of a permanent body of municipal experts. The new approach toward the urban environment that matured during this time, however, excluded seismic risk from its purview in spite of repeated warnings in 1894, 1905, and 1907, thus paving the way for the 1908 disaster. This cluster of urban plans, transformations, and unaddressed issues would constitute an important heritage in the aftermath of 1908.

Sanitizing the City

In 1861, when the new Kingdom of Italy annexed Sicily, Messina had some 60,000 inhabitants.[1] At that time, the city was mostly enclosed within the limits of its early modern boundaries, on the plain facing the "sickle" between the Torrente Portalegni (*torrente* meaning "small river, creek") on the south side and the Torrente Trapani on the north side. During the seventeenth century, a few urban interventions had modified the city's layout: the partial demolition of two old neighborhoods, the Amalfitani and the Giudeca, in order to create two new streets and the demolition of the old city walls along the waterfront.[2] As mentioned in chapter 1, the earthquake in 1783 had severely affected the city, causing the complete destruction of numerous buildings. The reconstruction brought about some alteration to the urban layout, but, despite initial plans, did not produce the massive transformation of the city and building structures that some had envisioned.[3]

Small fishing villages occupied the coastline up to Cape Peloro, at the northeast extremity of Sicily. South of the city lay a vast plain area called the Orti della Mosella, (see figure 2.2) which was largely devoted to agriculture, notably citrus and other kinds of fruit trees, as well as vegetables for the city's food markets.[4] Water sources located in the mountains surrounding the city supplied public fountains, while underground wells and the private market of barrels of water were a critical supplement to the urban supply. An old canal discharged sewage into the harbor, but most houses only had cesspools.[5] The small rivers that flowed through city had not undergone major transformations, except for the Torrente Portalegni. In the sixteenth century, after a disastrous flood had almost entirely filled the bay with sand and detritus, the city engineers had diverted the lower course of the Portalegni out of the bay and into the open sea, onto the beach of Maregrosso.[6] These early engineering works are explained by the importance of the harbor for the city's economy. Most of Messina's economic life revolved around its port. There, the agricultural and proto-industrial production from the city and its regional hinterland found its way toward national and international markets, and from there, merchandise from the most diverse corners of the globe was brought into Sicilian and Calabrian markets.[7]

After two centuries of low population growth, following a trend common to all Italian cities in an epoch of demographic transition and urbanization, Messina's population recommenced its rise.[8] In the early 1860s, alerted by the visible signs of growth, the city's authorities started to express increasing concerns about the size of the built space. In July 1861, arguing for the need to extend the urban area while boosting a stalling job market, the municipal council decided to expand the city beyond its early modern boundaries.[9] The following year two distinct groups of architects and engineers presented proposals for expansion. In spite of minor differences and disagreements, both plans envisaged the construction of four main roads, which would create a pattern for new urban development on the Orti della Mosella, the agricultural plain on the south side. In 1863, the municipal administration established a special commission to mediate between the two schemes and formulate a definitive plan. In the spring of 1864, the commission came out with a synthesis and, after lengthy debates, the municipal council appointed engineer Pasquale Spadaro to draw up a plan based on that synthesis.[10]

In the early 1860s, many Italian cities were debating similar plans for urban expansion, and a major issue they were all facing was the expropriation

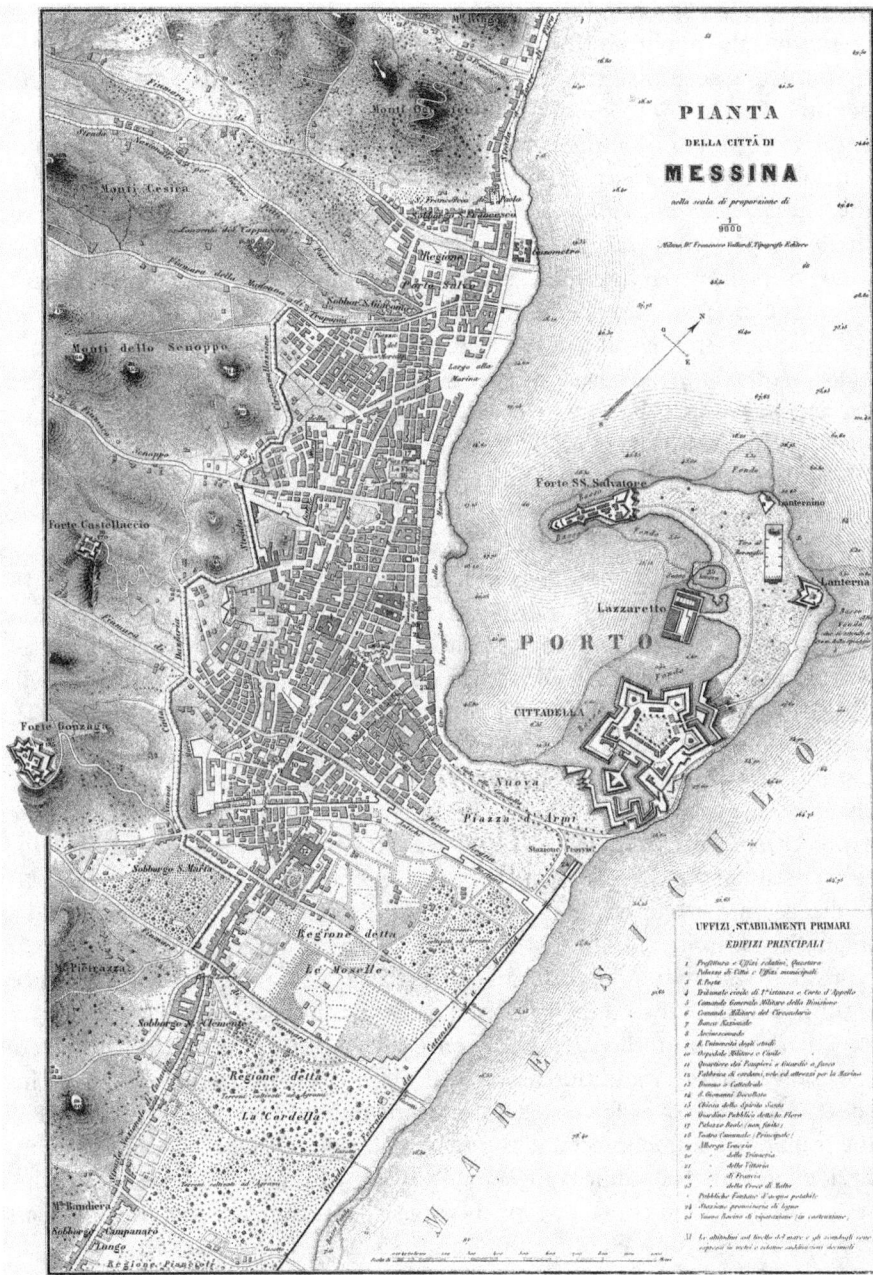

Figure 2.2. Messina, second half of the nineteenth century. Courtesy of GBM Edizioni.

of land needed to extend the built space.[11] The legislation that covered urban works and the public appropriation of real estate did not grant enough power to municipal administrations. Moreover, it was not consistent throughout the country. In 1865, in response to local needs, Parliament passed a new law to regulate the matter countrywide. This law, namely, regulated the procedures for public expropriation, and introduced two major innovations in planning: the *piano regolatore edilizio,* a plan for limited urban transformations, and the *piano di ampliamento,* a mandatory plan for new urban extensions. Both kinds of plan, when approved, entailed the definition of the related works as "of public interest," thereby limiting the rights of private owners in a substantial manner.[12] In the wake of that law, the Messina municipal council passed a *piano di ampliamento* based upon engineer Spadaro's plan. This way, the urban expansion towards the Orti della Mosella became a work of public interest and the required real estate expropriations could be speeded up. After defying legal suits from owners threatened by expropriation, the municipal authorities obtained national approval in 1869, when a deliberation by the Superior Council of Public Works validated the new development plan.[13]

Although solely based on road extensions, the Spadaro plan was still the first coordinated attempt to substantially modify the shape of the city. The final version included a smaller but significant expansion on the north side as well, which integrated the more substantial development on the Orti della Mosella. The topography of the city largely explains the directions of the growth. The surrounding mountains formed a significant barrier to the built space, leaving the narrow coastal plain as the best option for urban expansion. As we shall see, the north-south axis will become the focus of urban expansion after 1908. Urban development, however, was not the only issue debated at that time. Between the late 1850s and the early 1860s, the municipal council started to discuss the urban water supply.[14] In 1861, to face what many perceived as increasing scarcity, the council created a commission for investigating the urban water supply in and around Messina. The commission found the supply insufficient; thus the council decided to repair the old pipelines and tap unexploited sources in the surrounding area. The council, moreover, decided on the excavation of 12 additional wells within the city. These, however, were just short-term palliatives for a structural problem. Not long afterwards, in 1869, the municipal council, faced with the inadequacy of the recent interventions, decided to launch a public contest for a plan to substantially increase the urban water supply.[15] The contest never took place, and during the following years, the authorities proposed only minor improvements to the city's old aqueduct.[16]

During this period, urban gastrointestinal epidemics were a growing concern.[17] Local typographers and newspapers published an increasing number of pamphlets and articles on the issue, authored by members of the cultivated elite. In the beginning, none of these publications directly connected the epidemics to the city's water supply. Architect Giacomo Fiore, a key figure in the 1860s debates, wrote a booklet in 1867 in which he examined the causes of a cholera epidemic in the Portalegni neighborhood. In accordance with the then-popular miasma theory, he blamed the "deadly epidemic exhalations" that emanated from the old sewage canals, where human waste lingered until complete decomposition. To avoid that phenomenon, Fiore proposed isolating excrement in sealed cesspools, thus preventing contagious miasmas from spreading.[18] Similar beliefs influenced the rare municipal interventions in that matter. In 1873, indeed, after a public contest for new ideas, the municipal council voted to implement the cesspool system as the most suitable for human health.[19]

Texts arguing the existence of a relationship between the urban water cycle and gastrointestinal epidemics date back to the late 1870s. In 1877, engineer Domenico Ranieri published a detailed study on Messina's urban waters, in which he warned about the "intimate connection [of water] with cholera epidemics" and its contribution to "the destruction of citizens."[20] Ranieri claimed that the proximity of raw sewage to water pipes and wells caused the chemical by-products of putrefaction to infiltrate and contaminate potable water. Ranieri was a typical representative of a vocal group of scientists and engineers who sought to revise the dominant approach to health issues in the city. These professionals tried to demonstrate contamination by looking for nitrates in water, rather than miasmas. Accordingly, they directly linked epidemics to the urban water cycle, demonstrating that new impermeable pipelines and a waterborne sewage system were imperative in order to eliminate the risk of new epidemics on a permanent basis.[21] The bacteriological revolution was still ahead, but, as we shall see, its arrival would only modify the etiologic premises of that contamination theory, not its practical implications.[22]

Those early proposals did not visibly influence municipal policies. Nevertheless, they shed light on emerging arguments in favor of a more vigorous municipal engagement in urban health issues. Giacomo Fiore argued in favor of urban health improvements as a means to eradicate poverty, because "the races of the poor grow and multiply only where they have brothels and hovels to hide and procreate."[23] Domenico Ranieri maintained more soberly that the transformation of the hydraulic network of the city was necessary because the inefficiency of the system weighed so heavily on the economy.[24] Others, such as physicist Antonio Costa Saya, claimed that hygienic reform was a duty of "the State as protector of people."[25] Although their approaches were different, all these authors connected urban health with the social and economic conditions of the city and with the effectiveness and legitimacy of the authorities and their rule. Accordingly, in their opinion the municipal authorities had to regard structural health improvements as a matter of paramount importance. The ideas so passionately advocated by Messina's health promoters would find much more responsive ears after the advent of sanitation discourse and practices.

These arguments were common to other urban projects in nineteenth-century Europe. Public health debates were strongly related to major social and economic issues in rapidly industrializing and urbanizing cities and involved broader visions of power, economic efficiency, and governance of urban society.[26] In Italy, for urban sanitation to emerge as the dominant paradigm, some specific developments had to take place. Louis Pasteur's revolutionary discovery at the end of the 1870s followed by the identification of *Vibrio cholerae* by Robert Koch in 1884 were two such developments.[27] The new and fast-developing field of microbiology not only provided a scientific explanation for epidemics, but also legitimized the tentative theories that connected epidemics to water pollution and urban networks.[28] The deadly cholera epidemics that hit the city of Naples and other cities of Southern Italy in 1884–85 represented another turning point, although on a smaller scale. These were neither the first nor the last cholera outbreaks in Italy. On the contrary, cholera and typhus epidemics ravaged most Italian cities for the entire nineteenth century.[29] The 1884–85 epidemics, however, produced an outburst of fear and unrest, gained extensive media coverage, and spurred a nationwide debate on urban health issues, supported by new evidence provided by recent scientific discoveries.[30] This gave momentum to the discourses on urban reform that had been active in most Italian cities for at least a decade and stimulated important changes in Italian legislation and policies.

In 1885, responding to the cholera emergency, Parliament passed a law expressly designed to bolster urban health in Naples and prevent new epidemics. The keyword for the project was *risanamento*, which roughly corresponds to the English word "sanitation."[31] *Risanamento*'s main goals were to clean and sanitize the city by increasing air circulation, reducing population density, and creating an integrated urban water cycle. This would also have significant social consequences, including destruction of dwellings in the poorest neighborhoods and displacement of their inhabitants. To achieve such goals, the law accorded special powers to municipal authorities to appropriate real estate, and it offered privileged access to funding for urban renovations. While the law originally limited these concessions exclusively to Naples, the final version of the law extended them to all those cities that could prove a similar condition of need.[32] This was the beginning of a period of increased nationwide activism on the issue of sanitation. In 1886, the national authorities proposed a general survey on sanitary conditions in all Italian cities, which revealed that the situation of Naples was not an isolated case. In 1888, thus, Parliament passed new health legislation imposing certain hygiene standards on all the Italian cities.[33]

The *risanamento* approach synthesized diverse interventions on various features of the built space—water supply, solid and liquid waste disposal, street width, building features, and so forth—in a single schema with one unifying rationale. By doing so, it also aimed to address problems that were primarily social in nature by using technical and infrastructural solutions. The *risanamento* project, in other words, was not just a matter of sanitary regulations and infrastructure: it was a project of rule and reform that addressed the city as a social body and as a physical environment simultaneously. The new legislation introduced in the years following the Naples epidemics made health a priority in urban politics and policies and provided institutional and financial support to carry out major renewals. This new phase influenced debates about and plans for Messina's urban transformation, starting from the time immediately after the Naples emergency law. Article 18 of Law no. 2892 of 15 January 1885 extended certain concessions and special procedures to other municipalities in case of proven need. Amongst these concessions and advantages, as mentioned, was easier access to loans and faster procedures for real estate expropriation. The provisions of the special law for Naples represented an extraordinary opportunity for action. The 1884–85 outbreaks had already hit Sicily severely, but largely spared Messina.[34] In 1886, nonetheless, the city's administration started procedures to obtain concessions from the legislation for *risanamento*.

For the city to be eligible for benefits, the municipal authorities of Messina had to demonstrate an urgent need for urban health reform and propose a coherent and all-encompassing plan for urban renewal to the national authorities. Therefore, in October 1886 the municipal authorities established a special commission to prepare a sanitation plan. A plan like this was something new, for its scope would go beyond everything done or even debated up to that point. Two months later, on Christmas Eve 1886, the commission put forward an outline[35] that seems to be based on a report sponsored by the local association of engineers and agronomists at almost the same time.[36] For *risanamento* to be effective, the program could not limit its scope to the affluent neighborhoods: "The headquarters of cholera, smallpox, and all other infective diseases are the hovels of the poor. It is there, before anywhere else, that we must fight the enemy, in its quarters."[37] To protect the wealthy from epidemics, in other words, it was necessary to reverse the orientation of a class-based approach that, as the quote above seems to imply, had previously decided the distribution of public interventions. To protect the wealthy, it was necessary to "clean up" the poor, and the battlefield for that "fight" was the entire city.

Both the commission's scheme and the association's report referred to the conditions in Messina in grim terms, while touching on all the points on which the *risanamento* framework typically focused. No houses had a domestic water supply. According to the assessment of the engineers, moreover, the actual daily quantity of water per person was 18 liters, whereas hygienists prescribed a minimum of 150 liters per person. The existing sewage canals were judged largely insufficient and inefficient at evacuating waste materials. The lack of space between the buildings and the tortuousness of streets were also considered dangerous and unhealthy, for they hindered the circulation of light and air. Whereas these conditions affected the entire urban structure and infrastructure, the "hovels of the poor," as the commissioners called them, were seen as much more critical hotspots of infection. Dark, humid, crowded, and deprived of any kind of hygienic waste disposal, the working-class dwellings could not ensure "healthy" or "moral" conditions for the life of their inhabitants and thus represented a menace for the city.

In accordance with this vision, sanitation advocates envisioned extensive demolitions in many working-class neighborhoods and the creation of newer, broader, and straighter streets in order to guarantee the circulation of air and light. Moreover, they invoked the regulation of typology and structure of private dwellings in order to "ameliorate customs, habits, and the material and moral conditions of the population."[38] In their opinion, the most important issue was nonetheless the regulation of water circulation within the city. This involved a set of coordinated interventions. In the scheme presented to the national government, the commission highlighted the importance "of laying out the road surfaces, giving them a sufficient inclination for the easy draining of rainwater, and completely paving new roads as well as the existing ones which are not paved yet." This would help "prevent the rainwater from seeping into the surface of these roads and contaminating groundwater, and would render roads dryer and hence influencing the sanitary conditions of the ground floors of buildings." In addition, they continued, "it will be necessary to plan a functional sewerage system for the whole city, in order to quickly drive the enormous mass of putrid materials, originating from human excrements and from waste produced by industrial and domestic activities, away from the densely populated centers."[39]

The sanitation scheme, therefore, envisaged the creation of a complex system of water management, acting simultaneously on water circulation at several levels: supply, drainage, and disposal. Such a system would have had an important effect on the hygiene of individual families, dwellings, and streets, addressing "the poor" but ultimately benefitting all city inhabitants. The implementation of the plan nevertheless clashed with the chronic water scarcity that the municipal council had been unsuccessfully trying to overcome for at least two decades. "Among all interventions," the commissioners therefore concluded, "the most urgent is the provision of abundant potable water. Pure and abundant water has always been, and always will be, the basic element of cleanness and hygiene, and a condition for civilization of peoples; it would be vain to speak of sanitation without having considered its main element, which is water. Without water, there will be no cleanness, no sewerage, and no hygiene."[40]

The requirements for obtaining the concessions (and money) offered by the special legislation for Naples were far more complicated than compiling a generic list of intentions. Unsurprisingly, the first response from the ministry was negative: to be entitled to receive the concessions, the municipality should have presented a more detailed projection of the public works to be undertaken. Nonetheless, the officers from the ministry left the door open, allowing for the possibility to reconsider the application in presence of a truly adequate sanitation plan.[41] That early proposal, albeit unsuccessful, marked a turning point in debates on urban reform. From then on, all plans for urban improvements would be recast in the light of sanitation. In 1887, for example, the municipal council created another special commission to reconsider the city's new development plan in the Orti della Mosella. The commission advised making the streets larger than in the 1869 plan as well as reconsidering health issues in new houses. It would be "completely useless for a house to face a road of 30 meters in width," wrote the commissioners, "when internally it contains narrow, dark, humid, and fetid yards."[42] But an even greater achievement than stimulating dwelling reform, however, was the fact that the sanitation paradigm put the question of water supply at center stage. In the context of *risanamento*, water scarcity was something more than a matter of occasionally thirsty people: it meant a permanently unhealthy and unsafe city.

A New Geography of Urban Water

Debate over water scarcity had already gained new momentum in the early 1880s due to the sense that a major breakthrough was close.[43] In late 1881, recalling the disastrous impact of consecutive droughts on water supply, the mayor of Messina illustrated to the council a new project that envisioned channeling the water of the Alcantara, a major watercourse located some 60 kilometers south of Messina on the slopes of Mount Etna.[44] It was a considerable distance by contemporary standards, but the proponent, a private entrepreneur named Patricolo, promised that distance would not be a problem. He must have not been convincing enough, for in 1882, after lengthy discussions and much criticism, the council proposed to modify the project. Although everyone believed that the Alcantara could ensure plentiful water for the city's needs, most councilors considered it impossible to cover the more than 60 kilometers necessary to tap its flow. Rejecting Patricolo's proposal, the council deliberated instead to draw water from a source named La Santissima, which was located upstream of the Fiumedinisi River (see figure 2.3). The latter river was closer to the city, and the owner had expressed his willingness to rent it to the city. The source, then, seemed adequate to meet a demand that, in the word of a councilor "must grow with the population, the expansion of the built space, the desire for well-being of the contemporary generation, and the needs of public health, which seem to have no limits."[45]

Patricolo withdrew his offer after these substantial changes to his original project. A new local player, Antioci & Co., stepped in, and in 1883 the mayor signed a contract for the incorporation of the La Santissima water into the city's aqueduct. La Santissima was closer to Messina than the Alcantara, but still more than 30 kilometers away, and it was separated from the city by a mountain range and a sizable amount of private land that would have to be expropriated for the waterworks. Another company, Manganaro & Sons, stepped in to replace Antioci, but without any changes to the plan. As would soon become clear, carrying out the construction of an aqueduct of such length required money and skills that small private enterprises such as Antioci & Co. and its successor Manganaro & Sons lacked. Moreover, the companies had probably neither the means nor the intention to face strong local opposition. As soon as they knew about the project, local communities downstream of La Santissima and the local farmers' irrigation consortium asserted their rights to the water and announced their opposition the planned appropriation by Messina.[46] After a couple of years passed with no result, the municipality abandoned any hope and initiated a lengthy legal suit to get back the money it had advanced to the company.[47]

Another possible breakthrough seemed to be close in 1886, as the municipal commission was drafting his first, unsuccessful *risanamento* scheme. During the excavation of a rail tunnel through the Peloritani Mountains, workers had discovered a new source of water. The municipal authorities, alerted to the discovery, commissioned some preliminary studies and the water was shown to be drinkable.[48] At first, this discovery raised high expectations. Water seemed plentiful and was sufficiently close to the city to envision tapping it without too many problems. The *risanamento* scheme thus mentioned the water source in the railroad tunnel as the most promising solution to permanently increase Messina's water supply. In the following months, the municipal authorities negotiated successfully with the railroad company for the use of the source, and started undertaking the works. Yet even this attempt was doomed to failure. The water flow of the new source decreased year upon year, soon making it clear that this was not the permanent solution the authorities were looking for.[49]

Faced with repeated failures, confronted with ever new outbreaks of cholera, and under pressure from the new sense of urgency created by the *risanamento* plans, the municipal administration resorted to foreign expertise. In 1888, they hired Arnold Bürkli-Ziegler, a Swiss municipal engineer who had redesigned Zurich's water supply and sewage system in the late 1860s.[50] By the 1880s, Ziegler had already collaborated with other municipalities in Europe to solve their water issues, and Messina's authorities hoped he could come up with a definitive solution to the city's major problem. After having studied

Table 2.1 Overview of Planned Waterworks, 1861–1900.

YEAR	PROJECT	AUTHOR(S)	OUTCOME
1861	New small intakes in the city's environs and 12 new inner-city wells	Municipal commission	Insufficient to meet the demand, project contest for new improvements in 1869.
1881	Tapping the Alcantara River, 60 km south of Messina	Private entrepreneur Petricolo.	Municipal council rejected the plan as infeasible.
1882	Tapping the Fiumedinisi River, 30 km south of Messina, at La Santissima	Municipal council, outsourced first to private company Antioci & Co., then to Manganaro & Sons.	Opposition from local communities, contractor retires, legal suit between the city and the contractor.
1886	Tapping a newly discovered source in a railroad tunnel being excavated through the Peloritani Mountains.	Municipal council and hired local experts.	Decreasing water discharge, insufficient to meet the demand.
1888	Tapping sources on the other slope of the Peloritani Mountains using the railroad tunnel as a passage for pipes.	Swiss engineer Arnold Buerkli-Ziegler	Absence of detailed plan, nothing done.
1889	Tapping the Niceto River, 30 km north of the city, using the railroad tunnel as a passage through the Peloritani Mountains.	French engineer Georges Bechmann	Lack of funds, nothing done.
1895	Tapping both the Niceto and subsequently the Fiumedinisi with the same pipeline through the southern slope of the Peloritani Mountains.	Municipal engineers Leandro Caselli and Pietro Interdonato, outsourced to private contractor Vanni.	Opposition from Niceto Valley communities, legal suit between the city and the private contractor Vanni.
1900	Implemented version of previous project.	Municipal engineers Leandro Caselli and Pietro Interdonato.	The city obtains state capitals. Works to tap the Niceto started in 1901 and finished in 1905.

aquifers in the mountains surrounding the city, Ziegler concluded that the city's only viable solution was to tap water sources on the northwestern slope of the Peloritani Mountains. The recently excavated railroad tunnel would provide an easy access to the mountains' north side, thereby overcoming what had until then been the principal physical obstacle to tapping sources in the northwest: the mountains themselves.[51] Ziegler did not give any precise indication about which sources the city should actually tap. His proposal was thus inconclusive. Nevertheless, by suggesting a new way to extend the city's hydrological territory, Ziegler broke new ground, opening up a field of possibilities that none of the previous projects had considered.

To further the issue, the municipality hired another foreign expert in 1889: Georges Bechmann, chief engineer of municipal services and sanitation in Paris and professor at the École Nationale des Ponts et Chaussées. Like Ziegler, Bechmann was an authoritative representative of that corpus of municipal experts who led sanitation programs in many European cities, contributing to the diffusion of knowledge and technological solutions throughout the continent.[52] In Bechmann's opinion, Messina was "still in the same situation as most European cities at the beginning of the century," that is, without sufficient water provision to ensure adequate sanitation.[53] The inconsistent torrential flow of most local rivers, along with the presence of numerous communities and villages depending on them, shrank the options of the city dramatically. Accordingly, like Ziegler one year before, Bechmann urged his contemporaries in Messina to turn their attention to the northwest slope of the Peloritani. Unlike his Swiss colleague, though, Bechmann advanced a specific solution: he advised tapping the sources of the Niceto River, located 30 kilometers northwest of the city (see figure 2.3).[54] This seemed to be a concrete proposal to ameliorate the urban water supply to new sanitation standards. The water of the Niceto was pure, abundant, and constant enough to meet the city present and future demands. Moreover, thanks to the railroad tunnel, connecting it to the city's aqueduct was technically feasible.

Yet works such as those envisaged by Bechman required consistent funding, which the municipality did not have. The issue seemed to disappear from urban debate for a couple of years, only to resurface later in a different context. In 1888, a national reform had extended suffrage to municipalities, fuelling urban political struggles and giving room to the socialist movement emerging across the country.[55] In the new political climate of the 1890s, sanitation plans and water supply became something more than a solution to the fear of epidemics among the wealthiest citizens: they became a symbol of urban progress and emancipation. Socialist municipal councilors like Petrina became untiring advocates of sanitation in the name of the working class, and a progressive urban coalition would emerge in the late 1890s that embraced water supply and sanitation as one of its main goals.[56] This transformation in urban politics

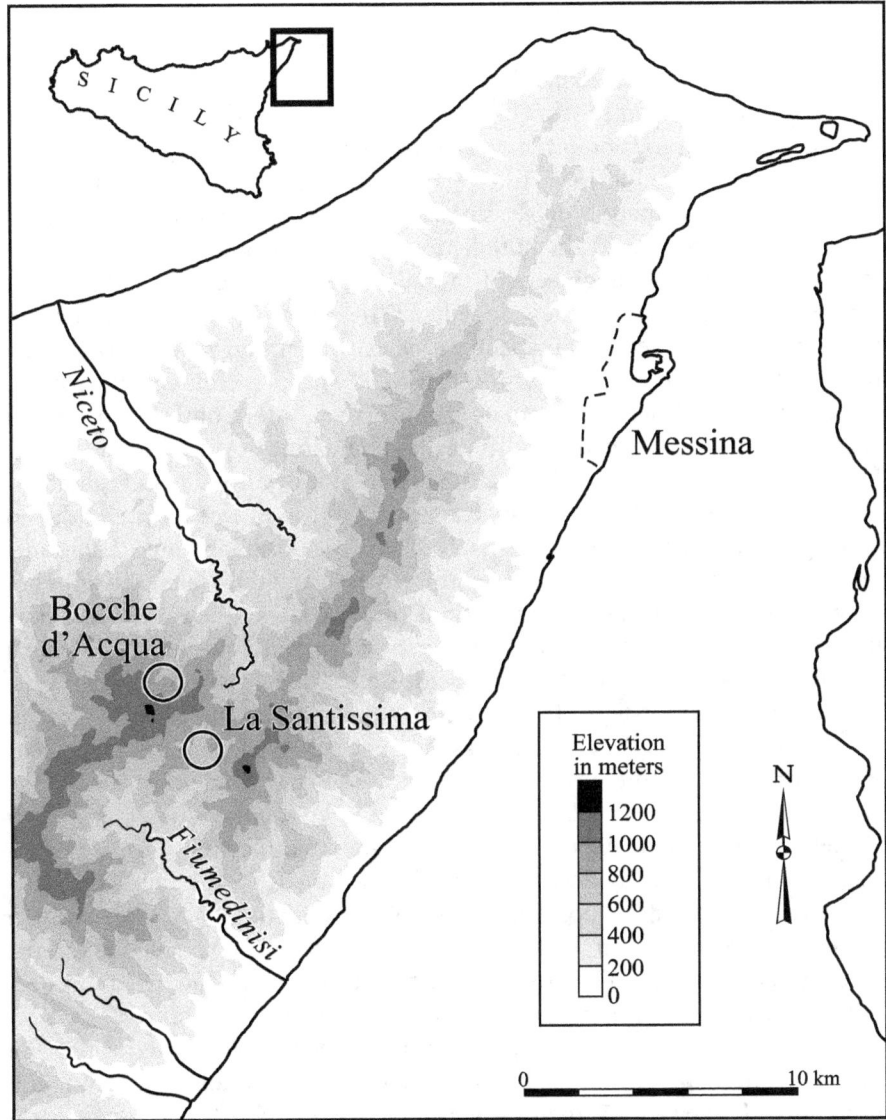

Figure 2.3. Messina and the planned water intakes for the new aqueduct. Cartography by Mary Lee Eggart.

went along with a broader change in urban administration. Starting in 1888, the municipal authorities undertook a substantial restructuring of municipal services. Convinced that the administration of the city required permanent technical expertise, they established the Ufficio Tecnico Municipale (Municipal Technical Bureau), followed two years later by the Ufficio d'Igiene (Bureau for Hygiene). These two bodies of professionals were modelled after similar services elsewhere in Italy and abroad to support urban reform initiatives with adequate knowledge and skills.[57]

In the mid-1890s, after years of inaction, the municipal authorities decided to retrieve the application for state funding for sanitation programs that had initially been rejected in 1887. In 1894, the municipal council requested a detailed report on sanitation in Messina from the newly established Bureau for Hygiene. Simultaneously, the authorities appointed Leandro Caselli and Pietro Interdonato, two engineers of the new Municipal Technical Bureau, to formulate a proposal for a new aqueduct. The report by the Bureau for Hygiene vividly described how inadequate the existing urban water network was, indulging in details such as rotting frogs and sheep excrement in open-air aqueduct canals. The most evident effect of these shortcomings, the report continued, was the recurrence of intestinal epidemics. According to the officer, between 1887 and 1894 the average rate of mortality due to typhoid fever was 14.2 per 10,000 inhabitants, and the average rate of mortality due to other gastrointestinal infections was 54.5 per 10,000 inhabitants. Additional figures for bacterial and chemical pollution clearly demonstrated the links between mortality rates and the quality of urban waters; therefore, the report insisted, a reform of the urban water cycle was urgently needed.[58] Municipal engineers Caselli and Interdonato provided a technical solution to this issue. Following in the footsteps of Bechmann, they identified the Niceto River, on the northern slope of the Peloritani, as the most suitable for meeting the needs of the current and future urban population. Like Bechmann before them, they claimed the Niceto River had limited agricultural potential and required only a small amount of land expropriations compared to other rivers. Unlike Bechmann, however, the engineers rejected the idea of using the railroad tunnel and revisited instead the possibility of tapping La Santissima on the southern slope of the Peloritani. In their opinion, by building just one aqueduct on the southern slope, it would be possible to tap first the Niceto and, when needed, the water from La Santissima, by means of the same infrastructure.[59]

This plan and the sanitary report by the Bureau for Hygiene formed the bulk of the new application to obtain the state concessions for urban sanitation programs. Unlike in 1887, the 1895 application was supported by adequate research, technical details, and sound plans. Consequently, the officers from the Ministry of Internal Affairs reopened the procedure and passed the project forward to a Technical Commission, whose members approved the request.[60] After a series of delays and further consultations, Royal Decree no. 6 of 5 January 1896 finally granted Messina special concessions for sanitation programs. This meant two things above all: first, favorable conditions for borrowing huge amounts of money; second, since the works were declared to be of public interest, the municipal authorities could count on expedited real estate expropriation procedures. Private business had failed to provide the capital and expertise to undertake long-distance water conveyance, but state money and municipal expertise would succeed. But not before a few more twists and turns in the story.

A few months after this state approval of the project, the mayor of Messina signed a preliminary agreement with an engineer and businessperson, Alessandro Vanni, for the construction of the new aqueduct.[61] This choice provoked strong opposition within the municipal council and from the Technical Bureau. The administration had just ended the lengthy legal suit against Antioci & Co and the choice of a private entrepreneur did not seem consistent with that past negative experience.[62] The Municipal Technical Bureau, moreover, possessed the necessary expertise to direct the works without resorting to an external contractor, and it publicly contested Vanni's ability to carry out the project.[63] The choice of Vanni as contractor is seemingly due to a suspicious financial connection between Vanni and the mayor and probably concealed a turbid story of corruption. Nevertheless, the council ultimately approved the mayor's choice.[64] In 1898, making use of the favorable conditions granted by the sanitation law, the municipality obtained a sizable loan from the Banque de Liège to finance Vanni.[65]

Stronger opposition to the project came from the inhabitants of the Niceto River valley. One of the main reasons for the choice of the Niceto River was that it would limit the number of real estate expropriations and would not significantly affect agricultural activities. Georges Bechmann had put forward this idea first, and Leandro Caselli and Pietro Interdonato reinforced it in their 1894 project. Despite these claims, once the council approved the project and the municipality obtained the loan, the inhabitants of the four main municipalities in the valley, Monforte San Giorgio, San Pier Niceto, Rocca Valdina, and Rometta, started to voice their growing concerns. More than ten years earlier, the communities of the Fiumedinisi River valley, directly downstream from La Santissima, had expressed similar concerns and obstructed the early plan of water conveyance by Antioci & Co. With direct support from their elected representatives, the Niceto communities tried to follow a similar path and organized themselves into committees, starting a legal suit in opposition to the plan.

In 1899, the Niceto Valley committees presented their formal opposition to the prime minister in Rome. The inhabitants claimed they lived solely from agriculture, "which is essentially made possible by irrigation due to the position and nature of these lands." The Niceto water, they continued, had been used "since time immemorial" to supply local aqueducts, fuel watermills, and irrigate large expanse of farmland. Moreover, countering one of the main arguments in favor of Messina's appropriation of water, the committees claimed that land property was highly fragmented, and thus the completion of the aqueduct required a huge amount of expropriations. "To modify the irrigation regime of the Niceto Valley," they concluded, "would provoke great damage and no small inconvenience to a large population of cultivators, who, having lost their vineyards because of phylloxera, are devoid of resources other than the cultivation of citrus and summer vegetables."[66] To strengthen their argument, finally, the committees appended a short historical study on the legal status of Niceto's waters, which aimed to demonstrate that all the authorities who had ruled Sicily over the centuries had expressly granted local communities access to Niceto water.[67]

The viewpoint represented here strongly contradicted what first Bechmann and later Caselli and Interdonato had claimed. Opponents to the aqueduct claimed that several communities depended on the use of the Niceto water, and the planned urban appropriation would have catastrophic effects on the local economy. They did not deny Messina the "right to drink," but at the same time they claimed their own "right to drink and eat."[68] Conflicts over the urban appropriation of water are common throughout Italy and elsewhere during this period. The transformation of urban ecosystems and metabolisms, and the increasing urban consumption of biogeophysical resources destabilized long-standing balances between urban and rural areas. Fast-changing urban environments were imposing their new ecologies onto the countryside and extending the reach of the urban water cycle over increasingly large territories.[69] Rural communities would bear the heavy burden of such dramatic changes, and they often tried to resist, as in the case of the Niceto Valley. In most cases, those conflicts ended in favor of the cities, while the long-standing rights of the countryside succumbed to the unstoppable wave of urban reform.[70]

The Messina aqueduct was no exception. After a vehement election campaign against the mayor centered on the aqueduct affair, a new progressive coalition took over the municipal council between the end of 1899 and the beginning of 1900. One of the first acts of the new majority was to dissolve the contract with Vanni and appoint the Municipal Technical Bureau to finalize a plan for the city aqueduct.[71] The new plan was far more detailed than any previous one. Preliminary works along the planned route preceded its completion, and the final version included fieldwork reports and new analysis of water composition and discharge, and it established a planning scheme for the urban network.[72] Despite these improvements, the main features of the plan remained the same as in 1895: the aqueduct would tap water from the sources of the Niceto and carry them via the southern slope of the Peloritani right to Messina. According to the municipal engineers, there were no valid alternatives to the Niceto water, and with the full backing of the national government, the council gave its definitive approval.[73] Messina's "right to drink" outweighed the claims of the Niceto Valley communities, and their voices disappear all of a sudden from official records.

On 25 May 1901, the works for the aqueduct finally started, undertaken directly by the Municipal Technical Bureau and financed by the state through the Cassa Depositi e Prestiti, a major Italian state-controlled bank. The route of the aqueduct had to go through 64 new tunnels for a total length of 24 kilometers. Construction work lasted more than three years and had to overcome severe technical and financial difficulties. These difficulties forced the engineers to implement changes in direction, and compelled the municipal administration to ask for new loans from the Cassa Depositi e Prestiti. Finally, at the beginning of 1905, the head of the new Ufficio Acquedotto (Bureau for the Aqueduct) could announce that "the long-invoked, clear, pure water of the Niceto ... has been dominated, won by the force of our will, and flows vivifying into the bosom of Messina."[74]

This emphatic announcement was definitely not justified. The aqueduct tapped only a part of the water it was supposed to bring to Messina, and apart from two urban reservoirs, there was no effective infrastructure for domestic distribution. The water of the Niceto River supplied only public fountains, and was thus nothing more than a slight improvement from the same old system.[75] Despite the absence of a distribution network, the conveyance of Niceto water was nonetheless a remarkable achievement and the result of an enormous accumulation of knowledge and expertise and of the efforts made by many individuals. Moreover, it was the first step towards environmental changes, the impact of which would last for generations, creating one of those structural path dependencies described by historian Martin Melosi.[76] The aqueduct established a new geography of urban water that extended the city's hydrological territory over an unprecedentedly large surface and reorganized priorities, rights, and access to water resources on multiple scales, from the built space to the hinterland.

Engineering the City's Environment

State capital and municipal expertise proved crucial to the completion of the Niceto aqueduct. This success, and the reasons for it, is the most eloquent testimony of a broader change. The authors of the early 1886 *risanamento* scheme had contended that the municipality had poor and insufficient knowledge of the urban environment. There were no comprehensive maps of existing water pipes.[77] The authorities also ignored the actual condition of operating sewage systems, or the quantity and quality of water resources within the municipal area.[78] The sanitation advocates deemed this lack of knowledge the first and most important obstacle to the realization of the public health program. Yet, even as the authors of the sanitation scheme were writing, new projects, studies, and reports were piling up, increasing the knowledge of the urban environment, of its inhabitants, and of the city hinterland and its resources. Local scientists and professionals published measurements of the hydraulic discharge of water sources across the municipal territory, analyses of the chemical and bacteriological composition of the water, studies of soil quality and permeability, and enquiries into hygiene conditions in dwellings and neighborhoods.[79] By the end of the 1880s, the information available was more detailed and richer than at any time before.

Until the end of the decade, though, this collection of knowledge had been added to only sporadically and unsystematically by individuals, private associations, or ad hoc municipal commissions. The creation of the Municipal Technical Bureau in 1888, and its definitive establishment two years later, was a fundamental turning point. With the establishment of this service, the municipal administration permanently incorporated technical knowledge and expertise on some crucial aspects of urban reform. The creation of the Technical Bureau was perhaps the most important instance of a larger urban administration reform. I have already mentioned earlier the establishment of the Bureau for Hygiene. In the same period, the municipality created myriad new bureaus and functions: a statistical service, a city archive, and so forth.[80] The establishment of a stable body of experts occurred in many other European and North American cities in a similar time frame and represented an essential step towards mastering the new problems of rapidly expanding cities.[81] In Messina, this new institutional expertise was essential in order to finalize the aqueduct project and obtain state funding for it, but had also other visible, if less remarkable, effects.

Another essential component of the original sanitation project of 1886 was urban sewage. In 1899, upon request of the authorities, engineers Leandro Caselli and Pietro Interdonato from the Municipal Technical Bureau drew up a plan for a comprehensive sewage system. The engineers planned to build a dense network for rainwater and wastewater collection covering the whole city and connecting every building with sewage canals. The lower course of the Torrente Portalegni would become the main collector, and bring wastewater and rainwater directly into the open sea and out of the bay. The plan then envisaged concreting over and paving the Portalegni "to transform it in a comfortable street." The engineers saw the sewage network as a necessary complement to the aqueduct. Only with a functional wastewater system would it be possible to create the integrated urban water cycle that the city's authorities wanted to achieve complete sanitation.[82] That plan, nevertheless, was not immediately followed up, apart from a small section of the new development area.[83] A reason for this may be that the authorities and the engineers of the bureau were largely occupied with the aqueduct construction. Another, perhaps more compelling reason is that an entirely new sewage system, unlike water conveyance, required major interventions in a heavily built-up and densely inhabited urban setting. As we shall see, that kind of extensive intervention would become possible only after the earthquake.

Although important, the reform of the urban water cycle was not the only issue concerning the city's infrastructure and its relationship with the biogeophysical environment. Among the most pressing concerns of the city's administrators in those years of tumultuous change was certainly also the port. Maritime commerce was the staple of Messina's economy and works to keep the deepwater bay in good condition were a constant in the city's history. The preservation of the harbor, for instance, was the main rationale behind the permanent diversion of the lower course of the Torrente Portalegni in the sixteenth century, as well as for the creation of a structure to retain sands and sediments carried by the Torrente Boccetta after it had almost entirely filled the bay with sand and detritus in 1754.[84] In the late nineteenth century, many of Messina's entrepreneurial activities still revolved around the port—navigation companies, businesses exporting agricultural and artisanal goods from a vast hinterland area, and companies engaged in the cultivation of citrus and production of citric acid.[85]

A functional harbor was essential for all these interests, and at the beginning of the twentieth century, debates increased regarding the role of the harbor in the economy of Messina and what interventions were necessary to improve its functioning. They stemmed from growing concerns about the appeal and competitiveness of Messina as a port city. In 1878, Messina lost its privileges as a "free port." Free ports enjoyed a special fiscal status that excluded the harbor and the ships sailing from it from normal taxation. It had been the traditional prerogative of the port of Messina throughout the ages, lost and regained at different times, and the local authorities and chamber of commerce considered it as an important basis for the city's prosperity.[86] In addition to having lost that privilege, local authorities and traders' associations were perhaps realizing that the "natural advantages" of Messina's deepwater harbor were not enough to guarantee its economic success. Improved infrastructure and new facilities were necessary to keep boats docking in, and sailing from, Messina's harbor. After a false start in 1900, a ministerial commission and the municipal administration negotiated a joint scheme of interventions and funding between 1903 and 1904. Although the parties formally reached a compromise, Messina's authorities judged the scheme insufficient and appointed the Municipal Technical Bureau to redact a new comprehensive plan for port renewals and submit it to the Ministry of Public Works for funding.[87]

Stating that the physical conditions of the port were responsible for its declining importance, municipal engineers Borzì and Sollima Novi included a number of important modifications of the shape of the harbor and of its visible infrastructures. They envisioned the construction of a new dry dock suitable for boats of bigger size, a new mechanical infrastructure for loading and unloading goods, a change in the length and size of wharfs, and similar improvements. The engineers also took into account the quality of the bay's water, thus linking the plans for the port directly to the restructuring of the city's sewage outflow. Furthermore, the plan included the management of the Torrente Boccetta. The Boccetta's estuary was located in front of the entrance to the harbor, and, just like the Portalegni, it threatened to clog the harbor with sand and detritus after heavy rain. According to the municipal engineers, it was necessary to modify the course and bed of the whole river in order to protect the harbor, and also to create a new and effective tank at the river's estuary to filter the sand. The plan also included the excavation of the bottom of the bay and the reinforcement of the underwater walls of the quays to make them more resistant to the strong currents of the strait. In conclusion, the authors claimed that "the physiognomy of a modern port cannot and must not derive from its natural features."[88] Engineers had to reshape nature to better suit the city's needs.

The debates about urban streams management reveal a similar attitude toward the biogeophysical features of the urban environment. The streams flowing down the Peloritani Mountains played a crucial role in making Messina's physical environment. The sediment the streams brought after each flood contributed to the creation of the thick, soft layer of sand on which the city stood—the alluvium that so many geologists and seismologists deemed co-responsible for the 1908 disaster. Flash floods had been also a constant in the human history of the city, constantly threatening the functionality of the harbor. Management of urban streams was therefore a recurring issue, and, as mentioned, these management attempts had brought about substantial modification of the various watercourses.[89] A number of flash floods in the late 1850s and 1860s, similar to many others in the city's history, led the municipal authorities to propose public works program in order to prevent new disasters, and local engineers and architects hotly debated the best solutions to adopt.[90] These proposals were in accordance with traditional solutions that focused entirely on the lower courses of the waterways and usually recommended the construction of embankments or the straightening the riverbeds. In the 1870s, new studies shifted the focus onto the entire catchment area. Ranieri, for instance, scrupulously analyzed the sites where floodwaters originated, their geological composition, and the rainfall regime of the area. Even Ranieri, though, concluded that the only strategy that could contain the fury of torrential waters was the construction of special embankments.[91]

Interestingly, despite paying attention to catchment area, Ranieri argued vigorously against any connection between deforestation and floods. The deforestation of peri-urban hills, the engineer claimed, was a much earlier phenomenon than the occurrence of the worst floods, and therefore did not constitute any meaningful correlation. Even if someone could prove a connection between the two phenomena, he continued, no law could prevent deforestation, which was nothing less than "the consequence of the progress of nations."[92] This view would soon find opponents. In 1901, agronomist Guido Inferrera wrote a pamphlet in which he made the case for the existence of a strong relationship between deforestation and floods. Inferrera stressed that the real problem was "the culpable negligence hitherto shown in ruling the water regime" and unawareness of the risks caused by deforestation.[93] Accordingly, in his view, reforestation was the only effective prevention measure against flash flooding, and a task that an efficient administration should tackle in earnest.

Inferrera demonstrated his point by considering the positive effects of the only reforestation program undertaken until then: the creation of a municipal forest in the Torrente Zaera catchment area. The municipal council had debated the creation of a municipal forest in that area from the late 1870s and proposed the first (unsuccessful) attempt at reforestation in 1881–82.[94] After 1890, the authorities revamped the initiative and promoted the establishment of a reforestation consortium.[95] Reforestation proceeded steadily and successfully during the 1890s, and during the heavy rain in 1901 the Torrente Zaera was the only urban stream that did not overflow. In Inferrera's opinion, this case showed clearly that the only effective measure for the protection of urban environments from flash flooding was the large-scale reforestation of peri-urban hills.[96]

In 1903, the municipal council appointed Inferrera as director of the municipal forest in Camaro.[97] This shows clearly how his approach was gaining supporters. What counts even more, however, is the attitude this reveals. Behind Inferrera's views, indeed, was a growing confidence in the ability to control and regulate the surrounding environment, and the conviction that engineering the biogeophysical features of the site was the most effective means to better the city and increase the safety and wellbeing of its inhabitants. This was the same attitude that we saw driving the aqueduct works, the new wastewater plan, and the scheduled port improvements. Inferrera expressed this principle clearly, arguing that engineering would turn "nature" from being a "cause of desolation and misery" into a "source of wealth" for the city.[98]

Much of this confidence did not necessarily correspond to real achievements. The sanitation plan of 1886 envisaged extensive changes to the urban environment: the expansion of the city beyond its old boundaries, the demolition of old neighborhoods, the creation of large boulevards and squares, and a comprehensive restructuring of the urban water cycle. On the eve of the earthquake, the only concrete result was the aqueduct, and even this, in the words of Messina's prefect in 1908, was in a "precarious and provisional state" and not yet fit for regular use.[99] Only a few scattered parts of the 1899 sewage plan had been completed, and the same holds true for the port renewals and the reforestation of peri-urban hills. The city had nevertheless changed profoundly, although not on an immediately material level. New branches of administration, such as the Municipal Technical Bureau, and new knowledge of the city's site, features, and resources, were produced and organized in the wake of sanitation plans. This in turn created the conditions for the extension of the discourse and practice of urban reform beyond the scope of sanitation itself. The *risanamento* had catalyzed an unprecedented project of increasing knowledge and governance in the city, seen now as a fully knowable and multi-dimensional environment, improvable in all possible aspects through technology and engineering.

To Live Happily and Forget the Quake

On the eve of the earthquake, the city was bubbling with plans and projects to make it fit for an upcoming era of progress. Given this remarkable activity, the absence of earthquakes from the urban debate is particularly striking, especially when considering that in the period covered by this chapter, the city experienced several earthquakes. According to the catalogue of historic seismicity in the Mediterranean, six earthquakes were felt in the city between 1870 and 1908.[100] The last three in this series had a magnitude attested to be around 6 points, they were felt by all inhabitants, and they produced serious damages

Figure 2.4. Garibaldi Street, Messina, before the earthquake. Courtesy of the University of Michigan Library.

to buildings. Nevertheless, they seemed to have had no impact on Messina's debates about urban reform, and did not produce any notable change in the features and conception of the urban environment.

As we have seen, the worst disaster prior to 1908 had occurred in 1783. That disaster related to a sequence of earthquakes that affected in particular the neighboring region of Calabria in 1783 and 1784. One of those earthquakes had a disastrous impact on Messina's built structure: many buildings crumbled because of poor engineering and unsuitable materials, and thousands of people died under the ruins.[101] Following the example of Portuguese authorities in 1755, the authorities of the Kingdom of Naples introduced a new building code into the stricken area. The code hinged upon the adoption of a special earthquake-resistant technology, the *casa baraccata*: an internal structure of interconnected wooden beams covered in masonry.[102] The *casa baraccata* was not adopted in Messina, but the city's authorities introduced an earthquake-resistant building code, which represented remarkable innovation and an unprecedented improvement in earthquake protection in Messina. Thanks to the adoption of the new building code, Messina would be better protected from the fury of any future earthquakes.

At first, the city's authorities enforced the building code. Some of the few buildings that withstood the 1908 earthquakes were engineered according to the principles of the *casa baraccata* technology, thus proving its effective adoption in the post-1783 reconstruction.[103] In a typical example of what some scholars call the erosion of social memory, however, city developers in later years were less and less respectful of the 1783 building code.[104] Throughout most of the nineteenth century, the city developed with no consideration given to seismic risk or the adoption of seismic-resistant engineering. In 1866, the city council passed a new building code; the Superior Council of Public Works rejected parts of the code in 1874, and a revised version only came into force in 1885. Despite the fact that memory of the 1783 earthquake had certainly not been lost, and many still recalled that disaster, the 1885 *regolamento edilizio* (building code) did not contain any specific provision concerning earthquake engineering.[105]

In the meantime, the urban population increased at a remarkable pace. According to national censuses, Messina city had 62,024 inhabitants in 1861. Forty years later, the number had risen to 93,672, and continued to grow.[106] As mentioned in chapter 1, the city had 109,516 inhabitants in 1907 according to a municipal statistical bulletin found in the state archives.[107] The city's new developments should have accommodated part of this new population in line with the Spadaro plan of 1869. Yet, according to both pre-1908 and post-1908 maps, only a few dozen new buildings had been completed in the new development areas north and south of the city, while most lots were still vacant.[108] The city must therefore have incorporated population growth mainly by increasing the number of dwellings in the same urban surface area. This goes some way to explain why so many post-earthquake observers, including Mario Baratta, noted that buildings that were already ill-equipped to withstand strong seismic shocks had been expanded by adding new floors to the existing ones, and therefore reducing further their already low stability and resistance.[109]

In 1894, an earthquake exposed the fragility of Messina's built environment. Preceded by other minor episodes during the previous decades, a tremor shook Calabria and Sicily on 16 November 1894. As in the past, the epicenter of this earthquake was on the continental side of the strait, and most damages were concentrated in a few Calabrian villages. Still, the material consequences of the earthquake were evident in Messina as well. Although no buildings collapsed completely, earthquake damage was severe, and a few edifices were almost toppled. There was one fatality, and many inhabitants were forced to abandon their homes for several weeks.[110] Commerce was halted and the municipal council established two committees, one for recovery and assistance of the injured and displaced, the other for the quantification of damages. The committee described the earthquake as a "calamity" and admitted it had renewed the memory of previous disasters, like the one in 1783.[111] Yet this was not enough.

After the emergency had passed, the mayor presented a report on the earthquake to the council. He briefly mentioned the costs required "to shore up crumbling buildings, to demolish buildings threatened with collapse, and to clear dangerous and uninhabitable premises." Nevertheless, his main concerns were of a different kind: the mayor proudly claimed he had avoided the creation of refugee camps and provisional shelters and successfully dealt with "the general crisis produced by the halt to commerce, the suspension of work, and the exodus of the upper class."[112] Impatient to re-establish social order and economic activities, the authorities encouraged people to go back to their homes, even if these were damaged. Most people repaired the earthquake damages quickly, often with the simple solutions such as holding together cracked walls by means of iron chains, or rebuilding damaged sections.[113] Almost nobody undertook major repair of internal structures, and to my knowledge the municipality did not establish any specific guidelines for repairing or securing damaged buildings. Moreover, in the printed minutes from the municipal council I have found no trace of any debate on a building code reform or earthquake-resistant engineering in the city. The only signs of risk awareness and actions taken as a consequence of this were the self-financed restructuring of a few residences by members of the upper-middle class, such as the Villino Cammareri that would become popular in the aftermath of 1908.[114]

This evidence (or rather the lack thereof) points to the conclusion that Messina's authorities perceived the 1894 earthquake and its aftershocks exclusively as a social and economic threat to the city and made no sustained reflection on the capability of the urban infrastructure to withstand similar events. A few years later, however, two new earthquakes loudly restated the existence of a serious seismic risk in the area. The first one was in 1905. The epicenter was, once again, located in Calabria, further away from the city of Messina than the 1894 one. In spite of this, and although damages were concentrated in a group of small towns and villages northeast of the strait, Messina's residents felt the earthquake distinctly.[115] Something similar happened in 1907: the village of Ferruzzano in southern Calabria was almost completely devastated, and the earthquake badly damaged many other towns.[116] The inhabitants of Messina once again perceived the tremor distinctly and fled out in the street. Even in 1905 and 1907, the authorities established recovery committees, and the population of the most affected villages and towns had to leave their houses to live in tents and other provisional shelters.

The emerging field of earthquake science scrutinized these earthquakes attentively. As we have seen in the previous chapter, two of the most prominent figures of earthquake science in Italy, Baratta and Mercalli, researched seismic activity in the strait area extensively. In the light of both immediately contemporary and more distant events, their studies stated insistently that earthquakes were a persistent phenomenon in the area and that poor engineering was responsible for their destructive effects. Local experts were likewise fully aware of the importance of earthquake-resistant engineering in order to prevent seismic disasters and criticized the inactivity of the authorities.[117] In both 1905 and 1907, the national authorities introduced norms for the prevention of earthquake damage. In some Calabrian towns, moreover, engineers experimented with reinforced concrete.[118] As usual, however, the national authorities enforced the new building code only in the most affected areas, which excluded Messina. The local authorities, for their part, continued seemingly unchecked along their path of inaction, and did not undertake any measures to secure the urban environment or reform the building code in the city.

The consequences of the erosion of social memory, uncontrolled urban growth, and institutional inaction would become evident in the 1908 earthquake and played a major role in determining the horrific scale of death and destruction in Messina. While describing in minute detail the ruined city in the aftermath of the quake, Mario Baratta pointed out not only that the 1784 building code had been completely forgotten, but also that the interventions made after the 1894 earthquake had been "absolutely inadequate."[119] The expansion of the urban environment and its human population without any attention to seismic safety had created the structural conditions for the disaster, whereas the inaction of the authorities and the lack of adequate intervention after the earthquake episodes in 1894, 1905, and 1907 increased the city's exposure to seismic hazards. As Baratta concluded sharply, "if certain facts had been considered and evaluated properly ... the catastrophe of 28 December 1908 would not have been as fatal to humans as it was."[120]

The history of urban disasters is dotted with similar cases of inaction and failed prevention.[121] Memory plays a relevant role in this regard, especially in seismic disasters. Strong earthquakes are often separated by several generations, and thus vivid memories of them easily fade, as in the case of 1783 earthquake. Knowledge painfully gained in past events gets lost over time, and careless practices emerge yet again. In addition, awareness of a particular risk does not necessarily lead to action, since other competing interests can gain priority.[122] This seems to have been the case with Messina in the late nineteenth century, when the need for urban development and the fears of social and economic disturbance clearly expressed by the mayor in 1895 were prioritized over seismic safety. Despite the occurrence of earthquakes, the city's authorities and most inhabitants disregarded the dangers and preferred easy and short-term solutions, while the national authorities continued their shortsighted policy of enforcing building codes only in places where a disaster had already happened.

There is perhaps also another explanation for the inaction in pre-1908 Messina. In order to deal effectively with seismic risk, it would have been necessary to radically change the mindset that guided urban reform during the pre-disaster years. This mindset was rooted in the conviction that the biogeophysical features of the site could be adapted to the needs of the city. Seismic prevention would require the opposite approach, e.g., the adaptation of the urban environment to the natural features of the site. This complete turnaround would happen only after the 1908 disaster.

Conclusion

On the eve of the 1908 earthquake, Messina was in the midst of change. The city was slowly expanding beyond its ancient borders and the built space was growing into part of the agricultural plain south to the city. The installation of the city's new sanitary infrastructure was modifying both the geography of urban water and the relationship between the city and the hinterland in profound ways. The transformation of the urban environment embraced the hydraulic regulation of urban streams, the reforestation of peri-urban hills, and the restructuring of the deepwater harbor. The city, in other words, was experiencing a process of modernization comparable to that undergone by other Italian and European cities in previous years, inclusive of the many environmental implications of modernization.

As we have seen, the authorities started to plan the transformation of at least some parts of Messina's urban environment as early as the early 1860s and 1870s. During those decades, the municipal council debated issues such as the expansion of the built space and the creation of new neighborhoods, the increase in urban water supply, the reform of working-class dwellings, and the modification of riverine hydrology. The authorities tried to address at least some of those issues with special plans and projects. The inception of the sanitation framework in the 1880s, however, produced a major shift, moving the comprehensive reform of the urban environment to the center of the municipal agenda.

A sizable amount of literature has brought into focus the importance of sanitation for the modernization of urban environments in Europe and North America.[123] Often, the specific impact of sanitation framework was the result of the combination of transnational processes such as scientific and technological innovations, national policies encouraging local change, and place-specific events and dynamics. Messina was no exception. The bacteriological revolution initiated by Pasteur's and Koch's epoch-making discoveries, and the new *risanamento* legislation that followed the cholera epidemics of the mid-1880s, reacted with Messina's specific context and ongoing debates, producing a significant modification of the approaches and scope of urban reform discourses. The wish to obtain state funding for urban renewals, and the consequent redaction of the first sanitation schemes for the city, indeed, allowed public health issues to reach out of the closed circle of local experts in public health and engineering. *Risanamento* proposals, nonetheless, were far from being merely technical or scientific: on the contrary, they promised solutions to social problems such as the living conditions of the urban working class via infrastructural and physical change. By so doing, they prompted a new holistic conception of the urban environment and its reform, which united previously discrete issues in a single vision of technological intervention and social improvement.

In this new context, securing a constant and abundant water supply soon became a priority. Messina depended upon the inconsistent torrential regime of its urban streams and its polluted groundwater and had no major watercourses in its vicinity. Given these specific geographical and environmental conditions, a constant and abundant water supply was not easy to find. The search for a suitable water source channeled the energy of many professionals and pushed the municipal authorities to hire foreign experts such as Arnold Bürkli-Ziegler and Georges Bechmann. The solution came in the end by means of a considerable expansion of the urban catchment area, incorporating distant watercourses such as the Niceto into the urban water cycle. That solution produced a radical reconfiguration of the geography of urban water, scaling up the city's ecology remarkably. Furthermore, it marked a turning point in the relationship between the city and the hinterland communities, as proved by the controversy over the use of the Niceto's water and its final resolution in favor of Messina.

The transformation of the geography of urban water was a direct effect of the new sanitation framework. A broader transformation, however, was underway. As we have seen, a remarkable accumulation of knowledge and data about the urban environment, as well as about the hinterland and its resources, preceded and facilitated the construction of the new aqueduct. This expertise and knowledge, previously scattered and sporadic, was now gathered systematically and incorporated into functioning of the municipal administration, becoming an essential feature of urban governance. The reform of municipal services in 1889 and the creation of the Municipal Technical Bureau was a turning point in that process, and it greatly enhanced the capability of the city's administrators to plan and enact all sorts of infrastructural improvements, from urban rivers' embankments and sewage canals to port renewals. In the early twentieth century, as a consequence, a large proportion of the biogeophysical features of Messina and its surroundings became the object of engineering projects proposed in order to bolster both the health of the population and city's economy.

When the 1908 earthquake struck, the envisaged multi-layered transformation of the urban environment was still largely unrealized. The aqueduct was still incomplete, the new sewage system was largely at the planning stage, and so were the comprehensive port renewals, the regulation of the rivers, and health improvements in working-class housing and neighborhoods. Most importantly, this new interventionist approach towards the biogeophysical features of the site did not take earthquake hazards into account. Despite the occurrence of at least three significant earthquakes at the turn of the century, the authorities did not take any measures to deal with the seismicity of Messina's site, for example by securing the urban infrastructure or modifying the building code. On the contrary, these decades of intense urban development and attempts at a comprehensive urban reform were also the years when the city's vulnerability to earthquakes increased, with tragic consequences. As we have seen, several elements contributed to this result, such as the absence of explicit earthquake-related provision in the existing building code, the reckless expansion of existing buildings to accommodate a growing population, and the irresponsible inaction after repeated wake-up calls. As a result, early twentieth-century Messina was even less prepared to face earthquakes than it had been thirty years earlier.

The 1908 disaster was a tragic confirmation of that unpreparedness, and of the limits of the concepts that had driven urban reform until then. The earthquake proved that the city's biogeophysical environment was not only a set of resources to exploit, or material obstacles to overcome via engineering for the benefit of an evolving urban society: they were also the source of ineradicable hazards. Overlooking that fact caused many thousands to die a terrible death and drove the city almost to extinction. The disaster thus called for the incorporation of hazard adaptation as a guiding principle and modification of the features of the urban environment in accordance with this. In the aftermath of 1908, this was clear to nearly everyone, and as we have seen in the previous chapter, that conviction was behind some of the most fundamental decisions concerning the future of the city. Nonetheless, the ruin of the earthquake did not bury the agenda for urban reform set during the pre-1908 decades. On the contrary, as we shall see in the next chapter, many saw the *ex novo* rebuilding of Messina as an unprecedented and unexpected opportunity to advance the modernization of the urban environment in a much more radical way, while protecting the urban environment and population from future seismic disasters.

Notes

1. Ministero di Agricoltura, Industria e Commercio [hereafter MAIC], Ufficio Centrale di Statistica. *Popolazione presente ed assente per Comuni, Centri e Frazioni di Comune, Censimento 31 dicembre 1871*, vol. 1 (Rome, 1874), xxxiv.
2. Amelia I. Gigante, *Le città nella storia d'Italia: Messina* (Rome, 1980), 53–54.
3. Michela D'Angelo and Marcello Sajia, "A City and Two Earthquakes: Messina 1783–1908," in *Cities and Catastrophes: Coping with Emergency in European History / Villes et catastrophes: Réaction face à l'urgence dans l'histoire européenne*, ed. Geneviève Massard-Guilbaud, Dieter Schott, and Harold L. Platt (Frankfurt am Main, 2002), 123–40. See also Vincenza Calascibetta, *Messina nel 1783* (Messina, 1995), 73–87; Nicola Aricò, "Cartografia di un terremoto: Messina 1783," in *Cartografia di un terremoto, Messina 1783*, ed. Enrico Guidoni and Nicola Aricò (Milan, 1988), esp. 17–20.
4. I gleaned this information by analyzing the maps of the mid-nineteenth century, such as the one reproduced later on in the chapter (figure 2.1) and by analyzing legal suits against public expropriations after the earthquake, discussed in the following chapter.
5. Franco Alibrandi and Adriana Salemi, "Dall'Unità al terremoto," in *Il progetto urbano di Messina: documenti per l'identita, 1860-1988*, ed. Giuseppe Campione (Rome, 1989), 1–131.
6. Luigi Borzì and Carlo Sollima-Novi, *Il Porto di Messina nel passato, nel presente e nell'avvenire* (Messina, 1907), 4.
7. Rosario Battaglia, *L'ultimo "splendore": Messina tra rilancio e decadenza (1815–1920)* (Soveria Mannelli, 2003), 23–53.
8. For data on Messina's population pre-1860, I refer to the database published by Paolo Malanima, "Italian Urban Population 1300-1861 (The Database)" (PDF file, 2005), http://www.paolomalanima.it/default_file/Italian%20Economy/Urban_Population.pdf.
9. Alibrandi and Salemi, "Dall'unità al terremoto," 18–19.
10. Atti Consiglio Comunale di Messina [hereafter Atti C.C.], 19 July 1864, reprinted in Alibrandi and Salemi, "Dall'unità al terremoto," 21–28.
11. An extensive overview is provided by Paolo Sica, *Storia dell'urbanistica*, vol. 2, *L'Ottocento* (Rome-Bari, 1985).
12. Law no. 2359, 25 June 1865, Articles 86–94. See P. Sica, *Storia dell'urbanistica*, 401–11.
13. Atti C.C., 3 April 186, reprinted in Alibrandi and Salemi, "Dall'unità al terremoto," 31–34.
14. Giacomo Fiore, *Delle pubbliche acque* (Messina, 1859), 4.

15. Atti C.C., 2 August 1869. Hereafter all quotes from Atti del Consiglio Comunale are taken directly from the printed minutes collected by the Biblioteca dell'Archivio Storico Comunale of Messina. See also Alibrandi and Salemi, "Dall'Unità al terremoto," 86.
16. Atti C.C., 19 April 1872, and 15 June 1874. On that issue, see also Luciana Caminiti, *Dalla pietà alla cura, Strutture sanitarie e società nella Messina dell'Ottocento* (Milan, 2002), 170–78.
17. On cholera epidemics in nineteenth-century Messina, see Caminiti, *Dalla pietà alla cura*, 153–70.
18. Giacomo Fiore. *Delle cause permanenti che hanno fatto imperversare il colera in Portalegni e modo come ripararsi* (Messina, 1867), 6.
19. See Alibrandi and Salemi, "Dall'Unità al terremoto," 90–93.
20. Domenico Ranieri, *Acque potabili e fognature* (Messina, 1877), 4.
21. See for example Antonio Costa Saya, *Delle acque potabili in relazione alla salute pubblica: Discorso letto innanti la Prima Classe dell'Accademia Peloritana nella tornata del 22 gennaio 1878* (Messina, 1879).
22. Ranieri and Costa Saya, like many others of the time, identified the polluting agent as the nitric acid produced by the decomposition of organic substances. The boundaries between different scientific explanations, however, were not so rigid, and Saya in particular insisted on the presence of unidentified germs that were responsible for the diseases together with the nitric acid.
23. Fiore, *Delle cause permanenti*, 12.
24. Costa Saya, *Delle acque potabili in relazione alla salute pubblica*, 8.
25. Ranieri, *Acque potabili e fognature*, 30.
26. See Christopher Hamlin, *Public Health and Social Justice in the Age of Chadwick* (Cambridge, 1998) and Patrick Joyce, *The Rule of Freedom: Liberalism and the Modern City* (London, 2003).
27. Norman Howard-Jones, "Robert Koch and the Cholera Vibrio: A Centenary," *British Medical Journal* 288 (1984): 379–81. For a larger historical narrative on the context of the discovery, as well as its impact on the scientific community, see Christopher Hamlin, *Cholera: The Biography* (Oxford and New York, 2009), 209–66.
28. On the transition from miasma theory to the "era of bacteriology" in the United States, see Martin V. Melosi, *The Sanitary City: Urban Infrastructure in America to Colonial Times to the Present* (Baltimore, 2000), 103–16. Simone Neri Serneri has argued for a different periodization in Italy in "The Construction of the Modern City and the Management of Water Resources in Italy, 1880–1920," *Journal of Urban History* 33 (2007): 814–15. The description of the transition to bacteriology is different here in some respects: the Messina case shows that bacteriology was incorporated into preexisting interpretations of urban diseases. Bacteriological contamination was used as a confirmation of the need for pure water and thus the further implementation of what Melosi dubbed "protosystems."
29. Annalucia Forti Messina, "L'Italia dell'Ottocento di fronte al colera," in *Storia d'Italia, Annali 7: Malattia e Medicina*, ed. Franco Della Peruta (Turin, 1984): 431–94.
30. Frank M. Snowden, *Naples in the Time of Cholera, 1884–1911* (Cambridge, 1995), especially chapters 4 and 5, 155–230.
31. Law no. 2892 of 15 January 1885 was entitled "Legge per il risanamento della città di Napoli."

32. Article 18 of Law no. 2892, 15 January 1885 reads: "Ai comuni che ne faranno richiesta nel termine di un anno dalla pubblicazione della presente legge, potranno essere estese, per Decreto Regio, udito il consiglio di Stato, tutte o parte delle disposizioni contenute negli articoli 12, 13, 15, 16 e 17, qualora le condizioni d'insalubrità delle abitazioni o della fognatura e delle acque ne facessero manifesto bisogno. La richiesta dovrà essere accompagnata dalla proposta delle opere necessarie al risanamento."
33. On these aspects, see Neri Serneri, "The Construction of the Modern City," 814–15, and Giovanna Vicarelli, *Alle origini della politica sanitaria in Italia: società e salute da Crispi al fascismo* (Bologna, 1997).
34. Caminiti, *Dalla pietà alla cura*, 227–38.
35. Commissione centrale to Illustrissimo Sindaco del Comune di Messina, "Risanamento della città di Messina: Relazione sommaria," manuscript, Messina, 24 December 1886, in box 55, folder 2, Ministero dell'Interno, Direzione Generale Sanità Pubblica 1861–1934 [hereafter MI DGSP 1882-1915], ACS.
36. Collegio degl'Ingegneri ed Agronomi di Messina, *Risanamento della città di Messina*, (Messina, 1886).
37. Ibid., 6.
38. Ibid., 78.
39. All quotes in this paragraph are from Commissione centrale to Illustrissimo Sindaco del Comune di Messina, "Risanamento della città di Messina: Relazione sommaria," manuscript, Messina, 24 December 1886, in box 55, folder 2, MI DGSP 1882-1915, ACS.
40. Ibid.
41. See the manuscript letter from the Ministero dell'Interno to the Prefetto di Messina on 11 February 1887, in box 55, folder 2, MI DGSP 1882-1915, ACS.
42. Report of the commission composed of Salvatore Buscemi, Antonino De Leo, Vincenzo Cammareri, Prof. Francesco Trombetta, and Giuseppe Papa, 18 January 1887, presented to the Municipal Council on 14 April 1887. Atti C.C. 14 April 1887.
43. ASCMe, Atti C.C., Conto Morale del Sindaco Comm. Cianciafara, 12 September 1882.
44. ASCMe, Atti C.C., 1 March 1882. See also S. Patricolo, *Conduttura di acque potabili per la citta di Messina* (Messina: Tipografia del Foro, 1882).
45. Councilor De Leo in Atti C.C., 10 August 1882.
46. Atti C.C., 10 April 1886.
47. For details on that legal suit, see Alibrandi and Salemi, "Dall'Unità al terremoto," 87.
48. Atti C.C., 16 March 1888.
49. The council approved a draft agreement with the railroad company in January 1887. By then, it was already clear that the water was not sufficient. Atti C.C., 24 January 1887.
50. Jean-Luc Bertrand-Krajewski, "Bürkli-Ziegler, Arnold," in *Short Historical Dictionary on Urban Hydrology and Drainage*, (PDF, 2006), http://jlbkpro.free.fr/shduhdfromatoz/buerkli-ziegler.pdf.
51. Atti C.C., 16 March 1888.
52. Stéphane Frioux, "'Amélioration de l'environnement urbain et transferts de technologie entre la France et ses voisins nord-européens, années 1870-années 1910," in *Innovations, réglementations et transferts de technologie en Europe du Nord-Ouest aux XIXe et XXe siècles*, ed. Jean-François Eck and Pierre Tilly (Berlin, 2011), 235–50; Pierre-

Yves Saunier and Shane Ewen, *Another Global City: Historical Explorations into the Transnational Municipal Moment, 1850-2000* (New York, 2008). Denis Bocquet, "Les villes italiennes et la circulation des savoirs municipaux: esprit local et 'Internationale des villes'(1860-1914)," *Histoire et Sociétés: Revue Européenne d'Histoire Sociale* 21 (2007): 18-30.

53. Georges Bechmann, *Assainissement de la ville de Messina* (Messina, 1890), 7.
54. In Bechmann's words: "Rien ne parait s'opposer à ce que prolongeant le collecteur plus à l'ouest on aille recueillir les eaux complémentaires dans le bassin suivant, celui du Noceto [sic] ... ," ibid., 15.
55. Law no. 5865 of 30 December 1888, later included in "Testo Unico della legge comunale e provinciale approvato con Regio decreto 10 febbraio 1889 n. 5921." See G. Barone, "Egemonie urbane e potere locale (1882-1913)," in *Sicilia*, ed. Giuseppe Giarrizzo (Turin, 1987), 280-81, 300-304.
56. The acts of the municipal council testify to socialist councilor Petrina's attention to urban health issues. On the birth and program of the new "progressive coalition" in Messina see Barone, "Egemonie urbane e potere locale (1882-1913)," in *Storia d'Italia: Le Regioni dall'Unità d'Italia ad oggi*, vol. 5, *La Sicilia*, ed. Maurice Aymard, and Giuseppe Giarrizzo (Turin, 1987), 355-58 and Antonino Cicala *Partiti e movimenti politici a Messina: Dal fulcismo al fascismo (1900-1926)* (Soveria Mannelli, 2000), 9-10. For a transnational perspective on municipal socialism, see Patrizia Dogliani, "European Municipalism in the First Half of the Twentieth Century: The Socialist Network," *Contemporary European History* 11, no. 4 (2002): 573-96.
57. Municipio di Messina, *Regolamento per l'Ufficio Tecnico del Comune di Messina,* approvato dal Consiglio Comunale nelle tornate del 20, 26 e 30 marzo 1889, Tipografia Filomena, Messina 1889, art. 1. The reform instituting the Ufficio Tecnico Municipale ended in 1888. Atti C.C., 23 June 1888.
58. Municipio di Messina, Ufficio d'Igiene, *Relazione sanitaria sulle acque potabili*, Messina, 4 September 1895, manuscript, in box 55, folder 2, MI DGSP 1882-1915, ACS.
59. Leandro Caselli and Pietro Interdonato, *Sui tracciati proposti per la provvista di acqua potabile della città* (Messina 1895).
60. See the letter manuscript in box 55, folder 2, MI DGSP 1882-1915, ACS.
61. Municipio di Messina, *Concessione del Comune di Messina all'Ing. Cav. Alessandro Vanni per la condotta di acque potabili e l'esercizio dell'acquidotto* (Messina, 1897).
62. Atti C.C., repeatedly through 1896 and 1897.
63. Municipio di Messina, Ufficio tecnico, *Relazione all'Ill.imo Signor Sindaco sul progetto particolareggiato dell'acquedotto presentato dal concessionario Cav. Ing. Alessandro Vanni* (Messina, 1897).
64. Barone, "Egemonie urbane e potere locale," 354.
65. Municipio di Messina, *Contratto con la Banca di Liegi e la Società dei Tramways Siciliani per il prestito per l'acqua potabile, la trazione e l'illuminazione elettrica* (Messina, 1899).
66. *In difesa delle acque del bacino del Niceto. Memoriale presentato al R.Governo*, manuscript, Rome, 31 May 1899, in box 55, folder 2. MI, DGSP, 1882-1915, ACS.
67. Pietro Mezzasalma, *Osservazioni di occasione sulle acque del bacino del Niceto* (Messina, 1899) in box 55, folder 2. MI, DGSP, 1882-1915, ACS.
68. "In difesa delle acque." See box 55, folder 2. MI, DGSP, 1882-1915, ACS.

69. See the contributions collected in *Urban Rivers: Remaking Rivers, Cities and Space in Europe and North America*, ed. Stéphane Castonguay and Matthew Evenden (Pittsburgh, PA, 2012), especially Frederic Graber, "Diverting Rivers for Paris, 1760–1820: Needs, Quality, Resistance," 183–200, and Craig E. Colten, "Fluid Geographies: Urbanizing River Basins," 201–18.
70. It is interesting to compare the case of Syracuse in Salvatore Adorno, "Luce e acque: Conflitti e risorse nella modernizzazione di una periferia meridionale; Il caso di Siracusa," in *Réseaux techniques et conflits de pouvoir: Les dynamiques historiques des villes contemporaines*, ed. Denis Bocquet and Samuel Fettah (Rome, 2007), 103–36.
71. Barone, "Egemonie urbane e potere locale," 191–370.
72. Municipio di Messina, Ufficio Tecnico, *Relazione sulle condizioni attuali del servizio delle acque nel Comune* (Messina, 1900).
73. Atti C.C., 22 December 1900. See also the correspondence in box 55, folder 2. MI, DGSP, 1882–1915, ACS.
74. Pietro Longo, *L'acquedotto civico di Messina* (Messina, 1905), 5.
75. Ibid., 38.
76. Melosi, *The Sanitary City*, esp. 10–12.
77. Collegio degl'Ingegneri ed Agronomi, *Risanamento della città di Messina*, 12.
78. In 1882, one of the points raised in the council was the need for a hydrographic map of the municipal territory, Atti C.C., 10 August 1882.
79. Other examples of such nonofficial studies are: Antonio Costa Saya, *Giudizio della Società italiana d'igiene sulla questione delle acque potabili di Messina* (Messina, 1880); L. Costa Saya, *Studi chimici intorno alle acque potabili di Messina* (Messina, 1881); Salvatore Giannetto, *Ricerche per determinare il grado di potabilità di un'acqua sorgiva nella contrada Santissima presso Fiumedinisi* (Messina, 1883); Luigi Costa Saya, *Studio su quattro campioni d'acqua della Santissima* (Messina, 1883); Gaetano Benigni, *Fognatura ed igiene pubblica in Messina* (Messina, 1884); Antonio Costa Saya, *L'acqua potabile e il colera epidemico* (Messina, 1888).
80. See the debate and outcome of the municipal reform of 1888. Atti C.C., 23 June 1888.
81. For a broader picture see Michèle Dagenais, Irene Maver, and Pierre-Yves Saunier, eds., *Municipal Services and Employees in the Modern City: New Historic Approaches* (Alderton, 2003). For the Italian case see in particular the chapter by Roberto Ferretti, "The Formation of a Bureaucratic Group between Centre and Periphery: Engineers and Local Government in Italy from the Liberal Period to Fascism (1861–1939)," 66–83. See also Salvatore Adorno and Filippo De Pieri, eds., "Burocrazie tecniche," special issue of *Città e storia* 5 (2011).
82. Municipio di Messina, *Fognatura della città: Relazione del Sindaco al C.C. Progetto Tecnico* (Messina, 1899), 37.
83. Pietro Interdonato confirms the presence of new sewage in the new development area in a contribution that appeared after the earthquake: Interdonato, "La catastrofe del 28 dicembre 1908—Impressioni di un tecnico superstite," *Annali della Società degli Ingegneri e degli Architetti Italiani*, 25, no. 20 (1909): 499–502.
84. Borzì and Sollima-Novi, *Il Porto di Messina*, 4.
85. Battaglia, *L'ultimo splendore*, 83–112.
86. Ibid., 11–23.

87. Borzì and Sollima-Novi, *Il Porto di Messina*, 10–11.
88. Ibid., 16.
89. Ibid., 4.
90. *Cenni critici sull'adozione del sistema chinese proposta dal Pittore D.Letterio Subba in rapporto ai torrenti di Messina, Porta Legni, Boccetta e Trapani*, n.d. (after 1856); Giacomo Fiore, *Sui progetti per frenare i torrenti Giostra e Camaro* (Messina, 1866); Riccardo Hopkins and Giuseppe Morabello, *Risposta ai pensieri del prof. Giacomo Fiore* (Messina, 1866); Domenico Ranieri, *Dei torrenti attraversanti Messina e dei mezzi diretti alla loro difesa* (Messina, 1871).
91. Ranieri, *Dei torrenti attraversanti Messina*, 72
92. Ibid., 43.
93. Guido Inferrera, *Il rimboschimento dei Peloritani in relazione con la sistemazione dei torrenti del messinese* (Messina, 1901), 1.
94. Atti C.C., 24 February 1882.
95. Atti C.C., 22 July 1890.
96. Guido Inferrera, *La sistemazione dei torrenti della Provincia di Messina e la sicurezza dei paesi rivieraschi* (Messina, 1907), 8–9.
97. Atti C.C., 5 January 1903.
98. Inferrera, *Il rimboschimento dei Peloritani*, 1.
99. Letter of the Prefetto della Provincia to the Minister of Internal Affairs, 23 October 1908, in box 103, folder 1271, Ministero dell'Interno, Direzione Generale dell'Amministrazione Civile, Commissione reale per il credito comunale e provinciale e la municipalizzazione dei servizi 1901-1923 [hereafter MI DGAC Comm.Mun.], ACS.
100. Emanuela Guidoboni, Graziano Ferrari, Dante Mariotti, Alberto Comastri, Gabriele Tarabusi, and Gianluca Valensise, "Felt Reports at: Messina(ME)," *Catalogue of Strong Earthquakes in Italy 461 B.C.–1997 and Mediterranean Area 760 B.C.–1500*, INGV-Istituto Nazionale di Geofisica e Vulcanologia, http://storing.ingv.it/cfti4med/localities/066973.html.
101. D'Angelo and Sajia, "A City and Two Earthquakes: Messina 1783–1908," 123–40.
102. Tobriner, "La Casa Baraccata," 131–38.
103. This is mentioned by all eyewitnesses' reports, starting with Mario Baratta, *La catastrofe sismica calabro-messinese (28 dicembre 1908): Relazione alla Società Geografica Italiana* (Rome, 1910), 25–26.
104. See W. Neil Adger, Terry P. Hughes, Carl Folke, Stephen R. Carpenter, and Johan Rockström, "Social-Ecological Resilience to Coastal Disasters," *Science* 309 (2005), 1037. See also Craig E. Colten, *Perilous Place, Powerful Storms: Hurricane Protection in Coastal Louisiana* (Jackson, MI, 2009) and Craig E. Colten and Amy R. Sumpter, "Social Memory and Resilience in New Orleans," *Natural Hazards* 48, no. 3 (2009): 355–64.
105. *Regolamento edilizio della citta di Messina: stabilito dal Consiglio comunale nelle adunanze del 12, 19 settembre 1873, 25 settembre 1874, 29 gennaro 1884; approvato dalla Deputazione provinciale nelle tornate dei 24 giugno 1875 e 8 aprile 1884; omologato dal Ministero dei L L. P P. addi 18 luglio*, Tipografia Filomena, Messina 1885.
106. Ministero dell'Agricoltura, Industria e Commercio, Direzione Generale di Statistica, *Censimento della Popolazione del regno d'Italia al 10 febbraio 1901*, vol. 1, *Popolazione*

dei comuni e delle rispettive frazioni divisa in agglomerata e sparsa e popolazione dei mandamenti amministrativi (Rome, 1902), 198.

107. Municipio di Messina, Ufficio Statistico Municipale, Bollettino Statistico del Comune di Messina, III Trimestre 1907, in box 38, Ministero dell'Interno, Direzione Generale dell'Amministrazione Civile "Terremoto calabro-siculo", ACS.

108. See for instance 'Pianta della città di Messina', in *La Patria, Geografia d'Italia*, vol. 5, ed. G. Strafforello (Torino, 1893) 402–3, and "Messina: gli effetti del terremoto del 1908" in L. V. Bertarelli, *Sicilia* (Rome, 1919), reproduced in full in chapter 3 of this book.

109. Baratta, *La catastrofe sismica calabro-messinese*, 27.

110. Guidoboni et al., "Earthquake Sequence 1894 11 16 Calabria meridionale," *Catalogue of Strong Earthquakes*, http://storing.ingv.it/cfti4med/quakes/14962.html. See also Emanuela Guidoboni and Gianluca Valensise, *Il peso economico e sociale dei disastri sismici in Italia negli ultimi 150 anni, 1861–2011* (Bologna, 2011), 81–90.

111. Comitato di Soccorso di Messina, *I terremoti del 1894 e 1895 nella Sicilia e nella Calabria* (Messina, 1895), 1.

112. Comune di Messina, *I terremoti del 1894–95 e la beneficenza pubblica in Messina*, Relazione alla Giunta del Sindaco Barone Natoli di Scaliti letta nella tornata del 21 giugno 1895 (Messina, 1895), 4.

113. This has been once again documented by Baratta, *La catastrofe sismica calabro-messinese*, 31.

114. Baratta described minutely the features of Villino Cammareri, see Baratta, *La catastrofe sismica calabro-messinese*, 6–7. Other isolated cases of preventions are documented by Luciana Caminiti, *La grande diaspora 28 dicembre 1908: La politica dei soccorsi tra carità e bilanci* (Messina, 2009), 35–37.

115. Guidoboni et al., "Earthquake Sequence 1905 09 08 Calabria," *Catalogue of Strong Earthquakes*, http://storing.ingv.it/cfti4med/quakes/19344.html. See also Guidoboni and Valensise, *Il peso economico e sociale die disastri sismici*, 91–104.

116. Guidoboni et al., "Earthquake Sequence 1907 10 23 Calabria meridionale," *Catalogue of Strong Earthquakes*, http://storing.ingv.it/cfti4med/quakes/20606.html; Guidoboni and Valensise, *Il peso economico e sociale dei disastri sismici*, 104–12.

117. See for example Michele Martone, *Studi preliminari sui terremoti della Calabria e della Sicilia* (Reggio Calabria, 1897), 35. The contemporary bibliography on these earthquakes is listed by Guidoboni et al. in the detailed *Catalogue of Strong Earthquakes*.

118. Crescentino Caveglia, "Pensieri sull'impiego del cemento armato," *Annali della società degli ingegneri e degli architetti italiani* 24, no. 6 (1909): 149–54.

119. Baratta, *La catastrofe sismica calabro-messinese*, 31.

120. Ibid., 41.

121. An excellent case in point is Colten and Sumpter, "Social Memory and Resilience in New Orleans," 355–64.

122. Theodore Steinberg shows a clear case of this in the aftermath of the 1906 San Francisco earthquake. See Theodore Steinberg, *Acts of God* (New York, 2000), chapter 2, esp. 27–36.

123. I refer extensively to that literature in the introduction of this volume.

CHAPTER 3

The Modern City 1909–1943

At the dawn of 1909, Messina was a wasteland. Churches and public edifices, houses and factories alike had disappeared, replaced by a landscape of ruins. Photographers rushing to the devastated city to record the event indulged in the material destruction: illusory shells of crumbled buildings, enormous heaps of rubble, corpses, contorted beams. Using realist aesthetics of death and devastation, they tried to represent the shocking event: the sudden and tragic disappearance of a whole city. Thirty years later, cameras captured a completely different scenario. Short, square buildings, wide roads, electric lights, and cars gave Messina the ordered appearance of a modern urban landscape. A new city had risen from the ashes of 1908. This chapter will recount the history of the rebuilding and transformation of Messina into a modern city in the years that span from the aftermath of the 1908 earthquake to the eve of World War II.

In 1886, the engineers who wrote the first *risanamento* program for Messina stressed how unrealistic it was to formulate plans of total urban transformation. "It is not possible to admit even as hypothesis," they wrote, "that for the city to be sanitized one must destroy two-thirds of its buildings and make them anew."[1] The 1908 earthquake, however, had produced exactly that unconceivable situation. Faced with the almost complete destruction of the urban environment, the comprehensive sanitation and infrastructural modernization program of the pre-1908 decades suddenly became a concrete option, and *ex novo* rebuilding an exceptional opportunity to realize it. Sanitation and modernization, though, were not enough. After the 1908 devastation, those envisioning a reconfiguration of the urban environment could not dismiss the need to adapt to the geophysical features of the site, and to seismicity in particular, in order to avoid the repetition of similar disasters in the future. As we have seen in chapter 1, this conviction underlay the new building and planning code introduced in April 1909. That code was the essential prerequisite for the rebuilding of Messina on the same site as before the quake and represented an inescapable constraint to planning.

The municipal and national authorities assigned the task of finding a synthesis between the opportunity for comprehensive sanitation and infrastructural modernization and the constraints of the earthquake code to Luigi

Borzì, director of the Municipal Technical Bureau. As we shall see, Borzì, a municipal engineer, succeeded in bringing together many factors, drawing up a plan for a more efficient, sanitary, and earthquake-proof new Messina. Nevertheless, during the years of reconstruction, unexpected events hindered the realization of his plan. Sustained demographic growth and the resilience of post-earthquake informal settlements complicated the rebuilding process. At the same time, the economy of the city slowly shifted away from maritime commerce, which had been a key element of the planning concept. This chapter will unravel the multi-layered interplay of long-term plans for reform, new post-earthquake priorities, urban developments, and unexpected outcomes in the making of a new Messina.

The Provisional City (and Its Permanent Consequences)

In the aftermath, it was common knowledge that little of the former city had survived the earthquake. How much of the city had survived was not that clear. Attempts to profile the exact extent of destruction went on for at least two years and involved the controversial decision to tear down certain historic buildings, thus bringing about the further destruction of a heritage that, according to architectural historian Oteri, could otherwise have survived.[2] An official assessment of damages stated that more than 90 percent of the buildings had been completely obliterated, and only a very few edifices were still standing on the outskirts of the city, largely in the new development area (figure 3.1). Such extensive destruction on the surface meant correspondingly serious damage to subterranean infrastructure, uncharted by maps but testified to in numerous reports. The seism affected aqueduct pipes, sewage canals, and the port, along with transportation and energy networks.[3] The earthquake, in summary, wrecked the physical structure of Messina even more thoroughly than the pictures and maps were able to show and transformed the historic city into an uninhabitable wasteland.[4]

As we have seen in chapter 1, survivors who had not left Messina and volunteers who had rushed to participate in the rescue and relief operations set up camps on the outskirts of Messina, south of the historic city center.[5] The location of "Michelopoli," the first organized survivors' camp, was not a carefully considered choice, but rather a direct outcome of both the condition of the city after the earthquake and the topography of the site. Due to the prevailing use of masonry in pre-1908 buildings, an enormous amount of rubble—later calculated as equivalent to one million cubic meters[6]—covered the entire surface of Messina, including most squares and streets. This meant that there were few clear areas, and even these were dangerous due to the presence of crumbling buildings and recurrent aftershocks. The mountains and the sea, unyielding

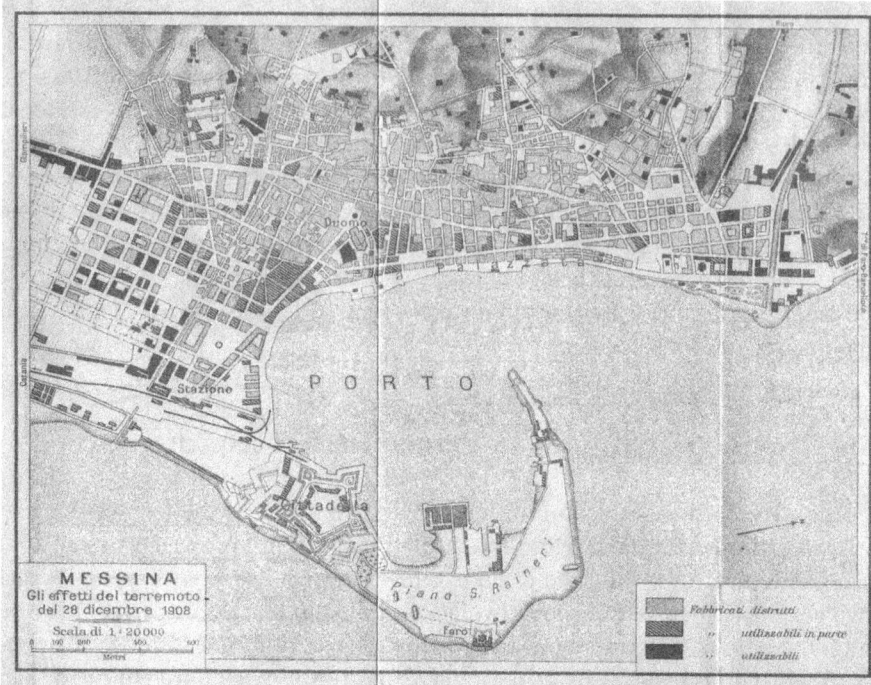

Figure 3.1. Extent of destruction. Light grey identifies completely destroyed buildings. Courtesy of Giorgio Stagni.

geographical boundaries to the city's expansion, further limited the possibilities of even a temporary settlement. However, due to low urban density, the incomplete urban development south to the city afforded enough rubble-free space for refugee camps, and its proximity to the port ensured a constant and direct connection with the outside world. Therefore volunteers created larger groups of shelters on this site. Despite the dangers, and in some cases without any formal authorization, some survivors erected huts in the few areas of the inner city that were clear of rubble.

Although Michelopoli and the other smaller camps could meet the most immediate needs of those survivors who still inhabited the site during the massive exodus after the quake, the reestablishment of a functional community required a different solution, and on a much bigger scale. As early as 12 January 1909, the Ministry of Public Works appointed Riccardo Simonini, an engineer from the Genio Civile (Civil Engineering Corps), as head of a special bureau for the provision of shelters. Simonini was to draw up a plan for a temporary settlement to shelter the earthquake survivors. He had to comply with two major requirements. First, the provisional settlements should be made to last for several years: this would give the authorities the time not only to clear

Figure 3.2. A poor woman's attempt to shelter her family in Messina. Courtesy of the Library of Congress, image LC-USZ62-73448.

the historic site of rubble, but also to rebuild a permanent urban environment. This meant that Simonini had to plan the settlement as a city in all respects and provide it with facilities such as electricity and fresh water. Second, the location of the provisional settlement was to help reestablish the connection with the harbor and bolster a quick restoration of maritime commerce.[7] As we have seen, many people considered the harbor and the maritime vocation of the city as the principal reason to rebuild the city where it was before; in the minds of the city's advocates, it would drive the economic rebirth of Messina's urban community.

From the beginning, Simonini seemed keen to recognize and sanction the status quo.[8] The provisional settlements that the volunteers had established south and north of the historic city were suitable for further expansion. In the final version of his plan, therefore, Simonini outlined two major settlements on the outskirts of the historic city, along the lines traced by the first camps. The first and bigger settlement would be on the Orti della Mosella, expanding Michelopoli further south into the rural surroundings. The second one would be in the Giostra Valley, extending the already existing group of huts into a more sizable settlement. The consequences of this operation were remarkable. Once completed, the two camps would occupy a surface that was roughly equivalent in size to the area of the old city, but located in previously rural areas of the hinterland.[9] This choice suited the ambitions of the local authorities. As we have seen, they had envisioned expanding the city along the north-south axis back in the 1860s, and in the pre-earthquake decades, private developers had built a few blocks in the new development areas. Consequently, in a meeting called to discuss the first draft of Simonini's plan, they encouraged his choice of the northern and southern plains, for they believed that this would facilitate the future incorporation of these areas into the built space. Therefore, they explicitly requested that Simonini take into account the ultimate plan for these areas, most notably the need for permanent sanitary and energy infrastructure and a space for industrial and commercial activities close to the port.[10]

If the choice of the areas for temporary shelter enjoyed a large consensus, their legal status was more controversial. As we have seen in chapter 2, the 1865 legislation on real estate appropriation in the public interest offered public administrators special legal powers, which greatly reduced the rights of owners and established rules for limited compensations. The amount of expropriations needed in this case, however, was extraordinary. The authorities would thus require even more far-reaching legal powers than those established by the 1865 law. In order to prevent any enduring resistance by the landowners and avoid unnecessary delays, Law no. 12 of 12 January 1909, the main piece of legislation to result from the 1908 earthquake, intervened in this matter. Articles 3 and 5 of that law granted special real estate appropriation powers to the authorities, rendering real estate appropriation procedures faster and less expensive.

The 1909 law established two different categories of expropriations: permanent and temporary. Depending on the category chosen, the amount of compensation paid to expropriated landowners varied considerably. After some hesitation, Simonini's bureau for provisional shelter and the Ministry of Public Works chose to proceed mainly with permanent expropriations. That choice was the result, first, of their awareness of the timescale of the reconstruction. Rebuilding Messina was not something that could be achieved in a few short months. In addition, the fact that the national authorities had yet to make a final decision on Messina's site certainly favored prudent estimates.[11] It would have been too risky to opt for temporary expropriations when facing such uncertainty about the rebuilding program. Secondly, from an economic point of view, permanent expropriation was more convenient than temporary occupation. The latter would imply restoring the property to its former condition at the end of the enforced occupation. Permanent expropriation, on the contrary, limited compensation to an initial lump sum. On their part, Messina's local authorities favored permanent expropriation as the more convenient option for a future incorporation of the areas into the new Messina.[12]

In order to complete the provisional settlements (known as *baraccamenti*) in Mosella and Giostra, the administration permanently expropriated almost 1,500,000 square meters of land and a further 500,000 on a temporary basis.[13] Unsurprisingly, such massive real estate expropriation raised strong opposition from landowners. Messina's prefect initially backed the opposition, but despite a few legal suits that lasted for years, the authorities were able to overcome most resistance.[14] The construction of the *baraccamenti* occupied officers and engineers from the Royal Army and the Genio Civile for several months, as well as construction workers who came to Messina specifically for this task. Construction materials from overseas—in particular wood from the United States, Canada, and Switzerland—and large donations from spontaneous committees formed in various Italian cities ensured that the construction of the camps progressed as quickly as possible.[15]

Before the earthquake, both the Orti della Mosella and the Giostra Valley were extensively cultivated, and the construction of housing and infrastructure often entailed the destruction of crops and eradication of orchards. While the internal report by the civil engineers and the printed report by the Ministry of Public Works give us only vague hints about the expropriated areas, the appeals landowners presented to the civil courts provide us with much more detail about the characteristics of the land and crops. The legal opposition by Domenico and Roberto Saccà, for instance, owners of 80,000 square meters in the Orti della Mosella, details that their property was cultivated through year-round irrigation and had more than 1,500 trees, mainly lemons, but also tangerines, figs, medlar trees, and mulberries.[16] The Saccà brothers' property was typical of the kind of agriculture common to most coastal areas of Sicily at that time: what were known as "citrus gardens," that is, irrigated citrus orchards mixed with other kinds of highly specialized fruit production. Prior to the earthquake, this production was strongly integrated with citric acid processing plants and shipping operations from Messina's port.[17] The post-earthquake *baraccamenti* dramatically altered the rural landscape and its industrial and commercial links, replacing orchards with thousands of wooden huts.[18]

The construction of shelters in Mosella and Giostra was in every respect an urbanization process. The prevailing housing unit was a one-storey wooden hut with two rooms and no sanitary facilities.[19] Thus, these dwellings could not be considered a permanent solution. The authorities nonetheless believed that the *baraccamenti* had to last for a period of several years, most probably followed by incorporation into the new city.[20] The settlements, therefore, needed basics of urban infrastructure such as electric lighting, roads, and a water supply. Considering the importance attached to water for public health, it is not surprising that a functioning aqueduct was of the utmost priority. The work teams of the Genio Civile and the army restored the Niceto aqueduct to basic functionality and built new pipelines to supply public fountains in the *baraccamenti*. In addition to infrastructure, the authorities sought to recreate a functional space for social and economic activities. Along with huts for families, therefore, the settlements had also huts for churches, schools, and public offices. There, the authorities could restore basic civic services and government offices: a statistical register of the population, urban police, a sanitation office, medical services, and education.[21] The *baraccamenti*, in summary, attempted to restore urban life and community, not simply an inhabitable, provisional urban environment.

The two camps boosted the expansion of Messina's built space enormously, accomplishing in a few months more than the authorities had done in the previous three decades.[22] Yet the construction of the huts had also other important, albeit unwanted consequences. Despite initial attempts to promote the ordered distribution and management of the new urban areas and of the huts,

Figure 3.3. Huts in the Mosella encampment, 1912. Courtesy of Bibliothèque Nationale de France.

survivors took possession of the space in a spontaneous and uncontrolled way from the very beginning. By the end of April 1909, the Genio Civile had started to denounce the "invasion" of expropriated land by unauthorized groups of families and the illegal occupation of unfinished huts both in Giostra and in Mosella.[23] A police report confirmed the extension of the phenomenon and noted that in many cases the squatters were the same workers who had built the huts. The report concluded that spontaneous occupation was an understandable recourse taken by a desperate population and warned about the risk of riots in case of forced evictions.[24]

In late May 1909, after yet more cases of occupation and resistance to eviction, the prefect of Messina wrote an alarmed letter to the prime minister, in which he claimed to have lost control over the settlements and asked for help. The population, he stated, did not respect official procedures for the allocation of dwellings, and they even occupied huts that were still under construction. "The idea of the most strenuous resistance to any order of eviction," he added, "is spreading everywhere, and the homeless population is multiplying its stratagems in order to invade those barracks that are still free and even those which have not been completed yet."[25] Despite the prefect's cry for help, the national authorities could not do much more to stop illegal occupation. On the contrary, they eventually acknowledged other shantytowns constructed by survivors on their own initiative amidst the rubble of the city center.[26] As the provisional city had firmly established the direction of the expansion of the urban space, it also had set in motion a process of uncontrolled appropriation. As we shall see, this would have important consequences for the duration and results of the rebuilding, and it would complicate the plans of the authorities.

The Master Plan

In many respects, the *baraccamenti* in Giostra and Mosella foreshadowed the shape of the city to come. Nonetheless, the rebuilding of a new Messina could start only after a ministerial decree had established its location, and thus the fate of the city's historic site. As we have seen in chapter 1, after lengthy studies and under enduring political pressure, a state geological commission led by member of Parliament and president of the Lincean Academy Pietro Blaserna had finally declared the site suitable for rebuilding in July 1909. The ensuing ministerial decree thus authorized the reconstruction on most of the soft, sandy plain facing Messina's harbor, under the condition of strict application of the new code for earthquake-resistant engineering and urban planning. The city could rise again, but the authorities had to redevelop it along new lines.

In the early twentieth century, urban planning was a fast-developing practice in European and North American cities, driven by concerns over public health and attempts to mitigate the worst consequences of urbanization and industrialization.[27] In Italy, as mentioned in the previous chapter, urban planning emerged as a response to the need for many cities to expand the built space and, concurrently, to better the socio-sanitary conditions of the old centers. Through their successions of failed attempts and unachieved plans, municipal authorities and professionals started to gain a more comprehensive vision of the urban space and a conception of planning as a practice addressing the city as a whole.[28] In 1908, though, this vision of the city and its complementary planning practice was still in the making. With the exception of planned industrial communities and the emerging garden city movement, pre–World War planning had rarely addressed the creation of an entire city from scratch.[29]

Post-disaster reconstructions, in fact, had offered opportunities for comprehensive urban plans on a large scale well before the conventional birth of modern planning. Lisbon after 1755 is perhaps the most widely known and successful example, but is not an isolated case.[30] In Italy, the authorities promoted comprehensive post-disaster planning after the 1693 Noto Valley earthquake and rebuilt the towns of Noto, Avola, Catania, and many others along new urban lines.[31] Something similar happened after the earthquake in 1783–84 in Calabria, and radically new plans for Messina were already debated in 1784.[32] The task required in Messina after 1908, however, was different from these cases, not just because of the size of the urban space to plan, but also because of the multiple layers that twentieth-century planning had to take into account. Unlike its early modern predecessors, the twentieth-century city was an elaborate and increasingly high-tech system involving the simultaneous interaction of energy networks, sanitary infrastructure, population management, and economic activities. The act of planning after 1908 had to take all these layers into account, which most previous post-disaster comprehensive restructurings of urban spaces simply could not have contemplated.

On 27 May 1909, a few weeks after the Ministry of Public Works promulgated the norms for earthquake-proof engineering and planning, the municipal council of Messina appointed engineer Luigi Borzì to draw up a *piano regolatore edilizio* for the new Messina. This planning tool had existed since 1865, but it was designed for partial renewals of existing urban space. Now that same tool was to aid in planning an entire city anew. Borzì had been a member of the Municipal Technical Bureau from 1891 and head of the bureau since 1907. He was also one of the few officers to have survived the earthquake. Because of his experience and rank, Borzì seemed the right person to undertake the crucial planning task. As head of the bureau, he had extensive knowledge of streets, networks, and underground infrastructure, and also of demographic dynamics and of the local economy and political milieu. Moreover, he had taken part in the pre-earthquake sanitation plans, which represented the most significant experiments in urban planning ever attempted in the city. Finally, being an engineer, he was in the best position to interpret and conform to the building and planning code for an earthquake-proof urban environment.

Local authorities were impatient to start the reconstruction of Messina regardless of any formal authorization from Rome, and appointing Borzì as early as May 1909 was, in all probability, a way to expedite the process. Borzì, however, could start his work only after the ministry passed the decree authorizing the reconstruction of Messina on the historic site. Following the decree, on 9 and 10 August 1909 two decisive meetings took place in Rome at the Ministry of Public Works. Several high-ranking officers of various ministries and members of the National Railroad Company attended the meeting, along with Edmondo Saint-Just di Teulada, chief engineer of the Genio Civile, who was responsible for the *piano regolatore* for the national capital. The purpose of these meetings was to establish guidelines for this unprecedented exercise in city planning through the cooperation of all the relevant local and national actors. The participants resolved to prioritize the economic and productive infrastructures of the city, with special emphasis on the creation of an industrial zone, a railroad network, and the reconstruction of the port infrastructure. Secondly, they agreed on the importance of harmonizing the plan with the building code and its rigorous standards. In addition, the ministry officers decided that Saint-Just de Teulada, a more experienced and influential planner, would supervise Luigi Borzì.[33]

Other claims and issues would also have a recognizable impact on the planning exercise. Professionals, entrepreneurs, and politicians strongly requested the restoration of industrial and commercial activities from the very first days, stating that it was of paramount importance for the future of the city.[34] To recover its maritime vocation and exploit the potential of its port, was indeed the ultimate reason for rebuilding Messina on the same dangerous site. Moreover, the earthquake building and planning code was not necessarily seen as a restrictive requirement imposed from above; an arguably large portion of the survivors must have been quite willing to cooperate with its enforcement. Many public figures had suffered personal losses among their close relatives, and they were sometimes the only surviving members of their family: that, for example, was the case with the engineer Borzì himself. In all probability, they were extremely aware of the importance of earthquake prevention. Finally, local authorities and municipal experts like Borzì had attempted for decades to sanitize the city in accordance with the new public health imperatives, and prior to the earthquake they had been broadening the scope of plans to incorporate other features of the urban environment. The large-scale urban planning required after 1908 was an unprecedented opportunity for comprehensive public health reform and the much-needed infrastructure, as well as other long-debated urban improvements.

Borzì completed the first version of the master plan at the beginning of 1910. The city's authorities then handed over the plan to the Superior Council of Public Works, a consultant body from the Ministry of Public Works. One of the main features of the plan, and a direct consequence of the building code, was the creation of entirely new building lots and new streets. The building code, indeed, required a minimum width for streets that rendered it impossible to entirely reproduce the former urban layout. This in turn entailed at least the partial reshaping of urban ownership and a considerable amount of real estate expropriation. Although the authorities did not consent to the most radical proposal of a "general expropriation"—immediate expropriation by the state of the entire surface area of the historic city—they nevertheless decided to proceed with partial expropriation and the reshaping of real estate parcels.[35] Some surviving property owners protested vigorously against the first version of the plan.[36] In June 1910, nevertheless, the authorities validated the overall scheme of the plan, designating a term of 25 years for the execution of works and expropriations. Following this decision, Borzì could draw up a more detailed version of the master plan, which the authorities finally approved in 1911.[37]

The master plan reshaped the layout of the city remarkably. The orientation of a few main streets remained the same, partly due to the attempt to retain the broad shape of the destroyed city whenever possible, and partly due to the physical constraints of the topography squeezed between the sea and the mountains.[38] Whenever possible, however, Borzì applied a grid, and even those streets that reproduced the old layout were much larger and straighter than before. In order to comply with the building code, the planner then divided the urban space into squared lots, *isolati*, which would host detached blocks of no more than two floors each.[39] Borzì had calculated that Messina's population would increase to 85,200 individuals within 25 years.[40] In order to accommodate this population in such a low-rise and generously spaced urban environment, and with the topographical constraints of the coastal site, there was no alternative to horizontal expansion. Accordingly, the surface area covered by the plan was almost double that of pre-earthquake Messina and occupied not only both pre-1908 new development areas, but a much more extended portion of the southern Orti della Mosella.

While scrupulously respecting the code for earthquake-proof planning, Borzì did not miss the opportunity to introduce most of those innovations planned in the pre-earthquake decades, thus advancing the urban sanitation program at the same time.[41] Consequently, he envisioned housing blocks built around large internal yards, which would facilitate light and air circulation and thus the sanitation of dwellings. Even more remarkably, he included a comprehensive network of pipelines to bring the water of the city's aqueduct into every dwelling and planned to connect each housing unit with an entirely new waterborne sewage system (see figure 3.4).[42] Revamping a core element of the

Figure 3.4. Master plan by Luigi Borzì with sewage pipes. Courtesy of Biblioteca Regionale di Messina.

1899 sewage plan, Borzì also envisioned transforming the Torrente Portalegni into a main wastewater and rainwater collector.[43] Moreover, he designed a system for rainwater drainage in the higher part of the city, to drain water flowing down from the surrounding mountains and to divert it into special canals.[44] This would minimize the risk of flash floods during heavy rains, as well as the health risks associated with freely flowing rainwater.

In addition to seismic safety and sanitation, the Borzì plan addressed the economic prospects of the new city. As we have seen, the local authorities and business community considered the port as key for the restoration of the city's economy. Even before the earthquake, however, they had contemplated the necessity of major renewals to adapt the "natural features" of the harbor to the needs of a "modern society."[45] Largely reprising the program he had drawn up in 1907, Borzì thus included in the final version of his master plan a renovated port, which he aimed to transform into a technologically equipped transport and commercial hub connected to a modern railroad station. This infrastructural complex, then, would function in strict connection with an adjacent industrial zone, which he located along the southern shore.[46] This industrial zone would benefit from the same rules and special fees as the industrial zone created in Naples in 1904 to encourage the installation of factories and production plants.[47] Finally, a dense network of tramway lines would guarantee the smooth circulation of people throughout the entire urban space.

For a long time, scholars have criticized or belittled this master plan as being a "bureaucratic plan"—the result of a compromise between different administrative instances, and therefore almost completely lacking in aesthetic value and originality.[48] More recently, others have opposed such an interpretation, pointing out some of the better qualities of the plan, such as its consistency with the morphology of the city, and stressing the ability of the planner to interpret the imperatives of the new earthquake legislation.[49] Even this latter position, however, ultimately seems to take into consideration the plan only from an aesthetic point of view and formulates value judgments based on this. I would suggest that we see the master plan from a different angle, taking into consideration the knowledge it mobilized, the conception of city that underpinned it, and the urban environmental transformation it entailed. In this regard, the definition of "bureaucratic plan" might still be of use, but rather than this being a pejorative term, it could help us in identifying some of its most interesting features.

The Borzì plan was largely the outcome of the knowledge of municipal experts, "bureaucrats," administrative bodies, and individuals that had been produced and accumulated over decades. Borzì was the efficient "terminal" of such knowledge and the executive of a consistent planning practice that mediated between different needs. The plan synthesized all the pre-earthquake ideas for urban reform into an integrated and comprehensive conception of the city and coupled these with post-1908 seismic adaptation requirements. Furthermore, the scale and scope of the exercise makes the plan at least unusual, if not exceptional, in an era that did not yet know modernist planning ideas. Borzì's master plan encompassed all the layers and components of an entire city as conceived at the beginning of the twentieth century: the street layout, the technical features of the buildings, a transport network, sanitary infrastructure, industrial development, and management of population growth. It is probably true that the Borzì plan was the outcome of bureaucratic mediation more than the aesthetic expression of an individual. Yet such mediation was a historically significant expression of the urban culture of the time.

Despite its all-encompassing ambition, two major flaws doomed the master plan. The most important was perhaps the calculation of population growth. Based on the disaster death toll and taking account of outward migration, Borzì expected the city to reach 85,000 inhabitants within 25 years.[50] The expected size of the population played a pivotal role in the whole planning exercise and determined the size of the plan and the extension of built space and infrastructure. Borzì clearly stated this in the lengthy text that accompanied the final published version of his plan.[51] His calculation, however, was dramatically wrong. The national census conducted in 1911 recorded a population of 68,138 inhabitants in the city center, and more than 120,000 in the entire municipal territory.[52] In less than three years, therefore, Messina had almost regained the same population it had had in 1881. In 1921, only 13 years after the earthquake, the population of the inner city reached 114,051 inhabitants, meaning almost 30,000 more people than Borzì had expected in only half of the time (see figure 3.6).[53] Such demographic growth, due to substantial inward migration driven by the building industry, invalidated a key assumption of Borzì's plan, thus undermining the success of the entire planning exercise.[54]

This demographic mistake was coupled with the failure of another key feature of the plan: the "land-rotation" method of reconstruction. According to Borzì's original vision, by concentrating the population in the peripheral *baraccamenti*, the historic city would be left empty and this would expedite the reclamation of wasteland and the construction of permanent buildings. This, in turn, would permit the gradual clearance of the *baraccamenti*, replacing these with permanent buildings, underground networks, and road infrastructure.[55] As we shall see, however, huts and provisional shelters proved much more resilient than imagined at the time of their construction. In the years to follow, they became the housing solution that allowed the city to keep up with the unexpected growth of the urban population, while other shantytowns mushroomed among the ruins of the old city. Before the official launch and beyond the edges of Borzì's planning exercise, a new informal city was born: the confrontation between the master plan and the resilience of that informal city and its inhabitants would leave a profound mark on the entire reconstruction process.

The City Developers versus the Hut Dwellers

Law no. 12 of 12 January 1909 had provided massive state funds for the reconstruction of Messina, establishing new taxes nationwide while exempting the damaged areas from most fiscal obligations. This was a significant innovation considering that, prior to 1908, the state had not funded any more than a very limited portion of any post-disaster reconstruction. The same interventionist approach animated another crucial piece of legislation that passed in 1910 to regulate one of the most pressing concerns: real estate ownership. As mentioned, the "general expropriation" that some had advocated as the best solution for the regulation of the reconstruction did not materialize. The implementation of the new master plan, and thus the creation of new building lots, however, entailed at least partial expropriation and redistribution of real estate.[56] Already in 1909, those among the survivors who owned real estate in the devastated city had formed a coalition of "damaged owners" to claim their rights and share financial resources. This coalition included some of the most influential personalities from local politics who had survived the disaster, and in 1910, the national government granted official status to this organization. Law no. 466 of 13 July 1910 established the "consortium of damaged owners" and recognized it as one of the main recipients of public funding.[57]

In the original version, the consortium would grant each of the "damaged owners" a mortgage loan covering 75 percent of the value of their lost property and a corresponding estate entitlement on the new building lots.[58] These were extremely advantageous conditions and soon triggered a whirlwind trade in estate and mortgage entitlements, as well as conflicts over new and old entitlements.[59] Even though this institution was originally only supposed to regulate the distribution of public funds to private owners, new legislation over the following years gradually extended its structure and functions, transforming the consortium into a more powerful institution called the Unione Edilizia, literally "Building Association." In its ultimate version, after 1915, this institution managed all the mortgages held by private owners with the state and directly managed contracts and works for private housing. In addition, it also managed the municipal properties and public works on behalf of the municipality and the Ministry of Public Works, and it could stipulate contracts with private enterprises for publicly funded construction. In the end, according to historian Guiseppe Barone, the Unione Edilizia had "the almost complete monopoly in the sector of building contracts," and was "the principal planning actor nationwide."[60] The only exceptions were those works that the municipal administration carried out directly, and that involved almost exclusively roads and underground infrastructure.

The consolidation of this institutional structure and the conspicuous flow of money associated with it did not lead to a correspondingly quick start in the rebuilding process. In 1913, while presenting the municipal administration's guidelines for the reconstruction, town councilor and former municipal engineer Pietro Interdonato expressed concerns with the rebuilding process. According to Interdonato, the master plan, although already approved by the authorities and in force by that time, was in fact provisional in respect to many important technical details. When tracing the lines of the new city, Borzì did not have complete and detailed information on the heights and topography of the land. He thus had to work largely by approximation and could take only the major elevations into account, not the minor gradients. This entailed several mistakes, which in turn required time-consuming modifications of the plan to adapt street angles and adapt the locations and sizes of buildings to the topography of each lot. Problems related to topography were intensified by the presence of enormous amounts of solid waste in the historic city. According to Borzì, the 1908 earthquake had generated around one million cubic meters of debris.[61] Dealing with such an enormous amount of matter was a major problem. The debris could not be dumped into the harbor without filling it almost entirely, which left no option other than dumping a portion of the rubble on the outskirts of the city; in other places, the rubble was leveled off, raising the ground level upon which the city was built.[62]

Other issues were complicating the rebuilding process. Among the most significant, according to Interdonato, were conflicts over property entitlement in the historic city. As Borzì himself had anticipated in the report accompanying his master plan, the extreme fragmentation of pre-earthquake property rendered it difficult to reach agreements between proprietors and thus the beginning of building operations was delayed.[63] Whereas this problem had been anticipated, this was not the case with another major issue: the unauthorized construction and occupation of shelters. The construction of permanent buildings was not keeping up with the speed of population growth, and the presence of temporary barracks both in the new development area and among the ruins of the historic center delayed the construction of private houses and public edifices. In Internonato's opinion, the only solution was to transfer the poorest inhabitants and their shelters into a "barracks concentration camp" (*campo di concentrazione di baracche*), and thus make room for permanent buildings for the middle and the upper classes.[64]

During wartime, the situation did not change much. The municipal authorities could hardly complete even the most essential tasks, such as establishing a functional road network, except for a few main roads. Justifying the delay and recalling the many material and political obstacles he and his team of engineers had to face, Luigi Borzì mentioned as an example the construction of Garibaldi Street, which was one of the main urban axes. In 1916, according to Borzì, the street was not yet complete due to technical difficulties with removing the excessive rubble, the opposition of the archbishop to the necessary expropriation of Church property, the continuous procrastination by the private contractor entrusted with the works, and especially the refusal of hut inhabitants to evacuate the site.[65] On the other hand, housing was not advancing any faster than streets were. In 1917, after five years of activity, the Unione Edilizia had completed only a few dozen houses for middle-class employees, dispersed around various points in the city. The rest of the urban population lived in some 17,000 shelters spread across the city's historic center and the new developments.[66]

Records of a major flood event in autumn of 1917 provide us with a vivid cross section of the state of the city. On 17 October, following intense precipitation, the streams flowing through the city flooded, as well as many others along the north and south coasts of Sicily.[67] Another similar event followed on 30 October.[68] In Messina, the consequences of the floods were tragic. Riverbeds were still largely obstructed by earthquake debris. When floods came, the piles of debris acted as involuntary dams and embankments, rerouting the flow out of the riverbeds and into the city. At least 20 people died, and the debris and solid material carried by floodwaters caused heavy damages. According to the Ministry of Public Works' inspector-general Pignatelli, who constantly reported on the floods and their aftermath, the disaster proved that management of Messina's urban streams had been "neglected for too long" and he called for a well-planned program of public works to secure them.[69] *Baraccamenti* and their inhabitants bore the most serious consequences of the flood. Water and debris damaged some 350 huts and destroyed around 50 more entirely.[70] Difficulties in finding new shelters for the survivors shed light on the state of post-earthquake huts and shacks and on the scant results of the reconstruction program a decade after the earthquake. A report by the Genio Civile on the state of the *baraccamenti* after the flood underlined the poor living conditions of the population, the general lack of dwelling space, and the unaffordable housing costs.[71] Then, in the years following the flood, the authorities claimed they had no choice but to authorize the construction of new shelters on private lots.[72]

A map drawn up at the end of World War I (figure 3.5) allows us to appreciate the slow progress of the reconstruction in the first decade following the earthquake. The most densely built area was the one along the railroad track. The two *baraccamenti* at opposite ends of the city were largely intact. In the central area, only a few edifices were completed or under construction. Nonetheless, the blank space at the center of the map was far from being empty. On the contrary, that area was a "full" space: full of physical debris still waiting

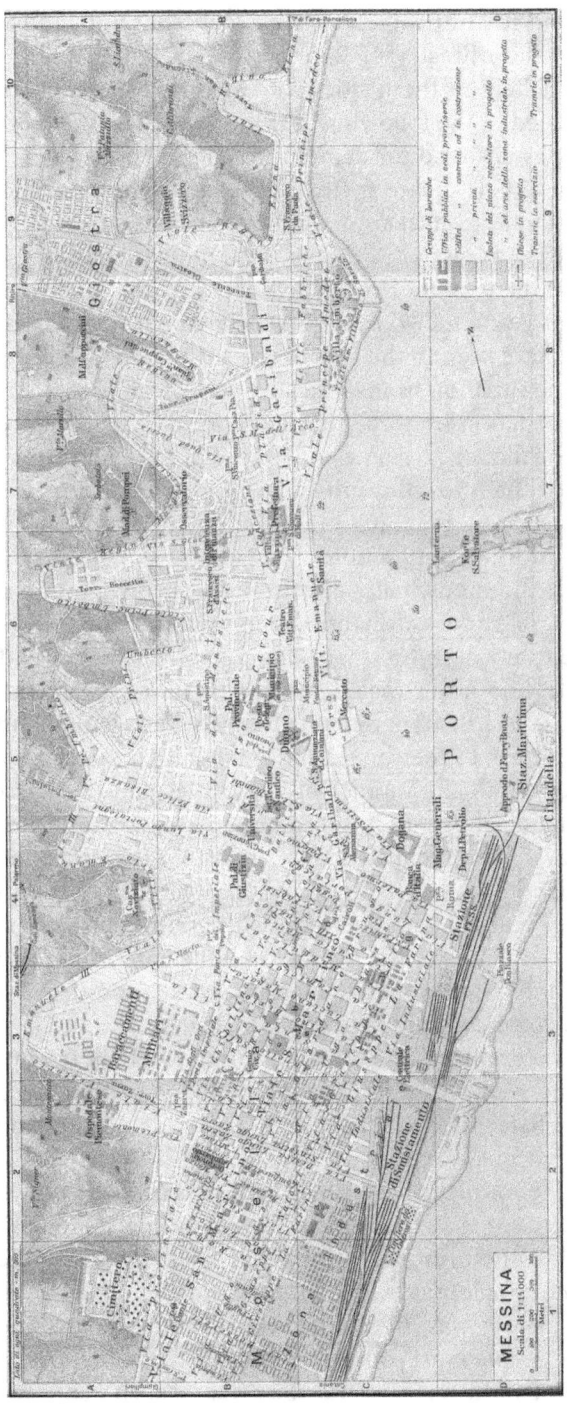

Figure 3.5. The state of reconstruction efforts in 1918. Courtesy of Guido Stagni.

for reclamation and full of people and their makeshift but enduring shelters. As we have seen, the Ministry of Public Works reported the unauthorized construction of shelters in the historic city as early as 1911.[73] Repopulation of Messina continued in the following years and included the reoccupation of crumbling buildings destined for demolition. In 1913, Interdonato wrote, for example, that on a 16,000-square-meter lot destined to become the courthouse there were more than 66 shacks. In addition, in the same area, people were squatting illegally in at least 144 "rooms" in crumbling buildings.[74] Later reports confirm that the unauthorized repopulation of the inner city continued during subsequent years, fueled by a growing number of urban dwellers and sometimes, as we have seen in the case of the 1917 flood, even encouraged by the authorities. The situation in the official *baraccamenti* was no different; the squatting and occupation by force that had already manifested itself in the aftermath of the earthquake became endemic. The 1917 report by the Unione Edilizia mentioned that most hut inhabitants did not pay any rent to the authorities.[75] In many cases, then, it seems that huts passed from one family to another through informal transactions.[76]

Over the years, the municipal authorities repeatedly announced the production of a cadastral survey of shanties, huts, and their populations, but this goal was never entirely accomplished. The figures on shacks and huts were often approximate, and never included the number of inhabitants except in small sample areas. The shelters remained largely outside the grasp of public powers, and the control of the communities inhabiting them was always limited and contested. Both the municipal authorities and the Unione Edilizia continuously denounced this informal and uncharted urbanization as responsible for the delay in the reconstruction program. The unauthorized occupation of urban land and the resistance of occupants to eviction shrunk the options of the city builders and delayed their actions considerably. As mentioned earlier, in the minds of the planner and the authorities, advancing the rebuilding in the inner city would allow for a gradual transfer of the population from the *baraccamenti* into concrete housing. This would in turn permit clearance of the *baraccamenti* and ultimately initiate rebuilding in these areas. Due to informal housing and resistance to eviction, however, there was a very limited amount of flat land available for building, and thus the "land-rotation" principle was largely unsuccessful.

Even though the municipal administration and the city's developer considered it a problem for the governance of the city, informal urbanization remained nonetheless the principal resource of a large working class with no other affordable housing options. The surge in population documented by the 1911 and 1921 censuses was due to the return migration of refugees and to the arrival of new people most probably attracted by the prospects of employment in the building industry.[77] Despite the needs of such a large population of earthquake survivors and new immigrants, the building program followed an explicit class agenda, prioritizing monumental public edifices, wealthy private residences, and housing for state employees.[78] As a result, in the early 1920s, a population of some 110,000 inhabitants could count on 1,483 dwellings.[79] Considering the disproportion of these figures, it should not come as a surprise to note that the shelters, instead of diminishing, had risen to up to 18,000 units, nor to discover that resistance to eviction was strong enough to compel the authorities to locate most new buildings outside the planned city.[80] Underrepresented and pushed to the margins of the official political agenda, the hut dwellers were nonetheless making their own, powerful urban politics and influencing the evolution of the built space.[81]

While a large population struggled to survive in overcrowded huts, decaying shanties, and crumbling buildings, local businesspeople, political representatives, and entrepreneurs' coalitions from Northern Italy struggled to gain control of the big money associated with the Unione Edilizia. A solid body of scholarship has shed light on this conflict at multiple levels: the control of the board of the Unione Edilizia, pressure on the national government for legislative reform, the movement of financial capital, and the mobilization of public opinion through the local press.[82] The transition to the Fascist regime marked a turning point. After Benito Mussolini visited Messina in 1923, the new regime tried to take control of the reconstruction. This operation was long and tormented. The resistance of local groups was difficult to eradicate, and the regime was not able to find reliable allies within the urban elites. Eventually, however, the regime was able to navigate the intricate local connections. In

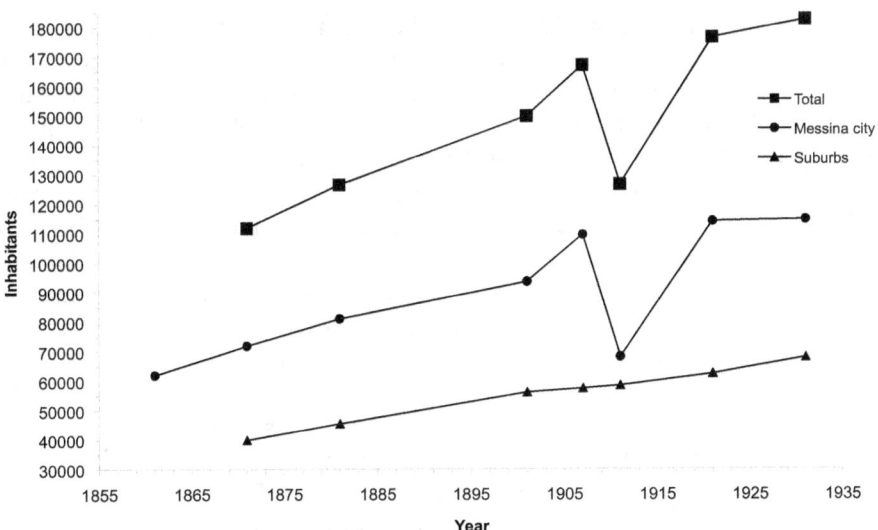

Figure 3.6. Population in Messina 1861–1931

1927, the government suppressed the Unione Edilizia and replaced it with a special section of the Genio Civile, operating in Messina under the direct control of the Ministry of Public Works.[83]

In 1912, the Ministry of Public Works claimed that reconstruction would be complete in a few years.[84] Fifteen years later, the condition of the city testified to the failure of such claims. The material living conditions of a large majority of Messina's inhabitants, if they hadn't actually worsened, had certainly not improved. To be sure, there were by then a few, elegant private residences, and massive public edifices such as the town hall, the courthouse, and the prefecture signaled the restoration of public functions and governance. The signs of the earthquake, however, still dominated the urban landscape, and the few permanent buildings were interspersed with ruins and shanties. The beginning of Fascism altered the political order of the post-earthquake city and had a significant impact on the power balance of the reconstruction economy. Yet it had hardly any effect on that landscape, at least in the first phase. Indeed, while gaining control over the reconstruction and pursuing the program of monumental rebuilding already initiated in the 1910s, the new Fascist rulers had to face the same issues as their predecessors: the constraints of Messina's topography and the presence of a large population that relied on shanties and huts as the only affordable form of housing. Without addressing the working-class housing problem, the reconstruction could hardly advance.

The New City and Its Darker Sides

Despite Mussolini's promises in 1923, the reconstruction proceeded in slow motion for almost another decade, while living conditions in the huts and shanties deteriorated. According to a sample inquiry led in 1930 by the municipality on an area of 31,000 square meters in the Orti della Mosella, life in the huts, if anything, had worsened. In 1930, the population density in the sample area was 1332 inhabitants for 259 huts, meaning more than 5 persons per hut. All huts dated back to 1909 and generally lacked sanitary facilities. Only 29 huts had running water and only 61 had private toilets, whereas the inhabitants of the remaining 198 huts had to share 21 open-air toilets.[85] Explaining the reasons why the population still refused to leave the huts, a couple of unusually perspicacious police officers reminded the oblivious prefect that there were "no houses outside the main streets," and that the rent of the few existing buildings was unaffordable even for the "middle class of the population"—an earth-shattering insight, no doubt.[86] A survey of private lots in the late 1920s largely confirmed that picture, proving the presence of vacant lots and the occupation of some of them by barracks and shanties.[87] This, coupled with rising unemployment figures from the mid-1920s onwards,[88] leaves no doubts as to why the large majority of the population obstinately defended their life in ramshackle and overcrowded huts and shanties. They simply had no other options.

In the late 1920s, after years of inaction, the regime launched a new, centrally funded program of social housing. The program was to give a boost to the rebuilding of Messina, and the demolition of huts and shanties.[89] According to the official report of the Ministry of Public Works that advertised the program in 1933, the number of barracks torn down prior to 1932 amounted to 13,791 units, of which more than 11,000 units had been torn down after 1926. Simultaneously, the regime directly undertook the construction of some 5,000 new dwellings.[90] Social housing mirrored the socioeconomic subdivision of the homeless population into three classes. For the middle class and the state employees—the first two classes—the regime followed in the footsteps of the Unione Edilizia: functional, earthquake-resistant, multi-apartment blocks with an internal yard and comprehensive sanitary facilities in each unit. For the larger class of urban poor, however, the regime introduced the more modest "ultra-popular" housing. This category admittedly included newly arrived immigrants in addition to the 1908 survivors.[91] The inclusion of immigrants among the beneficiaries of social housing along with earthquake survivors allowed a more effective response to the root causes of the chronic housing problem in post-earthquake Messina, largely contributing to the numbers advertised by the regime.

Several publications celebrated the results of the Fascist "new deal" on the ten-year anniversary of Benito Mussolini's first visit in Messina.[92] By 1933, the reconstruction had undeniably progressed. The implementation of the program, however, was not without its hardships. The civil engineers often requested police officers to accompany them to evict people from their huts and prevent new occupations.[93] The "ultra-popular houses" replacing the huts of the immediate aftermath were mostly one-storey buildings made of bricks, consisting of a single room, or a maximum of two: as a matter of fact, nothing more than a hut in brick. In addition, to complete some of the ultra-popular housing developments, the authorities had to expand the built space beyond the borders of the planned city.[94] Locations such as San Paolo were not included in the Borzì plan, which encouraged a spatial and social segregation, the effects of which are still visible today.[95] Many tenants refused to pay rent to the authorities, pursuing the pattern of illegal appropriation that had already emerged in the aftermath of the earthquake.[96] More importantly, despite the efforts made by the regime, huts and shanties had not disappeared, and in 1933 there were at least 5,000–6,000 shelters.[97] Nearly 25 years after the earthquake, provisional urbanization still marked the urban landscape.

The progress of urban infrastructure generally followed the sluggish pace of concrete housing construction and reproduced some of its fundamental contradictions. While planning the future city, Luigi Borzì envisioned the creation of a modern urban space, provided with features, services, and infrastructure to ensure public health, seismic safety, and economic development. During the twenty-five years following the earthquake, the authorities were able to provide many of these features, services, and infrastructure, making the Messina of the late 1930s a modern city. The modernity of Messina, however, had darker sides that rendered the city quite different from the harmonious, safe, technological urban environment the planner and the authorities imagined in the aftermath.

Management of water circulation was key for urban modernization, and, during the reconstruction years, the municipal authorities accomplished the construction of a comprehensive network of pipelines for freshwater distribution. The restoration of the Niceto aqueduct was relatively fast and helped the authorities to provide the *baraccamenti* with fresh water. The steady demographic growth of post-1908 Messina nonetheless soon convinced municipal engineers that the Niceto water would not be enough to supply the city's rising demand, especially once they completed the network for domestic supply. In 1916 the Municipal Technical Bureau introduced the possibility of tapping the Santissima sources in Fiumedinisi on the southern slope of the Peloritani into the aqueduct, thus realizing the aqueduct that the Municipal Technical Bureau had envisioned as far back as 1895.[98] The progress of urban aqueduct pipes along with the increasing number of permanent dwellings in the late 1920s raised awareness of water supply issues among the municipal administrators, and in the late 1920s they moved from plan to action.[99] The completion of the aqueduct and the comprehensive system for freshwater distribution within the city that Borzì had planned marked a turning point in Messina's history. The city's water cycle now extended over a far larger surface area, and for the first time in history, Messina's urban dwellings had tap water.

Along the same lines, *ex novo* urban reconstruction facilitated the construction of a sewage network. Sewage canals occupied the municipality for years, and were usually built alongside streets and freshwater pipes. Engineers designed canals made of masonry, covered with ceramic tiles, and protected by a shell of reinforced concrete. Following the 1899 scheme by the Municipal Technical Bureau, which the 1911 Borzì plan had entirely reproduced, the Torrente Portalegni became the main sewage collector for the entire city. To that purpose, its bed was entirely lined with concrete, and the estuary was embanked in a reinforced concrete structure to protect it from tidal streams and marine currents.[100] The urban portion of the stream was then entirely buried under a shell of reinforced concrete, and a paved surface transformed it into one of the city's main streets. In addition, this urban water system also incorporated the other streams that flow down from the Peloritani Mountains, connecting them to a rainwater drainage system that ran along a ring road in the higher part of the city.[101] By digging, canalizing, diverting, concreting, paving, connecting, and burying under cement, the new city had come closer than ever to fulfilling the vision of nineteenth-century public health reformers: an urban water cycle completely under human control.

The new Messina was also closer to the post-1908 ideal of an earthquake-proof city. Wartime aerial shots depict an urban environment corresponding to the lines traced by Luigi Borzì in the aftermath of the earthquake.[102] Building blocks were considerably spaced out, and all roads were in accordance with—and often exceeded—the minimum standard width of ten meters laid out in the 1909 code. The blocks were also considerably shorter than in the pre-earthquake city. A new set of norms for earthquake protection in 1927 had overcome some of the limitations imposed in 1909, but even with the new rules, no buildings could exceed three storeys.[103] While the rules established precise standards for the calculation of the static resistance of buildings and imposed some technical solutions, neither the 1909 nor the 1927 norms compelled planners and builders to use reinforced concrete. This technology, however, was widely considered as the most suitable to ensure both resistance to earthquakes and architectural versatility.[104] Numerous photographic records testify to the widespread use of reinforced concrete in private and public buildings alike, as well as in urban infrastructure.[105] The use of reinforced concrete in the rebuilding of Messina marked a substantial discontinuity with pre-earthquake construction methods. This technology, along with the adherence to earthquake-proof planning norms, certainly offered a better adaptation to the seismicity of the site than ever before in Messina's thousand-year history.[106]

Notwithstanding these remarkable accomplishments, the other qualifying points of the Borzì plan remained dead letters. The role of Messina as a Mediterranean port city was the most repeated argument in favor of rebuilding the city on the same site, in spite of the geological risk. Even if the supposed "natural advantages" of Messina's site and harbor made much of this argument's strength, the authorities knew already in the pre-earthquake years that they had to adapt the harbor to the needs of modern navigation. Its depth and width were insufficient for the increasingly large boats, whereas artificial modifications to the coastline allowed virtually every coastal city to build larger and better-equipped harbors than the one in Messina.[107] Despite the fact that the Borzì plan in 1911 had included significant port renewals, practically nothing happened until the 1920s, despite repeated appeals from local associations and the chamber of commerce.[108] The whole issue of the harbor redevelopment resurfaced only in the early 1920s, when the municipality proposed a new program of public works in the harbor.[109] In the following years, however, only a small portion of these improvements were realized, as the volume and importance of maritime traffic in the port of Messina dropped steadily.[110]

If port renovation stalled, the adjacent industrial zone turned into a complete fiasco. At least until the late 1920s, huts and shanties occupied much of the area, and no remarkable industrial initiative was ever launched, notwithstanding the aspirations and the claims of the local associations for special governmental initiatives.[111] Sea changes in the global markets had downgraded the traditional strengths of pre-earthquake Messina's industry, such as lemon-based products.[112] Initiatives such as the fiscal benefits for industrial plants and the creation of a "technical-industrial school"—the Verona-Trento—were not enough to balance the lack of capital investment.[113] Unsurprisingly, the only sector capable of a certain dynamism, at least in the first decades after the quake, was the heavily subsidized building industry. For thirty years, Messina was nothing but an enormous building site. All of the economic energy and industrial initiative was concentrated on this sector, ultimately producing what one scholar has called a "genetic mutation" of the city's economic system.[114] Construction slowly replaced maritime commerce, the backbone of Messina's economy for centuries, and, at the end of the rebuilding era, the city's economy showed signs of an anticipated expansion of the tertiary sector.[115] The "inescapable economic and geographic laws" that, according to geologist Secondo Franchi, would ensure the rebirth of Messina as a maritime city, were not so inescapable after all.[116]

Even public health and seismic adaptation were only partial achievements. As mentioned, to overcome the resistance of hut people to eviction, the authorities located a significant part of the new social housing outside the planned city. This meant that the new sanitary infrastructure did not reach these zones. Sanitation was often an impossible dream for "ultra-popular" houses and shanties even *within* the borders of the Borzì plan. Those dwellings generally had no sanitary furniture except for shared cesspools.[117] For those living there, the benefits of the post-earthquake sanitized city were out of reach. This was also true for seismic safety. "Ultra-popular" houses and post-1908 shanties were not built using the same earthquake-resistant technologies as middle-class blocks and wealthy residences, since they were always envisioned as a provisional solution. These constructions were thus more exposed to seismic hazards than the rest of the city. The local and national authorities explicitly designed earthquake protection and sanitation along the line of class, following a consistent pattern before and after Fascism took power. As a result, a twin Messina grew up alongside the safe and healthy urban environment designed for the upper class—a dark side of the city for which "modernity" translated as segregation and exclusion.

Conclusion

Three decades had elapsed between the wasteland left by the disaster to the cityscape captured on 1943 reconnaissance missions and military maps. After the initial depopulation, old and new inhabitants started to settle in the shattered city, and frail tents and shanties sprung up among heaps of rubble. Within a matter of months, two *baraccamenti* had replaced the agricultural landscape on the outskirts of the devastated city. Year after year, new inhabitants came to the site, debris slowly disappeared, and some pieces of the new city took shape along the lines of modernity traced out by Borzì. Whilst the permanent city was slowly consolidated, huts and shanties remained nonetheless the only housing solution for a large population of survivors and new immigrants, and the city's builders had to accommodate the enduring presence of "provisional" encampments. Underground pipelines, streams encased in concrete, wide roads, and earthquake-resistant buildings, therefore, materialized alongside unsafe and increasingly unhealthy slums. Over three decades, rebuilding profoundly transformed the urban landscape, many biogeophysical features of the site, and the hydrology of a larger region. Nevertheless, inequality persisted inside and outside the cityscape mapped by the Allies in 1943. Shortly after this, a new traumatic event would disrupt the urban configuration: the Allies bombed the city severely, closing one chapter of Messina's history and opening the era of postwar reconstruction.[118]

The 1908 earthquake was unprecedented in Italian history in terms of the extent of destruction and death it caused. Similarly, the rebuilding of Messina was a turning point in the history of post-disaster reconstruction. The massive public spending for the 1908 earthquake zone was a novelty in respect to the state's strategies and responses to earthquake destruction. In a sharp break with the past, the state not only provided massive funding for infrastructure and public edifices, but also assisted private owners, establishing itself as the principal—if not the only—financial player in post-disaster reconstruction.[119] The rebuilding of Messina also introduced a specific institutional arrangement: a special public body with the task of managing capital and building contracts, the Unione Edilizia. The Unione was the institutional complement to state-funded reconstruction. Although the creation of plenipotentiary bodies to supervise post-earthquake rebuilding was common well before Messina, the almost exclusive management of money flows and contracts by this single agency was a significant new development. After Messina, the national authorities repeatedly adopted a similar strategy, funding a large portion of the reconstruction work after the 1915 Marsica earthquake and the 1930 Irpinia earthquake.[120] As we shall see, national authorities largely conformed to this pattern throughout the twentieth century, although it was disguised in ever-changing legal and institutional forms.

The most severe consequences of the earthquake, nevertheless, were on the city itself. There, the earthquake proved to be an even more remarkable turning point, starting with the massive urban redevelopment planned by Borzì. It was the first time that anyone had attempted the planned *ex novo* reconstruction of a whole city of that size in Italy. To be sure, *ex novo* reconstructions after major earthquakes were the norm rather than the exception, at least starting in early modern times. After the 1693 earthquake, the Duke of Camastra, plenipotentiary of the Spanish viceroy of Sicily, oversaw the rebuilding of many towns in the Noto Valley according to new plans.[121] Similarly, the authorities of the Kingdom of Naples promoted the rebuilding of Reggio Calabria along new lines after the 1783 earthquake.[122] Nevertheless, none of the previous cases involved planning and rebuilding operations as vast, extensive, and complex as in Messina. There, as we have seen, the reconstruction included not only streets and buildings for a sizable city, which was already exceptional, but also a modern technological infrastructure. The creation from scratch of a city with all the features of early twentieth-century urban modernity was a landmark experiment, although largely undervalued by posterity. In many respects, it anticipated a form of comprehensive planning that addressed not only the layout of the built space, but also technological networks, modes of resources incorporation and circulation, hazard adaptation, and economic needs of the community. Despite its many shortcomings, the rebuilding of Messina was the first example of a trend that would characterize the entire century.[123]

In order to thoroughly understand the scope of the earthquake's impact and influence on the trajectory of Messina's urban change, it is vital to consider post-earthquake changes in the light of pre-earthquake plans and actions. This unfolds along several interrelated lines. We can certainly better explain the extent of destruction by looking at the intensification of the city's physical exposure during the last decades of the nineteenth century through the combined action of urban growth, erosion of social memory, and neglect of prevention measures. In comparison with the recklessness that had dominated urban growth and reform before 1908, moreover, the novelty of the earthquake adaptation strategy incorporated into the Borzì plan is all the more striking. Likewise, we can better understand the significance of the post-earthquake urban expansion only by taking into consideration the lengthy debate on new urban developments over the pre-disaster decades and the obstacles and delays in expanding the built space before 1908. Only by knowing the pre-1908 history, then, can we identify those features of the master plan that Borzì refashioned from the pre-earthquake plans for urban reform, from sanitation to port renewal. On the other hand, by looking at the pre-earthquake urban reform plans we can measure how high ambitions were able to rise after 1908, making possible renovations so extensive and radical that they had not even been considered possible before.

From this perspective, the earthquake of 28 December 1908 appears as a powerful trigger for innovation, and crucial in turning Messina's history in a new direction, by modifying the social and physical landscape radically and irreversibly. Its influence, however, cannot be measured only in terms of urban planning reactions. The unwanted consequences of emergency responses and unplanned social processes triggered by the new post-earthquake situation influenced the outcome as much as grandiose plans for urban renewal and modernization. The creation of the provisional settlements proved to be full of such unwanted consequences. The authorities made this choice in response to a perceived emergency in the turmoil of the aftermath. That emergency call made two weeks after the earthquake nevertheless affected the timing and outcome of the rebuilding program for nearly thirty years. Another example is the unprecedented money flow from the state to the earthquake zone. Decided in the wake of the disaster, it ended up being a crucial incentive to population growth, upper-class greed, and structural mutation of the city's economy. The (often undesirable) long-term effects of short-term responses to the earthquake made the new city as much as rational plans.

The new Messina was certainly unique in its blend of planned urban modernity and shantytowns, especially in a country like Italy, which is characterized by the persistence of historic urban environments. At the same time, it also had features, contradictions, and problems common to many other cities. The paradoxical outcomes of Messina's transformation depended upon the accumulation and overlapping of individual and collective human actions, plans, and choices, and their unpredictable interplay. In all these actions, plans, and choices, however, the voice of the earthquake resonates loudly: it was the initial call to which human actions tried to respond, although often in inconsistent, messy, unjust, and complicated ways. Something similar happened sixty years later, when a new seismic disaster hit another part of Sicily: the Belice Valley.

Notes

1. Collegio degli Ingegneri e degli Agronomi di Messina, *Risanamento della città di Messina* (Messina, 1886), 71.
2. Annunziata M. Otieri, "Memorie e trasformazioni nel processo di ricostruzione di Messina," *Storia Urbana* 26, no. 106–107 (2005), 13–65.
3. See Francesco Mazza, *Relazione sull'opera del R. Commissario Straordinario Tenente Generale Mazza nelle regioni sicule colpite dal terremoto del 28 dicembre 1908*, in box 380, folder 4, Presidenza del Consiglio dei Ministri 1909 [hereafter PCM 1909], Archivio Centrale dello Stato [ACS]. Nicola De Berardinis, *Relazione letta dal Commissario Straordinario Cav. Avv. Nicola De Berardinis, Consigliere Delegato dalla Prefettura di Messina, letta il 14 febbraio 1909, prima seduta del Consiglio Comunale dopo la catastrofe del 28 dicembre 1908* (Messina, 1909).
4. *Terremoto Calabro Messinese 1908–2008*, Dipartimento della Protezione Civile, Istituto Nazionale di Geofisica e Vulcanologia, Alinari Sole 24 Ore, Firenze 2008. The images reproduced in this book are taken from the Archivio Centrale dello Stato, Raccolte Museali Fratelli Alinari, INGV Biblioteca Centrale, and the private collection of Giovanni Ricciardi, Naples.

5. Dario Caroniti, "Michelopoli," in *Messina dalla vigilia del terremoto all'avvio della ricostruzione,* ed. Antonio Baglio and Salvatore Bottari (Messina, 2011), 331–38.
6. Luigi Borzì, *Il piano regolatore di Messina* (Messina, 1912), 6.
7. "Corpo Reale del Genio Civile, Ufficio Speciale di Messina pei baraccamenti in Sicilia e in Calabria, Relazione, Messina, 31 January 1910," in box 426, Prefettura Gabinetto 1909-1940 [hereafter Pref. Gab], Archivio di Stato di Messina [hereafter ASMe] and Ministero dei Lavori Pubblici, *L'opera del Ministero dei Lavori Pubblici per i danneggiati dal terremoto del 28 dicembre 1908* (Rome, 1912).
8. See the report from General Mazza 20 January 1909 in box 167, Ministero dell'Interno, Comitato Centrale di Soccorso pei danneggiati dal terremoto del 28 dicembre 1908 in Calabria e in Sicilia [hereafter MI CCS 1908], Archivio Centrale dello Stato [hereafter ACS].
9. A copy of the plan is in box 15, Ministero dei Lavori Pubblici, Direzione Generale Lavori Pubblici, Progetti stradali 1914–1926, ACS.
10. Telegram from General Mazza, 25 January 1909, reporting a meeting in box 167, MI CCS 1908, ACS.
11. That decision depended on the report of the geological commission led by Pietro Blaserna. The report was completed only in June 1909, and the subsequent decree was issued in mid-July 1909. See chapter 1.
12. Corpo Reale del Genio Civile, Ufficio Speciale pei baraccamenti in Sicilia e Calabria, Terremoto 28 dicembre 1908, *Relazione,* Messina, 31 January 1910, 11–12. In box 426, Pref. Gab., ASMe.
13. Ministero dei Lavori Pubblici, *L'opera del Ministero,* 67.
14. See telegrams from the expropriated owners to Minister Sonnino no. 2774, 4 February 1910 h.18, and the letter from Prefect Trincheri to the Prime Minister n.prot. 255-2, 17 March 1910 in box 11, folder "Baracche: Costruzione di casette in luogo di baracche; Affari diversi e complessivi," Ministero dell'Interno, Direzione Generale dell'Amministrazione Civile, Ufficio speciale dei servizi in dipendenza dei terremoti calabro-siculi e dell'eruzione dell'Etna, Affari Generali [hereafter Ufficio terremoti AaGg], ACS. See also the report of Prefect Trincheri expressing his opposition to the Genio Civile work, in box 1. Ufficio terremoti AaGg, ACS.
15. Civil engineers reported the creation of shared cesspools for groups of barracks, justifying the choice with the risk and complications of creating sanitary services in every barrack. Genio Civile, *Relazione,* Messina, 31 January 1910, 28. Box 426, Pref. Gab, ASMe.
16. *Stima analitica e brevi osservazioni per i Sigg. Roberto e Domenico Saccà contro il Signor Prefetto della Provincia di Messina nella rappresentanza del Ministero dei Lavori Pubblici* (Messina, 1912).
17. Rosario Battaglia, *L'ultimo "splendore": Messina tra rilancio e decadenza (1815–1920)* (Soveria Mannelli, 2003) 104–10.
18. The Ministry of Public Works calculated 14,439 units directly undertaken by the state plus 2,254 by other organs and committees. Ministero dei Lavori Pubblici, *L'opera del Ministero,* 41. Here "unit" indicates a room: most of the barracks had two rooms, but in some cases they could have one. According to special commissioner Salvadori, in two years the total number of barracks (not rooms) was 21,192. His calculation included all barracks, not only those built by the civil engineers. See Alessandro Sal-

vadori, *Relazione del Regio Commissario Comm. A.Salvadori al ricostituito Consiglio Comunale di Messina* (Messina 1913), 276.
19. Genio Civile, *Relazione,* Messina, 31 January 1910, 42–52, in box 426, Pref. Gab., ASMe.
20. Ministero dei Lavori Pubblici, *L'opera del Ministero,* 36.
21. On that first phase of administrative rebirth of the city see Nicola De Berardinis, *Relazione letta dal Commissario Straordinario Cav. Avv. Nicola De Berardinis, Consigliere Delegato dalla Prefettura di Messina, letta il 14 febbraio 1909, prima seduta del Consiglio Comunale dopo la catastrofe del 28 dicembre 1908* (Messina, 1909) and Alessandro Salvadori, *Relazione del Regio Commissario.*
22. Amelia I. Gigante, *Le città nella storia d'Italia: Messina* (Rome and Bari, 1980), 144.
23. Genio Civile, Ufficio Speciale di Messina per il baraccamento in Sicilia e Calabria, 30 April 1909, in box 48, Pref.-Gab., ASMe.
24. Regia Questura di Messina, Baraccamenti piano Moselle, 7 May 1909, in box 48, Pref.-Gab., ASMe.
25. "Occupazione di baracche per uso di ricovero," report of the Prefetto della Provincia di Messina to the Prime Minister and Minister of Internal Affairs, 5 May 1909, in box 11, Ufficio Terremoti Aa Gg, ACS.
26. Ministero dei Lavori Pubblici, *L'opera del Ministero,* 58–59.
27. See the classic comparative account by Anthony Suthcliffe, *Towards the Planned City: Germany, Britain, the United States and France, 1780–1914* (New York, 1981). See also Stephen V. Ward, *Planning the Twentieth-Century City: The Advanced Capitalist World* (Chichester, UK, 2002).
28. On the role of *risanamento* plans for Naples in nurturing a new approach to urban reform, already discussed chapter 2, see also Guido Zucconi, *La città contesa: Dagli ingegneri sanitari agli urbanisti (1885–1942)* (Milan, 1989), esp. 53.
29. For an overview of and bibliography on early planning experiments, see Peter Hall, *Urban and Regional Planning* (London, 2002), 27–54. On the emergence of modern planning, see also Ward, *Planning the Twentieth Century City,* 45–80.
30. Other examples include Chicago after the Great Fire of 1871; San Francisco after the 1906 earthquake and fire, but also earlier cases such as London after the Great Fire in 1666 or Lisbon after the 1755 earthquake. Some of those cases are examined in Greg Bankoff, Uwe Lübken, and Jordan Sand, eds., *Flammable Cities: Urban Conflagration and the Making of the Modern World* (Madison, 2012).
31. See Liliane Dufour, "Dopo il terremoto del 1693: La ricostruzione della Val di Noto," in *Storia d'Italia, Annali 8: Insediamenti e territorio,* ed. Cesare De Seta (Turin, 1985), 473–98.
32. Nicola Aricò and Ornella Milella, *Riedificare contro la storia: Una ricostruzione illuminista nella periferia del regno borbonico* (Rome, 1984).
33. Borzì, *Il piano regolatore,* 6. On those meetings see also Salvadori, *Relazione,* 282–83.
34. See for instance Mariano E. Cannizzaro, "Note al Memoriale per la resurrezione di Messina," 2 April 1909, later followed by "Note al Memoriale per la resurrezione di Messina," 14 September 1909. These documents, along with others of the same kind, are in box 379, folder 4, PCM 1909, ACS.
35. Mariano E. Cannizzaro. *Come ricostruire Messina: Il demanio comune* (Rome, 1909).
36. See Borzì, *Il piano regolatore,* 64–73, and Salvadori, *Relazione,* 287.

37. Decreto Reale 31 dicembre 1911 che approva le varianti al piano regolatore per la città di Messina ed il regolameno per l'esecuzione del piano regolatore stesso.
38. Borzì, *Il piano regolatore*, 19.
39. On the *isolato* in Borzì's plan, see Rita Simone, *La citta di Messina tra norma e forma* (Rome, 1996), 76–79.
40. Borzì, *Il piano regolatore*, 22.
41. Ibid., 20–21.
42. Ibid., 50.
43. Ibid., 36–40.
44. Ibid., 41.
45. Luigi Borzì and Carlo Sollima-Novi, *Il porto di Messina nel passato, nel presente e nell'avvenire* (Messina, 1907), 16.
46. Borzì, *Il piano regolatore*, 25–26.
47. On Naples and other cases, including Messina and Reggio Calabria, see Rolf Petri, *La frontiera industriale: Territorio, grande industria e leggi speciali prima della Cassa per il Mezzogiorno* (Milan, 1990).
48. See Gigante, *Le città nella storia d'Italia: Messina*, 145; Giuseppe Campione, *Il Progetto urbano di Messina: Documenti per l'identità 1860–1988* (Rome, 1988), 53.
49. See for example Massimo Lo Curzio, "Ricostruzione urbana e piano Borzì," in *Messina, una città ricostruita: Materiali per lo studio di una realtà urbana,* ed. G. Laura Di Leo and Massimo Lo Curzio (Bari, 1985), 19–29, and Francesco Cardullo, *La ricostruzione di Messina 1909–1940* (Rome, 1993). Both authors have developed their position further in a recent conference, "Messina: Dalla vigilia del terremoto all'avvio della ricostruzione," 20–21 March 2009, University of Messina; the proceedings are published in Baglio and Bottari, *Messina dalla vigilia del terremoto,* 483–562.
50. Borzì, *Il piano regolatore*, 22.
51. Ibid., 20.
52. Ministero dell'Agricoltura, Industria e Commercio, Direzione Generale Statistica e Lavoro, Ufficio Censimento, *Censimento della popolazione del Regno d'Italia al 10 giugno 1911,* vol. 1 (Rome, 1914), 285.
53. Presidenza del Consiglio dei Ministri, Istituto Centrale di Statistica, *Censimento della popolazione del Regno d'Italia al 1 dicembre 1921, XIII Sicilia* (Rome, 1927), 38–39.
54. Pietro Bruno, *Storia demografica di Messina* (Messina, 1951); Giuseppe Restifo, "Il vortice demografico dopo la catastrofe: Morti e movimenti di popolazione a Messina fra 1908 e 1911," in *Il terremoto e il maremoto del 28 dicembre 1908: Analisi sismologica impatto, prospettive,* ed. Guido Bertolaso, Enzo Boschi, Emanuela Guidoboni, and Gianluca Valensise (Rome and Bologna, 2008), 295–304.
55. This principle is expressed most clearly by Pietro Interdonato, *Relazione su criteri direttivi dell'Amministrazione comunale circa l'esecuzione del piano regolatore,* Seduta del Consiglio Comunale, 10 September 1913 (Messina, 1913), esp. 10–12.
56. Borzì, *Il piano regolatore,* 73–74.
57. Giuseppe Barone, "Sull'uso capitalistico del terremoto: Blocco urbano e ricostruzione edilizia a Messina durante il fascismo," *Storia Urbana* 10 (1982): 52.
58. Ibid., 52.
59. Ibid., 58.
60. Ibid., 68.

61. Borzì, *Il piano regolatore*, 12.
62. Pietro Longo, *Messina città rediviva: 1909-1933* (Messina, 1933), 85-86.
63. Borzì, *Il piano regolatore*, 63-64.
64. Interdonato, *Relazione*, 16.
65. Municipio di Messina, Ufficio Tecnico per il Piano regolatore, *Relazione riguardante gli studi fatti ed i lavori in corso fino a tutto il 31 maggio 1916 per l'attuazione del Piano regolatore* (Messina, 1916).
66. Unione Edilizia Messinese, *L'opera dell'Unione Edilizia Messinese per la ricostruzione di Messina (febbraio 1914-giugno 1917): Relazione del Regio Commissario Comm. Avv. Cesare Cagli* (Bergamo, 1917), 65.
67. Letter from Prefetto della Provincia di Messina to Ministero dell'Interno, Messina, 18 January 1918, in box 1, Ministero dell'Interno, Direzione Generale dell'Amministrazione Civile, Ufficio speciale dei servizi in dipendenza dei terremoti calabro-siculi e dell'eruzione dell'Etna "Alluvione di Messina 1917," [hereafter Ufficio terremoti 1917], ACS.
68. Telegram from Capitano dei Carabinieri Costa to Ministero dell'Interno, Gabinetto del Ministro Messina, 30 October 1917, in box 1, Ufficio terremoti 1917, ACS.
69. Telegram from Ispettore Generale Pignatelli to Ministero dell'Interno Messina, 28 October 1917, in box 1, Ufficio terremoti 1917, ACS.
70. Telegram from Ispettore Generale Pignatelli to Ministero dell'Interno Messina, 21 October 1917, in box 1, Ufficio terremoti 1917, ACS.
71. Corpo Reale del Genio Civile, Ufficio Speciale di Messina, Servizio terremoto to Prefettura di Messina, "Rapporto sulle attuali condizioni delle abitazioni baraccate in Messina," Messina, 3 February 1916, in box 1, Ufficio terremoti 1917, ACS.
72. Prefettura di Messina to Ministero dell'Interno, Direzione Generale dell'Amministrazione Civile, "Occupazione di aree demaniali," Messina, 10 June 1919; and Prefettura di Messina to Direttore Ufficio Fortificazioni del Genio Militare, "Occupazione di aree demaniali militari," Messina, 8 February 1919, in box 1, Ufficio terremoti 1917, ACS.
73. Ministero dei Lavori Pubblici, *L'opera del Ministero*, 59.
74. Interdonato, *Relazione*, 15.
75. Unione Edilizia Messinese, *Relazione*, 63-64.
76. Consorzio Industriale per la Ricostruzione di Messina, *Progetto tecnico-finanziario per la ricostruzione della città di Messina* (Messina, 1923), 16-18.
77. According to demographic studies, between 1911 and 1921, more than 70,000 people immigrated to Messina. In the same period, the building sector occupied a consistent portion of the working population. See Luigi Chiara, *La modernizzazione senza sviluppo: Messina a cento anni dal terremoto (1908-2008)* (Florence, 2011), 102-3 and 107.
78. Unione Edilizia Nazionale, *L'opera dell'Unione Edilizia Nazionale nel quadriennio 1917-1920: Relazione del Direttore Generale Gr. Uff. Avv. Cesare Cagli* (Rome, 1920). Ministero dei Lavori Pubblici, Direzione dei Servizi Speciali, *Gli edifici pubblici e le case degli impiegati dello Stato nei paesi colpiti dal terremoto* (Rome, 1912).
79. Municipio di Messina, *Relazione al Consiglio Comunale dell'Assessore ai LL.PP. Grand'Uff. Salvatore Siracusano sull'opera di ricostruzione della città, Maggio 1922* (Messina, 1922).
80. Unione Edilizia Nazionale, *L'opera dell'Unione Edilizia Nazionale*, 90-91.

81. On the possibility of considering as "political" some popular practices that exceed the bounds of political representation, see Partha Chatterjee, *The Politics of the Governed* (New York, 2004).
82. Besides the article by Barone, "Sull'uso capitalistico del terremoto" previously quoted, see also Marcello Sajia, "Messina 1923: la transizione dei poteri," in *Messina negli anni '20 e '30, Una città meridionale tra stagnazione e fermenti culturali*, ed. Rosario Battaglia, Michela D'Angelo, Santi Fedele, and Massimo Lo Curzio, vol. 1, (Catania, 1996), 13–32.
83. Barone, "Sull'uso capitalistico del terremoto," 47–104, and the edited collection by Battaglia et al., *Messina negli anni venti e trenta*.
84. Ministero dei Lavori Pubblici, *L'opera del Ministero*, 36.
85. Segretario federale prof. D'Addabbo to Ministero dei Lavori Pubblici, Memoriale: I maggiori bisogni della città di Messina, 1927, 4–5. In box 447, Segreteria Particolare del Duce, ACS.
86. Note from *Questura di Messina* to the Prefect of Messina, no. 3993, 9 July 1926, and Legione territoriale dei Carabinieri di Messina, "Crisi delle abitazioni nella città di Messina," 9 July 1926, box 34, Pref. Gab., ASMe.
87. See the list of private buildings and vacant private lots "Fabbricati privati," 1927, in box 12, Pref.-gab., ASMe.
88. Unemployment figures are provided by Chiara, *La modernizzazione senza sviluppo*, 100.
89. Ministero dei Lavori Pubblici, *L'azione del governo fascista*, 55.
90. Ibid., 15.
91. Ibid., 19.
92. Federazione Provinciale Fascista di Messina, *Le opere del Fascismo per la ricostruzione di Messina* (Messina, 1932); Longo, *Messina città rediviva*; Ministero dei Lavori Pubblici, Direzione Generale dei Servizi Speciali, *L'azione del Governo Fascista per la ricostruzione delle zone danneggiate da calamità* (Terni, 1933).
93. Corpo Reale del Genio Civile, Servizio Terremoto, "Militari dell'Arma die CC distaccati presso l'Ufficio," 23 June 1932, box 372, Pref.-Gab., ASMe.
94. G. Laura Di Leo, Elena La Spada, "La città dopo il terremoto: interventi pubblici e stratificazioni del patrimonio edilizio," in Di Leo and Lo Curzio, *Messina, una città ricostruita*, 15. The location of these new areas is mapped in Simone, *La città di Messina*, 85–92.
95. On social and urban inequities in today's Messina see Pietro Saitta, *Quota zero: Messina dopo il terremoto, la ricostruzione infinita* (Rome, 2013).
96. Segreteria personale del Duce, 1931, in box 447, Segreteria Particolare del Duce, ACS.
97. Unione Industriale Fascista della Provincia di Messina, *Relazione a sua Eccellenza il Prefetto*, typescript, 8 March 1933, ASMe, b.312. The numbers match with the figures in the 1922 report by Councilor Siracusano and those in the 1933 report by the Ministry of Public Works.
98. Municipio di Messina, *Relazione della Giunta Municipale all'Onorevole Consiglio Comunale sullo stato attuale del civico acquedotto e proposte relative a provvedimenti diversi* (Messina, 1916), 20.
99. "Federazione Provinciale Enti Autarchici, Commissione Tecnica, L'acquedotto civico e l'alimentazione idrica di Messina, relatore Gr. Uff. Siracusano, Messina, ottobre 1927,"

in ASMe, Pref. Gab.b.70. There are no records testifying of an opposition to the incorporation of Santissima sources comparable to that registered in the Niceto Valley. This, of course, could be simply due to the silence of the archives, all the more possible considering the repressive Fascist policy toward social opposition. However, it could also signal a muted context in the countryside: rural productions and interests such as those of the Niceto inhabitants had already declined in the late 1920s.

100. For pictures of sewage and the Portalegni estuary see Federazione provinciale fascista di Messina, *Le opere del fascismo*, 36–37.
101. The Archivio Comunale di Messina holds a rich photographical documentation of the realization of the sewage system. Photos of the transformation of the Torrente Boccetta are in box 20, Direzione Generale Viabilità e Porti 1903-38, ACS.
102. "Reconnaissance Photo Aerial View Messina Italy," 1941–1945, San Diego Air & Space Museum Archive, Catalog no. 10_0020716.
103. R.D.L. 13 March 1927, n. 431 "Recante norme tecniche e igieniche di edilizia per le località colpite da terremoti," art. 5.
104. See comments in "Norme edilizie per i paesi soggetti a terremoti: Relazione generale," *Annali della Società degli Ingegneri e degli Architetti Italiani* 24, no. 7 (1909): 177–205.
105. Almost all official publications by the Ministry of Public Works and the Unione Edilizia have rich photographic sections depicting buildings in construction with the characteristic iron bars. See also the photographic collection of the Archivio Comunale di Messina.
106. This statement is limited to the time we are discussing here. Nowadays, the safety of buildings dating back to that epoch is much less certain, due to the decay of reinforced concrete.
107. This is indeed what was happening in Milazzo and Messina. See Battaglia, *L'ultimo splendore*, 129.
108. See for instance Camera di Commercio e Industria di Messina, V. Furnari to Minister Sarocchi, Memoriale a S.E. Sarocchi, 23 July 1924, in box 255, Pref.Gab., ASMe, and Segretario e del Presidente della Federazione Provinciale di Messina to S.E. il Prefetto, "Il Porto di Messina," typescript, 30 December 1933, in box 376, Pref. Gab. ASMe.
109. See the records in box 20, Ministero dei Lavori Pubblici, Direzione Generale Viabilità e Porti, Porti 1903-38, ACS.
110. Rosario Battaglia, "Il porto di Messina nell'età della decadenza," in Battaglia et al., *Messina negli anni Venti e Trenta*, 217–32.
111. See, for instance, Associazione dei proprietari, Associazione dei Commercianti e degli Industriali, Collegio Ingegneri e Architetti, and Sindacato Costruttori, *Per la rinascita di Messina: Memoriale* (Messina, 1922).
112. See Chiara, *La modernizzazione senza sviluppo*, esp. 97–98. For a general overview of citrus production in Sicily see Salvatore Lupo, *Il giardino degli aranci: Il mondo degli agrumi nella storia del Mezzogiorno* (Venice, 1993).
113. The industrial zone in Messina was established by law with Decreto Luogotenenziale 29 luglio 1915, n. 1295. On the failure of the industrial zone, see for instance the records in box 135 folder "zona industriale," Pref. Gab. ASMe.
114. Antonino Checco, "Messina dal terremoto del 1908 al fascismo: La ricostruzione senza sviluppo," *Storia Urbana* 46 (1989), 161–92.

115. Ibid.; in addition to this study, see also Chiara, *La modernizzazione senza sviluppo,* 95–108.
116. Secondo Franchi, "Il terremoto del 28 dicembre 1908 a Messina in rapporto alla natura del terreno ed alla riedificazione della città," *Bollettino del R. Comitato Geologico d'Italia* 40, no. 2 (1909): 154.
117. In that letter, which responded to a request concerning the possibility of further expanding the program of ultra-popular housing in Messina, the chief engineer wrote: "With the data at your disposal concerning the living conditions and the social aspects of these settlements, Your Excellency could establish better than me the limit to which it is appropriate to insist upon such a practice." Corpo Reale del Genio Civile, Ufficio di Messina, Servizio Generale to the Prefetto della Provincia di Messina, "Costruzione di casette popolarissime," Messina, 14 November 1936, in box 89, Pref. Gab., ASMe.
118. On postwar reconstruction see Gigante, *Le città nella storia d'Italia: Messina,* 151–66 and Annunziata M. Oteri, "La città fantasma: Danni bellici e politiche di ricostruzione a Messina nel secondo dopoguerra (1943–1959)," *Storia Urbana* 30, no. 114–15 (2007), 63–112.
119. This is a significant difference compared to the practices diffused in other European and North American countries, where private capital and insurance companies played a substantial role. See Uwe Lübken and Christof Mauch, "Uncertain Environments: Natural Hazards, Risk, and Insurance in Historical Perspective," *Environment and History* 17, no. 1 (2011): 1–12.
120. See Emanuela Guidoboni and Gianluca Valensise, *Il peso economico e sociale dei disastri sismici in Italia negli ultimi 150 anni, 1861–2011* (Bologna, 2011), 157–73 and 232–47.
121. See Dufour, "Dopo il terremoto del 1693," 473–98.
122. Aricò and Milella, *Riedificare contro la storia.*
123. Ward refers to post-earthquake Messina in his overview of the birth of modern planning, but bases his considerations on a traditional interpretation of the Borzì plan that does not account for its complexity. See Ward, *Planning the Twentieth-Century City,* 68.

PART II

The 1968 Belice Valley Earthquake

 CHAPTER 4

The 1968 Belice Valley Earthquake

The geology of Sicily is spectacular. Sicily is the home of six of Italy's ten active volcanoes, and strong earthquakes have struck the island constantly throughout history. Nonetheless, no one knew that the Belice Valley was a seismic area until a devastating sequence of earthquakes occurred on 14 and 15 January 1968. This 1968 earthquake did not enjoy the same worldwide celebrity of its Sicilian predecessor in 1908. The Belice Valley was a largely unknown, rural, and impoverished area without any important urban center. The earthquakes, thanks to a series of fortuitous circumstances, did not result in mass fatalities, as in 1908. Yet, in January 1968, the Belice Valley was no less devastated than Messina in December 1908. The earthquakes affected the built environment across an area equivalent to one-tenth of the total surface area of the island. It obliterated fourteen towns completely or almost completely and left a population of 100,000 inhabitants homeless. There is no doubt that, in terms of material and social damage, the 1968 Belice earthquake was a major disaster.

National media coverage of the event was massive. Public and private organizations called for charitable donations and volunteers rushed to the disaster area from all over the country. In the process of making sense of what happened, the socioeconomic condition of the affected area captured the attention of contemporaries more than the physical causes of the earthquake. The Belice Valley that emerged from the ruins of the earthquake seemed trapped in the rural poverty of a past that had long since disappeared in the rest of the country. According to a multitude of commentators, poverty was far more responsible for the extent of destruction than geology or engineering. This dominant interpretation shaped the response to the earthquake. Since poverty was the real issue, economic development was the most adequate solution.

The two most important institutions directly responsible for the earthquake area, namely the Sicilian regional government and the Italian state, proposed two distinct pieces of legislation based on the same idea: the reconstruction of a safer Belice Valley could not be divorced from socioeconomic development of the area. Local committees and activists shared the same view and asked for the implementation of effective socioeconomic development policies. In addition, they demanded a locally based rebuilding process and asked the central authorities to include the local institutions and communities in the decision-making process. This chapter will recount these events and actors, and chronicle the emergence of a reconstruction strategy based on the radical redevelopment of the Belice Valley's environment and society.

"Like an Atomic Wasteland"

The Belice River originates in northwest Sicily from the confluence of two roughly equal branches, named Belice Sinistro (left fork) and Belice Destro (right fork). The rivers flow separately for more than fifty kilometers before their waters mingle into one stream. Another fifty kilometers after the confluence, the river joins the salt waters of the Strait of Sicily, which divides the island from the northernmost coast of Tunisia. Although the Belice is the second most important watercourse of the island and a perennial river, its discharge varies widely according to the season: torrential during the rainy autumn and winter, the flow almost disappears during the summer.[1] During its journey to the sea, the river crosses a landscape of gentle hills that stretch for hundreds of kilometers on both sides of the river. The Sicani, one of the indigenous peoples of Sicily, inhabited the region during the Bronze Age. In the seventh century BCE, colonizers from Greece settled there and founded the city of Selinunte. Unlike other Greek and Phoenician settlements in Sicily, however, Selinunte did not survive antiquity and its wars, and slowly faded into oblivion. After Selinunte, no major urban center ever prospered in this region, and each new epoch corresponded with the decline of some smaller settlements and the foundation of new ones.[2]

For centuries, human presence in the Belice River Valley was concentrated in densely populated hilltop towns that were dotted across a completely deserted countryside. Some of those towns dated back to antiquity or the early Middle Ages. Feudal seigniors and farmers founded new ones in early modern times during the colonization that accompanied the expansion of cereal crop cultivation in inland Sicily.[3] Historians and anthropologists have identified a specific urban pattern common to most centers in the Belice Valley, as well as others in the Mediterranean: the so-called "agro-town." Agro-towns were densely populated, urban-like centers, but lacking in industrial, administrative, or commercial functions and typically located in regions of extensive agriculture. The populations of these agro-towns consisted largely of impoverished peasants who worked for daily wages in large estates owned by a few landowners, the *feudatari*.[4] Surrounding these Belice towns, a belt of small subsistence gardens provided produce to supplement their meager and often unreliable income.[5]

Nowadays, we know this region is caught in the tectonic encounter of the African and the Eurasian plates, which is responsible for seismicity in the Strait of Messina and in other earthquake-prone regions of the Mediterranean.[6] Partly due to the unstable population and settlement dynamics, however, records on seismicity in this area are scarce. Although a few tremors occurred there over the centuries, none ever had impacts on the population and built environments comparable to the repeated earthquakes in eastern Sicily and Calabria.[7] In 1968, the memory of those past earthquakes was lost, and in the seminal work on historical seismology by Mario Baratta, updated in 1934, the Belice Valley was not included among the most earthquake-prone regions of Sicily.[8] Yet, throughout the centuries, the geology of the Mediterranean was at work beneath the gentle slopes of the Belice Valley. Although silent and until that time almost unnoticed, this fault system was slowly accumulating the energy that would explode into the devastating sequence of earthquakes in the winter of 1968.

The fourteenth of January 1968 was a Sunday, and in the Belice towns of Gibellina, Salaparuta, and Poggioreale the population was electing its municipal representatives. As a result, an unusually high number of officials and police officers were present in the towns in order to supervise the electoral operations. The ground shook for the first time at 13:28 hours. It was a relatively light tremor, with a magnitude of 4.7. Less than one hour later, at 14:15, another earthquake of the same intensity hit the same area, followed by a third one at 16:48.[9] The three earthquakes did not produced significant damage, but the population was scared. Recalling the first tremors of that Sunday afternoon, an activist living in the area at that time remembers that he spent some time reassuring friends and acquaintances: "There had been warnings the day before ... but I reassured everyone: 'don't worry, nothing will happen.'"[10] The police officers at the scene soon reported information about the earthquakes to the police and government offices in Trapani and Palermo, the nearest cities. That evening, the authorities in Palermo and Trapani started organizing a relief mission, sending supplies to the population, who refused to sleep inside their houses for fear of new tremors.[11]

The reports of the police officers, written soon after the event, offer us a vivid reconstruction of that frantic night. The spontaneous reaction of the population and the support offered by the officers at the scene seems to have been crucial in preventing mass loss of life. On 15 January, at 02:33 in the morning, another, stronger earthquake occurred in the area. Because of the tremors of the previous day, a number of inhabitants of Poggioreale, Salaparuta, and Gibellina were outside their houses, and some members of the police force were still there. In response to the new tremor, more people evacuated the buildings. Mr. Lo Presti, a police officer from Trapani, was in Gibellina from the morning of 14 January to supervise the election of mayor and municipal council, and he directed the relief operations on that day. According to his testimony, the tremor at 02:33 did not produce widespread damage. He and his subordinates, however, interpreted the earthquake as a "premonitory sign" and decided to proceed further with the evacuations of the inhabitants. Half an hour later, an even stronger earthquake struck the area.

That latter tremor had a magnitude of 6.5 and was the strongest of the entire sequence.[12] The earthquake surprised Lo Presti outside, where he was organizing the evacuation of the inhabitants of Gibellina. "Characterized by a dark prolonged roar, followed by a giant cloud of dust rising up to the sky," wrote Lo Presti in a report, "such a violent telluric movement seemed to liberate all the adverse forces of nature. The deafening crashing of masonry signaled the destruction of buildings, while the bitter and pungent smell of sulfurous anhydride infested all the surrounding area … Then silence, a silence of death and pain." This silence, however, continued Lo Presti, "lasted only for a few moments … With an almost uncontrollable desperation, invocations of help and excruciating cries arose." Lo Presti wrote that he tried to help some people buried underneath the ruins, and then tried to leave Gibellina. He did not succeed, because "rubble occupied all communication routes, so that any way of reaching the near towns was precluded."[13]

Meanwhile, in Poggioreale and Salaparuta, very similar scenes were taking place. Police officer Giuseppe Peri was part of the forces sent from Trapani to Gibellina on the evening of 14 January in order to support the early relief operation directed by Lo Presti. Lo Presti had sent him to the town of Poggioreale along with other colleagues to assist the local population. Even in Poggioreale some residents had already chosen to spend the night outside,

Figure 4.1. Aerial view of Gibellina, January 1968. Courtesy of Leonardo Mistretta.

fearing new tremors. Peri and his colleagues forced many of those who had not yet left their homes to evacuate and led the inhabitants outside the town. Around 02:00 in the morning, Peri moved to the nearby town of Salaparuta, only a couple of kilometers away from Poggioreale. The tremor at 02:33 surprised him while he was distributing supplies to the population of Salaparuta. He tried to go back to Poggioreale and was almost there when the strongest and most destructive earthquake occurred. Wishing to establish radio contact with somebody outside the area, Peri reached the highest possible ground and radioed SOS to Trapani, Palermo, Cagliari, Reggio Calabria, and Messina. Although none of these SOS messages received an answer, Peri was at least able to establish contact with officer Lo Presti, who was also radioing SOS from Gibellina.[14]

The officers first communicated with the authorities outside the disaster area three hours later, when Lo Presti finally talked with the head of the police in Trapani. By then, reports from other towns in the valley had reached Trapani and Palermo; it became known that something serious had happened in the area. Furthermore, many people in Trapani and Palermo had felt the two strong tremors in the night. The prefect of Trapani reported that "terrified people occupied the streets; some were crying, some shouting, others inside their cars were continuously sounding the horns. Everyone was trying to escape … and the traffic jam caused even more panic."[15] Most of the valley's residents, nonetheless, remained without assistance. Rubble and landslides obstructed all roads, and the rescue teams, although equipped with bulldozers, were not able to make their way through the debris. The only way to and from the most affected area was through the hiking trails across the hills. In the evening of 15 January, cars and trucks had not yet reached Gibellina, Poggioreale, and Salaparuta. Losing hope in the possibility of getting assistance where they were, survivors, including some injured, hiked out of the area.[16]

By that time, the authorities in Rome were just starting to organize an operation to support local forces. That same evening, nevertheless, the main channel on state television aired reassuring news about the earthquake and the relief operation. A helicopter with Minister of Home Affairs Taviani on board flew over the valley and filmed the destroyed towns. The report aimed to display the efficiency of the government and their ability to keep the situation under control and announced that Saragat, the president of the Republic, had scheduled a visit to the disaster area for the day after.[17] Tragically enough, Saragat did land in Gibellina the next morning, but without any useful items for the relief of victims. Although his helicopter was the first means of transportation to reach the earthquakes' epicenter, it did not offer any help or transport any injured person. This episode, initially unreported on the TV news, later became a symbol of the inefficiency of the rescue and relief operation, and of the incompetence and superficiality of the authorities.[18]

On 16 January, images and testimonies from the Belice Valley became front-page news, informing the public of the serious consequences of the earthquake. Quoting the words of an army pilot, the *Corriere della Sera* included the headline that the entire valley looked "like an atomic wasteland" in which there were no more traces of life, only devastation. The damages, in fact, extended over a considerably large surface area. Besides Gibellina, Poggioreale, and Salaparuta, the tremors had severely affected at least 10 other towns. Most buildings in Montevago, Partanna, Santa Ninfa, Menfi, Santa Margherita, Salemi, Contessa Entellina, Vita, Calatafimi, and Camporeale had crumbled or were uninhabitable. The earthquakes had also caused significant damage in many other towns. Thanks to the partial evacuation of the population after the tremors on 14 January, the number of people killed was not high when compared to the population affected by the quake: 400 deaths out of some 100,000 residents.[19] Nevertheless, the built environment of an area corresponding to one-tenth of the entire island was in ruins, and thousands of residents were homeless. New tremors in the following weeks worsened the already tragic situation.[20]

Despite reassuring reports by the state TV channel, the situation was far from being under control. Strong aftershocks increased the damage and injured more people, and worsened the condition of already wrecked routes in and out of the disaster area. It is not clear when the first land vehicles could

Figure 4.2. Ruins of Gibellina, January 1968. Courtesy of Leonardo Mistretta.

reach Gibellina, Salaparuta, and Poggioreale, where the ruins still trapped many people. It is certain that transportation in the whole area remained extremely arduous for days. The homeless population in need of assistance with food, shelter, and clothing was at least 20,000 people. These numbers were growing hour after hour, given the refusal of the population to sleep inside any sort of brick structure, even if undamaged. The absence of a coordinated center for the management of rescue and relief operations made the situation even worse. The national authorities struggled to coordinate all the organizations engaged in the relief operations. Moreover, the volunteers who had reached the area to help the survivors lacked coordination and clear instructions. The administrative division of the Belice Valley into three different administrative districts complicated coordination further, becoming an endless source of misunderstandings, conflicts of responsibility, and inefficiency.[21]

In this chaotic situation, the survivors themselves, with the aid of volunteers, erected the first tents using all the suitable materials they could salvage, and fled the ruined towns to set up camps in the open fields.[22] Local prefects, in the meantime, tried to provide further tents by buying them from private dealers. On 20 January, the prefect of Trapani reported that 8,300 refugees were sheltered in tent camps located in Castelvetrano, Salemi, Partanna, Santa Ninfa, and Sirignano (Alcamo), and a further 11,180 were sheltering "in suitable public and private buildings of various municipalities which had not been

Figure 4.3. Tent encampment in Santa Ninfa, January 1968. Courtesy of Leonardo Mistretta.

affected or which were less damaged."[23] On 28 January, there were 3,500 refugees sheltered indoors in the administrative district of Palermo and 2,100 in three tent camps located in Cinisi, Roccamena, and Camporeale.[24] In the district of Agrigento, finally, there were nearly 8,000 refugees in four tent camps.[25] It would take several weeks, however, before the army and the Genio Civile would clear the roads of rubble and landslides and restore basic services such as electricity and water.[26]

As had happened after the 1908 Messina earthquake, a great number of people tried to escape from the earthquake area in the aftermath. Whereas in 1908 the exodus took the authorities by surprise, in 1968 they encouraged evacuation from the outset, most likely as a means of relieving the pressure on the disaster area and facilitating relief operations. At least from 20 January, the public railroad company started providing free tickets for all the refugees who wanted to leave the island,[27] and the prefectures initiated accelerated procedures for the release of passports, encouraging the refugees to move to long-distance destinations.[28] Contemporary witnesses vividly remember this. Nicola Accardo and Gaspare Giglio recount that police officers visited the tent camps proposing the release of passports. According to their testimony, on that occasion it was sufficient to give one's name in order to obtain a passport, whereas it normally would have taken five to six months of bureaucratic procedures.[29]

The evacuation soon assumed massive proportions. On 23 January, the prefect of Messina reported to the Ministry of Internal Affairs that more than 7,000 refugees had been in transit through the local rail station heading for continental Italy.[30] Many refugees reached the industrial cities of northern Italy, such as Milan and Turin. Many others subsequently crossed the borders to France, Switzerland, and Germany. Some ultimately went overseas, to Australia, the United States, and Canada. These were the traditional destinations for emigration from the south. Most probably, these people took the opportunity afforded by free tickets and passports to emigrate, reaching relatives or friends already established in these destinations. In any case, the stream of refugees was conspicuous. In the railway station Rome Tiburtina, where all the trains heading north connected, a special police unit counted the Belice refugees who were on board. According to the calculations of this police unit, 29,445 people left from the station before 6 February 1968.[31]

The Disaster of Poverty

The sequence of earthquakes had caused immense devastation in the Belice Valley. Although not contaminated like a true "atomic wasteland," the region could nonetheless be understandably compared to a bombsite. Aerial pictures in the newspapers and magazines showed entirely flattened towns, scorched landscapes, and escaping refugees, like those images so often seen during World War II. On 17 January 1968, the national newspaper *Il Tempo* published an article in which the author tried to explain why the earthquakes had caused such immense destruction. The explanation took into account several concurrent causes: "1) a densely populated area; 2) an area which was considered to be "quiet" and therefore lacking in any earthquake-resistant measures; 3) old, unstable buildings, made of bricks and fragile mortar ... 4) the unstable nature of the soil and the probable position of towns on a faulted, tectonically tormented zone."[32]

This seems to be an accurate reading of the technical causes of the disaster. Yet, such an explanation was not enough to make sense of the tragedy. In 1968, scholars of geophysics and engineering could explain what had happened and how, and they could do that even more precisely than in 1908. They possessed instruments and scales to quantify the power of the earthquake, an advanced knowledge of interaction between seismic shocks, static features of buildings, and lithology.[33] Nevertheless, they did not seem capable of answering to another, more pressing question: why such devastation and despair? Faced with the post-earthquake landscape in the Belice Valley, contemporaries found the relatively low magnitude of the earthquakes striking. The strongest tremor, registered on 15 January at 03:02 hours, had barely reached a magnitude of 6.5, and the previous and subsequent tremors were all between 4.7 and 5.7.[34] Even considering their combined effects, there seemed to be a disproportion between the magnitude of the earthquakes and the intensity of their social and material effects. From the very beginning, commentators recounted and explained this disproportion as the tragic outcome of the poverty and "backwardness" of the Belice Valley and its people.

When national newsreels, TV, and newspapers presented the earthquake landscape and the tragedy of the Belice Valley people to the public, most of their audiences were discovering the existence of the Belice Valley for the first time. Deprived of major urban centers, located in the far south of Italy and dependent on archaic economic structures, the Belice Valley was not simply a marginal region: it was completely cut off from the rest of the country. Whereas Italy as a whole had experienced a rapid and tumultuous process of socioeconomic growth and a transition towards an affluent urban-industrial society, the Belice Valley and its inhabitants seemed trapped in a miserable past. Instead of middle-class families in Fiat 600s on *autostradas,* there were peasants riding donkeys on mountain trails; instead of factories and supermarkets, there were gravel roads and free-roaming animals; instead of modern apartment blocks in reinforced concrete, there were poorly engineered houses that had crumbled overnight. To many, that alien world from the deepest *Mezzogiorno* was in itself the explanation for the disaster. The Belice Valley, to them, was already a wasteland before the earthquake occurred.

The imagery of the post-earthquake valley reinforced such perceptions, depicting a landscape of deprivation and material and moral misery. Right after the earthquake, the weekly magazine *Epoca* issued a special issue entirely devoted to full color pictures from the Belice Valley, entitled "The Faces of the Tragedy." The narrative line of these photos presented defenseless, poor people in a dilapidated landscape of ruins, death, and suffering. Women stood expressionless with their heads covered by black shawls. Goats and barefoot children wandered among heaps of rubble in abandoned towns. Old men rode mules through bare fields and ruins.[35] TV reports and newsreels depicted similar scenes. On 19 January, for example, on the main TV channel, a journalist interviewed an old man and a woman in a tent camp. The old man looked ill and spoke towards the camera in deepest Sicilian dialect, all the more incomprehensible due to his lack of teeth. The woman, wearing a black shawl over her head, stated her refusal to leave the tent and take shelter indoors for fear of aftershocks.[36] Symbols of the "economic miracle" were absent from this depiction, and the inhabitants of the Belice Valley looked completely different from modern urban Italians.

Commentators constantly framed the Belice Valley as an unknown and uncharted territory. While images showed heaps of undistinguishable ruins, the voice-over by Sergio Zavoli, an RAI journalist, remarked rhetorically that "Gibellina was on no map" even before the earthquake. He continued in the same vein:

> Now, [Gibellina] has disappeared even from the hill that was once yellow during the summer and brown during the winter, where a thousand houses and a thousand doors gathered around three churches and three squares. To search for it on the map, now that one cannot even see which door belongs to which house, makes no sense at all. Yet it was a town, with its people and its stories … It contained the people of our country, and we did not know them well enough."[37]

It is likely that most Italians had never heard the name Gibellina before 1968. Nonetheless, by recalling the otherness of this town and people, the reportage was in effect framing the Belice Valley in a familiar, fixed narrative: the narrative of a persistent gap between a wealthy, modern Italy and a poor, archaic one. The Belice Valley was the epitome of this other Italy, and tangible proof of the persistence of a dark, backward, and immobile *Mezzogiorno*.

The mirror was a recurring metaphor used to describe rhetorically the Belice "otherness." In the Belice Valley and its poor agro-towns, in the black-veiled women and the barefoot children, in the yellow fields and the incomprehensible dialects, Italy could find its true self. The state-funded newsreel series "Tempi Nostri" devoted an episode to the Belice Valley, which was entitled exactly this, "Italy in the Mirror." The newsreel starts with some images of the earthquake area, the relief operations, and the refugees. Nonetheless, the Belice Valley soon disappears from the narrative, which begins to focus on the "backwardness" of the whole of Sicily. The reportage moves to Palermo and its most degraded slums, showing narrow streets crammed with children and animals. It then turns to day-to-day life in the countryside, depicting subjects such as a woman throwing waste and excrement out of her house and a peasant who rides a mule along a donkey trail on the outskirts of a city. In the end, images of modernity and development from other parts of Italy counterbalance these and other scenes of rural and urban degradation. The Belice Valley earthquake, in sum, became a symbol and an example of something else. Looking in the mirror held up by the earthquake, the country saw a "backwardness" that the celebrated postwar boom had not been able to overcome.[38]

Emigration had long been part of this picture. In the 1950s and 1960s, the Belice Valley had had high emigration rates, the prevailing emigrants being young males who left the valley in search of a better life.[39] After the earthquake, as we have seen, many refugees followed their example, heading northwards to Milan and Turin, or further to Germany and Switzerland, or even to destinations overseas. A documentary film dedicated to Italian emigration in Europe was therefore quite within reason to incorporate the Belice Valley earthquake into its larger narrative. The film showed industrial plants and mines all over Europe, and included interviews with Italian emigrants from various towns. Among them was also a group of Belice refugees, crammed into a railroad station in the week after the earthquake. Interviewed by the filmmakers, one of them declared bitterly that "[the authorities] do not know what the situation in Sicily is like; there is only hunger and misery, only hunger and misery."[40] From the Belice refugees, the documentary moves on to other stories of emigration from the South, hunger, and misery. The Belice Valley, once again, was just another example of a larger social problem, and a chapter in a broader narrative of "underdevelopment."

Such narratives allowed the framing of the extraordinary and shocking event of the earthquake within a set of well-known and ultimately reassuring cultural coordinates. At that time, the so-called "Southern question" was at the top of the political agendas of all the principal parties. The discourse on the country's poor regions and the nation's uneven development had deep roots in Italian politics that went back to national unification in 1861, and with the post–World War II developmental agenda, it had gained new energy.[41] Intellectuals and economists, politicians and commentators considered the lack of infrastructure and industries, along with archaic cultures and social relations, as the structural causes of a problematic divide between dynamic and depressed areas, and in particular between the urban-industrial North and the rural South.⁴² In the late 1960s, in the wake of a general radicalization of political discourse in Italy, left-wing parties, organizations, and intellectuals debated Southern "underdevelopment" in the light of a general critique of the triumph of industrial capitalism and expectations of social and economic justice.⁴³ By framing the Belice disaster within this pervasive developmental discourse, the exceptional could become normal and the uncharted familiar. More importantly, these cultural coordinates allowed the formulation of a convincing explanation of the perceived disproportion between the earthquake's magnitude and the intensity of its material and social effects.

Many reports and newspaper articles explicitly pointed out the connection between the social and economic "underdevelopment" of the Belice Valley and the consequences of the earthquakes. On 17 January 1968, the right-wing newspaper *Roma* published an editorial written by its director Alberto Giovannini. The earthquake, wrote Giovannini, had unveiled "the conditions of backwardness which are much too common in almost all regions and all sectors of national life, and which could be defined as archaic, in large parts of Sicily and many others areas of Southern Italy. The Belice Valley earthquake," he continued along a well-trodden path, "makes us look into the mirror and see ourselves for what we really are as a people and as a nation." The "underdevelopment" of Southern Italy, according to this reasoning, was not just the context of the disaster. It was its direct cause:

> The victims of Gibellina, Montevago, Salaparuta, and many of the other villages that the calamity "erased" are not just the unknown victims of an adverse destiny. They were also, and perhaps above all, the unjust victims of the existing gap between the "two Italys," a gap that the economic development of the country ... seems to exacerbate day by day, instead of making it less apparent.⁴⁴

Many other newspapers published similar content. On 20 January, in the pages of the left-wing newspaper *Paese Sera*, Giulio Goria claimed that the earthquake had struck "the poorest, most abandoned, and most defenseless part of Southern Italy." He also affirmed that it was necessary to acknowledge that the devastation was largely due to the conditions of poverty and abandonment. Most houses in the valley were made of tuff bricks—bricks made of the light, porous, and yellowish rock composed of solidified volcanic ash—and with poor building techniques, "because in Montevago, Gibellina, Salaparuta, Partanna, Santa Ninfa, Salemi, reinforced concrete never arrived."⁴⁵ Mino Monicelli from *Il Giorno* made a similar point. "On that catastrophe," he wrote, "there is the signature of poverty. The average income in these miserable, stunted hills is 172,000 lire. The heaps of rocks that once were Gibellina and Salaparuta were not houses, but shaky shelters built up bit by bit from the foundations ... with tuff bricks that were sealed together with a thread of thin mortar; shelters that fell down after the first tremor."⁴⁶ Poverty, not geology, was the true culprit of the devastation in the Belice Valley.

Road Maps to Development

As much as this explanation framed the earthquake in the discourse on the "underdevelopment" of the South, it also shaped the response to it. In the spotlights of national media, the post-earthquake Belice Valley had become a symbol of all that was wrong with Italy. The same country that had entered the exclusive club of the world industrial superpowers had, on its own territory, areas and people living in archaic, unacceptable conditions. The response to the earthquake should then become a symbol of the ability of the country to overcome these conditions. The authorities should give to the victims of the earthquake not simply the means to rebuild their homes and towns, but also the opportunity to enter into a new era of development. This idea, as we shall see, drove public intervention from day one.

The Regione Siciliana (Sicilian Regional Authority) took the first initiative. Established in 1946 to answer to the claims of the wartime Sicilian separatist movement, the institution granted a higher degree of autonomy to Sicilian residents than at any time in the recent past.⁴⁷ Sicily had its own government and an elected parliament, which had the power to write and pass laws concerning internal issues. As early as 17 January 1968, drawing on that prerogative, the principal political parties represented within the Sicilian parliament started debating the contents of a regional law on the Belice Valley earthquake crisis. To speed up the procedure, the parliament established a special commission. This commission was to discuss the contents of a draft law, which the parliament could then approve without further debate.⁴⁸

Much of the activity of the special commission focused on a controversial proposal by members of the PCI (Partito Comunista Italiano, the Italian Communist Party). According to the members of the PCI, the reconstruction of the Belice Valley should not "restore the intolerable situation that existed before the earthquake.... A new life and a new environment must emerge from the earthquake."⁴⁹ The creation of a "new environment" meant radical redevelopment and entailed the elaboration of an appropriate strategy and the provision of suitable instruments. Accordingly, PCI deputies proposed introducing a special planning tool: the *piano comprensoriale* ("area" or "district" plan). Unlike traditional town plans, each "district plan" would cover several urban centers and the surrounding region they shared. This planning platform would achieve two goals. First, it would guarantee a coherent and regulated rebuilding process across the entire disaster area, allowing the coordination of plans for all the affected towns. At the same time, it would be possible to incorporate the necessary interventions for the socioeconomic development of the Belice Valley through land-use planning and zoning.

The draft law by the Communist deputies detailed the contents and features of the new "district plan." According to Article 3 of that draft, the *piano comprensoriale* would perform several tasks:

> a) determine the centers to be relocated entirely or partially; b) contain provisions for the establishment, development, and transformation of urban and agricultural settlements by regulating their purpose and the respective norms; c) decide the infrastructural system, publicly run industrial plants, and equipment, and all the new construction necessary to develop the economic and social environment; d) determine the type of building work to undertake, based on the social and economic characteristics of the area, the needs of local employment and productive development, and the observation of technical norms for construction in earthquake zones; e) define the limits of the zones of special historic, artistic, or regional interest, their use and any special provisions; f) define programs and realization phases.[50]

The *piano comprensoriale*, in sum, would allow for an all-encompassing planning process covering not only housing and urban infrastructure, but also the geographical distribution of towns and production units, thus influencing the predominant economic activities of the area. After this comprehensive redesigning, the Belice Valley would never be the same again.

Arguing in favor of this proposal, Communist member of Parliament Pancrazio De Pasquale cited as a precedent the actions taken after the Vajont disaster of 1963.[51] In 1963, a landslide into the Vajont reservoir caused an immense wave that washed over the dam, destroying or seriously damaging a huge area. The authorities conceived the Vajont reconstruction as an opportunity to transform the area into a modern urbanized region by means of a new spatial layout and special policies for economic development. To coordinate reconstruction and investments and achieve that goal, the post-disaster legislation introduced an early version of the *piano comprensoriale*. Architect Giuseppe Samonà, in collaboration with sociologist Alessandro Pizzorno, drew up a special *piano comprensoriale* for the Vajont region that involved a general reshaping of the area, including settlement displacement, new industrial locations and new infrastructure.[52] De Pasquale used this example to assert the feasibility of his proposal. Moreover, he advocated better regulation of the entire process than in the Vajont, where lack of coordination had delayed the rebuilding. The main urban center in the Vajont region, De Pasquale recalled, "was supposed to become a new Brasilia and is not even a little village yet."[53] The Belice Valley should not be sentenced to the same fate, and in De

Pasquale's opinion this would be possible only by establishing efficient institutional and planning mechanisms.

Throughout the entire discussion, the commission never called into question the *piano comprensoriale* itself, nor its underlying vision. Instead, the deputies had a long and animated debate about whether it was for the Sicilian regional government to regulate such matters, or whether it was the exclusive responsibility of the central government. The members of the Communist Party argued vigorously in favor of the former option. They did not contest the fact that the central state would have to play a major role in funding the reconstruction. The Belice disaster was so great that it "can only be compared with the Messina one, and cannot be compared with any others," and thus was a matter of national importance requiring national funding.[54] Nevertheless, the regional government had to decide the final destination of these funds in the Belice Valley. The introduction of the *piano comprensoriale* could achieve that goal, by putting the entire planning activity in the earthquake area in the hands of the Sicilian authorities. Regardless of the precise terms of the draft legislation, the members of the Christian Democrat majority that held power in Sicily were firmly in favor of passing it by unanimous vote in a clear show of unity. This gave the Communists good leverage. In exchange for their vote, they were able to obtain the insertion of the *piano comprensoriale* into the final draft. Thus, after one week of discussion, the commission handed over the draft to the Sicilian parliament, which approved it almost immediately.[55]

The Sicilian law was unexpected from many viewpoints. In 1942, a pivotal piece of legislation had greatly modified the tools for urban planning in Italy.[56] Among many innovations, that law had introduced the possibility of extending the scope of urban planning beyond the strictly urban by incorporating multiple centers along with the surrounding shared territory into a single plan. Actual planning practice after the war did not make significant use of this innovation. In 1962, the planning reform of the center-left coalition had envisaged the introduction of the *piano comprensoriale*, but the reform by Minister Sullo had not overcome the opposition of their Christian Democrat allies.[57] The introduction of an extended version of the *piano comprensoriale*, although not entirely new, could thus still be considered an experiment in Italian planning. Furthermore, the regional parliament passed the law just a few days after the earthquakes of 15 January. The legislative activism of the regional government took the national authorities by surprise. The national government issued a first emergency decree on 22 January concerning the funding of rescue operations, allocation of monetary allowances to the victims, and some fiscal benefits for residents of the whole area.[58] The decree, though, did not include any measures on relief and reconstruction. The regional law thus happened to be the first piece of legislation to tackle post-earthquake reconstruction in the Belice Valley, and this inevitably conditioned efforts on the national level.

Although they were early and unexpected, the contents of the regional law advocated by the Communist Party did not represent an eccentric or isolated position. On the contrary, economic and territorial planning and large-scale redevelopment had many supporters during those years, especially among members of the national majority. In 1968, the so-called "center-left" coalition of Christian Democrats and Socialists held the Italian government, and one of the main exponents of the Socialist Party, Giacomo Mancini, was director of the Ministry of Public Works. From the beginnings of the center-left coalition in 1963, economic and large-scale spatial planning constituted one of the conditions of the participation of the Socialist Party in the coalition.[59] This meant that the idea of combining the reconstruction effort with wider socioeconomic development initiatives could easily find consensus among members of the government. The Socialist Party newspaper, moreover, had been endorsing this option since the end of January.[60]

Notwithstanding this cultural proximity, the government—more specifically Minister Mancini—initially considered the regional initiative to be an illegitimate interference in state activity and a potential source of problems.[61] Intervention in case of disasters was the prerogative of the national authorities—more precisely, it was the task of the Ministry of Public Works, at least since the precedent of the reconstruction of Messina after the 1908 earthquake. Moreover, Mancini hoped to use the symbolic status of the Belice Valley as an opportunity to showcase the efficacy of the Socialist Party and thus did not look favorably upon competition from the Sicilian regional government. Ultimately, ministry officials were able to find a compromise to avoid conflict between the two institutions. The Ministry of Public Works would negotiate the contents of the *piano comprensoriale* with the regional government, but would take full control of the infrastructural and urban planning for the most affected towns.[62]

The result of this compromise was Decree no. 79 of 26 February 1968, which established the scope and mode of the state's involvement in the reconstruction of the Belice Valley. The state was to support the reconstruction of private housing with special funds, and would undertake the reconstruction of all public edifices and infrastructure. The decree also specified the total amount of public funding, the extent and allocation of finances, and the duties and responsibilities of the state with regard to public works. Most importantly, it ultimately established a new institution to become the plenipotentiary body of the entire Belice Valley reconstruction: the Ispettorato Generale per la ricostruzione delle zone terremotate (General Inspectorate for the Reconstruction of the Earthquake-Damaged Area, hereafter General Inspectorate). Entrusted with supervising most public works and with allocating public money, the General Inspectorate would play a major role in the rebuilding process.[63]

The decree overtly mentioned the relocation of some of the destroyed towns. Article 11, in particular, specified that within thirty days the Ministry of Public Works would issue a special decree enumerating precisely the "settlements to be relocated."[64] Surprisingly, at this point there was still no official geological or seismological report on the disaster area that could justify a choice as drastic as the relocation of an entire town. In the aftermath of 1968, the Istituto Nazionale Geofisica (National Institute for Geophysics) had sent a couple of experts from Rome, Liliana Marcelli and Mario De Panfilis, to investigate the earthquake zone and produce a complete report for the authorities. In February, however, Marcelli and De Panfilis had just started their work, and they were not able to present any results before April of that year. In other words, the regional and the national authorities had already decided on the resettlement policy before experts could have the final word on the matter. To be sure, the intensity of destruction in some Belice towns could cast legitimate doubts on the chances of rebuilding them, even without precise scientific assessment. Yet the reason why the authorities anticipated resettlement so early, and without the support of scientific evidence, was its consistency with their development agenda. Rather than being a decision firmly supported by geological concerns, relocation was above all a function of redevelopment plans and stemmed directly from the aim of promoting social and economic change through the rebuilding process.

The decree addressed socioeconomic development directly. Article 59, most notably, established that the reconstruction of towns and infrastructure would go hand in hand with a larger investment plan. The aim of the plan was to create infrastructure and production units in the valley for the primary and secondary sectors, through the intervention of public financial and industrial bodies such as the Cassa per il Mezzogiorno (Fund for the South), the Ministry of Public Works, and the Ministero delle Partecipazioni Statali (Ministry for State-owned Industry). This article, in other words, laid down the precise commitment of the national institutions to the comprehensive economic development plan. To this purpose, it envisioned the coordinated activation of the entire governmental apparatus that had been created after World War II for economic planning and public funding for the industrialization of Southern Italy. This complex institutional system was at its apex in the late 1960s, bolstered by the planning-oriented culture of the center-left coalition. To counter the "disaster of poverty" in the Belice Valley, the state was committed to mobilizing the system entirely.[65]

The national parliament had to approve this decree for it to pass into law, and debate on the issue was to start on 4 March. That day, a delegation of survivors from the Belice Valley started camping in Montecitorio Square, in front of the Parliament building in Rome. They had arrived by train directly from Sicily, and intended to stay in Rome for the entire duration of the parliamentary debate. Their purpose was to make sure the voices of the local communities were heard, meet representatives of the national government, and make known their viewpoints and demands concerning the rebuilding.[66] They had organized the protest as soon as the government had passed the decree on 27 February. That day, several earthquake survivors held a meeting in the town of Partanna, in which they had discussed and criticized the contents of the decree. The participants, who also included several mayors from affected municipalities, had decided to organize a protest in Rome and appeal for participation.[67] Following that decision, they called a meeting on 2 March in Palermo and requested a special, low-priced train service to get them to Rome.[68] They then spent the following days promoting the protest throughout tent camps and refugee shelters in the valley. One meeting after another, tract after tract, with the result that more than one thousand survivors gathered in Palermo's central station on 2 March and took a train to Rome.[69]

This was not a spontaneous protest. An established network of activists had called the first meeting and supported the organization of the protest all along. These activists were all affiliated with the Centro Studi e Iniziative (Center for Studies and Activities), founded in 1958 by sociologist and activist Danilo Dolci. The mission of this center was to promote social and economic development in western Sicily through social services, irrigation, and infrastructural improvements. The appeal that announced the protest in Rome repeated long-standing demands made by the center, such as the construction of three reservoirs in the area, improvements to the road networks in the countryside, and a program of reforestation. In addition to these longstanding demands, the appeal included the construction of two express roads, new state-funded industrial plants in the area, and the massive financial and technical involvement of the state in the rebuilding of the Belice Valley.[70] The protesters' demands seemed to be fully in line with the intentions of the Regione Siciliana and the national government. Yet there was a fundamental difference. While the authorities planned their intervention entirely on a top-down basis, the people of Belice Valley were demanding control over the rebuilding process. "The population," stated the appeal, "must participate in the entire reconstruction process town by town, by means of the municipal administration, the municipal committees, the zone committee, and the popular assemblies."[71]

The presence of a thousand refugees camped out in the center of Rome was an unusual occurrence, and it granted the Belice protesters space and visibility in most national newspapers and on newsreels and television.[72] With their banners and slogans, they demanded the "elimination of large estates and illiteracy," the provision of "schools, houses, jobs, and hospitals," and stated that they would not leave Rome "until they give us what we are due."[73] This protest visibly countered the victimization of the survivors that was implicit in the post-earthquake mass-media imagery. The silent faces from archaic rural

Sicily were now voices shouting legitimate claims and making precise requests in the national capital. This empowering self-representation also gained the attention of the authorities. High-ranking officials from several ministries and even the Minister of Public Works himself received a delegation of protesters. The authorities assured the delegates that rebuilding would proceed quickly and would be part of a program of socioeconomic development. The final version of the law would provide all the necessary legal and administrative mechanisms and funds.

Parliament approved a revised version of the decree while the protesters were still outside the Parliament building. Minister Mancini himself presented the law to Parliament. The government action in the Belice Valley, he claimed, needed to address not only a post-earthquake crisis, but "an entire history of suffering and backwardness." The valley, he continued, had been "waiting for decades for some kind of intervention that would permit it to join the new reality of progress and democratic development." The time had come to fulfill these expectations. This meant, according to Mancini, that the national government should frame the post-disaster rebuilding plans in the broader context of nationwide economic planning initiatives.[74] Both houses of Parliament approved the law with only a few modifications. The most significant change was to Article 59, concerning the industrial development plan. Acceding to one of the requests made by the Belice protesters, the new version of Article 59 formalized a deadline: all institutions and ministries involved in developmental initiatives had to finalize a joint plan no later than 31 December 1968.[75] Besides this, Parliament confirmed all the other provisions of the initial decree, including the creation of a General Inspectorate.

After both chambers had passed the law, the protesters dismantled the camp. Members of the national government had received them, and Parliament had incorporated their requests into the final text of the law. Nonetheless, the protesters considered that one crucial point had gone unheard. Namely, the authorities had essentially ignored the requests for the direct participation of local institutions and communities in the decision-making processes. The law, on the contrary, concentrated the entire rebuilding into the hand of one agency, the General Inspectorate, directly dependent on the Ministry of Public Works. Before leaving Rome, therefore, the protesters announced they would keep making their voice heard via the national and regional institutions.[76] This was not an empty promise. A couple of months later, on 10 July, labor unions, the Communist Party, and the mayors from the affected localities organized a new protest in Palermo to demand greater allowances and benefits for the disaster area.[77] More than 10,000 people attended a march that ended in front of the Sicilian parliament building. This protest was not as peaceful as the tent camp in Rome. At the end of the demonstration, a riot erupted and the police fired shots into the crowd.[78] The following day, the Sicilian parliament approved a new law extending benefits and allowances to the disaster survivors and partially modified the features of the *piano comprensoriale* to facilitate the beginning of the reconstruction.[79]

As we shall see, local communities remained vocal during the following years, perpetuating a strong antagonism toward the central institutions. Otherwise, the objection raised in March 1968 about the role of local institutions and communities in the decision-making process would be key to the successes and failures of the rebuilding. In spite of the deep gulf between local communities and the national authorities regarding the decision-making process, all the actors agreed on one point: in order to respond adequately to the earthquake, the reconstruction would need to be accompanied by a comprehensive plan for socioeconomic development and industrialization. That idea was the basis not only of the two main pieces of legislation passed by the Regione Siciliana and the national government, but also the demands made by the protesters in Rome and in Palermo. A coordinated series of interventions were needed to redesign settlement patterns, infrastructure, and many features of the biogeophysical environment. All seemed to agree that this would allow the Belice Valley to rise again from the ruins of the earthquake in a completely new and better form.

Conclusion

The 1968 Belice earthquake struck after a sequence of other events with disastrous consequences in 1960s Italy. In 1962, a strong earthquake hit the Irpinia region, killing 20 people and leaving some 16,000 residents homeless.[80] The following year, in 1963, the Vajont Dam overflow killed several thousand people and devastated a large area between Veneto and Friuli Venezia Giulia.[81] In July 1966, a landslide destroyed an entire neighborhood in Agrigento (Sicily), and a few months later there were floods in Florence, Venice, and other Italian cities.[82] In each of those cases, the management of rescue operations provoked disputes and conflict. The 1968 Belice disaster was probably the most mismanaged of this sequence of disasters. The delays in rescue and relief, the absence of a coordinated center of management, and the lack of search and rescue teams and materials were all undeniable. As we have seen, most commentators deemed this failure responsible for exponentially increasing the impact of the earthquakes on the population. Following this calamitous failure in the Belice Valley, the organization of rescue and relief would be gradually but irreversibly changed, starting with the 1976 Friuli earthquake. Yet it took another earthquake disaster, the 1980 Irpinia earthquake, to lead to the creation of a permanent civil protection department.[83]

By the 1960s, earthquake science had changed considerably from its pioneering years around the Messina earthquake. At the beginning of the 1960s, Canadian scholar Tuzo Wilson was able to prove seafloor spreading convincingly. His contribution and that of other scholars in these years validated theories on faulting and paved the way for the uncontested confirmation of the theory of plate tectonics.[84] In this changed context, the 1968 Belice earthquake was certainly not as significant to transnational seismology as the 1908 Messina earthquake. Nevertheless, it stimulated an important development in Italian earthquake science and policy. In the wake of the Messina quake, the authorities had introduced several new measures for earthquake protection. Between 1916 and 1962, legislators passed several laws that elaborated the technical features of earthquake-resistant buildings and expanded the classification of earthquake-prone areas, creating a double zoning system based on the level of risk.[85] Yet, based on existing knowledge, the mapping of seismic risk in Italy did not include the Belice Valley. The location of the 1968 earthquakes thus implicitly reopened the problem of seismic risk classification and called into question the criteria through which scientists and authorities had implemented that classification.

Immediately after the 1968 earthquakes, the authorities declared the Belice Valley a seismic zone and enforced the existing earthquake-proof building code in all the affected towns. In addition, the authorities considered including a larger portion of western Sicily among the nation's seismic zones. Some municipalities, however, were fiercely opposed to this inclusion. They saw the constraints imposed by the earthquake building code as an obstacle to the construction industry. This was the case with Palermo. The authorities of that city engaged in a long legal and scientific dispute with the Ministry for Public Works to prove that the city should not be included in the seismic zones of Sicily. Despite the fact that Palermo inhabitants had distinctly felt the tremors of the 1968 quake, the authorities claimed that the city's site was safe and that a strict earthquake building code would only depress the local economy.[86] This resistance can be compared with the irresponsible inaction in Messina after the 1895, 1905, and 1907 earthquakes, and proves once again how easily economic priorities can overcome safety concerns.[87] Only in 1975 would the Ministry of Public Works finally pass a new decree on earthquake protection that modified the existing 1962 legislation. That decree elaborated the standards in construction engineering and, in addition, classified a large portion of western Sicily as a seismic zone.[88]

As we have seen, geology and engineering played a marginal role in the cultural perceptions of and response to the devastation of the Belice Valley in 1968. Earthquake science could provide a technical explanation as to why houses and public buildings had crumbled. Yet it could not explain why so many Italians were living in poverty on the outskirts of modern urban civilization and were so vulnerable to seismic hazards. As we have seen, the discourse about Southern "underdevelopment" provided a much more successful mode of understanding than earthquake science. After a decade of tumultuous economic growth that had transformed the life of many Italians and their environments, the Belice earthquake landscape looked like the return of an undesirable past. The earthquake displayed all too clearly that the achievements of the postwar economic miracle were unevenly distributed, and revealed to the public the persistence of the most archaic conditions of life and work in many parts of the country. The poverty of the Belice Valley thus became a symbol of and metaphor for the "backwardness" and poverty of the *Mezzogiorno*. This condition, more than geology, was deemed responsible for the disaster.

The most important consequence of this understanding was the incorporation of the development agenda and its corollary, socioeconomic and environmental engineering, into the earthquake response. The encounter between development agenda and post-earthquake reconstruction was indeed a perfect match. The development discourse confined its object structurally to zero degrees of modernity and assumed the obliteration of existing cultures, modes of production, and physical landscapes as a necessary step for improvement.[89] The wasteland of the earthquake's aftermath caused this zero degrees scenario to materialize. After the 1963 Skopje earthquake, many global development agencies were mobilized to help with rescue and recovery and promote the redevelopment of the Yugoslavian city.[90] In Latin America the implementation of developmental plans followed the 1970 Peru earthquake.[91] What happened in the case of Belice Valley, therefore, while it had particular resonance for the Italian developmental agenda and the latter's roots in post-unification *meridionalismo*, was also in tune with broader international trends. By incorporating development into reconstruction, the goal became the radical transformation of the affected area, its society, culture, and economy. Nothing in the Belice Valley was to ever be the same again.

The geological process that resulted in the 1968 tremors was a point of no return in the history of the Belice Valley. The unexpected occurrence of the earthquake devastated a conspicuous number of communities, triggered massive outward migration, and stimulated the development of a radical strategy of environmental and social reform. Nevertheless, however new it might have sounded at the time, the improvement and transformation of the Belice Valley's environment and society was not an entirely new proposal. As we shall see, a longstanding debate on rural reform and democratic planning in the Belice Valley, a conspicuous accumulation of knowledge and plans, and vocal local communities all preceded the post-earthquake debate. To understand the impact of the earthquake and its multiple facets we shall now turn to examine this story in detail.

Notes

1. Regione Siciliana, Assessorato Territorio e Ambiente, Dipartimento Territorio e ambiente, Piano Stralcio di Bacino per l'Assetto Idrogeologico (PAI) Bacino Idrografico del Fiume Belice (AG-PA-TP) *Relazione* (Palermo, n.d.), 9–11.
2. Agostino Renna, "La costruzione della città e della campagna," in *Costruzione e Progetto: La Valle del Belice*, ed. Agostino Renna, Antonio De Bonis, and Giuseppe Gangemi (Milan, 1979), 57.
3. Maurice Aymard, "Le città di nuova fondazione in Sicilia," in *Storia d'Italia, Annali 8: Insediamenti e Territorio*, ed. Cesare De Seta (Turin, 1985), 405–17; Timothy Davies, "La colonizzazione feudale della Sicilia," in De Seta, *Storia d'Italia Annali 8*, 419–75.
4. Anton Blok, "South Italian Agro-towns," *Comparative Studies in Society and History* 11, no. 2 (1969): 121–35; Russell King and Alan Stratchan, "Sicilian Agro-towns," *Erdkunde: Archive for Scientific Geography* 32, no. 2 (1978): 110–23; Daniel R. Curtis, "Is There an 'Agro-town' Model for Southern Italy? Exploring the Diverse Roots and Development of the Agro-town Structure through a Comparative Case study in Apulia," *Continuity and Change* 28, no. 3 (2013): 377–419.
5. On the subsistence belt, see Renna, "La costruzione della citta e della campagna," 52.
6. R. Rigano, B. Antichi, L. Arena, R. Azzaro, and M. S. Barbano, "Sismicità e zonazione sismogenetica in Sicilia occidentale," in *Consiglio Nazionale delle Ricerche, Gruppo Nazionale di Geofisica della Terra Solida, Atti del 17° Convegno Nazionale*, Rome, 10–12 November 1998, http://www2.ogs.trieste.it/gngts/gngts/convegniprecedenti/1998/Contents/ordinari/12/rrigano/htm/rrigano.htm.
7. An exception might have been the earthquake that hit Selinunte around 400 BCE: the archeological evidence suggests that the built environment of the already declining colony suffered hugely from the consequences of that seism. See Emanuela Guidoboni, Guido Ferrari, Dante Mariotti, Alberto Comastri, Gabriele Tarabusi, and Gianluca Valensise, "Earthquake Sequence -400 Selinunte," *Catalogue of Strong Earthquakes in Italy 461 B.C.–1997 and Mediterranean Area 760 B.C.–1500*, INGV-Istituto Nazionale di Geofisica e Vulcanologia, http://storing.ingv.it/cfti4med/quakes/42852.html. The same authors have also hypothesized the occurrence of another destructive earthquake in the same area around the eighth century CE. See "Earthquake Sequence 0701 Selinunte," http://storing.ingv.it/cfti4med/quakes/42853.html.
8. See Liliana Marcelli and Mario De Panfilis, "Il periodo sismico della Sicilia occidentale iniziato il 4 gennaio 1968," *Annali di Geofisica* 21, no. 4 (1968): 390.
9. The times given follow those reported in Emanuela Guidoboni and Gianluca Valensise, *Il peso economico e sociale dei disastri sismici in Italia negli ultimi 150 anni, 1861–2011* (Bologna, 2011), 287.
10. Lorenzo Barbera, interview by Giacomo Parrinello, Partanna, 17 March 2012, published in "Terremoti: storia memorie narrazioni," ed. Gabriella Gribaudi and Anna Maria Zaccaria, special issue of *Memoria/memorie: Materiali di storia* 8 (2012): 174.

11. Ministero dell'Interno, Direzione Generale della Protezione Civile e Servizio Antincendi, undated (but clearly 14 January 1968), in box 14 "Terremoto in Sicilia genn.1968," folder 16 "varie," Ministero dell'Interno, Gabinetto, Archivio Storico della Protezione Civile [hereafter ASPC].
12. Magnitude 6 according to the calculation of Marcelli and De Panfilis, "Il periodo sismico," 352; 6.5 of "equivalent magnitude" for Guidoboni and Valensise, *Il peso economico e sociale dei disastri sismici*, 389.
13. Questura di Trapani, Vice Questore Lo Presti to Questore di Trapani, Trapani, 27 February 1968, in box 14 "Terremoto in Sicilia genn.1968," folder 16 "varie," MI, Gabinetto, ASPC.
14. Questura di Trapani, Squadra Mobile, Report of Giuseppe Peri, Trapani, 9 February 1968, in box 14 "Terremoto in Sicilia genn.1968," folder 16 "varie," MI, Gabinetto, ASPC.
15. Questura di Trapani, Corpo delle Guardie di P.S., Impiego di personale nelle zone terremotate, Trapani, 17 February 1968, n.3.201.5.4/, p. 4, in box 14 "Terremoto in Sicilia genn.1968," folder 16 "varie," MI, Gabinetto, ASPC. See also Questura di Trapani, Rapporto del Questore di Trapani al Prefetto di Trapani, "Terremoto del gennaio 1968: compiti svolti dalla Polizia," Trapani, 23 February 1968, n.0/0185/Gab., p. 6, in box 14 "Terremoto in Sicilia genn.1968," folder 16 "varie," MI, Gabinetto, ASPC.
16. Questura di Trapani, Relazione di servizio dell'Isp. Amoroso al Questore di Trapani, Gibellina—scosse telluriche, 20 January 1968, in box 14 "Terremoto in Sicilia genn.1968," folder 16 "varie," MI, Gabinetto, ASPC.
17. Ministero dell'Interno, Ufficio Stampa, Appunto per il sig. Ministro, "Notizie del telegiornale del 15.1.1968," 15 January 1968, in box 14 "Terremoto in Sicilia genn.1968," folder 16 "varie," MI Gabinetto, ASPC.
18. A tragic and yet ironic report of that episode viewed "from the bottom up" can be found in Lorenzo Barbera, *I Ministri dal cielo: I contadini del Belice raccontano* (Milan, 1980): 20–22.
19. This is, moreover, the highest estimate. According to others, the figure was lower. See Guidoboni and Valensise, *Il peso economico e sociale dei disastri sismici*, 287.
20. Marcelli and De Panfilis, "Il periodo sismico," 343–442.
21. Comitato Interministeriale della Protezione Civile, Relazione sulle operazioni di soccorso svolte in Sicilia in occasione del terremoto del 15 gennaio 1968, 15 October 1968, in box 1, Ministero dell'Interno, Direzione Generale Protezione Civile e Servizi Antincendio 112 [hereafter MI DGPC 112] ASPC.
22. Barbera, interview by Parrinello, 174–75, and Enza Bellacera, video interview, 29 May 2009, 00:41:57, *Le Terre che Tremarono*, Centro di Ricerche Economiche e Sociali per il Meridione [hereafter CRESM].
23. Prefetto di Trapani Napoletano to Ministero dell'Interno, telegram no. 304, 21 January 1968, in box 14, "Terremoto in Sicilia genn.1968," folder 16 "varie," MI DGPC 112, ASPC.
24. Prefetto di Palermo to Ministero dell'Interno, telegram no. 46951, 28 January 1968, 12h 24', in box 5, MI DGPC 112, ASPC.
25. Prefettura di Agrigento, Terremoto in Sicilia—andamento delle operazioni di soccorso, Agrigento, 6 February 1968, in box 14 "Terremoto in Sicilia genn.1968," folder 16 "varie," MI DGPC 112, ASPC.

26. Prefettura di Trapani, "Relazione sui problemi conseguenti al terremoto del Belice e sulle attività svolte dalla Prefettura di Trapani fra il 14 gennaio ed il 14 luglio 1968," in box 2, folder 4 "Relazioni prefetture," sub-folder "Trapani," MI DGPC 112, ASPC.
27. Prefetto di Palermo to Ministero dell'Interno, telegram no. 35151, 21 January 1968, and the following two of 22 January 1968. On 28 January 1968, the Prefect wrote that in Palermo "the well-known assistance point activated in that station" had released 10,600 free tickets up to that day. Box 5 in MI DGPC 112, ASPC.
28. The massive release of passports is explicitly testified in a report of the Prefect of Agrigento, 14 February 1968, who wrote that until then the prefecture had released 2,409 passports. Box 14 "Terremoto in Sicilia genn.1968," folder 16 "varie," MI DGPC 112, ASPC.
29. Nicola Accardo and Gaspare Giglio, video interview, 7 April 2010, color, 01:54:42. *Le terre che tremarono*, CRESM.
30. Prefettura di Messina, Assistenza profughi delle zone terremotate, 23 January 1968, in box 2 in MI DGPC 112, ASPC.
31. Ministero dell'Interno, Direzione Generale della Protezione Civile, Comunicazione n. 15, 6 February 1968, in box 5, MI DGPC 112, ASPC.
32. Ivo Mataloni, "Perché tante vittime," *Il Tempo*, 17 January 1968, 1.
33. On advances in earthquake science and engineering before 1960 see Robert Reitherman, *Earthquakes and Engineers: An International History* (Reston, VA, 2012), esp. 241–304.
34. Again, these are the calculations by Marcelli and De Panfilis, "Il periodo sismico," 352, which do not necessarily correspond to today's estimates. They are relevant in this case, however, because they corresponded with the knowledge of the time and are a reference for popularized seismological knowledge.
35. *Epoca* 19, no. 105, 28 January 1968.
36. Mario Pogliotti, TG1, 19 January 1968, https://www.youtube.com/watch?v=KD8CKS Qkrj4.
37. Sergio Zavoli, Tv7, undated, http://www.youtube.com/watch?v=nIMFxzCoO7Y.
38. Tempi Nostri, *Italia allo specchio: Sicilia; Numero unico sulle condizioni socio-economiche della regione e sulle iniziative del governo per il suo sviluppo economico*, 00:08:30, b/w, sound, 1 March 1968, T1034, Archivio Storico dell'Istituto Luce [hereafter ASIL], http://www.archivioluce.com/archivio/jsp/schede/schedaCine.jsp?db=cinematograf icoDOCUMENTARI&section=/&physDoc=2994&theTerm=Italia+allo+specchio%3 A+Sicilia&qrId=3seb12fb468b22d9&findCine=true&findFoto=true. This special episode of the newsreel was just the first in a longer series that also examined the regions of Basilicata and Puglia: Tempi Nostri, *Italia allo specchio: Basilicata; Numero unico sulle condizioni socio-economiche della regione e sulle iniziative del governo per il suo sviluppo economico*, 00:07:37, b/w, sound, 01/03/1968, T1036, ASIL; Tempi Nostri, *Italia allo specchio: Puglia; Numero unico sulle condizioni socio-economiche della regione e sulle iniziative del governo per il suo sviluppo economico*, 00:08:05, b/w, sound, 01/06/1968, T1042, ASIL.
39. Carmelo Pennino, Antonino Pennino, and Alfonsa Carbone, *Analisi demografica dei Comuni della Valle del Belice colpiti dal sisma del 1968* (Palermo, 1976), 7–86.
40. Luigi Perelli, *Emigrazione 68: Italia oltre il confine*, 00:32:00, b/w, sound, Archivio Audiovisivo del Movimento Operaio e Democratico [hereafter AAMOD], http://www

.archivioluce.com/archivio/jsp/schede/schedaCine.jsp?db=partnerAAMOD&section=/&physDoc=1633&theTerm=emigrazione+68&qrId=3seb12fb4569704f&findCine=true&findFoto=true&findPartner=true.

41. Literature on Southern "underdevelopment" fills stacks. A few studies of cultural tropes underlying that discourse have appeared in the last decades. See for example Marta Petrusewicz, *Come il Meridione divenne una questione: Rappresentazioni del Sud prima e dopo il Quarantotto* (Soveria Mannelli, 1998); Robert Lumley, and Jonathan Morris, eds., *Oltre il meridionalismo: Nuove prospettive sul Mezzogiorno d'Italia* (Rome, 1999); Jane Schneider, ed., *Italy's 'Southern Question': Orientalism in One Country* (Oxford and New York, 1998).

42. For development policies and discourse after World War II and their interconnection with international policies, see Leandra D'Antone, ed., R*adici storiche ed esperienza dell'intervento straordinario nel Mezzogiorno* (Rome, 1996). See also Giuseppe Barone, "Stato e Mezzogiorno: Il primo tempo dell'intervento straordinario (1943–1960)," in *Storia dell'Italia repubblicana*, vol. 1, *La costruzione della democrazia*, ed. Francesco Barbagallo (Turin, 1994), 293–409. For an overview of the Italian historiographical debate on development policies for the South, see Alessandro Pavarin, *Lo sviluppo del Mezzogiorno: L'intervento dello Stato e il sistema bancario della nascita della Repubblica agli anni Sessanta* (Rome, 2011), esp. 15–103. For a historical overview on post–World War II development policies, see Gilbert Rist, *The History of Development: From Western Origins to Global Faith* (New York, 2008).

43. A good, if late, example of this tendency is Luciano Ferrari Bravo, *Stato e sottosviluppo: Il caso del Mezzogiorno italiano* (Milan, 1972).

44. Alberto Giovannini, "Il dovere di tutti," *Roma*, 17 January 1968, 1.

45. Giulio Goria, "L'Italia dalle case di tufo," *Paese Sera*, 20 January 1968, 1.

46. Mino Monicelli, "Sono crollate perché erano solo casette legate da un filo di calce," *Il Giorno*, 24 January 1968, 3.

47. On the history of Sicilian autonomy in the broader context of World War II and its aftermath see Rosario Mangiameli, "La regione in Guerra (1943–1950)," *Storia d'Italia: Le regioni dall'Unità a oggi*, vol. 5, *La Sicilia*, ed. Maurice Aymard and Giuseppe Giarrizzo (Turin, 1987) 485–600.

48. Commissione Speciale Terremotati, VI Legislatura, 1968–1971 [hereafter Comm. Terr.], Archivio Storico del Parlamento Siciliano [hereafter ASPS].

49. Decreto Legislativo Regionale (Regional Decree, hereafter DR) no. 168, 22 January 1968, "Formazione del piano urbanistico relativo alla zona colpita dal terremoto del 15 gennaio 1968," presented by De Pasquale, La Duca, Attardi, Scaturro, Grasso Anna, Giubilato, Giacalone Vito, La Torre, Colajanni, Rindone, Marraro, Marilli, Cagnes, Messina, in Comm. Terr., ASPS.

50. Ibid., Art. 3.

51. Meeting minutes of the Commissione Speciale Terremotati, 26 January 1968, p. 10, Comm. Terr, ASPS. For more on the Vajont disaster, see Ferruccio Vendramini, ed., *Disastro e ricostruzione nell'area del Vajont* (Longarone, 1994).

52. Giuseppe Samonà, *Piano urbanistico comprensoriale: Relazione generale* (Venice, 1965). On the reconstruction of Longarone see Luciana Palla, "La 'nuova città' e la sua gente: Un difficile percorso dal 1963 a oggi," in *Il Vajont dopo il Vajont 1963-2000,* ed. Ivo Matozzi and Maurizio Reberschak (Venice, 2009), 51–90.

53. Meeting minutes of the Commissione Speciale Terremotati, 24 January 1968, p. 6, Comm. Terr. ASPS.
54. Meeting minutes of the Commissione Speciale Terremotati 23 January 1968 at 22:30, p. 5, Comm.Terr. ASPS.
55. Regional Law no. 1, 3 February 1968, "Primi provvedimenti per la ripresa civile ed economica delle zone colpite dai terremoti del 1967 e 1968," Art. 2.
56. For the features of the urban law of 1942 and territorial planning see Vezio De Lucia, "Dalla legge del 1942 alle leggi di emergenza," *Cinquant'anni di urbanistica in Italia 1942-1992*, ed. Giuseppe Campos-Venuti and Federico Oliva (Rome and Bari, 1993), 87-102, and Valeria Erba and Laura Pogliani, "Il fallimento della pianificazione regionale," in Campos-Venuti and Oliva, *Cinquant'anni di urbanistica*, 133-50.
57. De Lucia, "Dalla legge del 1942," 92-93.
58. Decreto Legge (decree, hereafter DL) no. 12, 22 January 1968, "Provvidenze a favore delle popolazioni dei comuni della Sicilia colpiti dai terremoti del gennaio 1968."
59. On the center-left and the South see, among many other sources, Nicola Tranfaglia, "La modernità squilibrata: Dalla crisi del centrismo al compromesso storico," *Storia dell'Italia repubblicana*, vol. 2, *La trasformazione dell'Italia*, part 2, *Istituzioni, movimenti, culture*, ed. Francesco Barbagallo (Turin, 1995), 5-111, esp. 54-55, and Guido Crainz, *Storia del miracolo italiano: Culture, identità, trasformazioni tra anni cinquanta e sessanta* (Rome, 2003), 216-54. One of the principal documents testifying the planning ambitions of that period is Ugo La Malfa, *Nota aggiuntiva su problemi e prospettive dello sviluppo economico e della programmazione* (Rome, 1973; 1st ed. 1962).
60. Fabio Perini, "Ricostruzione programata," *L'Avanti*, 23 January 1968, 7.
61. Dir. Laudicina, Appunto per il Ministro, 1 February 1968, with the manuscript minutes of a meeting between Mancini, De Rossi, Giglia, Franco, Di Gioia, and the unnamed General Secretary of the Regione Siciliana, in box 26 "Terremoto del 68 varie," Ministero dei Lavori Pubblici Divisione 29, Affari Generali [hereafter MLP 29 AG], ASPC.
62. The Regione Siciliana claimed that its prerogative on urban planning was stated by the statute of autonomy of 1946. In the case of a major calamity, however, this prerogative passed to the national state. Relazione della Dir. Generale SS.SS. all'Ufficio Studi e Legislazione del 2 febbraio 1968 sulla legge regionale siciliana per le zone colpite, in MLP 29 AG, ASPC.
63. Decreto Legge no. 79, 27 February 1968, "Ulteriori interventi e provvidenze per la ricostruzione e per la ripresa economica dei comuni della Sicilia colpiti dai terremoti del gennaio 1968."
64. DL no. 79, 27 February 1968, Art. 11.
65. DL no. 79, 27 February 1968, Art. 59.
66. See the report of the police in: Roma, n.053581/U.P. della Questura di Roma, 3 March 1968, in box 248, folder 2, Ministero dell'Interno Gabinetto 1967-1970 [hereafter MI Gab 67-70] Archivio Centrale dello Stato.
67. Leonardo Barrile, Mayor of Montevago; Francesco Giovenco, member of the Municipal Committee of Gibellina; Vito Bellafiore, Mayor of Santa Ninfa; Lorenzo Barbera member of the Center for Studies and Initiatives; Nino D'Angelo, member of the Municipal Committee of Campobello di Mazara; Giambattista Giaccone, Mayor of Menfi, "Appello delle popolazioni terremotate," *Pianificazione Siciliana* 3, no. 1-4 (1968): 4.

68. Prefetto di Trapani to the Ministero dell'Interno, telegram no. 839, 26 February 1968, in box 3, folder 14, MI DGPC 112, ASPC.
69. Prefetto di Agrigento to Ministero dell'Interno, telegrams no. 548 and no. 550, 27 February 1968, in box 3, folder 14, MI DGPC 112, ASPC; Prefetto di Palermo to Ministero dell'Interno, telegram no. 1151, 1 March 1968, in box 3, folder 14, MI DGPC 112, ASPC.
70. Barrile et al., "Appello delle popolazioni terremotate," 5.
71. Ibid., 5.
72. "Mille terremotati siciliani protestano davanti a Montecitorio," *Il Corriere della Sera*, 3 March 1968, 7; "Nuova dimostrazione a Roma dei terremotati siciliani," *Il Corriere della Sera*, 4 March 1968, 2; "Bivacco presso Montecitorio dei terremotati della Sicilia," *Il Corriere della Sera*, 5 March 1968, 2.
73. Unitelefilm, "Manifestazione dei terremotati del Belice—Roma, 5 marzo 1968," 5 March 1968, 00:04:00, b/w, mute, AAMOD. http://www.archivioluce.com/archivio/jsp/schede/schedaCine.jsp?db=partnerAAMOD&section=/&physDoc=2512&theTerm=Manifestazione+dei+terremotati+del+Belice+&qrId=3seb12fb453e3050&findCine=true&findFoto=true&findPartner=true.
74. Giacomo Mancini to the Camera dei Deputati, 4 March 1968, in Atti Parlamentari, Camera dei Deputati, IV legislatura, discussioni, 44688. http://www.camera.it/_dati/leg04/lavori/stenografici/sed0836/sed0836.pdf.
75. Law no. 241, 18 March 1968, "Conversione in legge, con modificazioni, del Decreto-legge 27 febbraio 1968 n. 79, concernente ulteriori interventi e provvidenze per la ricostruzione e per la ripresa economica dei comuni della Sicilia colpiti dai terremoti del 1968," Art. 59.
76. Comunicato del comitato delle popolazioni terremotate siciliane a conclusione della pressione di Piazza Montecitorio, 8 March 1968, published in *Pianificazione Siciliana* 3, no. 1–4 (1968): 8.
77. "Il Convegno dei Sindaci del Belice fissa gli obiettivi della Marcia di protesta," *L'Ora*, 8–9 July 1968, 9.
78. Giuseppe Quatriglio, "Hanno vinto i terremotati," *Il Giornale di Sicilia*, 11 July 1968, 1.
79. Ibid., 1.
80. Guidoboni and Valensise, *Il peso economico e sociale dei disastri sismici*, 277–86.
81. Gian Battista Vai, "Vajont, 1963 cinquanta anni dopo: Cronaca, etica e scienza," in *L'Italia dei disastri: Dati e riflessioni sull'impatto degli eventi naturali, 1861–2013*, ed. Emanuela Guidoboni and Gianluca Valensise (Bologna, 2013), 43–72.
82. Giorgio Botta, "Ricordare e riflettere per conoscere: Alluvioni e frane in Italia dal dopoguerra a oggi," in Guidoboni and Valensise, *L'Italia dei disastri*, 99–108.
83. On the development of civil protection in Italy after the 1966 and 1968 disasters see David E. Alexander, "The Evolution of Civil Protection in Modern Italy," in *Disastro!*, ed. John Dickie, John Foot, and Frank M. Snowden, 165–85.
84. For details about the researchers and theories that brought about the consolidation of plate tectonics see Naomi Oreskes, "From Continental Drift to Plate Tectonics," *Plate Tectonics: An Insider's History of the Modern Theory of the Earth*, ed. Naomi Oreskes (Boulder, 2003), 3–27.
85. On the evolution of legislation for earthquake protection in Italy, see Sergio Castenetto and Massimiliano Severino, "Dalla prima normative antisismica del 1909 alle succes-

sive modifiche," in *Il terremoto e il maremoto del 28 dicembre 1908: Analisi sismologica impatto, prospettive,* ed. Guido Bertolaso, Enzo Boschi, Emanuela Guidoboni, and Gianluca Valensise (Rome and Bologna, 2008), 425–42.

86. See the reports from the Superior Council of Public Works and the attached documents and technical reports in box 1 "Terremoti 1968- Classificazioni zone sismiche" Ministero dei Lavori Pubblici Divisione 3 [hereafter MLP 3], ASPC.

87. A clear case in point is what happened in San Francisco after the 1906 earthquake. See Theodore Steinberg, *Acts of God* (New York, 2000), 26–36.

88. Decreto Ministeriale (ministerial decree), 3 March 1975, which followed Law no. 64, 2 February 1974.

89. On the development as a "discourse," see Arturo Escobar, *Encountering Development: The Making and Unmaking of the Third World* (Princeton, 1995), but also Tania Murray Li, *The Will to Improve: Governmentality, Development, and the Practice of Politics* (Durham and London, 2007). The idea of a "zero degree" is also articulated, with a different argument, by James C. Scott, *Seeing Like a State: How Certain Schemes to Improve the Human Condition Have Failed* (New Haven, 1998).

90. Ines Tolic, *Dopo il terremoto: La politica della ricostruzione negli anni della guerra fredda a Skopje* (Reggio Emilia, 2011).

91. See Nathan Clarke, "Reforming the Tragic City: Rebuilding after the 1970 Earthquake in Chimbote, Peru," paper presented at the 2013 ASEH Annual Conference, *Confluences, Crossings, and Power,* Toronto, Canada, 3–6 April 2013. More cases are discussed in the conclusion of this book.

CHAPTER 5

Rural Modernity 1933–1967

On the eve of the 1968 earthquake, the Belice Valley appeared to be scarcely different from the way it had been one or two centuries previously. The changing colors of the landscape, from brown bare fields to green shoots on gentle hills, and finally mature yellow ears of wheat, marked the rhythm of the seasons under the Mediterranean sun. Little hilltop villages and towns, crammed with humans and animals alike, were the backdrop for a rural life divided between intermittent labor in the wheat fields, the care of small subsistence gardens, and the arduous daily cycles of domestic work. Yet, in these little hilltop villages and towns, an attentive observer would have easily noticed signs of an ongoing transformation. A few cars were stationed along the main streets, or sped across the countryside on newly improved roads. Electrical cables connected the towns, and, at moments of silence, one could perhaps hear the ringing of telephones coming from a town hall or post office. If an observer lingered in those villages long enough, he or she would discover that certain groups of people were absent. Following the well-trodden path of labor migration, many young men had left the valley, heading towards the industrial cities of the *Pianura Padana* or beyond the border, to Germany, Switzerland, and France. For them, the winds of change had blown more strongly.

Emigrants and car drivers were not the only people on the move. In March 1967, a few months before the earthquake, a week-long protest march crossed the Belice Valley from the Mediterranean seaboard to Palermo, the regional capital. A network of local committees had organized the march to promote a community-based development plan that aimed to stimulate environmental and social reform in the valley. The initiative of the committees was the last and most radical version of plans for rural modernization proposed by a variety of public institutions and bodies from the late 1920s onwards. All the plans, including the one by the committees, revolved around the idea that water was essential to rural reform. In a dry region subject to seasonal and inconsistent rainfall, the access to a constant water supply could boost agricultural improvements and economic growth. The view of the local committees, however, was that the traditional goals of reclamation and development were not enough: environmental and economic reforms should aim for a better and more even distribution of wealth and resources to benefit the vast majority of poor and disenfranchised members of the local communities.

The 1968 earthquake abruptly interrupted the crescendo of initiatives and plans in the Belice Valley without any of the major goals having been achieved. Nonetheless, this does not mean that this history is unrelated or irrelevant to our understanding of the post-disaster context. On the contrary, the failure of reform initiatives paved the way for the devastating material and social effects of the earthquakes. Moreover, as we shall see, in the succession of plans and the confrontation between different visions of rural modernity, the Belice Valley itself emerged as the coherent unit for a broader socio-environmental reform, framing the scope and scale of future interventions. The constellation of pre-earthquake knowledge, expectations, and actors would contribute greatly to the orientation of the features, pace, and outcomes of the rebuilding process.

Reclamation and Redemption

In 1876, future Italian prime minister Sidney Sonnino left Tuscany in the company of Leopoldo Franchetti and Enea Cavalieri to undertake a journey around Sicily. Their purpose was to document the material and cultural conditions on the biggest island of the new Kingdom of Italy. During their five-month journey on horseback, the three voyagers also crossed the inland regions of western Sicily. The whole area was an uninterrupted sequence of wheat fields, pastures, and fallow land: "you can ride for five or six hours from one town to another," wrote Sonnino, "and never see a tree, nor a bush. You go up and down, now crossing fields, then climbing up steep trails devastated by water; you pass along streams, cross over the crests of the hills, one valley yields to another, but the scene is always the same: solitude everywhere and a desolation that grips your heart." In this desolation, there were no farmhouses to encounter. The dominant form of property ownership was the *latifondo*: a large estate owned by one of a tiny class of landowners, still called *feudatari* (feudal landlords), despite the formal abolition of feudal privileges in 1812. A large population of impoverished peasants, who worked the estates of the *feudatari*, resided in densely populated hilltop towns. To get to the fields in which they had to work, the peasants "must sometimes travel for 15 kilometers or more" along poorly maintained donkey trails.[1] In this comfortless landscape, violence prospered, and the Mafia ruled the economic life of the countryside and the relations between landowners and the multitude of impoverished daily laborers.[2]

The report that Sonnino and Franchetti made after this journey is a milestone in the history of the so-called "Southern Question" in Italy, and the first in a long series of enquiries and studies about Sicily and the rural regions of

Italy. Devoting to western Sicily perhaps the darkest pages of their generally grim text, Sonnino and Franchetti reported archaic forms of property ownership, violent social and labor relations, lack of transport infrastructure, lack of water resources, a deserted countryside, and dilapidated towns. That social and environmental landscape contained all the elements that authorities and social reformers would perceive for decades as the most acute manifestations of southern "backwardness."[3] In the following years, other, more official inquiries on behalf of the national parliament would fill library stacks and archival boxes on the subject of Southern Italy and the condition of its peasantry.[4] When describing Sicily, subsequent studies, such as the one led by Giovanni Lorenzoni in 1907 on behalf of the Italian parliament, returned a more nuanced and diverse image of the island than Sonnino and Franchetti. Still, more than thirty years after Sonnino and Franchetti, Lorenzoni still found western Sicily to be the island's "heart of darkness": the same dilapidated, arid, miserable and violent region of the *latifondo* as in 1876.[5] Small but dense hilltop towns were dotted across an otherwise deserted countryside, and water, roads, and trees were resources as scarce as land ownership.

From the late twentieth century onwards, historical studies have provided us with a more dynamic image of Southern Italy, and also of the Southern Italian *latifondo* and its social actors.[6] Against conventional portraits of unproductive units, dominated by a class of absentee, parasitic proprietors, some scholars have shown that, at least in some cases, the *latifondo* was a solid economic system that could sustain competition even in the international markets of the nineteenth century.[7] The same revisionist scholars have nonetheless pointed out that the Southern *latifondo* witnessed a steady decline from at least the late nineteenth century, becoming increasingly unsustainable from an economic point of view.[8] While *latifondo* economy declined, social unrest and conflicts in the countryside increased in intensity, especially in Sicily. At least two major waves of protest, the Fasci Siciliani between 1893 and 1894, and the land occupations in the *biennio rosso* (the "Red Biennium," 1919–1920) after World War I, perturbed the social order of the *latifondo*.[9] On both occasions, impoverished peasants unionized against *mafiosi* and landowners, demanding agrarian reform and better living and working conditions. Repercussions were on both occasions harsh and bloody, and most demands remained unanswered when Fascism took control. Meanwhile, the booming population of these poor rural areas was providing a high contribution to Italian emigration to the Americas. Between the late nineteenth century and the early twentieth, millions of Italians from the rural regions of the northeast and from most of Southern Italy sailed across the Atlantic, and many of them came from rural Sicily.[10]

The Belice Valley experienced these conflicts acutely. On 2 December 1894, the military killed twenty protesters in Gibellina in one of the bloodiest episodes of the Fasci Siciliani. During the *biennio rosso*, the Mafia killed several members of local cooperative unions and even the priest of Gibellina, Salvatore Caronia, who was actively engaged in supporting the unions.[11] The struggles were in vain, for in the early 1920s the material conditions of life were still bad for the vast majority of the population. Across the area that would be devastated by the earthquake in 1968, more than 100,000 individuals lived in a dozen hilltop towns and villages. These ranged in size from the two biggest agro-towns of the area—Salemi with almost 20,000 inhabitants, and Partanna with 18,000—to middle-sized centers such as Gibellina and Santa Ninfa with 6,000 inhabitants apiece to even smaller villages, such as Salaparuta, Poggioreale, and Contessa Entellina, with between 2,000 and 3,000 inhabitants each.[12] The principal occupation of most residents was agriculture, but only a very few of them had access to land of their own. The percentage of the entire cultivable surface taken up by large estates could sometimes reach and exceed 50 percent. This high proportion of land tied up in estates corresponded to an even smaller number of owners, since a landowner could often own more than one *latifondo*.[13] The rest of the population worked these fields for daily wages and supplemented their poor income with small-scale subsistence farming on the outskirts of the towns.

In the early 1920s, this region was on the verge of a slow but irreversible change. The transformation was initiated under the banner of *bonifica*, land reclamation. The Italian notion of *bonificia* refers to the management of the circulation of water to render land suitable for agriculture, i.e., draining water in excess from marshlands and routing water into arid regions where it was needed most. These interventions were a major factor in the environmental and social transformation in the whole country, especially in the South, where they became, in the wording of Piero Bevilacqua and Manlio Rossi-Doria, a "gigantic initiative of comprehensive reform of the territory."[14] The origins of *bonificia* in Italy date back to Roman times. During the nineteenth century, experts under the Bourbon administration developed a variant of *bonificia* conceived for the specific needs of Southern Italy's landscape and hydrology. The work of these Bourbon experts focused on the hydrological links between the mountains and the coastal plains. They thought that, in order to regulate the seasonal discharge of watercourses and eliminate malarial marshlands along the coast, it was necessary not only to canalize the rivers but to reforest the mountains as well. Innovative as this idea was, the new Kingdom of Italy quickly forgot it, and, especially in the first two decades of the kingdom's existence, the issue of land reclamation in the South was almost completely ignored.[15]

At the beginning of the twentieth century, the issue resurfaced in institutional and scientific debates, but now it was to follow a new set of guidelines. Reclamation was no longer conceived as simply the regulation of rivers to render the coastal plains suitable for agriculture. It was now intended as a series of interventions in the hydraulic regime of rivers, with multiple purposes: to irrigate large areas and transform their agriculture; to provide settlements with a greater quantity of drinkable water; and to obtain a new source of reliable and cheap energy by means of hydroelectric plants. Together with the transformation in water use and regulation, this new kind of reclamation included economic changes resulting from the unprecedented water supply for agriculture and the constant availability of electrical energy as the basis for industrial development.

The most explicit formulation of this new project was advanced by politician and academic Francesco Saverio Nitti. In 1904, Nitti proposed a special law to stimulate the economy of the Basilicata region through reforestation, dams, and hydroelectric plants. In Nitti's vision, the energy thus produced would in turn facilitate industrial development, while the regulation of the hydrological cycle would encourage agricultural improvements. A group of high-ranking officers from the state administration and experts in agronomy and economics elaborated on these ideas in the following years and sought to extend the scope and range of this kind of project across the entire Italian territory.[16] Even Giovanni Lorenzoni dedicated a great deal of attention to water in his 1907 technical report on Sicily for the Inchiesta parlamentare sulle condizioni dei contadini meridionali (Parliamentary Inquiry on the Condition of Southern Peasantry). Not only did he spend several pages describing the hydrological conditions of the island, he also insisted on the centrality of water management for the modernization of Sicilian agriculture via irrigation and the production of electricity, mentioning explicitly the Belice River. The authorities could consistently improve the conditions of western Sicily, he argued, by regulating the Belice River's hydrology through reforestation, the reclamation of malaria-infested floodplains, and the use of river water to irrigate farmland and produce hydroelectricity.[17]

His appeal remained unanswered initially, but more than a decade later, the Belice River would be the first Sicilian river to be involved in such an improvement project. As documented by the historian Giuseppe Barone, Aurelio Drago, a landowner from the region with good political and economic connections, was the first to take the initiative in the area in the early 1920s. He sought support for the construction of a dam and hydroelectric plant on the right branch of the Belice River. In his vision, this would create unprecedented amounts of water for irrigation, while boosting Palermo's energy supply. Between 1921 and 1923, Drago succeeded in bringing into existence the first modern reservoir in Sicily, Lake Piana degli Albanesi. The company that oversaw the work, however, encountered a number of financial problems and was not able to complete many of the planned projects (especially as regards irrigation) until the late 1920s. The Piana degli Albanesi reservoir was certainly a landmark in the process of transforming the landscape and hydrology of western Sicily. Nonetheless, its impact on inland communities was marginal. The energy produced by the reservoir was carried directly to Palermo, while the water provided exclusive irrigation for the agricultural plains upstream of the reservoir. None of the Belice communities and fields, located downstream, saw any of the benefits associated with the reservoir.[18]

The advent of the Fascist regime in 1922 enhanced reclamation in the region. Seduced by the idea of a technocratic solution to the agrarian question and to the social unrest among peasants, the new administrators framed the problems of the South as problems of resources and infrastructure, water supply and roads, rather than as issues of land ownership, labor relations, and living conditions. They consequently saw reclamation as the best and most effective solution at hand, and one that allowed for modernization without the redistribution of economic and political power. Reclamation became the pivot of Fascist rural policies, and in 1927, following a series of new laws in this area, the national parliament passed a new piece of legislation that established a number of specific districts of *trasformazione fondiaria* ("rural estate transformation"). In these newly established districts, those owners who were willing to form a "consortium" would benefit from special financial provisions. Included among these districts were the inland valley of the Belice River and its surroundings.[19] Public funding was a strong incentive for the biggest landowners to cooperate, possibly stronger than the obligation required of them by law, and it was a good opportunity to initiate some of the improvements that many of them had been procrastinating on for a long time.[20] While formally established in 1927, the Consorzio di Bonifica del Belice (Belice Reclamation Consortium) first began to function in earnest in 1929, when its board put engineer Ugo Sartori and agronomist Antonio Bianchi in charge of proposing a program of works to the Ministry of Agriculture for funding. Bianchi and Sartori envisioned improvements in road connections as well as water management works to prevent malaria. In addition, they proposed the creation of a new reservoir on the Belice River. The reservoir would ensure abundant water supply and so make possible a shift from cereals, which were predominant but increasingly unprofitable, to other crops. The Consiglio Superiore dei Lavori Pubblici (Superior Council of Public Works), which had decided on the feasibility of the program of works, accepted most of the proposal, but was unwilling to fund the dam. In the council's opinion, there was no significant potential for a radical agricultural transformation in the area based on large-scale irrigation, only for limited improvements of existing methods.[21]

In 1933, a new law revised the matter, extending the scope and aims of reclamation. Reclamation, according to the new law, was not to be limited to the amelioration of environmental conditions in rural areas; it was to promote a more radical transformation of agricultural systems and economies.

Accordingly, the law supported the formation of new reclamation districts and established a special institute in order to coordinate the consortia all across the island, the Istituto Vittorio Emanuele III per il bonificamento della Sicilia (Institute Vittorio Emanuele III for the Reclamation of Sicily).[22] The Belice Valley was once again the subject of special attention. A commission of experts then drafted a new plan of the works to be undertaken in the area.[23] Besides the classic concerns of reclamation, such as reforestation, water management, and irrigation networks, the 1933 plan insisted on the improvement of the road network and, more importantly, on the creation of new "rural villages" in the most depopulated areas. The idea of "colonizing" the deserted inland areas of Sicily was not new. Many of the towns in the valley were born as "colonial settlements" in the early modern period, when rising demand for cereals pushed *feudatari* to grant special privileges to rural settlers to expand crop cultivation in Sicily.[24] At the turn of the twentieth century, people such as the Parliament-appointed expert Giovanni Lorenzoni considered the settlement pattern of the region to be a major obstacle to the transformation of the rural economy. In these people's opinions, the workforce needed to move closer to the fields, rather than being concentrated in dense hilltop towns. The proposal of "rural villages" introduced in the 1933 reclamation program was, nonetheless, the first actual step in recent times to create the physical infrastructure that would "colonize" the deserted landscape of inland Sicily.

The 1933 program envisioned a broad transformation of the landscape, ecology, and settlement pattern of inland western Sicily. Yet no one believed that the consortium could achieve its ambitious goals in a few short years. As the consortium experts themselves stated, the planned works would "hew a jagged outline out of a featureless piece of stone, stone that is primordial and desert-like in nature." However, in order to "redeem" such a "desert-like" and "primordial" territory and transform it into a modern, productive agricultural area, the experts recognized, "the work of one generation" would not be enough.[25] Moreover, even if the long-term plan were to be accomplished, it would neither alter the structure of land property nor improve consistently the social and environmental lot of the majority of its inhabitants. The consortium had sketched out a path towards reshaping the desolated lands that Sonnino, Franchetti, and Cavalieri had traversed more than fifty years before, but this promised "redemption" would benefit the same old few.

Development Plans

On the eve of the Second World War, the Fascist regime launched a new campaign for the "colonization of the *latifondo*." The aim of this campaign was to stimulate increased settlement of the population in new rural villages dispersed throughout the countryside, and thus advance the transformation of the land. In order to promote this policy, the authorities transformed the Institute Vittorio Emanuele III for the Reclamation of Sicily into Ente per la Colonizzazione del Latifondo Siciliano (Agency for Agrarian Colonization of Sicilian Large Estates) and entrusted it with supporting and coordinating the colonization campaign.[26] Between 1939 and 1940, the new agency undertook the construction of a few villages in several parts of Sicily, where "colonizers" would promote the reclamation and agricultural transformation of the surrounding farmland. The best known and most representative of these settlements was perhaps Borgo Schirò in the Belice area. Mussolini celebrated its completion with a personal visit, and official newsreels disseminated images of the inauguration ceremony.[27] The war soon stopped the Fascist "colonization" of inland Sicily, and historians consider it to have been a failure.[28] Nonetheless, it marked a significant turning point, at least in methodology. All previous reclamation initiatives required the financial cooperation of landowners. The colonization of large estates, on the other hand, was a largely state-funded initiative.[29] In the postwar years, the governments of the new Italian republic would reprise this approach, making the state the principal financial actor in rural policies.

The transition from Fascist to republican rural policies in the Belice Valley did not bring about an immediate change in plans and undertakings. Thanks to funds from the European Recovery Plan—the so-called Marshall Plan—the Belice consortium completed many works initiated before the war, such as the drainage of marshland and floodplains, the chemical extermination of malaria-carrying mosquitoes, and improvements to the road network.[30] The beginning of the 1950s, however, saw a sharper discontinuity. In the aftermath of World War II, an unprecedented peasant movement rose up across the rural areas of Southern Italy.[31] Led by the reestablished labor unions and actively supported by the socialist and communist parties, peasants demanded the redistribution of underexploited large estates, the reform of agrarian labor laws, and the official recognition of cooperative production units. Once again, they faced violent repression, murders, and sometimes mass slaughters, committed either by the Mafia or by the police. This movement was intense in inland Sicily, and so was its repression.[32] On May Day 1947, Salvatore Giuliano's gang shot into the crowd occupying an estate in Portella della Ginestra, killing eleven people. Besides the countless police raids and the arrest of protesters, the Mafia also killed several union leaders in western Sicily. In 1950, bringing to a close a long cycle of peasant struggles, Parliament approved a law on agrarian reform. This law enabled the expropriation of a certain proportion of large estates and codified the redistribution of land property among poor peasants. In the same year, the Regione Siciliana, the island's newly established self-governing institution, adopted its own agrarian reform law. The regional authorities put the former Agency for Agrarian Colonization of Sicilian Large Estates in charge of supervising the process and renamed it Ente per la Riforma Agraria in Sicilia (Agency for Agrarian Reform in Sicily).[33]

Agrarian reform was only half of the picture. After the war, the U.S. administration and the recently established International Monetary Fund and World Bank became active advocates of "development." The postwar notion of "development" involved the stimulation of the economic growth and the social and cultural transformation of "poor" countries and regions by means of infrastructural improvements and legislative reforms.[34] On 10 August 1950, within this international framework, the Italian authorities established the Cassa per il Mezzogiorno (Fund for the South). The Cassa was the Italian version of a development institution, rooted in a longer national tradition of special policies for the South. Thanks to massive funding from the World Bank, the Cassa had an enormous amount of money at its disposal and the power to bypass ordinary procedures. The Cassa projected the modernization of agriculture and the rural landscape into a more ambitious long-term vision. Its goal was to reduce the gap between the South and the North via infrastructural and environmental improvements and create the material conditions for a "pre-industrialization" of the *Mezzogiorno*.[35] Alongside traditional rural improvement works, it promoted the construction of aqueducts, roads, telephone lines, railroads, and so forth. The Cassa per il Mezzogiorno became the most powerful actor in the enactment of national policies for the South, and thanks to its large financial resources and autonomy of action, it was able to boost the public intervention in the rural regions of Southern Italy enormously.[36]

From the start, the Cassa intervened in the Belice Valley, acting at multiple levels. The first intervention was the direct undertaking of infrastructural works. In the late 1920s, the Fascist administration had initiated the construction of a large aqueduct pipeline to tap water from the mountains of central Sicily to Trapani on the western coast.[37] Construction work on the aqueduct had stopped before the war, leaving the infrastructure only half-completed. The Cassa funded the completion of the aqueduct. The new "Montescuro West" aqueduct was completed in the mid-1950s, and on its way to the city of Trapani, it served several municipalities in the Belice Valley, bringing potable water to Poggioreale, Gibellina, and Salaparuta, among others.[38] In addition, the Cassa provided extensive funding to the newly established Agency for Agrarian Reform in Sicily and the Belice Reclamation Consortium.[39] In 1950, in the midst of a general reframing of the policy on Southern Italy, the authorities reclassified the Belice district yet again, renaming it a "district of integral transformation." The authorities reserved this label for only three areas of Sicily, in which the Cassa per il Mezzogiorno was to oversee a "special" and more comprehensive development "therapy." In the Belice "district of integral transformation," the Cassa would fund entirely the construction of roads and bridges, the regulation of the hydraulic regime of the Belice River, the complete eradication of malaria, the completion of water storage and irrigation infrastructure, and the creation of new "rural villages."[40] Actually, although they were appearing under a new label, these were the same objectives as in the reclamation plans of the 1930s, including the policy of inland colonization via new settlements. The ultimate purpose was, once again, to "redeem" the *latifondo* region by improving quantity and quality of agricultural production. This meant also bringing rural workforce nearer to the lands they farmed, creating in the process a new class of small landowners and producers who would act as a bulwark against social unrest.

In 1952, the renewed Belice Reclamation Consortium detailed its plan for the district. The 1950 reform of the consortium had consistently extended its surface area from that of the 1930s: from an original expanse of 79,528 hectares, it had now reached 103,000 hectares (see figure 5.1), covering nineteen municipalities and becoming, in the wording of its president, "the biggest consortium in Sicily."[41] The 1952 report analyzed the district's geological and lithological conditions, the hydrology of the Belice River, the climate and rainfall in the area, and the characteristics of human settlements and activities. The report claimed that malaria infestation was declining thanks to the eradication campaigns of the 1940s. Water shortage, however, remained a persistent obstacle to agricultural development. Average rainfall was only 92 days per year and most rainwater fell in a few prolonged showers. This caused extreme variation in the hydraulic discharge of the Belice tributaries, which turned from almost nonexistent trickles into torrential streams after heavy rain, and of Belice River itself, which ranged from hundreds of cubic meters per second in the winter to point zero in the summer. A predominance of impermeable soils, which were in turn susceptible to erosion, and the uneven distribution of other water sources worsened the situation. The lack of infrastructure was another major impediment to development. In spite of what the consortium had done in the 1930s and the 1940s, the road network was still inadequate for the needs of modern agriculture. Vehicles could hardly reach the internal part of the district, and this was all the more problematic when one considers that most of the workforce still resided far from cultivable areas.[42]

The consortium sought to address these issues in a coordinated manner. Consortium experts of course planned the further improvement of the road network. This had been on the reclamation agenda since the beginning of reclamation projects in the late 1920s, but the extent of the network envisioned by the 1952 plan was unprecedented. Moreover, to encourage the cultivation of even the most remote corners of the district, consortium experts planned the creation of new "rural villages" and the consolidation of the existing ones. The consortium then turned its attention to water storage and distribution. Given the climate and hydrology of the region, the only way to augment water supply was by promoting reforestation, terracing, the creation of reservoirs, and "rural aqueducts" to distribute water throughout the district. Trees and terraces would ensure that water flowed more slowly, thereby enhancing the penetration and retention of rainwater into the soil, reducing the risk of landslides, reinforcing groundwater sources, and enabling a more constant discharge of tributary creeks into the main rivers. Reservoirs and water pipes would ensure that even inconsistent rainwater would be enough to irrigate significant portions of the district. More importantly, the consortium experts revamped the idea of constructing two dams along the course of the Belice River to store water during the rainy seasons for use during the dry seasons. Thirteen smaller reservoirs and a network of pipelines would complete the system and allow the constant irrigation of large areas for four months every year, from June until September.[43]

Water storage and irrigation had, like roads, already been part of the 1933 plan. The 1933 plan had envisioned the construction of two dams on the Belice River as a means of converting the local agricultural system to irrigation. The Superior Council of Public Works, though, had discarded that part of the proposal as unlikely. The development goals and massive funding granted by the Cassa per il Mezzogiorno changed the rules of the game and justified the reintroduction of irrigation into the consortium program. The 1952 plan thus reprised the original 1933 idea of two reservoirs, but expanded its scope and ambition, envisioning the integration of the dams into a capillary system of smaller reservoirs and coupling all reservoirs with large-scale environmental engineering. With an increased and reliable water supply in place, it would then be possible for the area to move away from cereal monoculture. The cultivation of cereals occupied more than 80 percent of the entire surface area of the reclamation district as it was before the agrarian reform, and improvements in cereal cultivation were not enough to modernize the districts. Cultivating wheat, argued the report, even using more up-to-date methods, could never be economically sustainable in the smaller productive units envisioned by the agrarian reform. With reservoirs and aqueducts, however, it would become possible to shift to more profitable, water-intensive sorts of crops.

Despite some innovative proposals and the addition of many new technical details, the recurring ideas, such as the need for rural villages, were still largely dependent on an old-fashioned vision of the rural world. While the 1952 plan insisted on the potential for agricultural change, the conservative ideal of small-scale farming as a pillar of social order and stability was just as influential as the entire agrarian reform and the development agenda of the Cassa. The results of agrarian reform in the Belice Valley largely failed to live up to expectations. The district saw only a minor redistribution of property titles. Before the reform, large estates (more than 200 hectares) covered 21,190 hectares of the entire surface area of the district, whereas in 1952 they accounted for 18,000 hectares, a reduction of only 14 percent.⁴⁴ To be sure, raw data on property distribution does not count the land handed over to the care of peasants via long-term rental contracts known as *enfiteusi*. Yet *enfiteusi* could be hardly be considered equitable property redistribution: while they did not give full and complete propriety rights to the farmers, they burdened them with the labor and all the costs associated with cultivation and land improvement and granted only a yearly percentage of the profits to the owner.⁴⁵ Behind the propaganda of developmental agencies, therefore, social relations remained highly imbalanced in favor of large estate owners. Decision-making processes in the renewed reclamation consortium mirrored this inequality: the consortium assembly took decisions on investments and improvements using a weighted voting system based on the amount of land owned.⁴⁶ Small farmers did not have a voice in the decisions which mattered most to them.

Grassroots Countermeasures

While rural reformers held onto the dream of a conservative community of small farmers and simultaneously maintained the heavily imbalanced power relationships that contradicted their dream, Italy experienced one of the most rapid and tumultuous phases of economic growth and social transformation in its history. After the long and hard years of postwar reconstruction, all indicators of economic performance, from the GDP to energy consumption, were showing a rapid rise. Industrial production, once concentrated in a small portion of Northern Italy, expanded its presence and importance in other regions, while new products such as automobiles and home appliances transformed the everyday life of many Italians. At the end of this period, known as the Italian economic miracle, Italy joined the exclusive club of the most industrialized countries on the planet. According to these same statistics and indicators, however, the rural *Mezzogiorno* remained far behind. Despite the attempts of postwar reformers, industrialization in the South was nothing but a chimera and modern intensive farming had not taken off. In most rural areas, the average income was low, and unemployment was widespread.⁴⁷ The only "high performing" sector was emigration, which thrived during this period. Between 1955 and 1971, more than seven million people, mostly in Southern Italy, left their homes and towns to reach the industrial cities of Northern Italy, northern Europe, and overseas.⁴⁸

Faced with the failure of past initiatives, reformers tried to redress southern development policies. Whereas, in the postwar years, the Cassa per il Mezzogiorno and the other developmental agencies based their interventions on agricultural improvement and infrastructure, from the mid-1950s a new industrialist approach gained momentum. According to new ideas, the state should intervene in the country's most depressed area by encouraging the creation of industrial plants, either by providing advantageous conditions to attract private investors, or by directly establishing publicly owned companies. In 1957, a new law "for the industrial development of Southern Italy" tried to push this new direction in development policy, calling for the state to directly become involved in industrialization via special planning initiatives.[49] This would have important consequences for Sicily and, indirectly, for the Belice Valley. Sicily remained a crucial part of the new industrial strategy, and the authorities promoted the establishment of several factories on the island.[50] Yet the Belice Valley, which until that moment had been a core area in all reclamation and development initiatives, slowly but irreversibly fell off the new map of industrial development. In the new vision of change, investments in agriculture were no longer the priority; and a remote inland region such as the Belice district was certainly not well suited as a site for modern industrial plants.

While the Belice Valley disappeared from national development agendas, it captured the attention of a new breed of reformers. In 1951, Danilo Dolci, a young man from Trieste, decided to migrate from Northern Italy to the village of Trappeto in northwestern Sicily. Following his degree in architecture in Milan, and a short sojourn in Nomadelfia—a Christian community for orphaned children, founded by the Catholic priest Zeno Saltini after the war—Dolci was seeking a place where he could help people in need. He had visited Trappeto as a child, when he followed his father, an employee of the railroad company, and he remembered the place as the most miserable he had ever seen. In 1951, he found that little had changed. The population lived on the edge of survival, unemployment was rife, sanitary conditions were extremely bad, and there were almost no social services such as schools and hospitals. Once he was established there, he initiated an inquiry into the living conditions of the population and performed non-violent protests to draw the situation to the attention of the authorities and the press.[51] The visibility he obtained through his actions soon gained Dolci the support of a number of activists and intellectuals across Italy and allowed him to extend his research to cover "banditry" in the area round Trappeto and, later, social conditions in the city of Palermo.[52]

Dolci wrote up this later activity into two books, "*Banditi a Partinico*" (Bandits in Partinico) in 1955 and "*Inchiesta a Palermo*" (Report from Palermo) in 1956.[53] The books were a collage of different materials: short reflections and exposés written by Dolci himself; letters and documents; facts, figures, and reports on housing, work, health, and education; and transcripts of oral interviews with the locals. The use of interviews and first-hand accounts was the most unconventional and striking feature of Dolci's work. His inquiries reinstated personal experience and gave voice to the viewpoint and the words of those who had been until that time only the "object" of sociological research. The thesis of the books was simple and direct: the reasons for the existence of "bandits" in Partinico and crime in Palermo were the lack of education, resources, and employment in the area. The public authorities, Dolci maintained, had until then responded to a social and economic problem with weapons and violence. This strategy was illogical and had proved ineffective. In Dolci's opinion, it would be much more productive to invest money and resources in eradicating the causes of ignorance and poverty.

Local action to bring about change was essential to Dolci's vision. From 1954 onward, Dolci and his growing group of followers organized various activities together with the local population, circulated documents and reports, set up a "popular university," and organized public demonstrations. The goal of all these actions was to promote "development" in the area by prompting the authorities to intervene. According to Dolci and his collaborators, this meant two things in particular. First, the authorities had to improve infrastructure in the towns by providing them with a domestic water supply, sewage systems, and so forth. Second, they had to improve the environmental conditions of the region by undertaking those works already planned by the Cassa per il Mezzogiorno, the Agency for Agrarian Reform, and the Reclamation Consortia—works such as roads, dams, and irrigation canals. This would ameliorate the living conditions of the residents and create job opportunities.[54] The actions in this cause peaked with the *sciopero alla rovescia* (strike in reverse) on 3 February 1956. Revisiting a traditional form of protest by the peasantry, Dolci and his collaborators organized for a group of unemployed peasants from the area to repair an old, disused donkey trail. This initiative was designed to show how unemployed people could be a valuable resource in the improvement of local infrastructure. Although it was a non-violent protest, the police intervened to disperse the gathering and arrested many participants, including Dolci himself.[55]

While he was still in prison for the strike in reverse, the prefect of Rome denounced Dolci, together with the publisher Alberto Carocci, for their "obscenity and immoral behavior." Their alleged crime consisted in having reported, without censure, the life-story of Gino O., who recounted the practices of sexual initiation in which criminal organizations required aspiring young robbers in Palermo to participate. The trials resulting from the strike in reverse and the accusation of obscenity struck a chord with the general public. Both aspects of Dolci's activities—research and protest—were under attack, and widespread support for Dolci sprung up amongst Italian intellectuals and academics. Numerous committees were formed in many cities and organized support meetings and demonstrations in the name of free research and social inquiry, claiming that "public morality" could not obstruct access to knowledge and reporting on reality, even when this reality was at its darkest.[56] In the wake of the trials and the books, Dolci and his activities gathered more support in Italy and abroad. During this period, Dolci established relationships with Bertrand Russell, Jean-Paul Sartre, Eric Fromm, and Aldous Huxley; his books were translated and published in several countries (Huxley wrote the preface to the UK edition of *Report from Palermo*), and "Friends of Danilo Dolci" groups were formed in several European countries. These international networks enabled Dolci to raise funds for his projects in Sicily. His growing popularity then encouraged young activists to join his struggle.[57]

In the wake of the new legislation to encourage industrial development in the South, and thanks to increasing public approval of his activities, Dolci's protest took a step forward. At the end of 1957, he organized a meeting in Palermo devoted to the issue of "full employment." Several Italian politicians and scholars attended the meeting: the founder of the Cassa per il Mezzogiorno Pasquale Saraceno, union leaders Bruno Trentin and Vittorio Foa, politicians Giorgio Napolitano and Ferruccio Parri, economist Federico Caffè, sociologist Paolo Sylos Labini, and the researchers from the journal *Il Mulino*. This meeting directly addressed the main issues of the special policies for Southern Italy. As already discussed, by the mid-1950s political parties, economists, and scholars were openly debating the failures and shortcomings of postwar development policies, a debate that led to the so-called "second phase" of special intervention in the South. The prior environmental and infrastructural improvements undertaken by development agencies had not revitalized southern economy enough to provide employment and income to a large population of impoverished peasants, and emigration was rife once again. The 1957 meeting took up this general tenor and all participants seemed to acknowledge the need for new development policies based on economic plans. "The State"—reads the anonymous introduction to the proceedings—"... has the technical and political instruments for the realization of a plan: the financial and banking network, the industrial groups IRI and ENI. An important part of Italian society is now mature enough to pretend that ... these instruments would be controlled, directed, and used for the interest of society."[58]

Despite agreeing on a "planning turn," participants diverged over conceptions of the planning process itself. For the representatives of many institutions, the lack of success of special intervention in Southern Italy was due to the failure to embrace industrialization more fully. To obtain better results, they argued, the authorities would have to shift the focus away from rural restructuring and towards industrial development, as envisaged by the newly ratified legislation. For Dolci and his group, on the contrary, the main problem was the top-down approach that had held sway until then, with the national and regional authorities imposing overarching plans on local communities without their consent. Accordingly, Dolci and his group demanded a turn towards "democratic planning." They held that the planning authorities should involve local communities in their decision-making and allow them to supervise plans and their realization. If this principle, which was more attentive to the desires and needs of the locals, was applied, even traditional policies of rural modernization could still be effective and grant "full employment."⁵⁹ As a demonstration of his method and of its potential, Dolci presented the results of a survey he and a group of collaborators had carried out in the Palermo area. Researchers had interviewed locals about what they deemed necessary to improve their community. They had then combined their responses into a program of interventions to undertake, including the use of manure (usually dumped on the outskirts of towns) as a fertilizer in agriculture, the introduction of new kinds of crops (mainly olive trees and grapevines), the construction of roads and reservoirs for irrigation, the introduction of cattle-breeding, and reforestation.⁶⁰ The outline of this program was not so different from the reclamation plans elaborated in previous years. The specific contents, however, were more specifically targeted at the needs of peasants and small farmers, rather than those of large-estate owners, as had previously been the case.

In the following months and years, Dolci and his group began to apply this method to the Belice district. A few months after the meeting, Dolci was awarded the Lenin Prize, a Soviet version of the Nobel Peace Prize which—like its Swedish equivalent—came with a large amount of money. Thanks to this funding, Dolci was able to establish a network of Centers of Research and Initiatives for Full Employment (Centri studi e iniziative per la piena occupazione) across western Sicily, aimed at organizing and supporting protests and inquiries into development issues.⁶¹ The first public output of this new phase was the book *Spreco* ("Waste"), published in 1960.⁶² The book consisted of research carried out in various parts of western Sicily by the affiliated centers in collaboration with local communities and experts, and for the first time, several towns in the Belice Valley were included in Dolci's project. Using the voices of local people, the book described a world of violence, superstition, illiteracy, and oppression: overcrowded housing made of poor materials, villages without any sanitary infrastructure, rampant unemployment, absent public services, and a stronger-than-ever rural Mafia that violently opposed peasant unions. This "waste" of men and resources all across western Sicily could nonetheless be turned into its opposite by means of planning: the organized use of all the resources of the environment and the local communities in order to ensure their "development."⁶³

Just like the local reformers before them, Dolci and his group believed that water was key to developing the Belice Valley. The battle for dams and irrigation systems was integral to Dolci's activity from the very beginning. In 1955, Dolci pointed out that lack of water was the root cause of the presence of bandits in Partinico, and fought for the construction of a dam on the Jato River.⁶⁴ At the end of the 1950s, this battle had brought about its first results, and the construction of a dam on the Jato was underway.⁶⁵ This must therefore have seemed like a good angle of attack in the Belice Valley too. Dams and reservoirs could turn water into the principal instrument of development of the region by retaining and storing an average of 200 million cubic meters of water per year. The Belice Reclamation Consortium had envisioned the construction of the biggest reservoir in a place called Bruca, near the village of Roccamena. According to agronomist Malpede, the water from that reservoir would allow the constant irrigation of the surrounding region and thereby foster major agricultural change.[66] The locals clearly believed in the potential of water storage and irrigation. "If the Bruca dam existed," declared a local farmer, "the entire valley down to Menfi, everything below Poggioreale and Salaparuta, would be a wonderful garden, there would be cool air and one could work and eat in the shade; a new life. All cool air, all green, with orange trees too; the land that now costs one million, would cost four or five. Up to the mountains, where the steepest slopes are, it could all be woods and almond groves … and even some vineyards. … Below, if that lake were made, everything would change: a great garden 30 kilometers long, from Roccamena to Menfi, and we could also have electricity from the dam."[67] Dolci and his collaborators shared this vision entirely. Irrigation, to them, could be the basis of a social and environmental revolution.

The Many Virtues of Water

In the wake of the expansion of Dolci's activity in western Sicily, the Centers of Research and Initiatives for Full Employment established a new branch in the town of Roccamena, the closest town to the planned dam in the Belice reclamation district. In 1961, Lorenzo Barbera, an activist from Partinico who had joined Dolci in 1956, moved to Roccamena to lead this branch and experiment with the methods of social inquiry and mobilization that Dolci had used in previous years in Partinico. He started by facilitating regular discussions among the locals on various issues related to the prospects of development in the region. Discussions and meetings took place regularly over almost a year, and then Barbera and the most active participants decided to establish a comitato di sviluppo di Roccamenta (Roccamena Development Committee).[68] The founding charter stated the need to ignite a process of development based on local resources in order to stop emigration from Roccamena. The document of the committee, in particular, insisted on the construction of the dam on the Belice River. In April 1962, the newly established Roccamena Development Committee called a meeting of experts, social activists, and locals. The attendees stressed once again the importance of water storage and distribution. Irrigation, in their opinion, would also indirectly stimulate the creation of food-processing plants and so sow the seeds of industrial development.[69]

In 1961, construction on the dam on the Belice River had not yet started.[70] After making long and extensive inquiries of the authorities to establish why work on the dam was not underway, the Roccamena Development Committee and the network of centers led by Dolci scheduled a series of coordinated protest initiatives for the autumn of 1963. The first step was a postal campaign. The activists of the committees sent a number of letters to the responsible authorities simultaneously, trying to force them to reply. The campaign eventually gained the attention of the ministry for the Cassa per il Mezzogiorno, Giulio Pastore. Writing back directly to Danilo Dolci, Pastore retraced the bureaucratic history of the project and announced that the authorities had recently suspended it due to "perplexities of a technical and geological order."[71] Despite this letter, the mobilization went on as planned, and, on 3 November, the committees and Barbera's center organized a protest march to the location where the authorities had envisioned the dam. According to the police, more than 1,200 people attended the demonstration.[72] "A mass of people went to Bruca and Casalotto ..." recounted an inhabitant of Roccamena. "People from abroad, people from everywhere.... It seemed to be an enormous party with all of these people greeting each other.... I have never seen so many people in our town."[73] In the meantime, "Friends of Danilo Dolci" groups organized sit-ins in Bonn and London to support the protest in Sicily, and a filmmaker produced a documentary about the march.[74]

The initiative was not without consequences. A few months after the demonstration, a group of experts from the Ministry of Public Works came to Roccamena to study the geology of the area where the dam was to be built. After this field trip, the experts concluded that the original site was definitely not suitable for the dam. However, they proposed an alternative: a dam could be constructed far more safely on a lower part of the river, in a place named Garcia.[75] The Roccamena committee initially feared that the new project would exclude local landowners from irrigation and requested in vain to be included in the decision-making about the location.[76] The issue stalled for another year, and, not wanting the issue to be lost from sight, the committees organized a week-long protest in March 1965.[77] The protest ended with meetings with the authorities in Palermo and Rome, who once again promised to take care of the issue as soon as possible.[78] Whereas these demonstrations were somewhat inconclusive, they were accompanied by intense activism on the ground. While leading the campaign for the dam, Lorenzo Barbera and the small group of activists he had gathered in Roccamena were ceaselessly engaged in promoting new "development committees" in other towns in the Belice region. "At that time," recalled Lorenzo Barbera later, "my young first wife and I, with our two little children in our arms, went to a different town every night to have assemblies. Fabrizio was our oldest child, between two and a half and three and a half years old.... We were attending so many assemblies that every time we asked him what he wanted to do as a job, he replied he wanted to do the 'town committees.'"[79] Thanks to their hard work, new development committees formed in most towns and villages in the region, from Santa Ninfa to Partanna, involving not only researchers, activists, and local people, but also mayors and town councilors, such as Santa Ninfa's mayor and communist party member Vito Bellafiore.[80] These committees joined to form a larger *comitato intercomunale* (intermunicipal committee). The town of Partanna became the new headquarters, and Barbera transferred to there the branch of the Center of Research and Initiatives for Full Employment that had hitherto been located in Roccamena.[81]

In the wake of the protest over the dam in 1965, the Center of Research and Initiatives in Partanna published the first issue of a new journal entitled *Pianificazione Siciliana* (Sicilian Planning). The founders conceived *Pianificazione Siciliana* to be the voice of the newly established inter-municipal committee and "as an arena for in-depth discussions on local development."[82] "The entire area that we represent," explained Barbera in the first issue, "is unified by the presence of three dams, already built or to be built. The Carboi Dam, the dam on the left section of the Belice River, and the Piano di Campo Dam. These three dams will determine the irrigation of 25–30 thousand hectares: and subsequently, new developments, new jobs, the transformation of culture, the creation and commercial development of new [agricultural] products, etc., and the distribution of the water from the new reservoirs."[83] Irrigation-based development, in sum, was the core of a vision that bound together the network of committees and the geographical area they covered.

Pianificazione Siciliana did indeed become an arena for reports, plans, and debates on local development. Each issue contained a detailed "monograph" on one or more towns. These municipalities had in many cases never had the means to collect statistical data beyond the decennial national censuses, and even the studies by the various public agencies engaged in development projects did not usually contain any data on the living conditions of the population.[84] The "monographs" in *Pianificazione Siciliana*, therefore, offered what was in most cases the only available information on the evolving demography, health, education, income levels, jobs and productive activities, sanitary infrastructure, and the like. The journal in practice assumed those functions normally carried out by the public administration, gathering valuable knowledge on population, territory, and resources across the entire region. In addition, *Pianificazione Siciliana* was constantly scrutinizing institutional development plans, making counter-proposals regarding what these should address and why. Bit by bit, this research activity was producing an increasingly detailed picture of the area, and at the same time advancing a new program for rural reform. Unlike previous plans, the focus on water and irrigation pushed the committees to embrace the entire Belice River catchment area. Seeing the Belice River catchment area as a unit had no precedent, neither in the ordinary administrative division of the territory nor in the geographical understanding of the development agencies. The former was based on municipalities and provinces, both bureaucratic units that disregarded physical and hydrological formations; the latter was based on the "reclamation district," which had incorporated only a smaller portion of the river basin. The committees, however, believed the basin was the "ideal" political and social space for democratic planning and the "ideal" environmental unit for a coordinated project of rural reform and modernization based on irrigation.[85]

In 1967, the committees synthesized an overall development plan for the Belice Valley. First, the plan envisioned a radical reorganization of the admin-

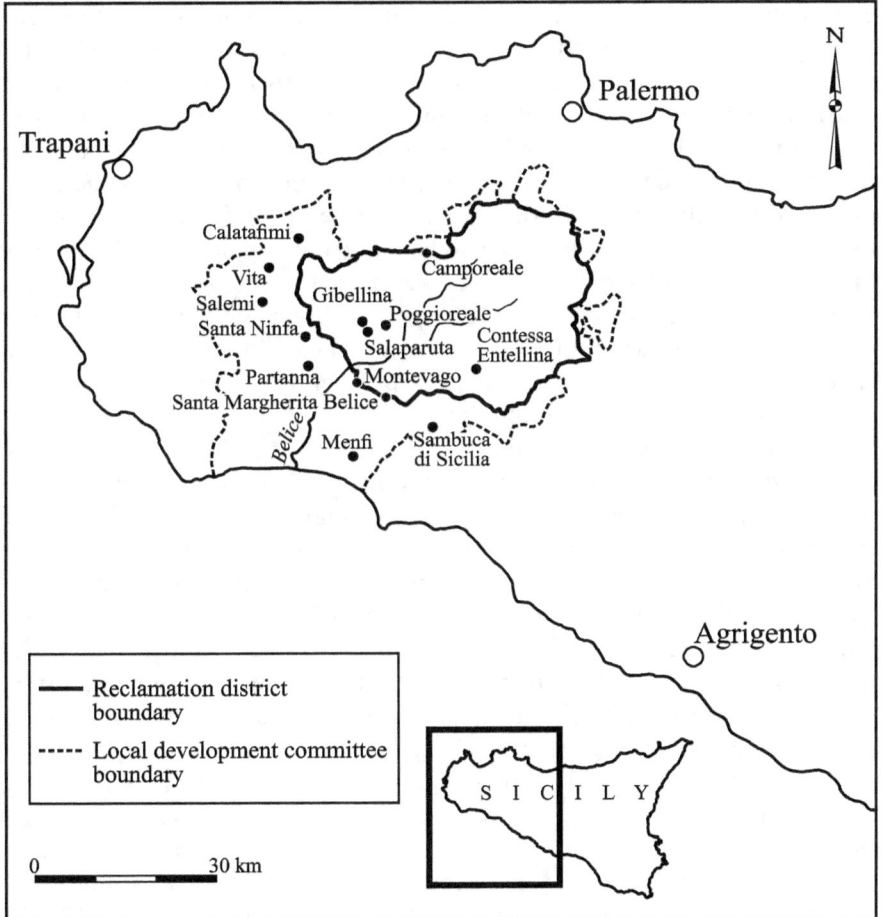

Figure 5.1. Boundaries of the Belice Reclamation District and of the Local Development Committee organization. Cartography by Mary Lee Eggart.

istrative division of the region, to eliminate overlapping tasks among agencies such as the Agency for Agrarian Reform, the Cassa per il Mezzogiorno, and the various reclamation consortia. The municipalities had to become the base units of planning, for they were seen as the most directly accessible institutions and the closest to the local population. The municipal plans, in turn, would be synthesized into broader district plans. A regional board covering the entire island would subsequently coordinate the district plans, reporting directly to the Regione Siciliana and the national government. The committees thus envisioned a bottom-up decision-making structure: from the local, represented by the municipalities, up to the national level. The river valley was the principal level of synthesis of the planning exercise. Their plan incorporated the infrastructure envisioned by the reclamation consortium in 1952 in its entirety. The committees mentioned by name the construction of five reservoirs among those planned or in construction, of which the one on the Belice River remained the most important. Reforestation, road network improvements, and districtwide irrigation would then complement water storage. According to the committees, irrigation could generate more than 30,000 new jobs in the valley, by integrating agricultural reform with the creation of infrastructure to process wine, oil, and milk.[86] The improvement in the living conditions of the local communities was as important as boosting the economic development of the area. The illiteracy rate in the area was more than 60 percent, so the plan stressed the importance of new public schools. Every house was also to have tap water and sewerage to improve the material conditions and the health of residents. Finally, the committees requested the exclusion of convicted or suspected *mafiosi* from all public appointments.[87]

This plan had clear progressive ambitions. The authorities had, until then, conceived development as a process of modernization and economic growth, but had not connected that to emancipation and social justice. The change the committees imagined, on the other hand, involved not just irrigation and agricultural modernization, but also social structures, culture, and power relations. These progressive goals could only be achieved by making the communities active players in the process, rather than solely passive targets of top-down schemes. Mobilization and protest were thus not only important tools in forcing the authorities to act, but also a means of reinforcing the role of the local inhabitants as agents of change. New protests and demonstrations preceded and accompanied the presentation of the plan to the public: namely, the committees organized a "March for Western Sicily," which started on 6 March 1967, beginning in the Belice Valley and ending in Palermo six days later. Police records downplayed the importance and success of this initiative, and apparently some local mayors who had previously been involved in the committees decided to boycott this particular initiative because they felt it was "too politicized."[88] Nevertheless, the March for Western Sicily gained media attention. On foot, on mule or horseback, or riding Vespas or horse-drawn carts, protesters crossed the entire valley, from Castelvetrano to Menfi, from Santa Margherita Belice to Roccamena (see figure 5.2). The march ended in front of the regional parliament building in Palermo, and a senior officer from the regional government received a representative from the committees, promising as always to consider their requests attentively.[89]

Yet more than thirty years after the first reclamation program, the dam on the Belice River was still only a promise, a promise which the authorities repeated reassuringly after every new protest. Despite the ceaseless activism of the committees, the various development agencies responsible for the area, from the Cassa to the Agency for Agrarian Reform and the Belice Reclamation Consortium, had done nothing or almost nothing towards either the dam or the other investment programs. The "industrial turn" in development policies

Figure 5.2. The March for Western Sicily. Picture by Toni Nicolini. Courtesy of CRAF (Centro di Ricerca e Archiviazione della Fotografia).

for the South after 1957 explains this inertia at least in part. Projections of employment patterns in the future showed that agricultural labor was shrinking and that, therefore, investments in agricultural modernization would not be effective in ensuring occupation. Between the 1950s and the 1960s, state planning agencies and private companies installed capital-intensive factories, often devoted to petrochemical processing, in coastal areas such as Milazzo in northern Sicily, Gela in the south, and Augusta in the east.[90] These industrial investments were the focus of all their efforts and resources, while attention to rural inland regions decreased. The strong uptake in migratory flows in the 1960s from all the Belice Valley towns most probably reinforced the conviction that any investment by the central state agencies in that area would be useless.[91]

During these years, the Regione Siciliana government put forward two plans for the economic development and spatial redistribution of economic activities across the island. In 1965, in particular, one of these plans proposed a program of urbanization in the Belice Valley. This included a main road connection from Palermo to the southern coast and shared infrastructure and "services," such as schools and hospitals, for the Belice towns. The ultimate goal was to create an "urbanization strip" in the inland area to balance increasing coastal urbanization.[92] This plan, however, did not include any industrial initiatives, and in 1967, the valley was omitted almost entirely from a new development scheme put forward by the socialist regional councilor for economic development, Calogero Mangione.[93] Whereas the committees did not succeed in convincing the authorities to invest in, or to substantially improve the living conditions in the valley and in the communities, their activity at least had the effect of keeping public attention focused on the area. The grassroots plans and protest initiatives raised awareness of the conditions and needs of the valley's communities, which persisted in spite of the new investment priorities of the public authorities.

This, then, was Belice Valley on the eve of the earthquake. Unforeseen by all, the earthquake extended over precisely the region that had been the site of so many planning and development initiatives. The disaster would propel the Belice Valley and its communities to the center of public debate, forcing the authorities to reconsider their plans and deal with radically new expectations.

Conclusions

On the eve of the 1968 earthquake, the Belice Valley was no longer the deserted and dilapidated landscape depicted by Sidney Sonnino in 1876. From 1930s to the 1950s, a carousel of agencies and bodies elaborated various plans for reforming the area. Despite the continuing polemical arguments, justified demands, and popular struggles for more substantial improvement, we should not overlook the fact that some of these initiatives *were* successful, and a transformation was already underway. Thanks to three decades of special funding, new roads connected not just the main centers of the valley but also some of the smallest ones, such as Gibellina, Poggioreale, and Salaparuta. These roads were for the most part suitable for motor vehicles and rendered the connection between the towns in the valley much easier than in the recent past. The funding from the Cassa per il Mezzogiorno had also been at work, consistently improving the technological infrastructure of the area, introducing telephone lines, electricity cables, and providing most towns with increased supply of potable water. The rural landscape was also changing. Malaria was no longer a menace, thanks to canalization of streams, the reclamation of floodplains, and the decisive contribution of chemicals after World War II. The law on agrarian reform in 1950 had favored a limited, often unjust, but still appreciable redistribution of cultivable land into smaller units to the benefit of a greater number of farmers.

The local communities had changed even more. As early as 1961, the population of the smallest towns, such as Poggioreale, Gibellina, and Salaparuta had diminished by several hundreds of people compared to the census in 1951, and in the biggest towns, such as Partanna and Salemi, the losses were even higher. In the following years, the migratory flow from the towns in the Belice Valley increased still further, reaching unprecedented numbers.[94] Those who remained, on the other hand, had become involved in protest and mobilization. The area had a long tradition of political activism and social struggle, dating back at least to the Fasci Siciliani in 1893–1894. After World War II, western inland Sicily had been one of the centers of land occupation and struggles for agrarian reform and land redistribution. The mobilization promoted by Danilo Dolci, Lorenzo Barbera, and their associates in the 1960s, however, had new features. The development committees associated plans for environmental and landscape transformation, until then exclusively promoted by top-down agencies, with their demands for social justice and emancipation. Those two aspects were interlaced into a comprehensive vision of socio-ecological reform that involved the rural environment, the infrastructure of the area, and the social and economic conditions of the local communities.

Despite the social and physical changes in the region, other things remained unaltered. As denounced by the inquiries and reports produced by the local committees, housing conditions in the valley's towns were extremely bad: no sanitary facilities, cohabitation with livestock, poor construction materials, no insulation, and so forth. Potable water supplied by means of the new Montescuro aqueduct was generally available only through public fountains, the transport situation, although improved, was still far from national standards, and unemployment and poverty were still rife. The dam on the Belice River, the pivot of rural modernization plans, was still at the planning stage, and cereal monoculture dominated the landscape. The new direction of public policies for Southern Italy, moreover, was bringing about a marginalization of the Belice Valley in the name of state-sponsored industry along the coasts. This largely justified the demands of the committees for more substantial improvements and for new investment from the national and regional authorities. The failure to realize these improvements, despite the ceaseless demands of the local communities, magnified the physical and social effects of the 1968 earthquakes. This increases the responsibility of the contemporary authorities for the immense material devastation and the tragic social impact of the earthquake.

Whilst unveiling the failures of an entire season of rural reforms, the earthquake would also reopen the debate on the valley's development and transformation, including the question of industrial development. The peculiar earthquake geography, which corresponded almost exactly to the borders of the Belice Valley according to the development committees, established the "Belice Valley" as the principal spatial unit for recovery and intervention in the region. Yet the absence of the pre-earthquake history from the aftermath debate is striking. As we have seen, TV and newspapers represented the Belice Valley as a relic from the past and the epitome of the stagnant and backward *Mezzogiorno*, without taking into account the dynamism and transformation of that area in the years leading up to the earthquake. Furthermore, the debate over reconstruction laws and policies seemed to completely ignore the existence of a long history of plans for the improvement and socio-environmental reform of the region. Most importantly, that debate, and most of its legislative outcomes, completely overlooked the existence of active local communities, at least until the protest in Montecitorio Square. The confrontation between residents and top-down plans, between long-standing claims for rural development policies and industrial horizons, between pre-earthquake plans and post-earthquake expectations would characterize and influence the entire reconstruction process.

Notes

1. Leopoldo Franchetti and Sidney Sonnino, *La Sicilia nel 1876* (Florence, 1925), 175. See Nelson J. Moe, "The Emergence of the Southern Question in Villari, Franchetti, and Sonnino," in *Italy's 'Southern Question': Orientalism in One Country*, ed. Jane Schneider (New York, 1998), 51–76. On agro-towns see chapter 4, note 4.
2. On the rural origins of the Mafia in western Sicily, see Salvatore Lupo, *Storia della mafia: Dalle origini ai giorni nostri* (Rome, 2004), esp. 49–61.
3. John Dickie, "Stereotipi del Sud d'Italia, 1860–1900," in *Oltre il meridionalismo: Nuove prospettive sul Mezzogiorno d'Italia*, ed. Robert Lumley and Jonathan Morris (Rome, 1999), 113–43.
4. See for example the notorious Inchiesta Jacini: Regno d'Italia, "Giunta per l'inchiesta agraria e sulle condizioni della classe agricola," *Atti della Giunta per la Inchiesta agraria*

sulle condizioni della classe agricola, vol. 1-15, (Rome, 1881-1890), and Regno d'Italia, Giunta parlamentare d'inchiesta sulle condizioni dei contadini nelle province meridionali e nella Sicilia, *Inchiesta parlamentare sulle condizioni dei contadini nelle province meridionali e nella Sicilia*, vol. 1-9 (Rome, 1909-1911).

5. Giovanni Lorenzoni, "Sicilia: Relazione del deputato tecnico," in *Inchiesta parlamentare sulle condizioni dei contadini meridionali*, vol. 6.1 (Rome, 1910), 11.

6. Numerous important studies carried out by historians like Piero Bevilacqua, Giuseppe Barone, Salvatore Lupo, and others have shown that between the nineteenth and the twentieth century Southern Italy was anything but a regressive or static society. Against the conventional image of an immobile *Mezzogiorno*, they stressed that large parts of Southern Italy's coastal areas were occupied by dynamic urban centers, by a new, specialized agriculture and by some important industrial and commercial activities. The "revisionist" approach toward Southern Italy has found a consolidated forum in the journal *Meridiana: Rivista di storia e scienze sociali*, an initiative by the Istituto meridionale di storia e scienze sociali. With specific regard to Sicily, see for example AA.VV. [various authors], *La modernizzazione difficile: Città e campagna nel Mezzogiorno dall'età giolittiana al fascismo* (Bari, 1983), but also Giuseppe Barone, "Egemonie urbane e potere locale (1882-1913)," in *Storie d'Italia: Le regioni dall'Unità a oggi*, vol. 5, *La Sicilia*, ed. Maurice Aymard and Giuseppe Giarrizzo (Turin, 1987), 191-370; Piero Bevilacqua, *Breve storia dell'Italia meridionale*, (Rome, 2005); Salvatore Lupo, *Il giardino degli aranci: Il mondo degli agrumi nella storia del Mezzogiorno* (Venice, 1990). For a comprehensive literature review on urban history in southern cities see Giuliano Lapesa, "Gli studi sulle città meridionali in età contemporanea: Tra storia del Mezzogiorno e storia urbana," *Meridiana* 57 (2006), 169-90.

7. Marta Petrusewicz, *Latifondo: Economia morale e vita materiale in una periferia dell'Ottocento* (Venice, 1990).

8. For an articulated examination of the reasons for the decline, see Marta Petrusewicz, "Il tramonto del latifondismo," in *Oltre il meridionalismo: Nuove prospettive sul Mezzogiorno d'Italia*, ed. Robert Lumley and Jonathan Morris (Rome, 1999), 31-50.

9. See the classic account by Giuseppe C. Marino, *Partiti e lotta di classe in Sicilia: Da Orlando a Mussolini* (Bari, 1976). See also Francesco Renda, *Storia della Sicilia dalle origini ai giorni nostri*, vol. 3, *Dall'Unità ai giorni nostri* (Palermo, 2003), 1039-78.

10. The first Italians to emigrate to the Americas notoriously were not from Southern Italy; however, the inhabitants of the *Mezzogiorno*, although latecomers, made a significant contribution in a second phase. See Andreina De Clementi "La 'grande emigrazione': Dalle origini alla chiusura degli sbocchi americani," in *Storia dell'emigrazione italiana: Partenze*, ed. Piero Bevilacqua, Andreina De Clementi, and Emilio Franzina (Rome, 2001), 186-211. For an overview and useful maps on Italian national and regional migration dynamics after unification see also Antonio Golini, Teresa Isenburg, and Eugenio Sonnino, "Demografia e movimenti migratori," in *Storia d'Italia Atlante*, ed. Ruggiero Romano (Turin, 1976), 696-736.

11. On peasant movement prior to 1945 in Gibellina, see Salvatore Costanza, *I giorni di Gibellina* (Palermo, 1980), esp. 55-102.

12. The exact data for the year 1921 are: Partanna 17,527; Salemi 19,374; Gibellina 6,264; Santa Ninfa 6,392; Salaparuta 2,730; Poggioreale 2,592; Contessa Entellina 2,018. Presidenza del consiglio dei ministri, Istituto centrale di statistica, *Censimento della*

popolazione del regno d'italia al 1 dicembre 1921 (XIII. Sicilia), series 6, vol. 13, (Rome, 1927), 22, 28–29.
13. See the statistics in Lorenzoni, "Sicilia," 355–60, and his comment on the difference between number of *latifondo* units and number of owners, 361.
14. Piero Bevilacqua and Manlio Rossi-Doria, "Lineamenti per una storia delle bonifiche in Italia dal XVIII al XX secolo," in *Le bonifiche in Italia dal '700 ad oggi*, ed. Piero Bevilacqua and Manlio Rossi-Doria (Rome and Bari, 1984), 37.
15. Bevilacqua, *Breve storia dell'Italia meridionale*, 32–39.
16. See Giuseppe Barone, *Mezzogiorno e modernizzazione: Elettricità, irrigazione e bonifica nell'Italia contemporanea* (Turin, 1986), and Bevilacqua and Rossi Doria, "Lineamenti per una storia delle bonifiche," 59–68.
17. Lorenzoni, "Sicilia," 635–36.
18. Barone, *Mezzogiorno e modernizzazione*, 175–88. This is still the case, as indicated in Regione Siciliana, Assessorato Territorio e Ambiente, *Relazione*, 11.
19. Royal Decree [hereafter RD] no. 2311, 27 October 1927, "Primo elenco dei comprensori soggetti a trasformazione fondiaria di pubblico interesse," *Gazzetta Ufficiale* 294, 21 December 1927. The decree in effect listed a series of "comprensori di trasformazione fondiaria" where to apply the disposition of an earlier decree, RD no. 753, 18 May 1924, "provvedimenti per le trasformazioni fondiarie di pubblico interesse," *Gazzetta Ufficiale* 122, 23 May 1924.
20. See the answers to the questionnaires reported by Lorenzoni, "Sicilia," 205–10.
21. Consiglio Superiore dei Lavori Pubblici, typescript, Adunanza generale del 30 giugno 1934, n.783, "Trasformazione fondiaria dell'Alto e Medio Belice—costruzione dei serbatoi montani di 'Maranfusa' e di 'Bruca,'" in box 89, folder a., Ministero Agricoltura e Foreste [hereafter MAF] Direzione Generale Bonifiche [hereafter DGB], Bonifiche Sicilia, Calabria e Sardegna [hereafter BSCS], Archivio Centrale dello Stato [hereafter ACS].
22. Royal Decree no. 215, 13 February 1933.
23. Consorzio per la Trasformazione Fondiaria del bacino dell'Alto e Medio Belice, *Criteri di classifica provvisoria: Relazione della commissione tecnica* (Palermo 1933); Consorzio di Bonifica del bacino dell'alto e medio Belice, *Le opere di bonifica: programma e realizzazioni* (Palermo 1952), 7–8.
24. Timothy Davies, "La colonizzazione feudale della Sicilia," in *Storia d'Italia, Annali 8: Insediamenti e Territorio*, ed. Cesare De Seta (Turin, 1985), 419–75. See also Maurice Aymard, "Le città di nuova fondazione in Sicilia," in De Seta, *Storia d'Italia, Annali 8*, 405–17.
25. *Relazione della commissione liquidatrice del costo effettivo dei lavori e interventi antianofelici concessi ai consorzio di bonifica del bacino dell'alto e medio Belice dal ministero dell'agricoltura e delle foreste*, DD.MM. 5 February 1943, no. 410, and 10 July 1946, no. 5883, in box 29, folder A/a., MAF, DGB, BSCS, ACS.
26. See Salvatore Lupo, "L'utopia totalitaria del fascismo (1918–1942)," in Aymard and Giarrizzo, *Storia d'Itali*, 464.
27. Giornale Luce, *Inizio della redenzione del latifondo siciliano*, 00:03:13, b/w, sound, 1939, Archivio Storico dell'Istituto Luce, B1609.
28. See Salvatore Lupo, "L'utopia totalitaria del fascismo," 475–81.
29. The Vittorio Emanuele III Institute could count on funding for one billion lire. See Lupo, "L'utopia totalitaria del fascismo," 464.

30. Relazione della commissione liquidatrice del costo effettivo dei lavori e interventi antianofelici concessi al Consorzio di bonifica del bacino dell'alto e medio Belice dal Ministero dell'Agricoltura e delle Foreste, DD.MM. 5 February 1943, n. 410 and 10 July 1946, n. 5883, in box 89, folder a, MAF, DGB, BSCS, ACS.
31. For an overview of peasant movement after the war and agrarian reform, see Paul Ginsborg, *Storia d'Italia dal dopoguerra a oggi: Società e politica 1943-1988* (Turin, 1989), 160-87. See also Bevilacqua, *Breve storia dell'Italia meridionale*, 133-36. See also Rosario Mangiameli, "La regione in guerra, 1943-1950," in Aymard and Giarrizzo, *Storia d'Italia*, 561-68 (on Sicily) and 578 (on Giuliano and Portella della Ginestra).
32. Giuseppe Montalbano, "La repressione del movimento contadino in Sicilia (1944-1950)," *Diacronie: Studi di Storia Contemporanea* 12, no. 4 (2012), http://www.studistorici.com/2012/12/29/montalbano_numero_12/.
33. Scholars have called into question success of the postwar agrarian reform in creating a large class of small farmers, especially in Sicily. Nevertheless, there is little doubt that the reform marked the definitive and irreversible decline of the *latifondo* and the political forces and interests which supported it. After 1950, the economic and social landscape that justified projects like the Fascist "colonization" began to disappear slowly but irreversibly. On the Sicilian agrarian reform see the articles collected by Giuseppe C. Marino, ed., *A cinquant'anni dalla riforma agraria in Sicilia* (Milan, 2003); Mangiameli, "La regione in Guerra (1943-1950)," 596-600, and Giuseppe Giarrizzo, "Sicilia oggi (1950-1980)", in Aymard and Giarrizzo, *Storia d'Italia*, 604-5.
34. See Arturo Escobar, *Encountering Development: The Making and Unmaking of the Third World* (Princeton, 1995), 1-4. Gilbert Rist, *The History of Development: From Western Origins to Global Faith* (London, 2008), 69-79. See also Marc Edelman and Angelique Haugerud, "Introduction," in *The Anthropology of Development and Globalization: From Classical Political Economy to Contemporary Liberalism*, ed. Marc Edelman and Alice Haugerud (Oxford, 2005), 1-74.
35. Leandra D'Antone, "L'interesse straordinario per il Mezzogiorno (1945-1960)," in *Alle radici dell'intervento straordinario*, ed. Leandra D'Antone (Naples, 1996), 51-109.
36. Giuseppe Barone, "Stato e Mezzogiorno: Il primo tempo dell'intervento straordinario (1943-1960)," in *Storia dell'Italia repubblicana*, vol. 1, *La costruzione della democrazia*, ed. Francesco Barbagallo (Turin, 1994), 293-409.
37. Alfredo Di Napoli and G. B. Mosca, "L'acquedotto del Littorio in Sicilia," *Annali dei Lavori Pubblici* 12 (1938), 1084-88.
38. Regione Siciliana, Cassa per il Mezzogiorno, *Gli interventi della Cassa per il Mezzogiorno in Sicilia* (Palermo, 1955), 173-74.
39. *Gli interventi della Cassa per il Mezzogiorno*, 18.
40. Consorzio di Bonifica del bacino dell'alto e medio Belice, *Statuto* (Palermo 1950).
41. Giovanni Misco, "Introduzione," in Consorzio di Bonifica, *Le opere di bonifica*, 5.
42. Ibid., 5.
43. On reclamation and irrigation in Southern Italy, see Piero Bevilacqua, "Le rivoluzioni dell'acqua: Irrigazioni e trasformazioni dell'agricoltura tra Sette e Novecento," in *Storia dell'agricoltura italiana in età contemporanea*, ed. Piero Bevilacqua (Venice, 1989), 255-318.
44. Consorzio di Bonifica, *Le opere di bonifica*, 14.

45. On *enfiteusi* in post-agrarian reform Sicily, see Centro studi e iniziative per la piena occupazione and Alleanza coltivatori siciliani, *L'enfiteusi in Sicilia: Atti del 1. Convegno regionale, Palermo, Fiera del Mediterraneo, 24 ottobre 1964* (Palermo, 1965).
46. Transcripts of interview with Lumia, ex vicecommissario Consorzio di Bonifica dell'Alto e Medio Belice, in box XXX, folder 3, Archivio-Dolci Barbera, Centro di Ricerche Economiche e Sociali per il Mezzogiorno [hereafter CRESM].
47. On the Italian miracle, see in particular Guido Crainz, *Storia del miracolo italiano: Culture, identità, trasformazioni tra anni cinquanta e sessanta* (Rome, 2003).
48. See Antonio Golini and Flavia Amato, "Uno sguardo a un secolo e mezzo di emigrazione italiana," in Bevilacqua, De Clementi, and Franzina, *Storia dell'emigrazione italiana,* 45–60; Eugenio Sonnino, "La popolazione italiana: Dall'espansione al contenimento," in *Storia dell'Italia repubblicana,* vol. 2, *La trasformazione dell'Italia,* part 1, *Politica, economia, società,* ed. Francesco Barbagallo (Turin, 1994), 531–75.
49. Law no. 634, 29 July 1957, "Provvedimenti per il Mezzogiorno," in *Gazzetta Ufficiale* no. 193, 3 August 1957. On the distinction between a first and a second phase of public intervention for the south, see Bevilacqua, *Breve storia dell'Italia meridionale,* 138–46.
50. Salvatore Adorno, "L'area industriale siracusana e la crisi ambientale degi anni Settanta," in *Industria, ambiente e territorio,* ed. Salvatore Adorno and Simone Neri Serneri (Bologna, 2009), 267–316. Also Francesco Martinico and Roberto Zancan, "Industria e ambiente nei piani d'area vasta dell'Italia repubblicana," in Adorno and Neri Serneri, *Industria, ambiente e territorio,* 339–61.
51. He collected and published documents about these first years of activity in Danilo Dolci, *Fare presto (e bene) perché si muore* (Turin 1954).
52. On the first phase of Dolci's activity, see Vincenzo Schirripa, *Borgo di Dio: La Sicilia di Danilo Dolci (1952–1956)* (Milan 2010). See also Giuseppe Barone, "Un mondo nuovo potrebbe crescere, diverso," in *Danilo Dolci: Una rivoluzione nonviolenta,* ed. Guiseppe Barone (Milan, 2007), 7–53.
53. Danilo Dolci, *Banditi a Partinico* (Rome and Bari, 1955; reprinted Palermo, 2009); Danilo Dolci, *Inchiesta a Palermo* (Turin, 1956).
54. See the letter by Dolci "to friends" in Dolci, *Banditi a Partinico,* 299.
55. Goffredo Fofi, by then Dolci's collaborator, has recounted that day in Goffredo Fofi, *Perché l'Italia diventi un paese civile: Palermo 1956; il processo a Danilo Dolci* (Naples, 2006), 31–35.
56. Danilo Dolci, *Processo all'articolo 4* (Turin, 1956); Dolci, "Pagine di un'inchiesta a Palermo," in *Nuovi Argomenti* 4, no. 17–18, (November 1955–February 1956), 136–78; Ignazio Silone, Vincenzo Arangio Ruiz, Carlo Antoni, and Guido Calogero, *Italia a porte chiuse: Inchiesta sociale od oltraggio al pudore? In merito al processo Dolci Carocci* (Rome, 1956).
57. This was the case of Lorenzo Barbera, who would soon become Dolci's closest collaborator.
58. "Introduction" to *Una politica per la piena occupazione,* ed. Danilo Dolci (Turin, 1958), 9.
59. Ibid., 13–15.
60. Lorenzo Barbera, Sandro Di Meo, Danilo Dolci, Goffredo Fofi, Franco Fontana, Grazia Di Fresco, Domenico Galliano, Luigi Guastamacchia, Iole Guerra, Carlo Ravasini, Ida Sacchetti, and Giorgina Vicquery, "Appunti sulle possibilità di piena occupazione,

nella sola agricoltura, in dieci paesi siciliani", in Dolci, *Una politica per la piena occupazione*, 27-78.
61. Letter no. 129, Partinico, 9 July 1958, in *Lettere 1952-1968: Aldo Capitini, Danilo Dolci*, ed. Guiseppe Barone and Sandro Mazzi (Rome, 2008), 137.
62. *Spreco: Documenti e inchieste su alcuni aspetti dello spreco nella Sicilia occidentale*, ed. Danilo Dolci (Turin, 1960).
63. Danilo Dolci, "Prefazione," in Dolci, *Spreco*, 25-26.
64. Danilo Dolci, *Banditi a Partinico*, 78-79.
65. The works started only in 1963. See Centro studi e iniziative, "Le ultime difficoltà circa la costruzione della diga sullo Jato," *Appunti per gli amici*, typescript no. 366, April–May 1965, box 30, folder 1, Archivio Dolci-Barbera, CRESM.
66. Pasquale Malpede, "Spreco di acqua nella Sicilia occidentale," in Dolci, *Spreco*, 413-34.
67. Ibid., 243.
68. Lorenzo Barbera, *La diga di Roccamena* (Rome and Bari, 1964), 135-39. See also the transcripts of the early meetings in box 30, folder 1, Archivio Dolci-Barbera, CRESM.
69. Malpede, "Spreco," esp. 135-37.
70. See the minutes of the meeting with engineer Indovina, head of the hydrogeological department of the ERAS in 1961, in box 30, folder 1, Archivio Dolci-Barbera, CRESM.
71. Although the letter does not provide other details, it is not difficult to imagine that it was a consequence of the Vajont Dam overflow on 9 October 1963. That day, a landslide caused a giant wave that literally leapt over the Vajont Dam in northeastern Italy and destroyed many towns and villages, causing almost 3,000 deaths. A complete copy of the letter, dated 25 October 1963, can be found in box 56, folder "attività Danilo Dolci," Ministero dell'Interno, Gabinetto 1964-66 [hereafter MI Gab. 64-66], ACS.
72. See Rapporto Prefettura di Palermo 10 December 1963, no. 5488, in box 56, folder "attività Danilo Dolci," MI Gab. 64-66, ACS.
73. Testimony reported in Barbera, *La diga di Roccamena*, 227. See also the record quoted in the preceding note.
74. The script of the documentary is in box 30, folder 3, Archivio Dolci-Barbera, CRESM.
75. Letter from Gabriele Pescatore to Danilo Dolci, 10 October 1964, in box 30, folder 1, Archivio Dolci-Barbera, CRESM. See also the letter from the President of the Cassa Gabriele Pescatore to the Minister of Home Affairs, 20 October 1964, in box 56, folder "attività Danilo Dolci," MI Gab. 64-66, ACS.
76. See minutes of the committee meetings in spring 1964, and the letter from Lorenzo Barbera to Giulio Pastore and President Leone, 31 August 1964, in box 30, folder 1, Archivio Dolci-Barbera, CRESM.
77. See "Programma del comitato cittadino di roccamena per l'anno 1965," typescript, in box 30, Folder 1, Archivio Dolci-Barbera, CRESM; and Appello del Comitato Cittadino per lo sviluppo di Roccamena, "Settimana di pressione" dal 7 al 14 marzo, in box 56, folder "attività Danilo Dolci," MI Gab. 64-66, ACS.
78. See the telegrams by the Prefect of Palermo following the protest almost day by day, in box 56, folder "attività Danilo Dolci," MI Gab. 64-66, ACS. See also the images of the march in Unitelefilm, *Dolci per l'acquedotto del Belice*, AAMOD.
79. Giacomo Parrinello, "Il terremoto del Belice: intervista a Lorenzo Barbera," in "Terremoti: Storia, memorie, narrazioni," ed. Gabriella Gribaudi and Anna Maria Zaccaria, special issue of *Memoria/memorie: Materiali di storia*, 5 (2012), 171-200.

80. Vito Bellafiore, video interview, 30 December 2009, color, 00:45:34, *Le terre che tremarono*, CRESM.
81. The main address of the new journal was indeed in Partanna, at the new center's facility.
82. Centro studi e iniziative di Partinico, *Un lavoro di sviluppo: Appunti dalla Sicilia occidentale; Rassegna bimestrale*, n.1 gen.-feb. 1964, Partinico.
83. Lorenzo Barbera, "Conoscere per capire," *Pianificazione Siciliana organo del Comitato Intercomunale per la Pianificazione organica della Valle del Belice* 1, no. 1 (November 1965), 1.
84. A minor anecdote can demonstrate this effectively. In the mid-1960s, a "trust" directed by UK Dolci supporters asked the Italian consulate for the authorization to lead an inquiry on the social conditions and agriculture potential of western Sicily. While doing so they also asked for the collaboration of the Italian institutions. The Cassa per il Mezzogiorno decided to collaborate because they wanted to gain more detailed knowledge of the area. See box 56, folder "attività Danilo Dolci," sub-folder "varie," MI Gab 64–66, ACS.
85. This vision of the river basin as unit for planning has a long transnational history that can be traced back as far as the creation of the Tennessee Valley Authority; see Fançois Molle, "River-Basin Planning and Management: The Social Life of a Concept," *Geoforum* 40 (2009), 484–94. The leaders of the Belice development committees were well aware of that history and its most recent developments in "developing" countries. See Danilo Dolci, *Verso un mondo nuovo* (Turin, 1964). Some sections of Dolci's book concerning planning experiments in other countries were republished in *Pianificazione Siciliana* between 1966 and 1967.
86. "'Le nostre dighe," *Pianificazione Siciliana* 2, no. 2 (February 1967), 3.
87. *Pianificazione Siciliana* 1, no. 2 (July 1966), 8.
88. Reports from local prefetti are in folder "Danilo Dolci attività," sub-folder 3, Ministero dell'Interno Gabinetto 1967–1970 [hereafter MI Gab 67–70], ACS.
89. Unitelefil, *Danilo Dolci e la marcia per la Sicilia occidentale e per un nuovo mondo*, 1967, b/w, silent, 00:09:00, AAMOD; and Report of the Prefect of Palermo, 14 March 1967, in folder "Danilo Dolci attività," sub-folder 3, MI Gab 67–70, ACS.
90. On industrial "poles" in Sicily, see Bevilacqua, *Breve storia dell'Italia meridionale*, 143 and 205–6 for extensive bibliographic references. For a periodization of state industry within the larger history of Italian industrial development, see Simone Neri Serneri and Salvatore Adorno, "Per una storia ambientale delle aree industriali in Italia: Introduzione," in Adorno and Nere Serneri, *Industria, ambiente e territorio*, 13–31.
91. Detailed analyses of migratory flows from the valley are in Carmelo Pennino, Antonino Pennino, and Alfonsa Carbone, *Analisi demografica dei Comuni della Valle del Belice colpiti dal sisma del 1968* (Palermo, 1976), 7–86.
92. Regione siciliana, Assessorato per lo sviluppo economico, *Progetto di programma di sviluppo economico della Regione siciliana per il quinquennio 1966–1970* (Palermo, 1965), 103–16 and the related maps.
93. Regione siciliana, Assessorato per lo sviluppo economico, *Progetto di piano di sviluppo economico e sociale della Regione siciliana per il quinquennio 1966–1970 / Regione siciliana, Assessorato allo sviluppo economico, presentato alla Giunta di governo nel marzo 1967 dall'assessore On. Calogero Mangione* (Palermo 1967).
94. Pennino, Pennino, and Carbone, *Analisi demografica*, 19–21.

 CHAPTER 6

Urbanized Countryside 1968–1993

On 16 January 1968, Gibellina, Poggioreale, Salaparuta, and Montevago were nothing but piles of ruins. In the following days, major aftershocks destroyed other towns to a similar extent. From the mountains to the estuary of the Belice River, there was nothing but ruined villages and towns, and the valley itself became indissolubly associated with the earthquake. Overnight, that remote part of the country gained intensive media coverage, and was propelled into the national limelight. The post-earthquake Belice Valley and its residents became the living symbol of "backwardness" and "underdevelopment" in the *Mezzogiorno*: a landscape of deprivation, misery, and abandonment, of archaic traditions and culture. Thirty years later, however, this landscape had disappeared. Highways and tract housing had replaced donkey trails and overcrowded hovels, and green fields and orchards surrounded modernist new towns.

In the aftermath of the earthquake, the valley drew unprecedented attention and was the focus of grand plans. Post-earthquake legislation envisioned the radical transformation of the valley's layout to stimulate its socioeconomic development. Dismissing the attempts of the local communities to get involved, the authorities scaled up pre-earthquake plans for rural reform into visions of revolutionary changes, and entrusted a special public institute, the ISES (Istituto per lo Sviluppo dell'Edilizia Sociale), with planning the outline of a new Belice Valley. The ISES experts imagined transforming the valley into a pioneering "city-territory": a network of interconnected settlements and facilities covering the entire region and functioning as a single urban unit. The city-territory would fit with the projected state-driven industrialization of the area and support the shift of the local communities from a rural to an urban culture. The partial or complete relocation of fourteen settlements was to make this ambitious redesign possible.

Nevertheless, actual reconstruction proved far more frustrating than expected. The local population resisted relocation, infrastructure advanced at a slow pace while housing construction stalled, and survivors remained for years in poorly built provisional shelters. In 1976, the authorities passed new legislation that gave more power to the local communities and supplied new funds for housing, boosting the completion of the new towns. Yet no money ever arrived to fund the promised state-driven industrialization, and in the early 1980s a parliamentary commission announced the failure of post-earthquake visions of socioeconomic revolution. Nevertheless, some important transformations had taken place in the valley. While industrial plants were never built, the new towns and transport infrastructure of the "city-territory" eventually materialized. In addition, the Cassa per il Mezzogiorno funded the construction of the long-awaited dam on the Belice River, which favored the ongoing transition from extensive cereal cultivation to intensive viticulture and olive groves. Thus, in today's Belice Valley, the suburban cityscape of earthquake-resistant new towns mingles with the new colors of a persistently agricultural region. This chapter will unravel the interplay of forces, actors, and processes that shaped this paradoxical post-earthquake landscape.

Tents, Barracks, and Committees

A few days after the strongest earthquakes, the devastation of the built environment of the entire valley was obvious. Yet in order to figure out the precise extent of destruction, officers from the Genio Civile (Civil Engineering Corps) had to spend weeks traveling across the region. Moreover, numerous aftershocks continuously altered the situation on the ground, increasing damage and thus the number of localities affected. As a result, the overall picture remained unclear. The first decree establishing special provisions for the disaster area listed 19 beneficiary localities, whereas a few months later the number had risen to 78.[1] Neither of the figures necessarily corresponds to the actual extent of the earthquake damage. Initially, some municipalities barely touched by the quake lobbied to get into the list to receive public funds. Others, conversely, even though seriously affected, tried to avoid inclusion in the list in order to escape the constraints of the earthquake building code, which they saw as an obstacle to the growth of the building industry.[2] Official geological reports by the National Institute of Geophysics and the Geological Service of Italy were unable to help with exact figures, since the authors based these reports upon what they admitted was insufficient fieldwork.[3] While the true dimensions of the damage were not clear, one thing was certain: in the valley of the Belice River, the effects of the earthquake had been "terrifying, and in some cases even apocalyptic," and at least four towns needed complete relocation to geologically safer localities.[4]

In this devastated region, there was little shelter for the several thousand homeless residents who did not emigrate. In the midst of the sequence of seismic events, having escaped the increasingly devastated towns in the valley, survivors erected tent camps on the outskirts of towns and in the open countryside, assisted by volunteers and members of the police and army.[5]

This, however, was just an interim measure. The amount of construction work needed to rebuild the towns was substantial. Considering what had happened after other such earthquakes, the authorities knew that rebuilding would take several years, and that they needed to provide medium-term shelter for the homeless in the meanwhile. As they had done in the past, the authorities decided to build ad hoc camps of huts (*baraccamenti*), with all the facilities and services needed to guarantee basic living standards and restore community life as far and as quickly as possible. Initially, the Ministry of Public Works estimated they would need approximately 8,000 units to shelter all the survivors.[6] This figure largely understated actual needs, as would soon become clear,[7] yet was still hard to meet, for the authorities had no stock of prefabricated units at hand. Officials thus tried to collect whatever kinds of shelters they could buy on the open market. Materials varied considerably, and included wood, steel, and, in many cases, asbestos. In general, each prefabricated unit was a two-room hut with basic sanitary facilities, such as a washbasin, toilet, and sink.[8]

In the spring of 1968, the Ministry of Public Works initiated the construction of the huts by employing one of its peripheral branches, the Provveditorato alle Opere Pubbliche. Wherever possible, the location of the huts followed the pre-earthquake subdivision of the valley's communities. The huts were divided in separate settlements, and most settlements were located near the towns that the survivors had formerly inhabited. Each of these settlements was supposed to last long enough to give the authorities time to complete the rebuilding. This entailed the construction of sewerage, aqueducts, electric lighting, and roads in these provisional camps. To expropriate the land for the camps and complete the infrastructure that was needed, Parliament had to increase the funding that had been established in January. Substantial donations came also from overseas, both in the form of money and in hut units.[9] In June, the prefect of Trapani sent the Minister of Public Works a set of photos in which largely completed *baraccamenti* in Gibellina, Salaparuta, Poggioreale, Vita, Salemi, Santa Ninfa, Partanna, and Castelvetrano can be seen.[10]

By the time the first *baraccamenti* were completed, demand for shelter had risen far higher than expected.[11] According to a report by the Provveditorato for the Minister of Public Works, the authorities would ultimately need 22,223 prefabricated units in order to shelter the entire homeless population in the Belice Valley, some 14,000 units more than initially estimated. Thus, in the following months, the Ministry of Public Works had to extend the size of the settlements considerably. At the beginning of 1969, the Ministry had completed 20,263 units and allocated 17,647 of them. The officer responsible, however, claimed that it was still hard to find appropriate sites for the remaining units and even harder to reach agreements with landowners.[12] In January 1969, while responding to public criticism about the shortcomings of the relief program in the earthquake area, the Minister of Public Works emphasized

Figure 6.1. Baraccamento Gibellina Rampinzeri, 1968. Courtesy of Dipartimento della Protezione Civile.

the unprecedented extent of the disaster. "Never in the recent history of Italy," declared the minister, "have we had to face such a complex problem … Other painful calamities have in the past required the state to work in extreme situations, but they had never been to the extent of this particular event or required work across such a huge area." The minister defended the significance of their achievements given the gargantuan task, despite a few undeniable shortcomings. The ministry had occupied approximately 3 million square meters of formerly agricultural land, constructed huts, provided 228 kilometers of new sewage pipes and 255 kilometers of new aqueduct pipes, and covered 1.5 million additional square meters with new roads.[13]

It was indeed an impressive transformation. The extent of construction work and the amount of money spent on infrastructure and housing for provisional post-earthquake settlements probably outweighed all previous public interventions in the valley. Despite facts advertised by the minister, however, life in the huts was harsh. In July 1968, the Sicilian newspaper *L'Ora* investigated the conditions in the *baraccamenti*. According to the newspaper, the provisional urbanization program was severely flawed. Not only were the prefabricated huts not enough to meet demand: in addition, they did not provide

Figure 6.2. Baraccamento Poggioreale, 1968. Courtesy of Dipartimento della Protezione Civile.

acceptable living standards, as they were overcrowded, exposed to extreme heat and cold, lacking in adequate air circulation, and often devoid of working sanitary facilities. In many cases, moreover, the ground was muddy and instable, and the settlements lacked schools, community centers, and commercial facilities.[14] According to the Sicilian writer Leonardo Sciascia, the conditions in the settlements were "no different from the most heinous and despicable concentration camps."[15]

Despite the investments and resources mobilized by the authorities, the ordeal of those men and women who had escaped homes and towns in ruins had not ended with the earthquakes. Nevertheless, while trying to find shelter in muddy tent cities and asbestos container homes, they did not cease to make their voices heard. As we have already seen, in March 1968, a thousand of these survivors had traveled to Rome to protest in front of the Parliament building. That initiative had been possible thanks to the activism of members of the local development committees. In the aftermath of the earthquakes, local activists had tried to re-establish the committees, organized informal relief operations, published appeals, and toured the tent cities untiringly to promote meetings and assemblies, sometimes whilst being actively obstructed by the police.[16] After the protest in Rome they published a special issue of the journal *Pianificazione Siciliana*. "The earthquake," explained the editorial of the journal, "abruptly stopped all activities and launched a new series of urgent problems: sheltering the population, feeding them, healthcare ... After this first period of disorientation, it has been necessary to reestablish the popular organization, to understand what should be done not only immediately, but also in the future, with respect to rebuilding, the reactivation of economic activities, and the development initiatives that were already necessary before [the earthquake] and now are even more necessary and urgent."[17] It was time, in other words, to resume the struggle for development in the new earthquake landscape and make local voices count in institutional plans.

The knowledge and data on local communities and their environment that the committees had produced throughout the years would have been of great value—had the government chosen to use it. Even in the midst of the great confusion of the first months, the committees showed themselves to be capable of gleaning a better picture of the situation than the authorities. While the Ministry of Public Works still believed that 8,000 huts would be enough to shelter the survivors, the committees were already maintaining that the actual need was for at least 22,000 hut units.[18] The latter was a much more accurate figure, as was proved by the fact that, three months later, the authorities reassessed their estimate, raising the figure to 22,000 units.[19] The competence of the committees in the earthquake area would have been even more valuable when planning reconstruction and development initiatives. They knew the valley, its geographical and topographical characteristics, the population and its social and economic conditions, and they already had precise and detailed plans and programs of things to do.[20] They had tried to display their competence and arguments during the protest in Rome and asked to be included in the decision-making process. The authorities, however, would follow a very different path—one in which there was no room for local ideas and bottom-up planning.

The City-Territory

As people on the ground were still struggling with mud and ruins, the regional and national authorities had already outlined a revolutionary future for the Belice Valley. They would not only aim to rebuild the destroyed towns, but also to transform the entire area to promote its social and economic development. The authorities had envisioned a significant redevelopment of the region at least from the late 1920s onwards. The vision underlying the post-earthquake legislation, however, largely overrode those early plans for a "rural modernity." After the earthquake, the authorities promised a complete reshaping of the spatial layout of the region, the rebuilding of most towns in new designs and in new locations, and a comprehensive program of state-funded industrialization. This program would bring the valley and its communities out of the dark era of rural "backwardness" and into urban-industrial civilization, eradicating the conditions that were ultimately responsible for the devastation witnessed in 1968.

To accomplish these ambitious aims, the authorities had introduced a plethora of planning platforms. The Regione Siciliana would draw up district plans (*piani comprensoriali*), town plans, plans for infrastructures such as roads and public facilities, and plans for those "productive initiatives" the Regione itself would fund. The Italian government, on the other hand, claimed the exclusive prerogative of deciding which towns to relocate partially or totally. For those towns, the Ministry of Public Works was to provide comprehensive "relocation plans." These relocation plans, formally distinct from the town plans, involved infrastructure (roads, electricity, aqueduct, sewage, and so forth), public facilities (schools, hospitals, public edifices) and social housing. The Ispettorato per le zone terremotate (General Inspectorate for the Earthquake-Damaged Zone), located in Palermo and acting as plenipotentiary body of the ministry, should supervise these "relocation plans" and the overall allocation of public funds.[21] Clearly, there was a great deal of overlap between the planning activities of the regional government and those of the Ministry for Public Works. As we shall see, confusion over roles and responsibilities between the different levels of the national and regional governments would affect the entire rebuilding process.

To mitigate the pitfalls of this complicated planning hierarchy, the authorities decided to entrust a third party with the entire planning exercise. This party would be the ISES, Istituto per lo Sviluppo dell'Edilizia Sociale (Institute for the Development of Social Housing). The ISES was a direct expression of the Italian planning culture of the 1960s. It had been established in 1963 as the newest reincarnation of a former institute responsible for social housing for homeless families (UNNRA-CASAS).[22] Since its inception, the ISES had managed several social housing projects all across the country, accumulating also significant experience in post-disaster reconstruction. After the Vajont Dam overflow in 1963, the Ministry of Public Works had appointed the ISES in charge of most public works in Longarone, the most affected town, which the authorities had decided to rebuild according to a new plan.[23] In 1966, after the landslide in Agrigento, the ISES had managed the rebuilding of the neighborhood of Villaseta. The ISES had interpreted this as an opportunity for creating an "ideal" neighborhood, with modern social services and facilities.[24] In 1968, the director of the ISES was the architect Fabrizio Giovenale: he was one of the key figures of the inner circle of the Minister of Public Works and a strong advocate of planning.[25] The ISES, in sum, was in a perfect position to interpret the ambitious program of rebuilding and development the authorities envisioned for the Belice Valley.

In January 1968, in a meeting at the Ministry of Public Works in Rome, a high-ranking officer mentioned the possibility of delegating the entire planning exercise to "the Institute."[26] In May 1968, the newly established General Inspectorate asked the ISES to carry out "demographic-economic, sociocultural, technical-urban, and technological studies" of the earthquake area, and in October 1968, the ministry charged the ISES formally with the "relocation plans," the plans for the towns that were to be rebuilt on new sites.[27] From the beginning, however, the authorities hoped that the ISES could also act as informal coordinator between the state and the Regione Siciliana.[28] To that end, a few weeks after the Ministry officially entrusted the ISES with the task, the Regione introduced yet another planning level, the Piano Territoriale di Coordinamento (PTC, territorial coordination plan). The scale of the PTC was much larger than a single district, and seemed the most suitable for the rebuilding and development program that was the ultimate goal of the post-disaster legislation.[29] In autumn 1969, then, even the Regione Siciliana appointed the ISES as official planner, entrusting the ISES architects with drawing up Territorial Plan no. 8. This latter plan encompassed the whole of the disaster area. From that moment on, thus, the ISES would be responsible for almost the whole planning operation in the Belice Valley.

Somewhat surprisingly, the outline of the new valley preceded all these complicated institutional negotiations. The Superior Council of Public Works had already produced the first draft of a plan for the valley in March 1968, after a field trip in the disaster area made by members of the council and experts on urban planning. This draft plan introduced two crucial goals for the future of the valley. First, it affirmed that the rebuilding had to promote the integration of the valley within a larger network of economic exchange, both on a regional and a national scale. The draft therefore took into consideration almost all of western Sicily, for which it established two main "development policies," one for the southern coastal areas and the other for the inland valley regions. Second, the draft outlined an urban system based on small and medium-sized centers linked to each other by an infrastructural network. According to this model, the network of centers would share various urban services and facilities (such as schools, hospitals, and recreational centers) and above all the same productive structure, which would guarantee jobs and income for the entire population. Permanent relocation, which the draft deemed inevitable for at least four of the stricken towns, was an important element of the project, and the location of the new settlements and transport networks would act as a pointer for state investments for industrialization of the area.[30]

The ISES would draw largely on the same ideas. In July 1968, before the ministry formalized its appointment, the ISES presented the first draft of a reconstruction and development plan. The ISES draft, like that by the Superior Council for Public Works, took into consideration a broader view of the regional and national situation. Within this broader context, the ISES study sketched out an "urban-territorial structure" covering the whole of western Sicily, in which the Belice Valley was to form the main core. This "urban-territorial structure" would reform the existing pattern of settlements—small towns dotted across the countryside—and integrate them by means of transport infrastructure and shared facilities. The physical interconnections of the towns would make them into a kind of cluster, which would function as a single urban unit for the whole area. This spatial layout would also guide the location of the industrial plants that the state and the Regione Siciliana had promised to fund. These plants would become the principal productive poles for the new urban-industrial network, providing jobs and income for the resident population. This plan ultimately aimed to trigger economic growth and, at the same time, create the right conditions for its continuation: "the goal [of the plan] should be the configuration of an urban plan and architecture for a developing area. This does not imply poorer urban planning and architecture, but the organization of the rebuilding as an engine for development." The purpose of the plan was to "lay the foundations for a self-propelling growth mechanism," eliminating the causes of emigration, and ultimately promoting "the shift from an archaic, rural culture to an urban culture."[31]

The authors of this draft plan laid down these radical aims without any sustained dialogue with the local communities. Yet the local committees had presented a set of detailed proposals, publicizing their willingness to contribute to the planning stage. Some of these proposals echoed the pre-earthquake plans for rural development, starting with the dam on the Belice River. Others were entirely new, such as a program of earthquake-resistant social housing encompassing some 50,000 dwellings and the installation of state-funded industrial plants.[32] The earthquake and the institutional response had clearly raised expectations. The valley seemed to be the focus of state initiative as never before, and this let local activists believe that change could finally happen, and on a bigger scale. "The earthquake," reads a document by the local development committees, "creates an undeniable turning point in the history of Belice Valley and western Sicily. The new course of development, the new expectations for the area are becoming ever more fixed in the people's consciousness." The documents continued with an exhortation: "Technicians and authorities have to listen to these claims and discuss the rebuilding plans with the locals."[33] Until that moment, though, this had not happened, and all the grandiose schemes for economic, social, and cultural improvements were being devised far from the Belice Valley.

In the following months, the committees put great effort into developing their proposals and organizing them into a structured plan. In September 1968, the Center of Research and Activities for Full Employment in Partinico put forward a "plan for the democratic development of the Belice, Carboy, and

Jato Valleys." It was a comprehensive scheme that architect Giuseppe Carta and economist Marziano De Maio had compiled from data and project work from the research activity of the local development committees. As with the institutional schemes, the committees' plan did not encompass just the Belice Valley in the strictest sense, but a much larger area, also including the smaller valleys of the Carboi River and the Jato River. The committees had included these two neighboring valleys in their 1967 development plan, the one put forward during the March for Western Sicily. Even back then, they considered this region as being a coherent territorial unit with common potential and similar prospects of development. In 1968, it also corresponded to the larger earthquake area: yet another reason to unify the region in a comprehensive redevelopment plan. Like the ISES experts, the authors of the committees' plan envisioned an experimental "city-territory": a network of interconnected urban centers working as one unit and served by a shared cluster of amenities. To support the economy of the new "city-territory," the authorities would have to invest in small industrial plants serving the needs of the building industry. The committees, nevertheless, believed that the main potential of the area lay in agriculture, and thus continued to make demands for the long-awaited construction of infrastructure for water storage and irrigation.[34]

Despite the emphasis on agriculture rather than industry, this latter plan was in tune with the institutional schemes. In particular, the idea of a "city-territory" was in all respects similar to the "urban-territorial unit" the ISES had envisioned in its draft. In October 1968, a few weeks after the committees had circulated their plan, the Ministry of Public Works called a meeting in Palermo. The aim of this meeting was to discuss all the existing draft plans for the earthquake area: the one by the Council of Public Works, the one by the ISES, and the "plan for democratic development" put forward by the committees. Representatives of all the bodies concerned were invited, among them the architect Giuseppe Carta, who presented the committees' plan. After Carta concluded his presentation, Giovenale, the director of the ISES, commented on the plan. Giovenale acknowledged the quality of the plan and the importance of the issues highlighted by the committees, especially irrigation and rural development, and pointed out existing similarities with the ISES plan. The only difference, according to Giovenale, was that the ISES had followed a much "more democratic" procedure than the committees, one based on "informal consultations" with the locals. Giovenale and the other participants ignored, or purported to ignore, that many years of research, inquiry, and mobilization with local communities and administrators underpinned the plan of the committees. It is hard to believe that the ISES could accomplish more in a few months than the committees had done in several years. Giovenale's comment, though, evidently closed the discussion. The ministry declared that it would adopt the ISES draft plan as the foundation for all planning in the earthquake region.[35]

New Towns and Ghost Factories

After that meeting, the committees developed a more elaborate version of their plan, which they presented officially at the beginning of 1969.[36] The authorities, though, did not give the committees any further formal opportunity to discuss their plan or any of its contents. By then the ISES was the sole body responsible for planning in the earthquake area. The time for democracy was over; now it was the turn of the experts. Territorial Plan no. 8, "the plan of plans" for the earthquake region, was only ready in 1972. In this plan the ISES planners, and in particular ISES director Fabrizio Giovenale, laid out the details of the proposed "city-territory." The PTC described the new automotive infrastructure and its interconnections with the existing one: a new motorway would cross the valley from north to south, and a high-speed road would run east–west. In addition, the plan envisioned a new railroad line, ports in the coastal localities, airports, and heliports. Secondly, the plan detailed land-use zoning: it identified a zone for mining, a zone for irrigation, a zone for intensive agriculture, but also an area for environmental conservation and another one of historic and artistic value for exploitation as a tourist destination. Consistent with this, the PTC detailed future industrial locations in accordance with the available resources and the location of transport infrastructures. Last but not least, the plan detailed the urban layout of the area—the position of shared facilities such as schools, hospitals, and amenities, placed at strategic points to render them easily accessible to all. Beneath these features, the choice of "network" model could be discerned: the city-territory was ultimately an extensive urban network, adapting the traditional polycentrism of that rural area to the needs and functions of an urban-industrial society. The underlying assumption of the model was the widespread diffusion of car-based mobility: only the automobile, indeed, could render that networked urban system possible.[37]

Town relocation would play a major role in this ambitious design. In April 1968, the report by the ING experts Marcelli and De Panfilis had clearly stated that the "geological and topographical" conditions of Gibellina, Salaparuta, Poggioreale, and Montevago were unable to provide the necessary solidity for building foundations. The topsoil on the hills was unstable and subject to erosion, and the earthquakes had only exacerbated these conditions, provoking several landslides. This advised against rebuilding on the same site. Clearing the ruins, moreover, would be an arduous task, and one that the condition of the soil did not justify: it would be much more simple and efficient to abandon the destroyed sites completely. According to the state geologists, the authorities should identify different and better sites on which to rebuild these towns. A similar verdict was applied to many other devastated towns in the valley. In these towns, only a portion of the former settlement could remain where it was.

The rest had to be relocated to a more stable site. A presidential decree in May 1968 listed a first group of nine towns to relocate, which was later extended to fourteen towns. Besides Gibellina, Salaparuta, Poggioreale, and Montevago, towns earmarked for relocation were Vita, Salemi, Calatafimi, Partanna, Santa Margherita, Santa Ninfa, Camporeale, Contessa Entellina, Sambuca di Sicilia, and Menfi.[38]

The ISES planners considered relocation a great opportunity to plan the settlements along new lines, using the space "as a resource to build new social relations." They saw rural tradition and the types of housing and settlements that had existed before the earthquake as part of the "backwardness" they wanted to eradicate from the valley. Architecture and planning in the relocated towns and neighborhoods was thus to follow a new, modern style, suitable for a pop-

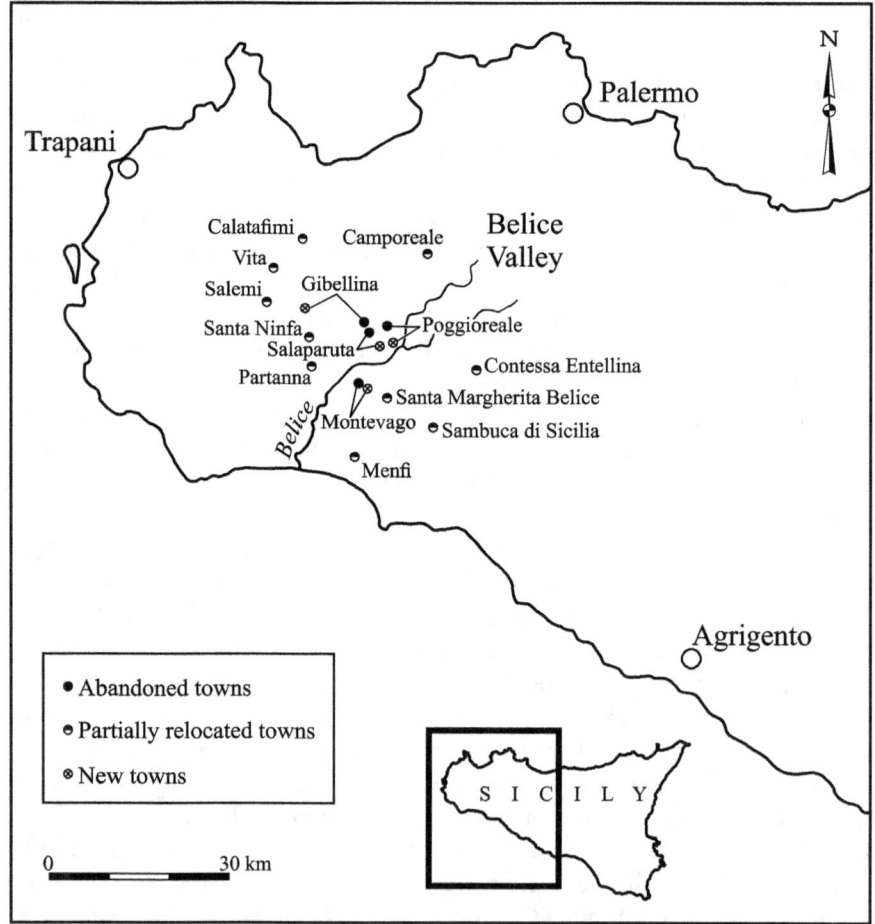

Figure 6.3. Partially or entirely relocated towns. Cartography by Mary Lee Eggart.

ulation of modern citizens with new cultural values and new lifestyles and adapted to car-based mobility.[39] Whereas Fabrizio Giovenale, the director of the ISES, was chiefly responsible for the large-scale framework, the architect Marcello Fabbri, a long-time friend and collaborator of his, personally drew up the plans for Gibellina and Poggioreale and supervised the planning for almost all of the fourteen towns.[40] Inspired by the example of British planners in the postwar United Kingdom, Fabbri planned the Belice relocated settlements as suburban "new towns." The Belice new towns would have modernist urban lines and would be spread over a larger area, featuring low tract housing with backyards and garages, wide roads, and generous open spaces.[41]

The complete eradication of the past that underlay this vision of urbanism was rooted in the conviction that the Belice Valley would eventually boast an industrial economy. The urban-industrial future of the valley was at the core of the ISES "city-territory" idea and supported the radical modernization the planners incorporated into the design of the new towns. From a contemporary perspective, this was not necessarily an extravagant expectation. As we have seen, post-disaster legislation had explicitly mentioned a state-driven program for economic development. According to Article 59 of the national law passed on the reconstruction of the Belice Valley, the relevant development agencies and branches of the state administration, from the Cassa per il Mezzogiorno (Fund for the South) to the Ministero delle Partecipazioni Statali (Ministry of State-Owned Industry) were to define a joint program of intervention. The Comitato Interministeriale per lo Sviluppo Economico (CIPE, Inter-Ministerial Committee for Economic Development), was supposed to have approved this program by the end of 1968. The official deadline of 31 December 1968, however, passed without any action being taken, and at the beginning of 1969, only the Regione Siciliana and the Ministry of Public Works had made a few proposals for investments in the valley, namely concerning the construction of an express road from Trapani to Sciacca (east–west) and an *autostrada* from Palermo to Mazara del Vallo (north–south).[42]

This was not what the state had promised in the aftermath of the earthquakes. On 11 April 1969, after vigorous protests by the Regione Siciliana, the CIPE organized a meeting between all of the institutions concerned to discuss the subject of investments in the valley. During this meeting, participants heatedly debated the interpretation of Article 59. The Regione Siciliana argued that Article 59 committed the national authorities to the implementation of a special program of investment within the disaster area. The national authorities argued the opposite, claiming they would not invest outside the overall frame of economic planning for Southern Italy. This meant no investment for the Belice Valley, for the authorities had excluded the valley from industrial development initiatives in the early 1960s. The Regione Siciliana was not willing to accept that interpretation without a fight and tried to oppose the decision over the following months.⁴³ The national authorities, nevertheless, did not reconsider their position. On 30 November 1969, the CIPE approved a funding program for the valley that exclusively supported the *autostrada* between Palermo and Mazara and the express road between Trapani and Sciacca. The government, in sum, had entirely dismissed their original ambitions of economic development for the Belice area, and therefore deprived the city-territory of its very raison d'être.⁴⁴

While the planners were drawing up their visionary plans for modernist towns and "urban-territorial units" and the authorities were breaking their promises of economic investment, the committees did not remain silent. In the fall of 1968, it was already evident that the authorities were not proceeding at the pace they should. At that time, the exact number of towns to be relocated was still not clear, and above all, there were few hints about the new sites for relocation.⁴⁵ The committees feared that this would affect the entire rebuilding program and condemn survivors to a protracted and uncertain existence in the *baraccamenti*. To counter this pernicious trend, they tried to keep up the media focus on the issue and put the authorities under pressure. While circulating the *piano di sviluppo democratico,* the committees promoted yet another week-long series of demonstrations, including feasts and a protest march.⁴⁶ On 1 November 1968, a group of protesters covered the walls of public offices in Palermo with graffiti and political slogans, demanding "houses, geological surveys, work, dams, water, schools, industries" and "work for all," and proclaiming "one can die of bureaucracy."⁴⁷

The committees fought to counter the authorities' visible lack of commitment to the economic development program. In October 1968, a popular protest in Roccamena revisited the longstanding question of a dam on the Belice River, denouncing the long list of broken promises by the authorities, who were "condemned" by a "popular jury" in the main square of the town.⁴⁸ This protest marked the split between Danilo Dolci and Lorenzo Barbera, but did not stop the activism of the committees.⁴⁹ Between 1969 and 1970, the committees launched another campaign, in which they declared the government itself "illegal" because it had not respected the deadline of Article 59, and they encouraged the residents to stop paying utility bills and local taxes.⁵⁰ After a few months, a thousand quake survivors repeated the journey to Rome and stood in front of the Parliament building for more than one week, despite a brutal intervention by the police.⁵¹ The same year, Danilo Dolci performed a 24-hour pirate radio broadcast from the valley, in which he denounced the poor living conditions of the survivors and the repeated delays in reconstruction.⁵² The protest peaked between 1970 and 1971, when several young men in the valley refused to be conscripted into the armed services, requesting instead to complete their national service in the reconstruction program.⁵³ The police initially arrested some of these *obiettori di coscienza* (conscientious objectors), but the action eventually succeeded in bringing about the first law that established conscientious objection and alternative civilian service in Italy; this, in turn, authorized civilian service in the Belice Valley.[54]

In spite of persistent outspoken protests by the locals and repeated promises from the authorities, there were still no traces of economic investment in the region, and even the rebuilding program had made very limited progress. As we have seen, the idea of relocation had circulated among officers and members of the government well before it appeared in the first geological and technical reports. When relocation was finally formally sanctioned, the motives varied: while the soft soil of the Belice hills was a recurring argument, technical reports also mentioned the unsanitary conditions of the old town centers, their lack of space and the difficulty of applying technical norms to them.[55] Completing relocation plans for Gibellina, Salaparuta, and Poggioreale proved particularly difficult, for there were few areas geologically stable and large enough for the new towns.[56] Former residents, for their part, were not comfortable with the idea of relocation. Several inhabitants of Salemi put their formal opposition to the relocation of certain neighborhoods into writing. They overtly contested the claims of geologists, affirming that the area to abandon was "not subject to landslides" and in fact was "pleasant ... and full of many noble historical traditions."[57] The initial proposal the authorities made for the relocation of Gibellina, namely to an area in the proximity of the barrack camp "Rampizeri," provoked a serious protest and the municipality subsequently rejected it.[58] Only in 1973 were the authorities able to establish definitive locations for all the new towns and neighborhoods and overcome the resistance of the locals.[59] The new Montevago was located on an adjacent site, and Salaparuta and Poggioreale a few kilometers away from their previous locations. Gibellina, however, was located almost 18 kilometers from its former site, within the municipal area of Salemi and near Santa Ninfa. In the remaining ten towns, relocation was partial and did not break entirely with the old center.

Establishing the location of the new towns and neighborhoods allowed the ISES to initiate "primary urbanization," that is, roads, underground pipe work, telephone connections, and electricity. The planners had sized new towns and infrastructure in accordance with expectations of economic growth and radical changes in the residents' daily life. Land use, therefore, increased exponentially: for instance, while the old Gibellina had occupied a surface area of less than 1 square kilometer, the new Gibellina occupied more than 45 square kilometers.[60] The new urban infrastructure, nonetheless, was not accompanied by substantial advancements in the housing program, and most new towns were nothing more than empty grids of roads, pipes, and cables.[61] Furthermore, the Territorial Coordination Plan, the overarching scheme responsible for the design of the city-territory, was still lying on the desk of the regional authorities, pending approval that would never arrive. The new towns and neighborhoods thus materialized without the formal overall planning framework that should have defined them and that justified their very existence. To mark the definitive abandonment of all planning ambitions, in 1973 a presidential decree dissolved the ISES: this product of the center-left season did not outlive the political coalition that created it.[62] The ISES survived in name for a few more years, managing ongoing business, but the planning and political culture the ISES embodied had decidedly gone.

Whereas the prospects for the rebuilding program were not promising, industrial development policies had no future at all. On 28 January 1971, the CIPE approved a development plan for Sicily and Calabria, the "Pacchetto Sicilia-Calabria." This plan seemed to counter the strategy of disengagement in the Belice Valley, because it proposed the construction of an electro-metallurgical plant for the production of aluminum near the earthquake-affected area.[63] Over the following months and years that plan seemed to make progress, and the government put a public industrial group, Enfim, in charge of building and running the plant. In 1973, however, the authorities revoked their promises of funding, and so Enfim abandoned the whole project before it had even got off the ground.[64] By the mid-1970s, various other minor industrialization schemes put forward by the Regione Siciliana had also failed.[65] This was yet another confirmation that the national authorities had neither the resources nor the intention of promoting industrial development in the area. The only successful initiative, ultimately, was the construction of the *autostrada* between Palermo and Mazara del Vallo planned by the Regione Siciliana in the aftermath of the earthquake and begun by the CIPE in 1969. The *autostrada* was completed in the mid-1970s. Yet the industrial economy that such infrastructure had been built to serve was no more than a chimera, and the completion of the highway contrasted tragically with the delays in the housing program.

By the mid-1970s, the locals were still living in the increasingly dilapidated shantytowns. Many residents and some municipal administrations had repeatedly complained about moisture on the walls and floors, flooding, and the deterioration of the building materials.[66] They claimed that the electricity supply was sporadic and running water was available for less than one hour per day.[67] The public authorities recognized that most of these claims were true, and, in some instances, initiated legal suits against the private contractors responsible.[68] The committees, however, no longer had the same power as in the aftermath of the earthquake, and the voice of the local communities was not as loud as it had been in the early 1970s. After the campaign against compulsory military service, the participation of the locals in the local development committees declined steadily. In 1973, the journal *Pianificazione Siciliana* ceased publication, and Lorenzo Barbera dissolved the Center for Studies and Activities that he had established in Partanna almost ten years before. Barbera and a small group of associates founded a new venture, the Center for Economic and Social Research for the South (CRESM, Centro di ricerche economiche e sociali per il Meridione), which focused more on social research than on political activism. Thus, in spite of the miserable living conditions in the *baraccamenti*, there were no visible protest initiatives comparable to those of the first years.

Eight years after the earthquake, the reconstruction of the Belice Valley was well on the way to becoming a spectacular failure. In 1976, an internal inquiry by the Ministry of Public Works highlighted unjustifiable delays and shortcomings in the rebuilding program and the oversized infrastructure and urbanized spaces, and advised legislative reform and new funds to boost the housing program.[69] Acknowledging the inefficacy of the 1968 legislation and related initiatives, Parliament started debating a new law to drive the reconstruction. In the wake of this debate, protest rose once again among the locals. In March 1976, following what was by now tradition, a group of residents traveled to Rome. They were demanding new funding to support the reconstruction of private housing, an extensive program of social housing, and, above all, the drastic revision of the entire institutional architecture of the reconstruction program in favor of local communities.[70] Under pressure from the protesters and faced with undeniable claims of inefficacy that were largely being echoed in the newspapers, Parliament approved a new law for the Belice Valley. Law no. 178 of 26 April 1976 established new funding for the reconstruction and modified the entire institutional organization of the rebuilding process. The government gave the local municipalities control of the allocation of funding to private citizens and limited the role of the General Inspectorate to the final supervision.[71]

Rural Urbanism

As Parliament passed the new legislation, the Belice Valley regained the national limelight. Scholars initiated sociological inquiries on post-earthquake changes in local communities, architects dissected the plans of the ISES, and journalists denounced the misconduct and corruption in the use of public funds.[72] The Belice Valley reconstruction, which the authorities had imbued with the symbolic purpose of overcoming "backwardness" and "underdevelopment," and which was to be a successful example of state-driven modernization, had turned into the exact opposite: it had become the example of what the authorities should *not* do after an earthquake disaster, and a symbol of the inefficiency of public action. Following the legislative reform in 1976, Parliament established a bicameral commission to investigate the shortcomings of the rebuilding and development program in the Belice Valley. The commission published its report only in 1981: commissioners had had to garner and examine an impressive amount of evidence and interrogate the most important representatives at every level, from the Regione Siciliana to the General Inspectorate, from the ISES to the Cassa per il Mezzogiorno. The inquiry became an opportunity for a global examination of the reconstruction, of its successes and failures, and of the actions of all the major development departments and agencies of the state.[73]

The first and most difficult task the commissioners had to face was to distinguish duties and responsibilities. A plethora of different agencies and institutions were directly or indirectly involved in the reconstruction, and this resulted in a continuous and systematic confusion of roles and made room for fraud and corruption. This confusion of roles and responsibilities also had a negative impact on planning. Laws and decrees by the national and regional authorities had established too many planning levels, and the corresponding plans had not always been implemented. The most significant case was the Territorial Coordination Plan, the overarching plan for the "city-territory," which the Regione Siciliana had never formally approved. Furthermore, some plans, such as the *piani comprensoriali* (district plans) were drawn *after* the relocation plans, rather than *before*, as they should have been, and then usually by a different team of planners than those responsible for relocation. The most substantial failure of the reconstruction program, though, was the lack of economic investment in development. "Nothing had been done with regard to productive initiatives," the commissioners stated harshly, and as a result, the new and oversized valley infrastructure "had no structures to serve."[74] Twelve years after the earthquake, in stark contrast to the high expectations of state-driven modernization, the valley showed "the conditions of backwardness in the local economy that still make western Sicily one of the most depressed areas in Italy."[75]

The condition of the valley in the late 1970s largely justified the commission's scathing comments. Nevertheless, the situation was on the verge of a change. The 1976 law and funds lent substantial new momentum to the rebuilding process. Whereas the inspectorate had funded only 1,198 private dwellings by 1975, between 1976 and 1980 the number rose to 6,000, covering more than 50 percent of housing demand.[76] The new valley was taking shape, and from 1977, the first group of families could finally leave the *baraccamenti* for real houses in real towns.[77] In sharp contrast to the rural hilltop towns that the earthquake had blanketed with ruins, all houses in the new towns were provided with adequate living space, sanitary facilities, and even individual backyards and garages like in northern European and North American suburbs. The ecologies of the old rural settlements had disappeared, together with the subsistence gardens, chickens, pigs, and burning piles of manure on the outskirts of towns. Sewage networks, telephone lines, and electricity cables wired up the valley, and a high-speed road network ensured the connection between the new towns and the rest of the island. By the late 1980s, the material conditions of life in the Belice Valley new towns were similar to many Italian and European suburbs, and radically different from the poor agro-towns of 1968.

The modernization of new towns and neighborhoods was spectacular. This new, modern urbanism in the Belice Valley, however, did not bring about the disappearance of rural life. On the contrary, rising out of the wreckage of industrial dreams, agriculture remained the principal economic activity in the valley and even experienced remarkable growth. From the 1970s onwards, all across the valley, farmers undertook a slow but steady conversion from cereal cultivation to olive trees and grapevines. From being almost the only crop cultivated in the valley until the 1950s, wheat had dropped to 60 percent of the cultivated surface by 1990, with the remaining 40 percent devoted to grapes and fruit trees.[78] This transformation in land use that was already evident in the early 1990s would continue at an increased pace during this decade, resulting in a spectacular metamorphosis of the rural landscape in the entire Belice Valley. Visitors looking for the yellow, bare fields described by Sidney Sonnino in 1876, and still depicted by so many reporters in 1968, would now look for them in vain. A carefully cultivated landscape of farms had replaced the cereal *latifondo* and its colors.

This transformation was also the unforeseen outcome of the public money that had flowed into the area after the earthquake. Building activity, although tarnished by corruption and fraud, had nonetheless been an unprecedented source of income for many residents and had produced a significant transformation in the social composition of the local communities.[79] The economic status of many families subsequently increased further due to the payment of a monetary allowance for earthquake survivors. Every household that had suffered the loss or serious injury of one or more of its members was entitled to receive a significant sum from both the national and regional authorities.[80] These sums were added to the money allocated for private housing, and many residents then invested their small capital in the few economic activities of the region, among which agriculture still dominated. "With all this money coming from the earthquake," explained the former activist Lorenzo Barbera, "those local workers who did not own farmland before [the earthquake] could buy some. Those who already had a piece of farmland cultivated with cereal crops transformed it into vineyards, olive groves, orchards, and so forth."[81] Investments like these were not the result of any planned policy, since the authorities had not distributed the allowances for this purpose. Nonetheless, the unprecedented availability of capital allowed many farmers to meet the costs of agricultural conversion even on small properties, a process documented in the early 1990s in a pilot study by the Belice Reclamation Consortium.[82]

As the two generations of reformers from the late 1920s onwards had envisioned, water storage proved key to this spectacular agricultural conversion. The construction of a dam on the Belice River had been the subject of debate since the founding of the Belice Reclamation Consortium in 1933 and was one of the principal demands of the local communities both before and after the earthquake. After yet another protest action by the local committees in late 1968, the president of the Cassa per il Mezzogiorno, Gabriele Pescatore, had explained that plans for the dam were still not complete due to "technical problems" and that the technicians needed to undertake a "more detailed examination" of the site.[83] In the early 1970s, agricultural development plans put forward by the Regione Siciliana still listed the dam among the most important works to undertake.[84] While none of the other promised investments ever came to pass, the dam did. In 1974, forty years after the first proposal by the experts of the reclamation consortium, the Cassa and the consortium put forward a detailed plan. The dam would materialize on the site selected in 1964—a locality named Garcia—and would become the pivot of a complex irrigation system.[85] This reservoir would become the biggest reservoir of the island, and the water supply would allow for the irrigation of a territory of more than 19,000 hectares and increase the urban water supply in many towns in the valley.[86]

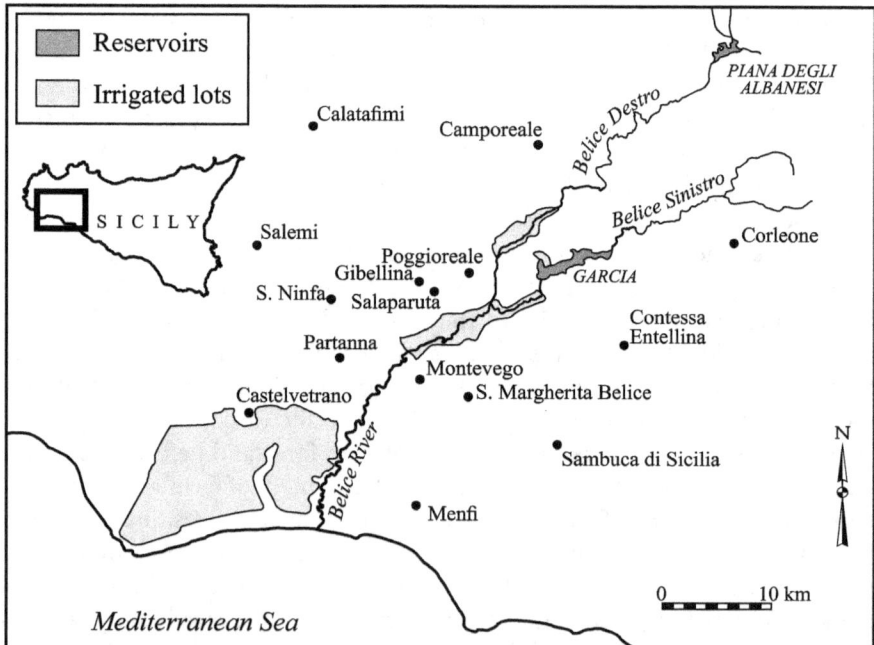

Figure 6.4. The Garcia Dam and irrigated lots in a project from 1974. Cartography by Mary Lee Eggart.

Works for the dam started shortly after this, although sources are not clear about the timing. It seems certain that the construction of the dam had already started in 1976, under the direction of a company from Milan, Lodigiani S.p.a. The reasons for this lack of detail may well be the presence of the local Mafia in the business, which a source from the Ministry of Public Works had already confirmed in 1976.[87] Sicilian journalist Mario Francese also publicly denounced the presence of the Mafia in the construction of the dam in his detailed reportage for the *Giornale di Sicilia*. According to Francese, the Mafia was taking advantage of the substantial investments in infrastructure and had killed several people to protect its interest.[88] Two years later, because of his reporting, a Mafia killer murdered Francese himself in front of his home.[89] The construction of the Garcia Dam was an important step in the rise of the Mafia clan from Corleone. In these years, the clan led by Salvatore Riina and Bernardo Provenzano took control of licit and illicit activities across much of the island and committed dozens of murders, including the bombing that killed judges Giovanni Falcone and Paolo Borsellino in the summer of 1992.

The Garcia Dam was completed in the mid-1980s. The new reservoir extended for 5.7 square kilometers, permanently reshaping the landscape of this once arid region and allowing the irrigation of large expanses of farmland in the valley and in neighboring areas.[90] Although the extent of its influence is unclear, the Garcia Dam's water certainly contributed to the agricultural transformation in the valley. Yet this process was not without contradictions and drawbacks. The rise of viticulture, the driving sector of Belice Valley new agriculture, relied largely upon *cantine sociali* (cellar cooperatives): that is, facilities for processing wine owned jointly by groups of farmers. This system allows small producers to share the cost of processing, which was otherwise unaffordable. This system, however, could only support low quality production with very low profit margins, and was not enough to sustain a strong agricultural economy.[91] Since the mid-1990s, some wine producers in the valley have been trying to raise quality standards, and the cultivation of olive trees is evolving towards specialized and certified production. Overall, however, the agricultural sector has suffered major reductions in employment levels and in economic importance compared with the 1980s, as in the rest of Southern Italy. No other economic sector has emerged to compensate for the loss of jobs in agriculture.[92]

During the 1980s, the mayor of Gibellina, Ludovico Corrao, tried to encourage economic growth based on tourism and culture, making Gibellina a little "capital" of contemporary art. Corrao successfully invited famous contemporary artists to donate artworks and permanent installations to decorate Gibellina's public spaces, gaining a great deal of attention and much criticism.[93] Yet no other town followed in the footsteps of Gibellina, and this has remained an isolated experiment.[94] Despite agricultural improvements and the limited development of secondary and tertiary sectors, the economy in the area is weak, and income levels are still amongst the lowest in the country, largely below the average of a "poor" region such as Sicily.[95] Perhaps the most evident sign of this is in the changing demography. While western Sicily was becoming the choice destination for immigrants coming from Mediterranean countries such as Tunisia, most of the fourteen towns totally or partially relocated after the disaster have never recovered from post-earthquake population losses. Over the decades, the area has continued to lose people and has further reduced its demographic weight. According to national censuses, Gibellina, which in 1961 still had more than 6,700 inhabitants, had only 4,677 in 2001; Poggioreale went from 2,698 in 1961 to 1,715 in 2001, Salaparuta from 2,943 in 1961 to 1,835 in 2001.[96] A similar decrease was registered almost everywhere, with a very few exceptions, such as Montevago and Menfi. The visions of affluence that underpinned and legitimated the massive reshaping of the Belice Valley after the earthquake never come true, and the region's future is still uncertain.

Conclusions

The Belice Valley has been a true landmark in the history of post-earthquake rebuilding in Italy. The disorganization of relief operations and the alleged corruption, the grandiose plans for new towns and the "city-territory," and the demographic decline made the Belice Valley reconstruction an example of the shortcomings of state-led intervention. Nonetheless, the manifest failures paid for so dearly by Belice residents have brought about some significant changes on a larger scale. Whereas the 1968 legislation conceded some power to the Regione Siciliana, the 1976 law transformed the system for allocating funding and contracts profoundly, devolving both to the local municipalities.[97] The authorities continued this new strategy in subsequent seismic disasters. In both the 1976 Friuli earthquake and the 1980 Irpinia earthquake, the state covered most rebuilding costs, but the allocation of money was managed at least in part by local institutions, with uneven results. In addition, the radical reshaping of urban environments and spatial layouts undertaken in the Belice Valley has never been attempted again to anything like this extent. In Friuli, the authorities planned and rebuilt Gemona and Venzone following their original urban shape and housing style. In Irpinia, a few towns opted for modernist reshaping, whereas many other communities restored the destroyed urban environments as they had been before.[98]

Among the artists Mayor Corrao invited to Gibellina in the mid-1980s was the painter and sculptor Alberto Burri. Unlike the other contributors, Burri refused to produce a permanent installation for the new town. Instead, he decided to work on the abandoned ruins of the old Gibellina. "[The abandoned town] was almost 20 kilometers away. I was really struck," recounted Burri in a late interview, "I almost felt like crying. And suddenly I had the idea: I feel I can do something here. I would do like that: We can compact the rubble … reinforce it properly, and create an immense white *cretto* in concrete, so as to leave an enduring memory of this event."[99] The *Cretto* (meaning crack, rift) was built between 1985 and 1989 on a portion of the surface planned by Burri, along the slope where Gibellina once stood. Visitors can see the *Cretto* from kilometers away, and can walk across it, along the traces of the former streets. Some have celebrated Burri's *Cretto* as the first memorial to the victims of seismic disasters in Italy.[100] Others have criticized it as being yet another expression of intellectual hubris: to meet some abstract aesthetic ideals, the artist has deprived survivors of their last tangible connection with the past.[101] Whichever side one takes, in the cracked white concrete shaped by the artist's vision, the voice of the earthquake still resounds powerfully.

Although for different reasons than the ones that drove Burri's remaking of old Gibellina, the entire Belice Valley has been similarly transformed following the earthquake. Many residents have gone away, never to return. Those who remained after the long and harsh years in tent cities and decaying asbestos huts, marked by outspoken protest and silent endurance, have become dwellers of a truly new environment. Black stripes of asphalt roads cover the hilltops and slopes. New towns and neighborhoods have permanently altered the geography of human settlement in the region. Small earthquake-resistant

Figure 6.5. The construction of the Cretto by Alberto Burri, 1987. Copyright Osvaldo Amari, used with permission.

houses, all connected to modern water and energy networks, have filled the empty lots of the ISES modernist plans. The colors of grapes and olive trees have spread across the valley, replacing the vivid yellow of mature wheat and the dark brown of bare fields. An artificial lake has materialized in the high valley, while the scant stream of the Belice River is now barely discernible among the cane thickets in the lowlands. The Belice Valley of today is no longer the dilapidated rural region of 1968, and the material life of its inhabitants has changed dramatically. Yet the valley is not the urban-industrial "city-territory" imagined by the planners in the aftermath of the quake. Today's Belice Valley can be better described as a hybrid of advanced urban modernity and a persistently rural environment and economy; an urbanized countryside that exaggerates and at the same time epitomizes the transformation of most of rural Italy in the late twentieth century.

Tectonics have actively participated in this astonishing transformation. The fault lines underneath the Belice Valley were unknown before 1968, and the region was not on contemporary seismic maps. This, along with the extremely poor housing and infrastructure of the impoverished region, magnified the impact of the earthquakes. The unexpected activation of the fault not only destroyed houses and infrastructure: it also modified the status of the Belice Valley in Sicilian and Italian social and economic hierarchies, raising ambitions and expectations to new heights. Reconstruction and relocation provided the opportunity for an unprecedented large-scale planning experiment. This plan failed to fulfill most of its grand goals of social regeneration and modernization. Yet it provided the layout according to which the new valley has materialized: new roads and new towns, sanitary infrastructure, and energy networks. The earthquake repositioned the valley in the geography of state-led development policies. Generations of local reformers had envisioned rural modernization from at least the late 1920s. Local peasants and farmers had dreamed and fought for development for at least a decade before the earthquake. Yet despite these ideas and struggles, pre-earthquake development plans had only marginalized the valley further and excluded the possibility of major investments there. After the earthquake, the money for earthquake recovery and victim compensation created the economic conditions for agricultural change. In addition, while the promised industrialization never arrived, the post-earthquake funds contributed to the long-awaited dam on the Belice River, albeit by means of the unwanted and murderous participation of the Mafia. The water from this dam contributed to the spectacular conversion of land use and the shift to viticulture and olive groves, and thus also to the making of the paradoxical new landscape of the Belice Valley that we see today.

The hybridization of rural and urban settings is a typical feature of many global landscapes in the late twentieth century. The urbanized countryside of the Belice Valley can be seen as an example of this widespread phenomenon, which defies the common dichotomy between city and countryside.[102] Nevertheless, the history and features of this particular case render it unique. Here, unlike most of Europe's urbanized countryside, there are few traces of old rural built environments. They have been largely replaced by a suburban cityscape with radically new and distinctive architectural and technological features. This cityscape is surrounded by a developed rural landscape that bears no trace of industrialism and remains far from the biggest population centers of the island. This configuration is extremely unusual and, like the paradoxical modernity of Messina, is by no means the product of solely human activity. The earthquake has shaped this landscape of the Belice Valley as much as the actions and the ideas of human beings.

Notes

1. Decreto Legge (decree) no. 12, 22 January 1968, "Provvidenze a favore delle popolazioni dei comuni della Sicilia colpiti dai terremoti del gennaio 1968"; Decreto Ministeriale (ministerial decree), 10 May 1968, "Elenco dei comuni delle provincie di Agrigento, Palermo e Trapani colpiti dai terremoti del gennaio 1968 che possono beneficiare delle provvidenze previste dal decreto-legge 27 febbraio 1968, n.79, convertito nella legge 18 marzo 1968, n.241."
2. Minutes of a meeting held on 1 July 1968 in the Prefecture of Trapani, in box 1 "Terremoti 1968- Classificazioni zone sismiche," Ministero dei Lavori Pubblici Divisione 3 [hereafter MLP 3], Archivio Storico della Protezione Civile [hereafter ASPC].
3. Servizio Geologico d'Italia, Divisione di Geologia Applicata, "I comuni delle province di Agrigento, Palermo, Trapani ed i movimenti sismici del gennaio 1968," Rome, 9 April 1978, (undersigned by ing. Amedeo Balbani, typescript), in box 1 "Terremoti 1968—Classificazioni zone sismiche," MLP 3, ASPC.
4. Mario De Panfilis and Liliana Marcelli, "Relazione sismologica sui terremoti di Sicilia iniziatisi il 14 gennaio 1968," n.7, in box 1 "Terremoti 1968—Classificazioni zone sismiche," MLP 3, ASPC.
5. Lorenzo Barbera, interview by Giacomo Parrinello, Partanna, 17 March 2012, unpublished part, and Enza Bellacera, video interview, 29 May 2009, color, 00:41:57, *Le terre che tremarono*, CRESM.
6. See Ministro dei Lavori Pubblici to Presidente del Consiglio Leone, Rome n.d., in box 26 "Terremoto del 1968 varie," Ministero dei Lavori Pubblici Divisione 29, Affari Generali [hereafter MLP 29 AG], ASPC.
7. Indeed, one year later, on 8 January 1969, the Minister of Home Affairs wrote to the ISTAT (Istituto Centrale di Statistica) asking for a detailed survey of the camps' population, which was not known at all. The letter is in box 250, folder 1, Ministero dell'Interno, Gabinetto 1967–1970 [hereafter MI Gab 67-70], Archivio Centrale dello Stato [hereafter ACS].
8. "Rapporto sulle opere di pronto soccorso attuate in dipendenza del terremoto 1968 nella Sicilia Occidentale, in riferimento agli articoli apparsi sul giornale 'Il Tempo' n.168 del 24.6.1969 e n.170 del 26.6.1969," in box 26 "Terremoto del 1968 varie," MLP 29 AG, ASPC.

9. See table of foreign contributions in box 3 "Terremoto in Sicilia gen.1968," sub-folder "Paesi Esteri—aiuti e offerte varie," Ministero dell'Interno, Direzione Generale Protezione Civile e Servizi Antincendio 112 [hereafter MI DGPC 112], ASPC.
10. Pictures attached to the report from the Provveditorato alle Opere Pubbliche of Palermo to the Ministry of Public Works, 11 June 1968, in box 26 "Terremoto del 1968 varie," MLP 29 AG, ASPC.
11. Note (typescript) concerning a meeting on 3 July 1968 in the Ministry of Public Works, in box 26 "Terremoto del 1968 varie," MLP 29 AG, ASPC.
12. Provveditorato alla Opere Pubbliche di Palermo to Ministry of Public Works, "In occasione della visita del Ministro del 21 e 22 gennaio 1969," in box 2 "Terremoto del 1968 Belice (Sicilia) articoli originali, visita ministro Mancini-Nenni, decreto legge, quantificazione danni ecc ecc.," Ministero dei Lavori Pubblici, Divisione 29 Direzione Generale Servizi Speciali, Ufficio Stampa [hereafter MLP 29 Stampa], ASPC.
13. Press release by the Ministry of Public Works, Rome, 23 January 1969, in box 2 "Terremoto del 1968 Belice (Sicilia) articoli originali, visita ministro Mancini-Nenni, decreto legge, quantificazione danni ecc ecc.," MLP 29 Stampa, ASPC.
14. "Nell'inferno dei terremotati," *L'Ora,* 10 July 1968, 5–12.
15. Leonardo Sciascia, "Sono stato nei 'lager' della Valle del Belice," *L'Ora,* 10 July 1968, 9.
16. See report by Questore Marangio, Trapani, 6 February 1968, in box 3, folder "proteste e scioperi inerenti al terremoto della Sicilia," MI DGPC 112, ASPC.
17. Untitled text in bold, *Pianificazione Siciliana* 3–4 (March–April 1968): 2.
18. "Notizie dai Comuni della Valle del Belice," *Pianificazione Siciliana* 3–4 (March–April 1968): 10–11.
19. Provveditorato alla Opere Pubbliche di Palermo to Ministry of Public Works, "In occasione della visita del Ministro del 21 e 22 gennaio 1969," in box 2 "Terremoto del 1968 Belice (Sicilia) articoli originali, visita ministro Mancini-Nenni, decreto legge, quantificazione danni ecc ecc.," MLP 29 Stampa, ASPC.
20. "Premessa," in "Alcune indicazioni operative per lo sviluppo della Valle del Belice," special issue, *Pianifacazione Siciliana* 5 (April 1968): 3–5.
21. Law no. 241, 18 March 1968, Article 16.
22. Marcello Mamoli and Giorgio Trebbi, *Storia dell'urbanistica: L'Europa del secondo dopoguerra* (Rome and Bari, 1988), 512.
23. See Luciana Palla, "La 'nuova città' e la sua gente: Un difficile percorso dal 1963 ad oggi," *Il Vajont dopo il Vajont, 1963–2000,* ed. Maurizio Reberschak and Ivo Mattozzi (Venice, 2009), 56.
24. Teresa Cannarozzo, "Agrigento: Risorse, strumenti, attori; Percorsi verso nuovi orizzonti di sviluppo locale," *Progettare le identità e il territorio,* ed. Francesco Lo Piccolo (Florence, 2009), 90–91.
25. Fabrizio Giovenale spent his entire career within public agencies: the INA-Casa, the GESCAL, and then the Servizio Studi e programmazione-SSP of the Ministry of Public Works, before he became director of the ISES in 1968. See the biographical profile by the Centro di Cultura Ecologica—Archivio Ambientalista, "Biografia di Fabrizio Giovenale," http://www.centrodiculturaecologica.it/home/node/285 (accessed 11 November 2014).
26. Minutes of a meeting between Mancini, De Rossi, Giglia, Franco, Di Gioia, and the General Secretary of the Regione Siciliana, n.d. but most probably 29 January 1968, as

emerges from an enclosed letter, in box 26 "Terremoto del 1968 varie," MLP 29 AG, ASPC.
27. Ispettorato Generale per la ricostruzione nelle zone terremotate, "Relazione sull'organizzazione e sull'attività svolta dall'Ispettorato dalla sua costituzione," Palermo, 30 May 1968, n.1473, in box 4 "Atti vari Terremoto gennaio 1968," MLP 3, ASPC.
28. Ispettorato generale per le zone colpite dai terremoti del gennaio 1968, Report on a meeting in the office of the Presidenza della Regione Siciliana, Palermo, 8 July 1968, signed by Inspector Luigi Corona, in box 2 "Leggi decreti circolari su quesiti terremoto 68," MLP 3, ASPC. The meeting was attended by: "Presidente Regione, Capo di Gabinetto Min Int, Prefetto Giordano del Min.Int, Prefetti di Agrigento Palermo e Trapani, vice pres. GESCAL dott. Chirosi, ISES, Provv.OOPP per la Sicilia, Capo Ispettorato Generale, Ing. Capi GC Agrigento, Palermo Trapani, Assessori a LL.PP. Agricoltura e Foreste, Enti Locali, Sviluppo Economico, Sanità della Regione Siciliana e Presidente ESA."
29. Decreto del Presidente della Regione Siciliana (decree of the President of the Sicilian Region) no. 147, 25 October 1968.
30. I have not found the complete text of the plan, but merely a summary produced one year later: Ministero dei Lavori Pubblici, Servizio Studi e Programmazione—Ufficio Coordinamento dei Piani Territoriali, "Rapporto sui provvedimenti destinati a favorire la rinascita economica e sociale dei comuni terremotati ai sensi dell'art.59 del D.L. 27.2.1968, n.79 e successive modificazioni," Rome, February 1969, in box 4, MLP 3, ASPC.
31. ISES, "Stato attuale dello Studio per la ricostruzione e lo sviluppo economico delle zone terremotate siciliane," typescript, 15 July 1968, in box 6 "Ispettorato generale per le zone colpite dal terremoto 68: Programmi di intervento per la programmazione economica," folder "programmi di intervento per la ripresa economica delle zone terremotate C.I.P.E.," MLP 3, ASPC.
32. Leonardo Barrile, Mayor of Montevago; Francesco Giovenco, from the Comitato Cittadino (town committee) of Gibellina; Vito Bellafiore, Mayor of Santa Ninfa; Lorenzo Barbera from the Center for Studies and Activities; Nino D'Angelo from the Comitato Cittadino of Campobello di Mazara; and Giambattista Giaccone, Mayor of Menfi, "Appello delle popolazioni terremotate," *Pianificazione Siciliana* 3–4 (March–April 1968): 4.
33. "Premessa," in "Alcune indicazioni operative," 3–4.
34. Centro studi e iniziative, *Piano di sviluppo democratico per le valli Belice, Carboi, Jato*, typescript (Partinico, 1968).
35. Minutes of a meeting of the sub-commission for the coordination of *piani comprensoriali* (district plans) held on 12 October 1968 in Palermo, attachment A to the report of the Ispettorato per le zone terremotate, 21 November 1968, in box 4 "Atti vari Terremoto gennaio 1968," MLP 3, ASPC.
36. Marziano Di Maio, "Il piano di sviluppo democratico delle valli Belice, Carboi e Jato: Piano di sviluppo agricolo," *Urbanistica: Bollettino della sezione regionale piemontese dell'Istituto nazionale di urbanistica* 56 (1970): 66–67; Giuseppe Carta, "Il Piano di sviluppo democratico delle valli del Belice, del Carboi e dello Jato: Piano di sviluppo urbanistico," *Urbanistica: Bollettino della sezione regionale piemontese dell'Istituto nazionale di urbanistica* 56 (1970): 78–90. A polemic report of that public meeting is in

Lorenzo Barbera, *I ministri dal cielo: I contadini del Belice raccontano* (Milan, 1980), 80–84.

37. An outline of PTC no. 8 and the related maps are in Agostino Renna, Antonio De Bonis, and Giuseppe Gangemi, eds., *Costruzione e progetto: La valle del Belice* (Milan, 1979). These considerations are explicated and developed in an official publication by the ISES, in which the ISES presented to the public all the works done in the Valley. ISES, "L'ISES nella Valle del Belice: La ricostruzione dopo il terremoto del gennaio 1968," special issue, *Quaderni di Edilizia Sociale* 6 (1972), entire issue.
38. Copies of the presidential decrees (the first of which dates to 30 May 1968) and of technical reports on relocations are in box 3 "Trasferimento di abitati terremoto 68," MLP 3, ASPC.
39. ISES, "L'ISES nella Valle del Belice," quotes 56 and 58.
40. See the credits in ISES, "L'ISES nella Valle del Belice," 185–90. Giovenale and Fabbri had coauthored a paper for the 1963 conference of the INU (Istituto Nazionale di Urbanistica), on the city-region. See Marcello Fabbri and Fabrizio Giovenale, "Dalla città-regione alla regione urbanizzata," typescript, 1963, in folder 34, Collection Giovenale, Centro di Cultura Ecologica.
41. Agostino Renna, "La costruzione della città e della campagna," in Renna, De Bonis, and Gangemi, *Costruzione e progetto*, 104–5.
42. Regione Siciliana, *Proposte di provvedimenti per favorire la rinascita economica e sociale dei comuni terremotati (art.59 della legge 18-3-1968, n.241)* (Palermo 1969); "Proposte e programmi di intervento del Ministero dei LL.PP. nelle zone terremotate (art.59)," in box 4 "Atti vari Terremoto gennaio 1968," MLP 3, ASPC.
43. Regione Siciliana to CIPE, "Provvedimenti per la rinascita economica e sociale delle zone terremotate della Sicilia," 7 May 1969, in box 4 "Atti vari Terremoto gennaio 1968," MLP 3, ASPC.
44. Ministero del Bilancio e della Programmazione Economica, "Piano di interventi a favore dei comuni siciliani colpiti dal terremoto ai sensi dell'articolo 59 della legge 241/1968," 23 July 1968, in box 4 "Atti vari Terremoto gennaio 1968," MLP 3, ASPC.
45. See Direttore Generale Servizi Speciali to Ministro dei Lavori Pubblici, Rome, 17 December 1968, in box 2 "Leggi decreti circolari su quesiti terremoto 68," MLP 3, ASPC.
46. See the report of the Prefect of Trapani to the Ministero dell'Interno, 15 October 1968, in box 86, folder "Danilo Dolci attività," sub-folder "Centro studi e iniziative," MI Gab 67–70, ACS.
47. Provveditore Grappelli to Direzione Generale Servizi Speciali del Ministero dei Lavori Pubblici, 1 November 1968, telegram n.544, in box 26, folder 3, MLP 29 AG, ASPC.
48. The protest was reported in a document of the committees, "Il giudizio popolare di Roccamena," April 1969, in box 248, folder 14519/98/1/1/1, sub-folder 2, MI Gab 67–70 ACS. See also Barbera, *I ministri dal cielo*, 66–71.
49. See the testimony by Lorenzo Barbera reported in Carola Susani, *L'infanzia è un terremoto* (Rome and Bari, 2008), 62–63.
50. *Pianificazione Siciliana* 5, no. 1 (1970).
51. *Pianificazione Siciliana* 5, no. 10 (1970), special issue.
52. See Guido Orlando and Salvo Vitale, *Danilo Dolci, La radio dei poveri cristi: Il progetto, la realizzazione, i testi della prima radio libera in Italia* (Marsala, 2008).

53. See the vivid testimony by Vito Accardo, one of the leaders of that protest. Vito Accardo, video interview, 20 May 2009, 00:56:07, *Le Terre che Tremarono*, Centro di Ricerche Economiche e Sociali per il Meridione [hereafter CRESM].
54. This protest, which joined the claims of the anti-recruitment movements, was instrumental for the creation of the first law for the "obiezione di coscienza": Law no. 772 of 15 December 1972, the so-called "Legge Marcora." The protest is documented by various prefects' reports in box 297, folder G/5/8/44, Ministero dell Interno, Pubblica Sicurezza, G-Associazioni, ACS.
55. See for example Genio Civile di Agrigento, "Relazione sul trasferimento totale di Montevago e parziale di Santa Margherita," 5 March 1968, in box 3 "Trasferimento di abitati terremoto 68," MLP 3, ASPC.
56. Manuscript minutes of a meeting with Mangione (Regione Siciliana), De Rossi and Giovenale (ISES), Corona (Ispettorato), Franco (Consiglio Superiore del lavori Pubblici), and Giacomo Mancini, in box 2, MLP 3 Stampa, ASPC. Similar difficulties are also testified in a report of the General Inspectorate: Ispettorato Generale, "Relazione sull'attività dell'Ispettorato," Palermo, 10 October 1968, no. 4032, in box 4, MLP 3, ASPC.
57. Signed letter to Presidente del Consiglio dei Ministri, received on 24 May 1969, in box 3 "Trasferimento di abitati terremoto 68," MLP 3, ASPC. It has to be highlighted that even the parliamentary commission expressed serious doubts about the accuracy of geological reports, as reported in Senato della Repubblica, *Relazione della Commissione Parlamentare d'inchiesta sull'attuazione degli interventi per la ricostruzione e la ripresa socio-economica dei territori della Valle del Belice colpiti dai terremoti del gennaio 1968* (Rome, 1981), 133–38.
58. As reported in Senato della Repubblica, *Relazione della Commissione Parlamentare*, 130.
59. Ispettorato generale per le zone terremotate, Trasferimento degli abitati e Situazione dei lavori affidati all'ISES, not dated but updated until 1973, in box 3 "Trasferimento di abitati terremoto 68," MLP 3, ASPC.
60. See the plans of the old and the new Gibellina in Renna, De Bonis, and Gangemi, *Costruzione e progetto*, 255–56.
61. ISES, "L'ISES nella Valle del Belice," 25.
62. Decreto del Presidente della Repubblica (presidential decree) no. 1036, 30 December 1972, "Norme per la riorganizzazione delle amministrazioni e degli enti pubblici operanti nel settore della edilizia residenziale pubblica," *Gazzetta Ufficiale* 58, 3 March 1973.
63. Senato della Repubblica, *Relazione della Commissione Parlamentare*, 374.
64. Ibid., 393–94.
65. Ibid., 405–15.
66. See for instance "Esposto baraccati di Gibellina per pessimo stato baracche," 29 November 1969, in box 26, folder 3, MLP 29 AG, ASPC and "Esposto dei baraccati della baraccopoli Santo Monte di Campobello Mazara," 26 October 1969, in box 28, folder 1, MLP 29 AG, ASPC. See also "Delibera Consiglio Comunale di Menfi," 31 December 1969, in box 27, MLP 29 AG, ASPC.
67. See the testimony by Vanni Giustizia in Barbera, *I ministri dal cielo*, 109.

68. Ministero dei Lavori Pubblici, Direzione Generale Servizi Speciali, "Indagini per irregolarità commesse nella costruzione di opere per terremotati della Sicilia 1968," Trapani, 10 July 1971, in box 27 "corrispondenza 1970," MLP 29 AG, ASPC.
69. Giovanni Abbati and Filippo Rossi, "Rapporto-accertamento tecnico aministrativo e proposte per l'utilizzazione di fondi disponibili per opere di competenza dell'Ispettorato Generale per le zone colpite dal terremoto del gennaio del 1968 in alcuni centri delle provincie di Agrigento, Palermo e Trapani," 26 January 1976, in box without number, MLP 3, ASPC.
70. Lorenzo Barbera, "La disgregazione della solidarietà e delle lotte popolari," *Casabella: Rivista di urbanistica architettura e disegno industriale* 420 (1976): 10.
71. Law no. 178, 29 April 1976, "Ulteriori norme per la ricostruzione delle zone del Belice distrutte dal terremoto del gennaio 1968," Article 5. See Judith Chubb, "Three Earthquakes: Political Response, Reconstruction and the Institutions: Belice (1968), Friuli (1976), Irpinia (1980)," in *Disastro! Disasters in Italy since 1860: Culture, Politics, Society*, ed. John Dickie, John Foot, and Frank M. Snowden (New York and Basingstoke, 2002), 197.
72. In 1976 a sociological inquiry led by Aldo Musacchio investigated the effects of the reconstruction and public policies for socioeconomic development: Aldo Musacchio, ed., *Stato e società nel Belice: La gestione del terremoto 1968–1976* (Milan, 1981). The same year a special issue by Agostino Renna and Giuseppe Gangemi of *Casabella: Rivista di urbanistica architettura e disegno industriale* 420 (December 1976) scrutinizes the results of the ISES action for town planning and architecture. The issue was later expanded into a book (Renna, De Bonis, and Gangemi, *Costruzione e progetto*). In the same years, the weekly review *L'Espresso* was publishing the articles of the investigative journalist Mario La Ferla, and Lorenzo Barbera published in 1980 his books on the experience of popular mobilization, Barbera, *I ministri dal cielo*.
73. Senato della Repubblica, *Relazione della Commissione Parlamentare d'inchiesta sull'attuazione degli interventi per la ricostruzione e la ripresa socio-economica dei territori della Valle del Belice colpiti dai terremoti del gennaio 1968* (Rome, 1981).
74. Ibid., 403.
75. Ibid., 431.
76. Ibid., 147.
77. Ibid., 154.
78. Maria Crescimanno, Gian Gaspare Fardella, and Salvatore Tudisca, *L'agricoltura nella valle del Belice* (Palermo, 1993).
79. For a thorough analysis of social and economic changes in the late 1970s Belice Valley, see Musacchio, *Stato e società nel Belice: La gestione del terremoto 1968–1976*, esp. 151–56.
80. Article 41 of Law no. 241 of 18 March 1968 assigned 1 million lire to each family who had lost a member because of the earthquake. The amount added half a million for each additional family loss.
81. Interview with Lorenzo Barbera by Giacomo Parrinello, Partanna, 17 April 2012, in "Terremoti: Storia, memorie, narrazioni," ed. Gabriella Gribaudi and Anna Maria Zaccaria, special issue of *Memoria/Memorie: Materiali di Storia* 5 (2012): 171–200.
82. The redistribution of land property and agricultural converions on small properties are largely confirmed by Ministero dell'Agricoltura e delle Foreste, Consorzio di Bon-

ifica del Bacino dell'Alto e Medio Belice Palermo, *Ricerca pilota a valenza interregionale sulla riconversione colturale ed ammodernamento delle strutture nel comprensorio dell'alto e medio Belice* (Palermo, 1993), 18–19 and 26.

83. See the letter from Gabriele Pescatore to President Saragat, 30 November 1968, in box 248, folder 14519/98/1/1/1, sub-folder 2, MI Gab 67–70, ACS.
84. The disaster area was divided into three regions with a separate plan for each: no. 25, no. 2, and no. 4. Regione Siciliana, Ente di Sviluppo Agricolo, *Piano di Sviluppo Agricolo n.25 "Valli del Belice e del Platani"* (Palermo, 1970); Regione Siciliana, Ente di Sviluppo Agricolo, *Piano di Sviluppo Agricolo n.2 "Collinare del Trapanese"* (Palermo, 1971); Regione Siciliana, Ente di Sviluppo Agricolo, *Piano di sviluppo agricolo n.4 "del Monrealese"* (Palermo, 1974).
85. Cassa per il Mezzogiorno, Consorzio di Bonifica dell'Alto e Medio Belice, *Serbatoio di Garcia sul fiume Belice sinistro* (Palermo, 1974), 4.
86. Cassa per il Mezzogiorno, Regione Siciliana, Ente di Sviluppo Agricolo, *Progetto di massima per la utilizzazione dell'acqua a scopo irriguo: Serbatoio Garcia; Relazione economica agraria* (Palermo, 1973), 4.
87. Letter to Lorenzo Barbera (signed by "Giulio"), Milan, 10 January 1976, in folder II, 19, Archivio Dolci-Barbera, CRESM.
88. The articles, formerly published between September and October 1977, are now on the website of the Foundation "Francese": http://www.fondazionefrancese.org/inchieste.htm (accessed 6 June 2011).
89. See the biographic profile of Mario Francese on the site http://www.fondazionefrancese.org/biografia.htm (accessed 6 June 2011), and also Giovanna Fiume and Salvo LoNardo, *Mario Francese: Una vita in cronaca* (Palermo, 2000).
90. The exact amount of water for irrigation in the valley is not clear. According to the reclamation consortium, in 1993 a significant part of the Garcia Dam water served to irrigate other areas and to increase Palermo's water supply. See Consorzio di bonifica, *Ricerca pilota*, 55.
91. On Sicilian "cellar cooperatives" see Antonio Simeti, "Le cantine sociali," in *Storia della cooperazione Siciliana*, ed. Orazio Cancila (Palermo, 1993): 441–52.
92. There are significant internal differences, as shown by the case of Santa Ninfa studied by Michele Rostan, *La terribile occasione: Imprenditorialità e sviluppo in una comunità del Belice* (Bologna, 1998).
93. Federico Zeri, "La piovra culturale," *La Stampa*, 6 February 1988, 3. Corrao always defended the value of what he had done in Gibellina, including the choice of relocation. See Ludovico Corrao, video interview, 7 April 2010, 00:56:33, *Le Terre che Tremarono*, CRESM.
94. See for instance Massimo Bignardi, Davide Lacagnina and Paola Mantovani, eds., *Cantiere Gibellina: Una ricerca sul campo* (Rome, 2008).
95. See the interactive map based on the official data of the tax declaration IRPEF in 2007 by the financial newspaper *Il Sole 24 Ore*, http://www.ilsole24ore.com/art/SoleOnLine4/Italia/2008/08/italia-redditi-comuni.shtml (accessed 11 November 2014). In the last several years even viticulture has experienced a drastic contraction with respect to the 1990s, as stated in a report by Alessandro La Grassa and Giampaolo Grillo, "Il vino siciliano: Un gigante con i piedi di argilla," *Partecipare* 2, no. 2 (2005): 2–5.

96. For 1961 see Istituto Centrale di Statistica, *10° Censimento generale della popolazione, 15 ottobre 1961 Popolazione legale dei comuni* (Rome, 1963), 6, 119, 120, 164, 165. For the 2001 data see Istituto Centrale di Statistica, *Atlante statistico dei comuni*, database and software, 2014. http://www.istat.it/it/archivio/113712.
97. On this change and comparisons with the 1976 Friuli and the 1980 Irpinia earthquakes, see Chubb, "Three Earthquakes," 186–233.
98. See Emanuela Guidoboni and Gianluca Valensise, eds., *Il peso economico e sociale dei disastri sismici in Italia negli ultimi 150 anni* (Bologna, 2011), 316–18, 355–57.
99. See Stefano Zorzi, *Parola di Burri* (Turin, 1995): 59. A biography of Burri in Italian is available on the website of his namesake foundation: http://www.fondazioneburri.org/ita/pdf/biografia.pdf.
100. See for example Emanuela Guidoboni, "Upside-Down Landscapes: Seismicity and Seismic Disasters in Italy," *Nature and History in Modern Italy*, ed. Marco Armiero and Marcus Hall, (Athens, OH, 2010), 52.
101. The documentary directed by Emanuele Svezia, *Earthquake 68: Gente di Gibellina*, 2008, color, 01:38:08, reports several criticisms.
102. As I remarked in the introduction, this phenomenon has been largely studied from the viewpoint of large metropolitan areas and their "in-between" spaces. See Edward W. Soja, *Postmetropolis: Critical Studies of Cities and Regions* (Malden, MA, 2000); Stephen Graham, and Simon Marvin, *Splintering Urbanism: Networked Infrastructures, Technological Mobilities and the Urban Condition* (London and New York, 2001); Thomas Sieverts, *Cities without Cities: An Interpretation of the Zwischenstadt* (London and New York, 2003); Marc Antrop, "Changing Patterns in the Urbanized Countryside of Western Europe," *Landscape Ecology* 15 (2000): 257–70. In terms of physical forms, ecological impact, and material cultures, however, even regions that are distant from major population centers, such as the Belice Valley, should be considered part of a blended urban-rural experience and be subject to more sustained attention.

 CONCLUSION

Fault Lines

Earthquakes come and go. Many years have elapsed since those that destroyed Messina and the Belice Valley, and human memory of the terrible disasters has faded. Eyewitnesses of the 1908 disaster are long gone; in the Belice Valley, a new generation that never experienced the disaster has come of age. The earthquakes and the devastation, the odyssey of the survivors; the painful and tormented decades of rebuilding that were once the vivid and tragic experiences of thousands of men and women—today these are nothing more than an echo preserved in the faint images and crackling voices of old pictures and films, or words in history books. Yet, these events are deeply inscribed on the landscape of those two corners of Sicily. In the Belice Valley, the material remembrance of the earthquake is not simply confined to spectacular artworks such as the *Cretto* by Alberto Burri. It is also in the ruins that overlook the new town of Santa Margherita Belice. It takes the shape of the wasteland where Montevago once stood. It has the perturbing concreteness of the ghost town of Poggioreale, where everything remains unchanged but for the tall rank weeds. Even in Messina, the memory and experience of the earthquake is a material part of the urban landscape, albeit more subtly. Interestingly, no memorial has ever been built there, and only a few plaques affixed to the walls of buildings explicitly commemorate the disaster. However, the shantytowns that still persist in Messina—in some cases even with the same huts erected in 1909,[1]—the scattered wastelands, or the ruins of the monumental Monte di Pietà in the center of the city, still embody the tragic events of 1908.

The persistent materiality of the earthquake is not limited to ruins, dilapidation, and emptiness. The new buildings, the new urban plans, and the new infrastructure are also parts of an earthquake "memoryscape," although the inhabitants do not always recognize them as such. These traces are what make Messina and the Belice Valley two exceptional places. In a country famous for its historic urban and rural environments, where transformations have taken the shape of the gradual overlapping and integration of urban forms and features, Messina and the Belice Valley have been violently unmade and remade anew. In Messina, broad, square roads, compact and resistant buildings, and a comprehensive sanitary network are coupled with the almost complete absence of any traces of its pre-earthquake urban past. In the Belice Valley, new settlements and infrastructure form a suburban cityscape in the hearth of inland rural Sicily. Only a few traces of the past have survived in the inhabited built environment, and even the rural landscape has changed profoundly due to the combined effects of property redistribution, agricultural conversion, and irrigation. In all these features, the environments in both today's Belice Valley and Messina are a material legacy of and memorial to the earthquakes that once destroyed them. The voice of the earthquake still rings powerfully and resoundingly through the landscape, even after human memories of it are gone.

Tales of Earthquake Urbanism

The fault lines of Sicily set in motion the unmaking and remaking of Messina and the Belice Valley. Yet historical changes, as we all know, do not happen in a vacuum. Telluric forces acted upon a thick tapestry of ongoing transformations on multiple scales. The voice of the earthquake speaks through these interwoven transformations, and thus we can understand it only by means of historical explanation and its painstaking untangling of multiple threads.

By the late nineteenth century Messina was a typical Southern Italian city with a rich urban past, a growing population, and problematic urban ecologies. As in many other Italian cities, plans and projects for reform, initially limited to the expansion of the built space outside the city walls, increasingly embraced the physical and social transformation of the inner city. In the wake of *risanamento* policies in the early 1880s, these attempts crystallized into plans for comprehensive urban reform. This included the enlargement of streets, the demolition of working-class housing and neighborhoods, and the creation of a comprehensive system for water circulation. Following this plan, after multiple failed attempts, the newly established Municipal Technical Bureau succeeded in tapping the sources of the Niceto River at the expense of the local communities, increasing Messina's water supply substantially. Other parts of the *risanamento* ideal remained confined to the planning stages, however, and the same was true for other projects of urban improvement, such as port renewals and flood control measures. Furthermore, in spite of the occurrence of several earthquakes between 1895 and 1907, urban reformers and local authorities never factored in seismicity in their debates and plans for urban change. Over these years, Messina's built environment grew considerably, but without regard for seismic risk or the implementation of any prudent anti-seismic measures, and the significant damages produced by the 1895 earthquake were treated only with non-structural interventions, paving the way for the tragic consequences of the 1908 earthquake.

The earthquake was a crossroads. Messina's weak urban environment crumbled overnight. Thousands of inhabitants died and the survivors were sheltered in temporary huts. The existence of the city itself was called into question, and the opportunity to rebuild Messina on the same hazardous site sparked a countrywide debate. The presumed "natural advantages" of the site and the evidence of urban recovery ultimately led the authorities to sanction the permanence of Messina in its historic location, on condition that the reconstruction followed a strict code for earthquake-resistant engineering and planning. As a result, the city had to be planned along new lines, and that imperative provided the opportunity to combine the creation of an earthquake-proof urban environment with an upgraded version of pre-earthquake schemes for urban reform and expansion. The earthquake, moreover, produced other, more indirect effects. The massive funding that the state provided to subsidize the reconstruction transformed the local economy, encouraging a shift from maritime commerce to the building industry and tertiary activities. In addition, it also stimulated labor migration from the countryside despite the poor condition of the urban environment. These inward migrations, combined with a structural housing shortage, greatly influenced the pace and results of the reconstruction. The longevity of provisional huts and shelters proved greater than expected, and the new urban environment took shape by incorporating some of the huts or refashioning them into "ultra-popular" housing. In sum, then, the shape and features of the new city certainly drew on pre-earthquake processes and plans. However, the 1908 earthquake twisted these plans and processes, removed persistent obstacles, imposed new priorities, and spurred new and unexpected phenomena; it thus played a determining role in the making of the new Messina. To dismiss this fact by exclusively recalling the deep continuities would signify a deterministic understanding of historical processes, and one that downplays the role of contingency.

The earthquake of 1968 is as significant for the history of the Belice Valley. The valley of the Belice River was one of the poorest regions of Italy, and was repeatedly at the center of waves of social unrest. From the 1920s, the authorities targeted this region with experimental plans for rural modernization based on a set of coordinated interventions including land reclamation, anti-malaria campaigns, improvements to the road network, and modifications in the settlement pattern. The Belice Valley was one of the key areas for integrated reclamation in the 1930s, and one of the centers of the Fascist "colonization of large estates" before World War II. In the postwar climate, those plans were reframed under the banner of development and extensively funded by agencies such as the Cassa per il Mezzogiorno, with the aim of stimulating a broader process of economic growth. In the late 1950s, despite some improvements in infrastructure, most development goals were unachieved, and many residents chose the road of long-distance labor migration. In response to the failures of development policies, grassroots committees formed with the purpose of encouraging "local development" through water storage and irrigation. Through studies, inquiries and protest initiatives, mass mailing, marches, feasts, and other demonstrations, these committees tried to both monitor and provoke action on the part of the authorities, while extending their influence and support throughout the region. Despite this, the new industrial course of development policies in the South marginalized the Belice Valley, and the most significant investment plans excluded the area.

The 1968 earthquakes came as a tragic surprise. At that time, western Sicily was not on seismic maps. The complete absence of earthquake prevention measures and the poor condition of the built environment amplified the effects of the tremors, and the material devastation was immense. Their lack of economic means magnified this devastation for local residents, many of whom chose to emigrate in the very first weeks. Public debates in the aftermath of the quake deemed the poverty of the earthquake-affected region responsible for the devastation, and post-earthquake legislation tied the reconstruction to a revolutionary transformation of the valley into an urban-industrial region. Taking advantage of the relocation of fourteen affected towns, the ISES planners drew up the layout of a "city-territory," a network of interconnected, modernist new towns working as a single urban unit and with an industrial economy. While the expected industrialization never came to pass, the reconstruction permanently altered the pattern of human settlement in the valley. Furthermore, income redistribution brought about by post-earthquake state subsidies, along with the long-awaited infrastructure for water storage and irrigation on the Belice River, prompted a spectacular change in land use. The earthquake therefore not only paved the way for profound transformations in the features and locations of settlements, but also stimulated a substantial modification of the geography of public investment and money flows, creating unexpected opportunities for rural development and resuming marginalized projects such as the dam on the Belice River. Today's Belice Valley would be unimaginably different without the unexpected irruption of telluric forces.

While Messina and the Belice Valley were changing so profoundly, the rest of the country also witnessed significant transformations. Between 1880 and 1920, most Italian cities experienced massive population growth, largely driven by rural inward migration. The cities created comprehensive sanitary infrastructure, cleared old working-class neighborhoods, and built new boulevards. They expanded beyond the boundaries of the old medieval walls, adapted their built environment to new functions, and dealt with conflicts and competition for resources. The making of the new, modern Messina is a piece of this larger history. So is the making of the new Belice Valley. Roads, energy networks, and sanitary infrastructure reached the most remote corners of the country in the second half of the twentieth century. Large portions of the rural landscape changed in this process, resource use and ecosystems were transformed, old economies were forced to adapt, and ties with centuries of tradition were radically severed. The life of country inhabitants changed profoundly, as they adopted habits and cultures much more similar to those of urban citizens than of their forebears. From an environmental and a social point of view, these two processes have much more in common than usually acknowledged. Despite the obvious differences between large urban centers and smaller rural locations, Messina and the Belice Valley exemplify two phases of the same epoch-making process: the transformation of Italy into a largely urbanized country.

While recognizing the common historical context in which these two histories took place, it is nevertheless vital to acknowledge their peculiarities. For instance, it is not enough to simply note that inward migration and population growth, such as that witnessed in Messina, happened simultaneously in other cities. One should also understand why they *also* happened in Messina, despite the terrible and tragic effects of the earthquake, despite a city that lay in ruins for decades, and despite the decline of traditional economic activities such as maritime commerce. As we have seen, the institutional response to the earthquake in Messina, and particularly the prominent amounts of money freed up for the reconstruction, played a crucial role in driving inward migration. Likewise, it is not enough to state that highways and new urban infrastructure were built in most of Italian countryside in the second half of the twentieth century. One should ask why this process in the Belice Valley took the form that it did: that is, with a complete reshaping of architectural style and settlement patterns. Here, the role of the earthquake was crucial too, in giving free rein to radical modernization plans. The histories of Messina and the Belice Valley thus are thus also histories of differences. They are histories of the fault lines that divide "before" from "after," and those that divide these two places from others in the country. These historical fault lines are, in many respects, the products of geological ones.

Earthquakes shaped the urbanism of Messina and the Belice Valley in many ways. The first, critical effect was the devastation and ruin of existing built environments. Almost complete destruction was the unavoidable starting point for the remaking of Messina and the Belice Valley. The occurrence of earthquakes exposed the inadequacy of the existing built environments. In both cases, the experience prompted contemporaries to rethink human settlements in order to make them more resistant, and their residents less vulnerable to earthquakes. In the first case, this resulted in the 1909 building and planning code, whereas in the second case it resulted in a combination of town relocations and socioeconomic development policies. Both these responses to the earthquakes, although quite different, had an enormous and long-lasting impact on the material configurations of Messina and the Belice Valley. The earthquakes also exerted indirect influence. The need for *ex novo* reconstruction gave developers the opportunity to realize long-debated plans. This was certainly the case with *risanamento* in Messina: the rebuilding plan provided the opportunity to implement the comprehensive sanitation plan of the late nineteenth century. In the Belice Valley, *ex novo* rebuilding allowed for the first time the realization of the infrastructural improvements that rural reformers had planned in the 1930s. The earthquakes, finally, prompted choices and actions that had unforeseen but substantial consequences for the making of the new Messina and Belice Valley, such as economic and demographic changes due to migration and public money earmarked for the reconstruction. The urbanism that emerged through these processes was largely the combination of the direct and indirect effects of the earthquakes.

The environments that resulted from the combination and interaction of all these different layers are specific and unique. In addition, the multiple influences of the earthquakes were conditioned by, and interacted with specific historical and geographical features of the place, with diverse cultures and social actors at a local, regional, and national levels, and with different historical times, producing outcomes that are essentially *incomparable*. From this point of view, one could dismiss these two histories as fascinating curiosities or bizarre accidents, certainly too exceptional to be the expression of a noteworthy historical phenomenon. And they surely are exceptional and unrepeatable, as every place and every history is. Yet the voice of the earthquake that spoke so clearly in the texts of Messina and the Belice Valley urbanism is not such a rare occurrence in history. Many other regions of Italy have been reshaped due to major earthquake disasters. Although each of those cases is an irretrievably singular historical occurrence, taken as a whole they outline a larger, albeit seldom acknowledged picture.[2] It would be helpful, I believe, to review some of the most significant seismic disasters I mentioned in the course of this book on a geographical basis. This would not only reinforce the point I make, but also help place the stories I have told into the broader context of seismicity and urbanism in Italy.

Fault Lines in a Seismic Country

In 1693, the Val di Noto, in southeastern Sicily, suffered the consequences of a major earthquake. The earthquakes obliterated at least fifteen towns and cities almost completely, among them Noto, at that time one of the biggest urban centers in the region; others, such as Catania, were severely damaged. The reconstruction process lasted for several years under the supervision of Giovanni Lanza, plenipotentiary of the Spanish Viceroy of Sicily. Most towns were rebuilt according to entirely new plans, in line with ideals of aesthetic harmony and rational design.[3] Some were also relocated to sites that were deemed safer and more suitable for reconstruction according to a new plan. The reconstruction thus resulted in a permanent modification of the urban patterns and of the settlement geography of the region.[4] Besides the transformation in urban shape and location, post-1693 rebuilding also introduced remarkable innovations in architectural style. Most public edifices and private houses in the affected localities were rebuilt a particular variant of the baroque style, later recognized as the most representative expression of the Sicilian Late Baroque, and incorporated limited measures to protect against seismic damage.[5] As a consequence of the earthquake and the subsequent reconstruction, the 1693 earthquake area has acquired unique architectural and urban features, thanks to which the Noto Valley's "earthquake urbanism" is today protected by the UNESCO as a World Heritage Site.[6]

Strong earthquakes have reshaped Calabria as much as Sicily, if not more. In particular, the years 1783 and 1784 are remembered for one of the most devastating seismic sequences in modern history. The combined effects of five major tremors reconfigured the landscape of southern Calabria: hills disappeared, rivers changed their courses, and new lakes materialized overnight. The consequences for the built environment were just as impressive. The quakes almost completely destroyed 182 towns and villages in Calabria, and 33 of these were subsequently relocated.[7] Even in these cases, radical urban redesign accompanied rebuilding and relocation, and the Bourbon administration introduced an innovative building code to ensure earthquake-resistant engineering, the *casa baraccata* technique.[8] The authorities also took the opportunity provided by the earthquake to promote the expropriation of Church properties to fund the reconstruction and, additionally, the redistribution of land ownership.[9] As we have seen, the twentieth century witnessed yet another sequence of devastating earthquakes in Calabria—1905, 1907, 1908, and 1913. The cumulative effects of these events led to the decline and abandonment of several small villages and the relocation of many others.[10] In addition, the adoption of the same building and planning code as in Messina encouraged a profound shift in building techniques and urban designs in many places.

Ascending the peninsula to the north, we encounter Irpinia, a seismic mountain region between Calabria and Naples. In 1857, a strong earthquake devastated several towns and villages. The administrative machine of the late Bourbon kingdom was unable to provide sufficient money and assistance, and the authorities that succeeded the Bourbons after national unification disregarded the earthquake area. The missed reconstruction resulted in a demographic shrinkage of the most affected towns, reflected in their simultaneous economic decline.[11] In the twentieth century, other earthquakes hit the region, namely in 1933 and 1962. The strongest and most destructive, however, happened in 1980. The authorities relocated the most affected towns, or rebuilt them to new designs. Other towns were reconstructed according to the pre-existing urban plan, but with substantially different features due to the adoption of earthquake-resistant technologies. Following the 1980 earthquake, the authorities funded the construction of new infrastructure to stimulate the socioeconomic development of the area, as with the Belice Valley after 1968. This state funding subsequently stimulated a trend of partial return migration from northern Italy and northern European countries.[12]

Irpinia is not the only region along the Apennine fault lines to have experienced seismic disasters in recent times. In 1915, a strong earthquake hit the Marsica region, a mountain area east of Rome. The earthquake devastated the city of Avezzano, at that time in the midst of rapid growth due to the drainage of the nearby Fucino Lake, and severely affected at least ten other towns. The authorities rebuilt Avezzano along new lines to comply with the 1909 earthquake building code and relocated some other towns. Relocation, however, was not always successful, and in some instances, the communities were split in two: some citizens remained in the old center, while others moved to the new location.[13] In 2009, another earthquake occurred a few kilometers further to the north, which devastated the city of L'Aquila and many other neighboring towns and villages and caused more than 300 fatalities.[14] The L'Aquila crisis is still far from resolution, and more than five years later the historic city center still lies in ruins, despite protests by the locals. However, due to a widely criticized decision by the government led by former Prime Minister Berlusconi, the authorities have already built new neighborhoods on the outskirts of the city. The houses built in these new settlements incorporate new building technology, designed to absorb possible tremors. It is not clear what the outcome for this region will be and whether the inhabitants will succeed in restoring the old town or not. In either case, the earthquake will have had a profound influence on urbanism in L'Aquila and the surrounding area.[15]

Climbing further north, we reach Umbria and Le Marche, affected by a seismic sequence in 1997. The earthquakes damaged not only private houses and edifices but also some of the most valuable examples of Italy's national heritage, such as the medieval Basilica of Saint Francis in Assisi. The most affected area comprised more than thirty villages and towns, where the state funded the rebuilding of private dwellings on condition that the owners undertook structural interventions to help them withstand earthquakes better.[16] In Friuli Venezia Giulia, in the far northeast of Italy, a seismic sequence in 1976 determined yet another significant transformation of the built environment. The earthquakes destroyed a number of towns across a large area. Unlike the Belice Valley, protests by associations and institutions led to the restoration of some of the destroyed localities exactly as they were before the earthquake, due to their special historic and artistic value. Gemona and the cathedral of Venzone were rebuilt "stone by stone," like some European cities were after World War II.[17] In the case of Gemona, historical restoration was limited to the street pattern and orientation and the external aspects of buildings. The building technologies were different from the past and were designed to ensure they would withstand earthquakes better. The exclusive focus on the restoration of the old town had the paradoxical effect of allowing a disordered urban expansion outside the preserved center, which is still largely depopulated today.[18]

Sicily, Calabria, Irpinia, Abruzzi, Umbria, and Friuli are just the most ravaged regions of Italy, where the presence of a modern "earthquake urbanism" is most evident and has assumed particularly interesting forms. Many other examples, however, could find a place into this overview, and many more are likely to be added in the future along the fault lines that run underneath the land mass of Italy. In 2012, another seismic sequence hit an area erroneously held to be immune from earthquakes by the local population, the lower plain of Emilia Romagna. These earthquakes caused significant damages to the built environment of many towns. They also caused minor damages in cities such as Bologna and Modena. Despite the lack of earthquake knowledge within the local population, evidence of past quakes in the region is substantial, starting from the 1570 Ferrara earthquake, and scholars knew the area was as a seismic one.[19] In a pioneering article, historian Piero Bevilacqua pointed out the need to incorporate earthquakes into historical narratives of southern Italy as "agents of historical change."[20] Almost no corner of the country, in fact, could be deemed immune to seismicity. In a hard-hitting recent compendium of Italian seismic disasters over the last 150 years, Emanuela Guidoboni and Gianluca Valensise have pointed out that the economic and social impact of these events parallels the absence of a consistent public prevention policy. While scientific evidence shows that they are a regular occurrence, the authorities tend to treat earthquakes as one-off emergencies. The lack of awareness and farsighted prevention policies, they argue, has made a constant environmental feature the cause of tragically recurrent disasters and a heavy burden on the country's social and economic development.[21]

I would also argue that recurring earthquakes have played a significant role in the unmaking and remaking of built environments across the country. In all the examples that I have recalled, as much as in Messina and the Belice Valley, earthquakes have been an important factor in urban transformation. They have stimulated radical innovations in urban design, the permanent transformation of the geography of urban settlement, the creation of new infrastructure, and last but not least, in many cases a better (if not ideal) adaptation of the built environment to seismicity. A pattern of recurring responses has emerged through time, including building and planning codes, town relocation, special legislation, and substantial public funding. In several cases, solutions, laws, and expertise that matured in one place, such as the seismic code introduced in 1909, migrated from there and eventually extended to cover most of the nation's territory. Earthquakes have also contributed to enhancing the widespread affirmation of certain technologies, such as reinforced concrete, which is now the principal building material for private housing, public edifices, and infrastructure alike, its success largely due to its tremor-resistant properties.[22] In conclusion, the recurrence, geographical diffusion, and local and national impact of earthquakes on urban environments and landscapes, render earthquakes a primary force in the history of urbanization processes in Italy, and one that deserves careful scrutiny. Any narrative of Italian modernity and urbanization that disregards seismicity should be deemed incomplete.

Hazards, Urbanization, and Nature

Italy lies in an extremely volatile location, along the faulting system between the African and the Eurasian plates: the particular significance of earthquakes in its environmental history is clearly related to this fact. Yet plate tectonics is a planetary phenomenon, and no continent is immune from seismicity. California and Alaska, Peru and Chile, Portugal and Morocco, Iran and China, Japan and New Zealand share the slow but powerful encounters of underground plates of solid rocks floating on a sea of magma. The consequences of the sudden release of energy along the global fault lines have shaped their built environments too, making the history of earthquake urbanism a truly global history. Due to strong earthquakes, human settlements have been destroyed and rebuilt countless times throughout human history in virtually every known civilization on Earth. However, this is simultaneously an inescapably local history. Faulting has different characteristics in different places, and each release of energy is different from every other in terms of intensity, duration, and locality. Energy strikes specific combinations of surface elements—rocks, alluvial soils, water—producing largely divergent effects. Energy, moreover, interacts in multiple and mutable ways with human-crafted environments in places that are shaped by history as much as humans themselves. The response to destruction and the choices about reconstruction are also deeply entrenched with the particular experience, knowledge, and expectations of distinct places and periods. A global history of earthquakes and urbanism, therefore, cannot be but the history of how the infinite variety of human societies, cultures, and places interact with a fundamental and perennial feature of our planet—seismicity and its multifarious expressions.

The growing historical literature on earthquakes does allow us to identify some major threads, however, at least over the last few centuries. Modern earthquakes often resulted in bold projects for social and material improvements. Following both the 1746 Lima earthquake and the 1755 Lisbon earthquake, the ruling authorities interpreted the almost total destruction as an opportunity to drastically transform the urban environment and society. In Lima, the Viceroy tried, not entirely successfully, to reshape the urban environment by eliminating all traces of the baroque and imposing sobriety and uniformity of architectural style on the reluctant higher classes.[23] In Lisbon, the firm direction of Sebastião de Melo, Marquise of Pombal, transformed the reconstruction into an opportunity to reform the urban design and architectural style of downtown Lisbon.[24] In both Lima and Lisbon, moreover, the better adaptation of the settlements to the seismicity of the sites was also at stake. The ruling authorities seriously considered permanent relocation and introduced new codes for earthquake-resistant (and, in the case of Lisbon, fire-resistant) engineering and planning.[25] These measures appear to have been more successful in Lisbon than in Lima, but in both cases adaptation to seismicity brought about transformations of the built environment. In addition, other side-effects, such as the redistribution of land or the substantial modification of the urban economy, influenced post-earthquake urban developments.[26]

Post-earthquake reconstruction, however, did not always take a radical turn. Perhaps the most striking example of this is San Francisco, California. In 1906, a combination of earthquake and fire wiped out most of San Francisco's built environment. The site looked like an empty brown field after the disaster, and this fact would theoretically have allowed the radical reshaping of the city, as had happened in Lisbon, and as would happen again in Messina just two years later. Architect Daniel Burnham had already drawn up a new urban plan for San Francisco in 1905, and some of the city authorities certainly considered the possibility of implementing it after the earthquake. Nevertheless, in the end, the city regained its former shape, in order to prevent delays in the rebuilding process.[27] For different reasons, even the planned relocation of San Francisco's Chinatown failed: the resistance of the local Chinese community, backed by the Chinese authorities, successfully imposed reconstruction *in situ*.[28] Moreover, no open debate took place concerning adaptation to seismicity: to avoid the booming metropolis of the West being labeled as a risky location, boosters successfully publicized the event itself as a fire disaster rather than an earthquake disaster.[29] The rebuilding became an opportunity to make some changes in urban infrastructure and environment, such as a comprehensive sanitary network and the paving of all streets, but not for an explicit seismic adaptation strategy.[30]

The absence of seismic prevention in post-1906 San Francisco contrasts with the intensive efforts for earthquake-resistant urbanism in Japan. There, modern strategies of adaptation to seismicity were debated within the framework of opposition between "native" Japanese and "foreign" (mostly Western) cultures and technologies. The Great Nōbi Earthquake of 1891 provoked criticism of the Western masonry building style that had recently been adopted and a favorable re-evaluation of traditional building techniques, and later, a local interpretation of reinforced concrete.[31] While improvements in adaptation to seismicity were a constant feature in Japan seismic history, major post-earthquake urban changes were implemented only where there were pre-existing plans and only in presence of a "broader societal mandate for change."[32] The Great Kanto Earthquake in 1923, which, in combination with a conflagration, flattened Tokyo, stimulated ambitious modernization projects. In the aftermath, former mayor of Tokyo and Home Minister Gotō Shinpei envisioned a radical reshaping of the capital.[33] The plan, strongly contested and debated by different offices of the Japanese government, was almost entirely dismissed. The reconstruction, nevertheless, produced remarkable transformations, including street widening and the displacement of inhabitants, the creation of green areas, and implementation of sanitary infrastructure.[34] After the 1995 Kobe earthquake, the uneven spread of the damages provided opportunities to devise grand plans for urban renewal along with urban zoning and new building codes. Existing planning procedures and contestations, however, complicated the implementation of those plans, and the overall results appear largely uneven.[35]

In the second half of the twentieth century, radical post-earthquake modernization projects are a recurring feature. After the 1944 San Juan earthquake in Argentina, architects and planners envisioned remaking the built environment not only to increase its resistance to future earthquakes, but also to foster social change. The authorities ultimately dismissed this project, which is considered by historian Mark Healey to be the incubator of Peronism, and the rebuilding followed a less ambitious plan. Post-earthquake San Juan was nevertheless substantially altered, both in the layout of the city and in the technical features of the buildings (with a shift from adobe to concrete), and it boasted a more even distribution of resources and wealth through different social groups.[36] In Peru, after the 1970 earthquake, the authorities tried to connect seismic adaptation to ambitions of social and economic reform. They relocated and rebuilt Yungay along new lines, despite opposition from the survivors,[37] whereas in Chimbote they tried to implement a large-scale plan for urban reform and industrial development.[38] In Managua, after the 1972 earthquake, the ruling dictator Somoza envisioned the transformation of the capital according to a new urban model, turning Managua into a sprawling city with all the markers of North American urban modernity.[39] In China, after the 1976 Tangshan earthquake, the Maoist leaders redesigned the city following a new earthquake building code. The plan for a modern Tangshan also introduced new kinds of housing units (deemed more appropriate to a good communist life), proposed a rigorous system of functional zoning, and created a new transport infrastructure for the city.[40]

These mid-twentieth-century post-earthquake modernization projects in Asia and Latin America seem to be literal representations of the "high modernism" criticized by James Scott. Experts and bureaucrats saw post-earthquake landscapes as blank spaces onto which they could inscribe authoritarian schemes of radical social and economic change, usually without any consideration of local needs, knowledge, and preferences. A new built environment would give inescapable concreteness to the new social and economic landscape. When considering similarities to earlier cases, such as Lisbon under Pombal, or to democratic regimes such as Italy in 1968, it occurs to me that we need a different label to describe the ambitious visions of regeneration and renewal that earthquakes have so often triggered across the centuries and the continents. However, regardless of how we define these visions, fault lines will not disappear, and earthquakes will continue to occur, destroying the work of human hands, taking lives, and reshaping landscapes. Earthquake urbanism may take different forms through time and space, but it will remain one of the key processes in the making, unmaking, and remaking of our world.

As recalled in the introduction to this volume, earthquakes are a very particular natural phenomenon. Different timescales overlap when an earthquake occurs. Geological processes taking millions of years, the few thousand years of history of our kind on Earth, and built environments that are a couple of hundred years old all collapse into the shortest point in time: a dozen seconds, a violent tremor of the ground, and an echo that can be heard down the centuries. Nevertheless, other nonhuman forces, elements, and processes have been constantly and ubiquitously active in human history: climatic events such as storms, hurricanes, and tornadoes; conflagrations; floods and landslides; epidemics. Virtually every city and region on the planet, in every epoch of human history, has experienced the impact of nonhuman forces. Chicago would not be the same without the conflagration that destroyed its timber buildings in 1871 and the subsequent reconstruction, nor New Orleans without the constant presence of water hazards and the insufficient solutions adopted to cope with them.[41] The 1842 conflagration and the 1862 flood profoundly reshaped Hamburg in Germany.[42] The urban environment of Manila is the product of the concurrent influences of fire and earthquake hazards.[43]

The extent of post-disaster transformations partly depended on how much of the former built environment had survived intact, but also on the strength of pre-existing interests and aftermath contestations. Strong central authorities were often of pivotal importance in enforcing the ambitious plans that tried to give shape to visions of change. Nonetheless, the tragic irony of natural hazards is that as much as they provide opportunities for unleashing the most radical expressions of human intentionality, they also represent the factual contestation of human control over the material world. Every reconstruction plan, while giving free rein to human ambition, has to take into account the failure that generated it in the first place and implicitly respond to that failure. These responses are not always effective, as we know, but they are generally consistent with the explanation of disastrous event and of its causes, and they play a central role in reshaping the built environment. Processes directly or indirectly triggered by the hazard itself, on the other hand, like migration, property redistribution, and emergency resettlement, often frustrate the expectations of even the most carefully designed plans and attempts to adapt. These processes interact in often unforeseen and always uncontrollable ways with human plans and programs. In this sense, post-disaster transformations are by no means the "pure" expression of human intentionality, but rather the outcome of more-than-human interplay.[44]

Natural hazards are recurrent and ubiquitous. Acknowledging this simple and well-known, and yet too often overlooked fact should encourage us to see natural hazards as the norm rather than the exception in the history of urbanization, and a major factor in the way built environments develop. Nonhuman forces and features have reshaped urban environments as much as their human inhabitants have. From this perspective, the environmental history of modern urbanization would appear to be a history of clashes, compromises, crises, and provisional stalemates—the history of attempts to shape a built environment entirely according to human will and plans, and the irreducible presence of forces and features that, in effect, participate in the development, failure, and unexpected outcomes of such plans. Acknowledging the place of natural hazards in urbanization, in other words, advises us to adopt an understanding of urbanization itself as a hybrid process of human and more-than-human actions and forces interacting on an always-revocable basis, rather than solely the story of how we remake the natural world through the construction of urban habitats.

If we are to rethink the place of natural hazards in urban environmental histories, then we need to strive for new narratives. We need to push our understanding beyond the dichotomy between event and process, between humans and nature, and embrace a different concept of historical change. We need to acknowledge that we can never imagine change as the sole product of human agents interacting between themselves and imposing their will upon passive matter. Matter is not passive by any means. On the contrary, the material world in which the historical existence of our species plays out is dense and constantly in motion, a field of forces, organisms, and elements that we have to come to terms with over and over again. There may be no such thing as the "agency of nature," as some claim. The active, historical existence of myriad "natures," however, challenges and in many respects complicates notions of human agency, of social structures and systems, and of their transformation over time, as it challenges and complicates our understanding of urban change. Yet acknowledging the limits of human agency does not limit our responsibility, it increases it; for it requires us to situate our past and our possible futures in a more-than-human world and rethink our actions accordingly. Earthquakes, it turns out, can speak, and they are speaking to us.

Notes

1. See Pasquale Filippone, "Intervista a Giovanna," *Cent'anni di baracche*, Istituto per la formazione al giornalismo, Urbino 2008, https://www.youtube.com/watch?v=yRh-U2TDM8M&index=11&list=UUf9-qsNeUAQpLvWfYuS-igg
2. That picture is emerging due to the painstaking work of recollection and analysis by historical seismologists such as Emanuela Guidoboni. See Emanuela Guidoboni and Gianluca Valensise, *Il peso economico e sociale dei disastri sismici in Italia negli ultimi 150 anni, 1861–2011* (Bologna 2011); and Emanuela Guidoboni, Guido Ferrari, Dante Mariotti, Alberto Comastri, Gabriele Tarabusi, and Gianluca Valensise, *Catalogue of Strong Earthquakes in Italy 461 B.C–1997 and Mediterranean Area 760 B.C.–1500*, INGV-Istituto Nazionale di Geofisica e Vulcanologia, http://storing.ingv.it/cfti4med/, both quoted several times in this book.
3. Liliane Dufour and Henri Raymond, *1693: Catania, rinascita di una città* (Catania, 1992).
4. Liliane Dufour, "Dopo il terremoto del 1693: La ricostruzione della Val di Noto," *Storia d'Italia, Annali 8: Insediamenti e territorio*, ed. Cesare De Seta (Turin, 1985), 476–98. Also Henri Raymond and Liliane Dufour, *1693: Val di Noto, la rinascita dopo il disastro* (Catania, 1994); Maria Teresa Campisi, "Il terremoto del 1693 in Val di Noto: Permanenze e trasformazioni nei centri urbani," *Storia Urbana* 23, no. 106–107 (2005): 111–66.
5. See Lucia Trigilia, "Dispositivi 'antisismici' nella ricostruzione del Val di Noto dopo il terremoto del 1693," in *Presidi antisismici nell'architettura storica e monumentale*, ed. Angela Marino (Rome, 2000), 95–97.
6. UNESCO, World Heritage Convention, *Late Baroque Towns of the Val di Noto (South-Eastern Sicily), Advisory Board Evaluation*, 2002, http://whc.unesco.org/archive/advisory_body_evaluation/1024rev.pdf.
7. For a comprehensive overview of the earthquakes, their material and social effects, and the sources available see Guidoboni et al., *Catalogue of Strong Earthquakes in Italy*, especially the section "Reconstructions and Relocations" at http://storing.ingv.it/cfti4med/quakes/02700.html#comment_12.
8. Stephan Tobriner, "La Casa Baraccata: Earthquake-Resistant Construction in 18th-Century Calabria," *Journal of the Society of Architectural Historians* 42, no. 2 (1983): 131–38.
9. The *Cassa Sacra* has been extensively examined by Augusto Placanica, *Cassa sacra e beni della Chiesa nella Calabria del Settecento* (Ercolano, 1970).
10. On Calabria in particular see Emanuela Guidoboni, "Upside-Down Landscapes: Seismicity and Seismic Disasters in Italy," in *Nature and History in Modern Italy*, ed. Marco Armiero and Marcus Hall (Athens, OH, 2010), 42–51.
11. Guidoboni and Valensise, *Il peso economico e sociale dei disastri sismici*, 25–26.
12. Stefano Ventura, "I ragazzi dell'Ufficio di Piano: La ricostruzione urbanistica in Irpinia," *I Frutti di Demetra* 22 (2010): esp. 41–51. See also Stefano Ventura, *Non sembrava novembre quella sera: Il terremoto del 1980 tra storia e memoria* (Avellino, 2010).
13. Guidoboni et al. "Earthquake sequence 13 01 1915, Marsica," in *Catalogue of Strong Earthquakes*, http://storing.ingv.it/cfti4med/quakes/24751.html. On that case, see also

the documented monograph by Sergio Castenetto and Fabrizio Galadini, eds., *13 gennaio 1915: Il terremoto nella Marsica* (Rome, 1999).
14. Carlo Ciavoni, "Il sisma che ha squassato la notte: I danni, la paura, la solidarietà," *La Repubblica*, 6 April 2009, archived online at: http://www.repubblica.it/2009/04/sezioni/cronaca/terremoto-nord-roma/terremoto-il-punto/terremoto-il-punto.html?ref=search. The names and pictures of all the victims are on the webpage of the newspaper of *Il Centro*: "Abruzzo, 6 aprile 2009: Le vittime del terremoto," http://racconta.kataweb.it/terremotoabruzzo/index.php.
15. Osservatorio sul terremoto dell'Università degli Studi dell'Aquila, *Il terremoto dell'Aquila: analisi e riflessioni sull'emergenza* (L'Aquila, 2011).
16. On the 1997 earthquakes and reconstruction see the rich collection of official data in http://www.osservatorioricostruzione.regione.umbria.it/. See also Gianluigi Nigro and Francesco Fazzio, eds., *Il territorio rinnovato: Uno sguardo urbanistico sulla ricostruzione postsismica in Umbria 1997-2007* (Perugia, 2007).
17. Guidoboni and Valensise, *Il peso economico e sociale dei disastri sismici*, 319.
18. Claudia Battaino and Luca Zecchin, "Traumatic Scapes: Gemona del Fruli e il suo paesaggio 35 anni dopo" (paper presented at the 5th Conference of the AISU, *Fuori dall'ordinario: Le città di fronte a catastrofi ed eventi eccezionali*, session "I disastri di origine naturale," panel "Città territori e società urbane di fronte ai disastri naturali del XX secolo," Rome 8–10 September 2011).
19. On this sequence see the articles collected by Marco Anzidei, Alessandra Maramai, and Paola Montone, eds., "The Emilia (Northern Italy) Seismic Sequence of May-June, 2012: Preliminary Data and Results," special issue of *Annals of Geophysics*, 55, no. 4: http://www.annalsofgeophysics.eu/index.php/annals/issue/view/483.
20. See Piero Bevilacqua, *Tra Natura e storia* (Rome, 1996), 73–112. The piece was originally published in 1981.
21. Guidoboni and Valensise, *Il peso economico e sociale dei disastri sismici*, 411–16.
22. Tullia Iori and Alessandro Marzo Magno, eds. *150 anni di storia del cemento in Italia: Le opere, gli uomini, le imprese* (Rome, 2011), esp. 70–71.
23. Charles Walker, *Shaky Colonialism: The 1746 Earthquake-Tsunami in Lima, Peru, and Its Long Aftermath* (Durham, 2008), 90–105.
24. John R. Mullin, "The Reconstruction of Lisbon Following the Earthquake of 1755: A Study in Despotic Planning," *Planning Perspectives: An International Journal of History, Planning, and the Environment* 7, no. 2 (1992): 157–79; Maria Helena Barreiros, "Urban Landscapes: Houses, Streets and Squares of 18th Century Lisbon," *Journal of Early Modern History* 12 (2008), 205–32.
25. For Lima see Walker, *Shaky Colonialism*, 91–92. For Lisbon see Mullin, "The Reconstruction of Lisbon," esp. 163–64, and Mark Molesky, "The Great Fire of Lisbon, 1755," in *Flammable Cities: Urban Conflagration and the Making of the Modern World*, ed. Greg Bankoff, Uwe Luebken, and Jordan Sand (Madison, 2012), esp. 161–62.
26. Beside Walker's *Shaky Colonialism*, for Lima see also Maria H. Ribeiro dos Santos and Ferran Sagarra I Trias, "Trading Properties after the Earthquake: The Rebuilding of Eighteenth-century Lisbon," *Planning Perspectives: An International Journal of History, Planning, and the Environment* 26, no. 2 (2011): 301–11. See also Alvaro S. Pereira, "The Opportunity of a Disaster: The Economic Impact of the 1755 Lisbon Earthquake," *The Journal of Economic History* 69, no. 2 (2009): 466–99.

27. Simon Winchester, *A Crack in the Edge of the World: America and the Great California Earthquake of 1906* (New York, 2005), 356–59.
28. Erica Y. Z. Pan, *The Impact of the 1906 Earthquake on San Francisco's Chinatown* (New York, 1995).
29. Carl H. Geschwind, *California Earthquakes: Science, Risk, and the Politics of Hazard Mitigation* (Baltimore, 2001), 19–42; and Theodore Steinberg, *Acts of God: The Unnatural History of Natural Disaster in America* (New York, 2006), 25–42.
30. Johanna Dyl, "The War on Rats versus the Right to Keep Chickens: Plague and the Paving of San Francisco, 1907–1908," in *The Nature of Cities*, ed. Andrew C. Isenberg (Rochester, 2006), 38–61.
31. See Gregory Clancey, *Earthquake Nation: The Cultural Politics of Japanese Seismicity, 1868–1930* (Berkeley, 2006), esp. 180–216.
32. Carola Hein, "Resilient Tokyo: Disaster and Transformation in the Japanese City," in *The Resilient City: How Modern Cities Recover from Disaster*, ed. Lawrence J. Vale and Thomas J. Campanella (Oxford and New York, 2005), 216.
33. Charles J. Schencking, "Catastrophe, Opportunism, Contestation: The Fractured Politics of Reconstructing Tokyo Following the Great Kantô Earthquake of 1923," *Modern Asian Studies* 40, no. 4 (2006): 833–73.
34. See Carola Hein, "Resilient Tokyo," 213–34; Hein, "Shaping Tokyo: Land Development and Planning Practice in the Early Modern Japanese Metropolis," *Journal of Urban History* 36, no. 4 (2010): 447–84. See also Edward Seidensticker, *Tokyo Rising: The City since the Last Earthquake* (New York, 1994).
35. David Edgington, *Reconstructing Kobe: The Geography of Crisis and Opportunity* (Vancouver and Toronto, 2010).
36. Mark Healey, *The Ruins of the New Argentina: Peronism and the Remaking of San Juan after the 1944 Earthquake* (Durham, 2011).
37. Anthony Oliver Smith, *The Martyred City: Death and Rebirth in the Andes* (Albuquerque, 1986), esp. 235–69.
38. Nathan Clarke, "Reforming the Tragic City: Rebuilding after the 1970 Earthquake in Chimbote, Peru" (paper for the 2013 ASEH Annual Conference, *Confluences, Crossings, and Power*, Toronto Canada, 3–6 April 2013, unpublished).
39. According to Dosal, "[Somoza] envisioned a sprawling new city that ironically would resemble the Managua that came into being in the 1990s, long after his death." Paul J. Dosal, "Natural Disaster, Political Earthquake: The 1972 Destruction of Managua and the Somoza Dynasty," in *Aftershocks: Earthquakes and Popular Politics in Latin America*, ed. Jürgen Buchenau and Lyman L. Johnson (Albuquerque, 2009), 141.
40. Beatrice Chen, "'Resist the Earthquake and Rescue Ourselves': The Reconstruction of Tangshan after the 1976 Earthquake," in Vale and Campanella, *The Resilient City*, 235–53.
41. Craig E. Colten, *Unnatural Metropolis: Wrestling New Orleans from Nature* (Baton Rouge, 2006).
42. Dieter Schott, "One City—Three Catastrophes: Hamburg from the Great Fire 1842 to the Great Flood 1962," in *Cities and Catastrophes: Coping with Emergency in European History / Villes et catastrophes: Réaction face à l'urgence dans l'histoire européenne*, ed. Geneviève Massard-Guilbaud, Dieter Schott, and Harold L. Platt (Frankfurt am Main, 2002), 185–204. Dirk Schubert, "The Great Fire of Hamburg, 1842: From Catastrophe to Reform," in Bankoff, Lübken, and Sand, *Flammable Cities*, 212–34.

43. Greg Bankoff, "A Tale of Two Cities: The Pyro-Seismic Morphology of Nineteenth-Century Manila," in Bankoff, Lübken, and Sand, *Flammable Cities,* 170–89.
44. Thomas Puelo offers an insightful elaboration of this idea in "Baroque Disruptions in Val di Noto, Sicily," *Geographical Review* 100 (2010): 476–93, in which he intriguingly applies Michel Serres's concept of "parasite" to earthquakes.

Bibliography

Archival Collections

Archivio Centrale dello Stato
Ministero dell'Agricoltura e delle Foreste, Direzione Generale Bonifiche, Bonifiche Sicilia, Calabria e Sardegna
Ministero dell'Interno, Comitato centrale di Soccorso danneggiati del terremoto calabro-siculo del 1908
Ministero dell'Interno, Commissione Reale per Credito Comunale e Provinciale e per la Municipalizzazione dei Pubblici Servizi.
Ministero dell'Interno, Direzione Generale Amministrazione Civile, Ufficio speciale dei servizi in dipendenza dei terremoti calabro-siculi e dell'eruzione dell'Etna
Ministero dell'Interno, Pubblica Sicurezza, G-Associazioni
Ministero dell'Interno, Direzione Generale di Sanità Pubblica, 1896-1934
Ministero dell'Interno, Gabinetto, 1964-1970
Ministero dei Lavori Pubblici, Direzione Generale Viabilità e Porti, Porti 1903-1938
Ministero dei Lavori Pubblici, Direzione Generale Lavori Pubblici, Progetti stradali 1914-1926
Presidenza del Consiglio dei Ministri
Segreteria Particolare del Duce

Archivio di Stato di Messina
Prefettura, Gabinetto, 1909-1940

Archivio Storico della Protezione Civile – via Affile Rome
Ministero dell'Interno, Direzione Generale della Protezione Civile e Servizio Antincendi
Ministero del Lavori Pubblici, Divisione 29°, Affari Generali
Ministero dei Lavori Pubblici, Divisione 3°, Affari Generali

Archivio Dolci-Barbera – CRESM Gibellina

Archivio Storico del Parlamento Siciliano
Commissione Speciale Terremotati, 1968-1971

Centro di Cultura Ecologica – Archivio Ambientalista
Fondo Fabrizio Giovenale

Printed Sources

Associazione dei Proprietari, Associazione dei Commercianti e degli Industriali, Collegio Ingegneri e Architetti, and Sindacato Costruttori. *Per la rinascita di Messina: Memoriale*. Messina, 1922.
Atti del Consiglio Comunale di Messina, 1861–1908.
Baratta, Mario. *I terremoti d'Italia: Saggio di storia, geografia e bibliografia sismica italiana*. Turin, 1901.
———. "Carta sismica d'Italia." In *Sulle aree sismiche italiane*. Voghera, 1901.
———. *Il grande terremoto calabro dell'8 settembre 1905: Alcune considerazioni sulla distribuzione topografica dei danni*. Pisa, 1906.
———. *Il nuovo massimo sismico calabrese, 23 ottobre 1907*. Rome, 1907.
———. *La catastrofe sismica calabro messinese (28 dicembre 1908): Relazione alla Società Geografica Italiana*. Rome, 1910.
———. *I terremoti d'Italia*. Florence, 1936.
Barbera, Lorenzo. *La diga di Roccamena*. Bari, 1964.
———. "La disgregazione della solidarietà e delle lotte popolari." *Casabella: Rivista di urbanistica architettura e disegno industriale* 420, no. 10 (1976): 10.
———. *I ministri dal cielo: I contadini del Belice raccontano*. Milan, 1980.
Barbera, Lorenzo, Sandro Di Meo, Danilo Dolci, Goffredo Fofi, Franco Fontana, Grazia Di Fresco, Domenico Galliano, Luigi Guastamacchia, Iole Guerra, Carlo Ravasini, Ida Sacchetti, and Giorgina Vicquery. "Appunti sulle possibilità di piena occupazione, nella sola agricoltura, in dieci paesi siciliani." In *Una politica per la piena occupazione*, edited by Danilo Dolci, 27–78. Turin, 1958.
Barone, Giuseppe, and Sandro Mazzi, eds. *Lettere 1952–1968: Aldo Capitini, Danilo Dolci*. Rome, 2008.
Bechmann, Georges. *Assainissement de la ville de Messina*. Messina, 1890.
Benigni, Gaetano. *Fognatura ed igiene pubblica in Messina*. Messina, 1884.
Borzì, Luigi. *Piano Regolatore di Messina*. Messina, 1912.
Borzì, Luigi, and Carlo Sollima Novi. *Il Porto di Messina nel passato, nel presente e nell'avvenire*. Messina, 1907.
Cannizzaro, Mariano E. *Come ricostruire Messina: Il demanio comune*. Rome, 1909.
Carta, Giuseppe. "Il Piano di sviluppo democratico delle valli del Belice, del Carboi e dello Jato: Piano di sviluppo urbanistico." *Urbanistica: Bollettino della sezione regionale piemontese dell'Istituto nazionale di urbanistica* 56 (1970): 78–90.
Caselli, Leandro, and Pietro Interdonato. *Sui tracciati proposti per la provvista di acqua potabile della città*. Messina, 1895.
Cassa per il Mezzogiorno and Consorzio di Bonifica dell'Alto e Medio Belice. *Serbatoio di Garcia sul fiume Belice sinistro*. Palermo, 1974.
Cassa per il Mezzogiorno, Consorzio di Bonifica dell'Alto e Medio Belice, Regione Siciliana, and Ente di Sviluppo Agricolo. *Progetto di massima per la utilizzazione dell'acqua a scopo irriguo: Serbatoio Garcia; Relazione economica agraria*. Palermo, 1973.
Caveglia, Crescentino. "Pensieri sull'impiego del cemento armato in località soggette a terremoti." *Annali della Società degli Ingegneri e degli Architetti Italiani* 24, no. 6 (1909): 149–54.
Centro studi e iniziative. *Un lavoro di sviluppo: Appunti dalla Sicilia occidentale; rassegna bimestrale*, no. 1 (1964).

———. *Piano di sviluppo democratico per le valli Belice, Carboi, Jato*. Typescript. Partinico, 1968.
Centro studi e iniziative and Alleanza coltivatori siciliani. *L' enfiteusi in Sicilia: Atti del 1; Convegno regionale, Palermo, Fiera del Mediterraneo, 24 ottobre 1964*. Palermo, 1965.
Collegio degl'Ingegneri ed Agronomi di Messina. *Risanamento della città di Messina*. Messina, 1886.
Comitato di Soccorso di Messina. *I terremoti del 1894 e 1895 nella Sicilia e nella Calabria*. Messina, 1895.
Commissione per le prescrizioni edilizie dell'isola di Ischia. *Relazione della Commissione per le prescrizioni edilizie dell'isola d'Ischia istituita dal Ministro dei Lavori Pubblici dopo il terremoto del luglio 1883*. Rome, 1883.
Commissione Reale incaricata di designare le zone più adatte per la ricostruzione degli abitati colpiti dal terremoto del 28 dicembre 1908 o da altri precedenti. *Relazione*. Rome, 1909.
Commissione Reale incaricata di studiare e proporre norme edilizie obbligatorie per i comuni colpiti dal terremoto del 28 dicembre 1908 e da altri anteriori. *Relazione*. Rome, 1909.
Commissione Speciale del Reale Istituto di Incoraggiamento di Napoli. "Contributo del R.Istituto d'Incoraggiamento di Napoli alla ricerca delle norme edilizie per le regioni sismiche," *Atti del Reale Istituto d'Incoraggiamento di Napoli* 6 (1909): iii–xxv.
Commissione Speciale della Società degli Ingegneri e degli Architetti Italiani. "Norme edilizie per i paesi soggetti a terremoti: Relazione generale." *Annali della Società degli Ingegneri e degli Architetti Italiani* 24, no. 7 (1909): 177–217.
Consorzio Industriale per la Ricostruzione di Messina. *Progetto tecnico-finanziario per la ricostruzione della città di Messina*. Messina, 1913.
Consorzio per la Trasformazione Fondiaria del bacino dell'Alto e Medio Belice. *Criteri di classifica provvisoria: Relazione della commissione tecnica*. Palermo, 1933.
Consorzio di Bonifica del bacino dell'alto e medio Belice. *Le opere di bonifica: programma e realizzazioni*. Palermo, 1952.
———. *Statuto*. Palermo, 1950.
———. *Ricerca pilota a valenza interregionale sulla riconversione colturale ed ammodernamento delle strutture nel comprensorio dell'alto e medio Belice*. Palermo, 1993.
Costa Saya, Antonio. *Delle acque potabili in relazione alla salute pubblica: Discorso letto innanti la Prima Classe dell'Accademia Peloritana nella tornata del 22 gennaro 1878*. Messina, 1879.
———. *Giudizio della Società italiana d'igiene sulla questione delle acque potabili di Messina*. Messina, 1880.
———. *L'acqua potabile e il colera epidemico*. Messina, 1888.
Costa Saya, Luigi. *Studi chimici intorno alle acque potabili di Messina*. Messina, 1881.
———. *Studio su quattro campioni d'acqua della Santissima*. Messina, 1883.
Crescimanno, Maria-Fardella, Gian Gaspare, and Salvatore Tudisca. *L'agricoltura nella valle del Belice*. Palermo, 1993.
De Berardinis, Nicola. *Relazione letta dal Commissario Straordinario Cav. Avv. Nicola De Berardinis, Consigliere Delegato dalla Prefettura di Messina, letta il 14 febbraio 1909, prima seduta del Consiglio Comunale dopei la catastrofe del 28 dicembre 1908*. Messina, 1909.

Di Maio, Marziano. "Il piano di sviluppo democratico delle valli Belice, Carboi e Jato: Piano di sviluppo agricolo." *Urbanistica: Bollettino della sezione regionale piemontese dell'Istituto nazionale di urbanistica* 56 (1970): 66–77.

Di Naples, Alfredo, and Giovanni B. Mosca. "L'acquedotto del Littorio in Sicilia." *Annali dei Lavori Pubblici* 12 (1938): 1084–88.

Dolci, Danilo. *Fare presto (e bene) perché si muore.* Turin, 1954.

———. *Banditi a Partinico.* Rome and Bari, 1956. Reprinted Palermo, 2009.

———. *Inchiesta a Palermo.* Turin, 1956.

———. *Processo all'articolo 4.* Turin, 1956.

———, ed. *Una politica per la piena occupazione.* Turin, 1958.

———. *Spreco: Documenti e inchieste su alcuni aspetti dello spreco nella Sicilia occidentale.* Turin, 1960.

———. *Verso un mondo nuovo.* Turin, 1965.

Federazione Provinciale Fascista di Messina. *Le opere del Fascismo per la ricostruzione di Messina.* Messina, 1932.

Fiore, Giacomo. *Delle pubbliche acque.* Messina, 1859.

———. *Sui progetti per frenare i torrenti Giostra e Camaro.* Messina, 1866.

———. *Delle cause permanenti che hanno fatto imperversare il colera in Portalegni e modo come ripararsi.* Messina, 1867.

Fofi, Goffredo. *Perché l'Italia diventi un paese civile; Palermo 1956: Il processo a Danilo Dolci.* Naples, 2006.

Franchetti, Leopoldo, and Sidney Sonnino. *La Sicilia nel 1876.* Florence, 1925.

Franchi, Secondo. "Il terremoto del 28 dicembre 1908 a Messina in rapporto alla natura del terreno ed alla riedificazione della città." *Bollettino del Regio Comitato Geologico d'Italia* 40, no. 2 (1909): 111–57.

Giannetto, Salvatore. *Ricerche per determinare il grado di potabilità di un'acqua sorgiva nella contrada Santissima presso Fiumedinisi.* Messina, 1883.

Hopkins, Riccardo, and Giuseppe Morabello. *Risposta ai pensieri del prof. Giacomo Fiore.* Messina, 1866.

Inferrera, Guido. *Il rimboschimento dei Peloritani in relazione con la sistemazione dei torrenti del messinese.* Messina, 1901.

———. *La sistemazione dei torrenti della Provincia di Messina e la sicurezza dei paesi rivieraschi.* Messina, 1907.

Interdonato, Pietro. "La catastrofe del 28 dicembre 1908—Impressioni di un tecnico superstite." *Annali della Società degli Ingegneri e degli Architetti Italiani* 24, no. 20 (1909): 499–502.

———. *Relazione su criteri direttivi dell'Amministrazione comunale circa l'esecuzione del piano regolatore, Seduta del Consiglio Comunale 10 settembre 1913.* Messina, 1913.

Istituto Centrale di Statistica. *VII Censimento generale della popolazione 21 aprile 1931.* Volume 2, *Popolazione dei comuni e delle frazioni di censimento.* Part 2, *Italia centrale, meridionale e insulare.* Rome, 1933.

Istituto Centrale di Statistica. *10° Censimento generale della popolazione, 15 ottobre 1961 Popolazione legale dei comuni.* Rome, 1963.

Istituto di Sociologia di Catania. "Pel risorgimento di Messina: inchiesta dell'Istituto di sociologia di Catania." Special issue, *La Scienza Sociale* 11, no. 1 (1909).

Istituto per lo Sviluppo dell'Edilizia Sociale. "L'ISES nella Valle del Belice: la ricostruzione dopo il terremoto del gennaio 1968." Special issue, *Quaderni di Edilizia Sociale* 6 (1972).

Longo, Pietro. *L'acquedotto civico di Messina.* Messina, 1905.

———. *Messina città rediviva: 1909–1933.* Messina, 1933.

Lorenzoni, Giovanni. "Sicilia: Relazione del deputato tecnico." In *Inchiesta parlamentare sulle condizioni dei contadini meridionali,* vol. 6.1. Rome, 1910.

Mallet, Robert. *Great Neapolitan Earthquake of 1857: The First Principles of Observational Seismology.* London, 1862.

Marcelli, Liliana, and Mario De Panfilis. "Il periodo sismico della Sicilia occidentale iniziato il 4 gennaio 1968." *Annali di Geofisica* 21, no. 4 (1968): 343–442.

Martone, Michele. *Studi preliminari sui terremoti della Calabria e della Sicilia.* Reggio Calabria, 1897.

Mercadante, Francesco, ed. *Il terremoto di Messina: Corrispondenze, testimonianze e polemiche giornalistiche.* Messina, 1958. Reprinted Reggio Calabria, 2006.

Mercalli, Giuseppe. *Vulcani e fenomeni vulcanici in Italia.* Milan, 1883.

———. *L' isola d'Ischia ed il terremoto del 28 luglio 1883.* Milan, 1884.

———. *I terremoti della Calabria Meridionale e del Messinese: Saggio di una monografia sismica regionale.* Rome, 1897.

———. *Sulle modificazioni proposte alla scala sismica De Rossi-Forel.* Modena, 1902.

———. *Alcuni risultati ottenuti dallo studio del terremoto calabrese dell'8 settembre 1905.* Naples, 1906.

———. "Contributo allo studio del terremoto calabro-messinese del 28 dicembre 1908." *Atti del Reale Istituto d'Incoraggiamento di Naples* 6 (1909): 249–89.

Mezzasalma, Pietro. *Osservazioni di occasione sulle acque del bacino del Niceto.* Messina, 1899.

Ministero dei Lavori Pubblici Direzione Generale dei Servizi Speciali. *L'opera del Ministero dei Lavori Pubblici per i danneggiati dal terremoto del 28 dicembre 1908.* Rome, 1911.

———. *Gli edifici pubblici e le case degli impiegati dello Stato nei paesi colpiti dal terremoto.* Rome, 1912.

———. *L'azione del Governo Fascista per la ricostruzione delle zone danneggiate da calamità.* Terni, 1933.

Ministero dell'Agricoltura Industria e Commercio, Ufficio Centrale di Statistica. *Popolazione presente ed assente per comuni, centri e frazioni di comune. Censimento 31 dicembre 1871.* Vol. 1. Rome, 1874.

Ministero dell'Agricoltura Industria e Commercio, Ufficio Centrale di Statistica, Direzione Generale di Statistica. *Censimento della popolazione del Regno d'Italia al 31 dicembre 1881, Volume I Parte I: Popolazione dei comuni e dei mandamenti.* Rome, 1883.

———. *Censimento della popolazione del regno d'Italia al 10 febbraio 1901, Volume I: Popolazione dei comuni e delle rispettive frazioni divise in agglomerate e sparse e popolazione dei mandamenti amministrativi.* Rome, 1902.

Ministero dell'Agricoltura Industria e Commercio, Ufficio Centrale di Statistica, Direzione Generale di Statistica e Lavoro, Ufficio Censimento. *Censimento della popolazione del Regno d'Italia al 10 giugno 1911.* Vol. 1. Rome, 1914.

Municipio di Messina. *Atti del Consiglio Comunale.* Messina, 1861–1908.

———. *Regolamento edilizio della citta di Messina: Stabilito dal Consiglio comunale nelle adunanze del 12, 19 settembre 1873, 25 settembre 1874, 29 gennaio 1884; approvato dalla Deputazione provinciale nelle tornate dei 24 giugno 1875 e 8 aprile 1884; omologato dal Ministero dei L L. P P. addi 18 luglio.* Messina, 1885.

———. *Regolamento per l'ufficio Tecnico del Comune di Messina, approvato dal Consiglio Comunale nelle tornate del 20, 26 e 30 marzo 1889.* Messina, 1889.

———. *I terremoti del 1894–95 e la beneficenza pubblica in Messina: Relazione alla Giunta del Sindaco Barone Natoli di Scaliti letta nella tornata del 21 giugno 1895.* Messina, 1895.

———. *Concessione del Comune di Messina all'Ing. Cav. Alessandro Vanni per la condotta di acque potabili e l'esercizio dell'acquedotto.* Messina, 1897.

———. *Contratto con la Banca di Liegi e la Società dei Tramways Siciliani per il prestito per l'acqua potabile, la trazione e l'illuminazione elettrica.* Messina, 1899.

———. *Relazione della Giunta Municipale all'Onorevole Consiglio Comunale sullo stato attuale del civico acquedotto e proposte relative a provvedimenti diversi.* Messina, 1916.

———. *Relazione al Consiglio Comunale dell'Assessore ai LL.PP. Grand'Uff. Salvatore Siracusano sull'opera di ricostruzione della città, Maggio 1922.* Messina, 1922.

Municipio di Messina, Ufficio tecnico *Relazione all'Ill.imo Signor Sindaco sul progetto particolareggiato dell'acquedotto presentato dal concessionario Cav. Ing. Alessandro Vanni.* Messina, 1897.

———. *Fognatura della città: Relazione del Sindaco al C.C. Progetto Tecnico.* Messina, 1899

———. *Relazione sulle condizioni attuali del servizio delle acque nel Comune.* Messina, 1900.

Municipio di Messina, Ufficio Tecnico per il Piano regolatore. *Relazione riguardante gli studi fatti ed i lavori in corso fino a tutto il 31 maggio 1916 per l'attuazione del Piano regolatore.* Messina, 1916.

Patricolo, Salvatore. *Condutture di acque potabili per la città di Messina.* Messina, 1882.

Pianificazione siciliana. 1966–1973.

Platania, Giovanni. "Il maremoto dello Stretto di Messina del 28 Dicembre 1908." *Bollettino della Società Sismologica d'Italia* 13 (1909): 369–458.

Presidenza del Consiglio dei Ministri, Istituto Centrale di Statistica. *Censimento della Popolazione del Regno d'Italia al 1 dicembre 1921: XIII Sicilia.* Rome, 1927.

Ranieri, Domenico. *Dei torrenti attraversanti Messina e dei mezzi diretti alla loro difesa.* Messina, 1871.

———. *Acque potabili e fognature.* Messina, 1877.

Regione Siciliana, Assessorato Territorio e Ambiente, Dipartimento Territorio e Ambiente, Piano Stralcio di Bacino per l'Assetto Idrogeologico (P.A.I. Bacino Idrografico del Fiume Belice (AG-PA-TP) Relazione.

Regione Siciliana, Cassa per il Mezzogiorno. *Gli interventi della Cassa per il Mezzogiorno in Sicilia.* Palermo, 1955.

———. *Proposte di provvedimenti per favorire la rinascita economica e sociale dei comuni terremotati (art.59 della legge 18-3-1968, n.241).* Palermo, 1969.

Regione Siciliana, Cassa per il Mezzogiorno, and Assessorato per lo sviluppo economico. *Progetto di programma di sviluppo economico della Regione siciliana per il quinquennio 1966-1970.* Palermo, 1965.

———. *Regione siciliana, Assessorato allo sviluppo economico, presentato alla Giunta di governo nel marzo 1967 dall'assessore On. Calogero Mangione.* Palermo, 1967.

Regione Siciliana, Cassa per il Mezzogiorno, and Ente per lo Sviluppo Agricolo. *Piano di Sviluppo Agricolo n.25 "Valli del Belice e del Platani."* Palermo, 1970.
——. *Piano di Sviluppo Agricolo n.2 "Collinare del Trapanese."* Palermo, 1971.
——. *Piano di sviluppo agricolo n.4 "del Monrealese."* Palermo, 1974.
Salvadori, Alessandro. *Relazione del Regio Commissario Comm. A.Salvadori al ricostituito Consiglio Comunale di Messina.* Messina, 1913.
Samonà, Giuseppe. *Piano urbanistico comprensoriale: Relazione generale.* Venice, 1965.
Senato della Repubblica. *Relazione della Commissione Parlamentare d'inchiesta sull'attuazione degli interventi per la ricostruzione e la ripresa socio-economica dei territori della Valle del Belice colpiti dai terremoti del gennaio 1968.* Rome, 1981.
Silone, Ignazio, Vincenzo Arangio Ruiz, Carlo Antoni, and Guido Calogero. *Italia a porte chiuse: Inchiesta sociale od oltraggio al pudore? In merito al processo Dolci Carocci.* Rome, 1956.
Subba, Domenico. *Cenni critici sull'adozione del sistema chinese proposta dal Pittore D.Letterio Subba in rapporto ai torrenti di Messina, Porta Legni, Boccetta e Trapani*, Messina, after 1956.
Stima analitica e brevi osservazioni per i Sigg. Roberto e Domenico Saccà contro il Signor Prefetto della Provincia di Messina nella rappresentanza del Ministero dei Lavori Pubblici. Messina, 1912.
Unione Edilizia Messinese. *L'opera dell'Unione Edilizia Messinese per la ricostruzione di Messina (febbraio 1914–giugno 1917): Relazione del Regio Commissario Comm. Avv. Cesare Cagli.* Bergamo, 1917.
Unione Edilizia Nazionale. *L'opera dell'Unione Edilizia Nazionale nel quadriennio 1917–1920 Relazione del Direttore Generale Gr. Uff. Avv. Cesare Cagli.* Rome, 1920.
Zorzi, Stefano. *Parola di Burri.* Turin, 1995.

Audiovisual Sources

CRESM. "Intervista a Gaspare Giglio e Nicola Accardo," *Le terre che tremarono.* 7 April 2010, color, 01:54:42.
——. "Intervista a Vito Bellafiore," *Le terre che tremarono.* 30 December 2009, color, 00:45:34.
——. "Intervista a Vito Accardo," *Le terre che tremarono.* 20 May 2009, color, 00:56:07.
——. "Intervista a Ludovico Corrao," *Le terre che tremarono.* 7 April 2010, 00:56:33.
——. "Intervista a Enza Bellacera," *Le terre che tremarono.* 29 May 2009, color, 00:41:57.
Giornale Luce. *Inizio della redenzione del latifondo siciliano,* 00:03:13, b/w, sound, 1939, B1609, Archivio Storico dell'Istituto Luce.
Perelli, Luigi. *Emigrazione 68: Italia oltre il confine,* 00:32:00, b/w, sound, 1968, Archivio Audiovisivo del Movimento Operaio e Democratico.
Svezia, Emanuele. *Earthquake 68: Gente di Gibellina,* color, 01:38:08, 2008, Centro di Ricerche Economiche e Sociali per il Meridione.
Tempi Nostri. *Italia allo specchio: Sicilia; Numero unico sulle condizioni socio-economiche della regione e sulle iniziative del governo per il suo sviluppo economico,* 00:08:30, b/w, sound, 1968, T103, Archivio Storico dell'Istituto Luce.

———. *Italia allo specchio: Basilicata; Numero unico sulle condizioni socio-economiche della regione e sulle iniziative del governo per il suo sviluppo economico,* 00:07:37, b/w, sound, 1968, T1036, Archivio Storico dell'Istituto Luce.

———. *Italia allo specchio: Puglia; Numero unico sulle condizioni socio-economiche della regione e sulle iniziative del governo per il suo sviluppo economico,* 00:08:05, b/w, sound, 01/06/1968, 1968, T1042. Archivio Storico dell'Istituto Luce.

Unitelefilm. *Danilo Dolci e la lotta per l'acquedotto del Belice,* 00:32:00, b/w, silent, 1965, Archivio Audiovisivo del Movimento Operaio e Democratico.

———. *Danilo Dolci e la marcia per la Sicilia occidentale e per un nuovo mondo,* 00:09:00, b/w, silent, 1967, Archivio Audiovisivo del Movimento Operaio e Democratico.

———. *Manifestazione dei terremotati del Belice – Rome, 5 marzo 1968,* 00:04:00, b/w, silent, 1968, Archivio Audiovisivo del Movimento Operaio e Democratico.

——— *Per uno sviluppo organico delle valli dello Jato, del Belice, del Carboi,* 00:11:00, b/w, silent, 1968, Archivio Audiovisivo del Movimento Operaio e Democratico.

Secondary Sources

AA.VV. [various authors]. *La modernizzazione difficile: Città e campagna nel Mezzogiorno dall'età giolittiana al fascismo.* Bari, 1983.

Adger, W. Neil, Terry P. Hughes, Carl Folke, Stephen. R. Carpenter, and Johan Rockström. "Social-Ecological Resilience to Coastal Disasters." *Science* 309 (2005): 1036–39.

Adorno, Salvatore. "Luce e acque: Conflitti e risorse nella modernizzazione di una periferia meridionale; Il caso di Siracusa." In *Réseaux techniques et conflits de pouvoir: Les dynamiques historiques des villes contemporaines,* edited by Denis Bocquet and Samuel Fettah, 103–36. Rome, 2007.

Adorno, Salvatore, and Filippo De Pieri, eds. "Burocrazie tecniche." Special issue, *Città e storia* 5 (2011).

Adorno, Salvatore, and Simone Neri Serneri, eds. *Industria, ambiente e territorio: Per una storia delle aree industriali in Italia.* Bologna, 2009.

Agnoletti, Mauro, ed. *Italian Historical Rural Landscapes.* New York and Berlin, 2013.

Alexander, David E. "The Evolution of Civil Protection in Modern Italy." In Dickie, Foote, and Snowden, *Disastro!,* 165–85.

Antrop, Marc. "Changing Patterns in the Urbanized Countryside of Western Europe." *Landscape Ecology* 15 (2000): 257–70.

———. "Landscape Change and the Urbanization Process in Europe." *Landscape and Urban Planning* 67 (2004): 9–26.

Anzidei, Marco, Alessandra Maramai, and Paola Montone, eds. "The Emilia (Northern Italy) Seismic Sequence of May–June, 2012: Preliminary Data and Results." Special issue, *Annals of Geophysics* 55, no. 4 (2012).

Aricò, Nicola. "Cartografia di un terremoto: Messina 1783." In *Cartografia di un terremoto, Messina 1783,* edited by Enrico Guidoni and Nicola Aricò, 7–53. Milan, 1988.

Aricò, Nicola, and Milella Ornella. *Riedificare contro la storia: Una ricostruzione illuminista nella periferia del regno borbonico.* Rome, 1984.

Aymard, Maurice. "Le città di nuova fondazione in Sicilia." In *Storia d'Italia, Annali 8: Insediamenti e Territorio,* edited by Cesare De Seta, 405–17. Turin, 1985.

Aymard, Maurice, and Giuseppe Giarrizzo, eds. *Storia d'Italia: Le regioni dall'Unità a oggi,* vol. 5, *La Sicilia,* Turin, 1987.
Baglio, Antonio, and Salvatore Bottari, ed. *Messina dalla vigilia del terremoto all'avvio della ricostruzione.* Messina, 2010.
Bankoff, Greg. *Cultures of Disaster: Society and Natural Hazards in the Philippines.* London, 2003.
———. "Time is of the Essence: Disasters, Vulnerability, and History." *International Journal of Mass Emergencies and Disasters* 22, no. 3 (2004): 23–42.
———. "A Tale of Two Cities: The Pyro-Seismic Morphology of Nineteenth-Century Manila." In Bankoff, Lübken, Sand, *Flammable Cities,* 170–89.
Bankoff, Greg, Uwe Lübken and Jordan Sand, eds. *Flammable Cities: Urban Conflagration and the Making of the Modern World.* Madison, 2012.
Barone, Giuseppe. "Sull'uso capitalistico del terremoto: Blocco urbano e ricostruzione edilizia a Messina durante il fascismo." *Storia Urbana* 10 (1982): 47–104.
———. *Mezzogiorno e modernizzazione: Elettricità, irrigazione e bonifica nell'Italia contemporanea.* Turin, 1986.
———. "Egemonie urbane e potere locale (1882–1913)." In Aymard and Giarizzo, *Storia d'Italia,* 191–370.
———. "Stato e Mezzogiorno: Il primo tempo dell'intervento straordinario (1943–1960)." In *Storia dell'Italia repubblicana,* vol 1, *La costruzione della democrazia,* edited by Francesco Barbagallo, 293–409. Turin, 1994.
Barone, Giuseppe [1970-]. "Un mondo nuovo potrebbe crescere, diverso." In *Danilo Dolci: Una rivoluzione nonviolenta,* edited by Giuseppe Barone, 7–53. Milan, 2007.
Barreiros, Maria Helena. "Urban Landscapes: Houses, Streets and Squares of 18th Century Lisbon." *Journal of Early Modern History* 12 (2008): 205–32.
Battaino, Claudia, and Luca Zecchin. "Traumatic Scapes: Gemona del Fruli e il suo paesaggio 35 anni dopo." Paper presented at the 5th Conference of the AISU, *Fuori dall'ordinario: le città di fronte a catastrofi ed eventi eccezionali,* session "I disastri di origine naturale," panel "Città territori e società urbane di fronte ai disastri naturali del XX secolo," Rome, 8–10 September 2011.
Battaglia, Rosario. *L'ultimo splendore: Messina tra rilancio e decadenza.* Soveria Mannelli, 2003.
———. "Il porto di Messina nell'età della decadenza." In Battaglia et al., *Messina negli anni venti e trenta,* 217–32.
Battaglia, Rosario, Michela D'Angelo, Santi Fedele, and Massimo Lo Curzio, eds. *Messina negli anni venti e trenta: Una città meridionale tra stagnazione e fermenti culturali.* Catania, 1997.
Bertolaso, Guido, Enzo Boschi, Emanuela Guidoboni, and Gianluca Valensise, eds. *Il terremoto e il maremoto del 28 dicembre 1908: Analisi sismologica impatto, prospettive.* Rome and Bologna, 2008.
Bevilacqua, Piero. "Le rivoluzioni dell'acqua: Irrigazioni e trasformazioni dell'agricoltura tra Sette e Novecento." In *Storia dell'agricoltura italiana in età contemporanea,* edited by Piero Bevilacqua, 255–318. Venice, 1989.
———. *Tra Natura e Storia: Ambiente, economia, risorse in Italia.* Rome, 1996.
———. *Breve storia dell'Italia meridionale.* Rome, 2005.

Bevilacqua, Piero, and Gabriella Corona, eds. *Ambiente e risorse nel Mezzogiorno contemporaneo.* Conigliano Calderaro, 2000.
Bevilacqua, Piero, Andreina De Clementi, and Emilio Franzina, eds. *Storia dell'emigrazione italiana: Partenze.* Rome, 2001.
Bevilacqua, Piero, and Manlio Rossi-Doria. "Lineamenti per una storia delle bonifiche in Italia dal XVIII al XX secolo." In *Le bonifiche in Italia dal'700 ad oggi,* edited by Piero Bevilacqua and Manlio Rossi-Doria, 5–78. Bari, 1984.
Bignardi, Massimo, Davide Lacagnina, and Paola Mantovani, eds. *Cantiere Gibellina: Una ricerca sul campo.* Rome, 2008.
Billen, Gilles, Josette Garnier, and Sabine Barles, eds. "History of the Urban Environmental Imprint." Special issue, *Regional Environmental Change* 12, no. 2 (2012): 249–405.
Blok, Anton. "South Italian Agro-Towns." *Comparative Studies in Society and History* 11, no. 2 (1969): 121–35.
Boatti, Giorgio. *La terra trema: Messina 28 dicembre 1908; I trenta secondi che cambiarono l'Italia, non gli italiani.* Milan, 2004.
Bonini, Lorenzo, Daniela Di Bucci, Giovanni Toscani, Silvio Seno, and Gianluca Valensise. "Reconciling Deep Seismogenic and Shallow Active Faults through Analogue Modelling: The Case of the Messina Strait (Southern Italy)." *Journal of the Geological Society* 168, no. 1 (2011): 191–99.
Botta, Giorgio. "Ricordare e riflettere per conoscere: Alluvioni e frane in Italia dal dopoguerra a oggi." In *L'Italia dei disastri: Dati e riflessioni sull'impatto degli eventi naturali, 1861–2013,* edited by Emanuela Guidoboni and Gianluca Valensise, 99–108. Bologna, 2013.
Boucquet, Denis, and Samuel Fettah, eds. *Réseaux techniques et conflits de pouvoir: Les dynamiques historiques des villes contemporaines.* Rome, 2007.
———. *Rome, ville technique (1870–1925): Une modernisation conflictuelle de l'espace urbain.* Rome, 2007.
———. "Les villes italiennes et la circulation des savoirs municipaux: Esprit local et 'Internationale des villes' (1860–1914)." *Histoire et Sociétés: Revue Européenne d'Histoire Sociale* 21 (2007): 18–30.
Braun, Bruce. "Environmental Issues: Writing a More-Than-Human Urban Geography." *Progress in Human Geography* 29, no. 5 (2005): 635–50.
Bruegmann, Robert. *Sprawl: A Compact History.* Chicago, 2005.
Buchenau, Jürgen, and Lyman L. Johnson, eds. *Aftershocks: Earthquakes and Popular Politics in Latin America.* Albuquerque, 2009.
Calascibetta, Vincenza. *Messina nel 1783.* Messina 1937. Reprinted 1995.
Calcara, Geppi."Breve profilo dell'Istituto Nazionale di Geofisica, 1936–1963." *Quaderni di Geofisica* 36 (2004): 5–21.
Caminiti, Luciana. *Dalla pietà alla cura: Strutture sanitarie e società nella Messina dell'Ottocento.* Milan, 2002.
———. *La Grande Diaspora: 28 dicembre 1908 la politica dei soccorsi tra carità e bilanci.* Messina, 2009.
Campione, Giuseppe. *Il progetto urbano di Messina: Documenti per l'identità 1860–1988.* Rome, 1988.
Campisi, Maria Teresa. "Il terremoto del 1693 in Val di Noto: Permanenze e trasformazioni nei centri urbani." *Storia Urbana* 23, no. 106–107 (2005): 111–66.

Campos-Venuti, Giuseppe, and Federico Oliva, eds. *Cinquant'anni di urbanistica in Italia 1942–1992*. Rome and Bari, 2003.
Cannarozzo, Teresa. "La ricostruzione del Belice: Il difficile dialogo tra luogo e progetto." *Archivio di studi urbani e regionali* 55 (1996): 5–50.
———. "Agrigento: Risorse, strumenti, attori; Percorsi verso nuovi orizzonti di sviluppo locale." In *Progettare le identità e il territorio*, edited by Francesco Lo Piccolo, 90–91. Florence, 2009.
Cantarella, Laura, and Lucia Giuliano, eds. *Topography of Trauma: Belice Valley Sicily; A Landscape Survey*. Catania, 2012.
Cardoso, Rafael, Mario Lopes, Rita Bento. "Earthquake Resistant Structures of Portuguese Old 'Pombalino' Buildings," Paper no. 918, presented at the 13th World Conference on Earthquake Engineering, Vancouver, Canada, August 1–6, 2004, http://www.iitk.ac.in/nicee/wcee/article/13_918.pdf.
Cardullo, Francesco. *La ricostruzione di Messina: L'architettura dei servizi pubblici e la città 1909–1940*. Rome, 1993.
Castenetto, Sergio, and Fabrizio Galadini, eds. *13 gennaio 1915: Il terremoto nella Marsica*. Rome, 1999.
Castenetto, Sergio, Mirella Sebastiano, Fosca Pizzaroni. *La gestione dell'emergenza nel terrremoto calabro-siculo del 28 dicembre 1908*. Rome, 2008.
Castenetto, Sergio, and Massimiliano Severino. "Dalla prima normativa antisismica del 1909 alle successive modifiche." In Bertolaso et al., *Il terremoto e il maremoto del 28 dicembre 1908*, 425–40.
Castonguay, Stéphane. "The production of Flood as Natural Catastrophe: Extreme Events and the Construction of Vulnerability in the Drainage Basins of the St. Francis River (Quebec): Mid-Nineteenth Century." *Environmental History* 12 (2007): 820–44.
Chatterjee, Partha. *The Politics of the Governed*. New York, 2004.
Checco, Antonino. "Messina dal terremoto del 1908 al fascismo: La ricostruzione senza sviluppo." *Storia Urbana* 46 (1989): 161–92.
Chen, Beatrice. "'Resist the Earthquake and Rescue Ourselves': The Reconstruction of Tangshan after the 1976 Earthquake." In *The Resilient City: How Modern Cities Recover from Disaster*, edited by Lawrence J. Vale and Thomas J. Campanella, 235–53. Oxford, 2005.
Chubb, Judith. "Three Earthquakes: Political Response, Reconstruction and the Institutions: Belice (1968): Friuli (1976): Irpinia (1980)." In Dickie, Foot, and Snowden, *Disastro!*, 186–233.
Ciacagli, Massimo. "Cento anni di studi scientifici sul terremoto e maremoto del 1908." In Bertolaso et al., *Il terremoto e il maremoto del 28 dicembre 1908*, 255–70.
Clancey, Gregory. *Earthquake Nation: The Cultural Politics of Japanese Seismicity, 1868–1930*. Berkeley, 2006.
Clarke, Nathan. "Reforming the Tragic City: Rebuilding after the 1970 Earthquake in Chimbote, Peru." Paper presented at the American Society for Environmental History Annual Conference, Toronto Canada, 3–6 April, 2013.
Coen, Deborah. "Witness to Disaster: Comparative Histories of Earthquake Science and Response." *Science in Context* 25 (2012): 1–15.
———. *The Earthquake Observers: Disaster Science from Lisbon to Richter*. Chicago, 2013.
Colten, Craig E. *Unnatural Metropolis: Wrestling New Orleans from Nature*. Baton Rouge, 2006.

———. *Perilous Place, Powerful Storms: Hurricane Protection in Coastal Louisiana.* Jackson, 2009.

Colten, Craig E., and Amy R. Sumpter. "Social Memory and Resilience in New Orleans." *Natural Hazards* 48, no. 3 (2009): 355–64.

Condie, Kent C. "Crustal Composition and Recycling." In *The Oxford Companion to the Earth,* edited by Paul L. Hancock and Brian J. Skinner, 192–95. Oxford, 2000.

Corona, Gabriella and Simone Neri Serneri, eds. *Storia e ambiente: Città, risorse e territori nell'Italia contemporanea.* Rome, 2007.

Costanza, Salvatore. *I giorni di Gibellina,* Palermo 1980.

Crainz, Guido. *Storia del miracolo italiano: Culture, identità, trasformazioni tra anni cinquanta e sessanta.* Rome, 2003.

Cronon, William. *Nature's Metropolis: Chicago and the Great West.* New York and London, 1991.

Curtis, Daniel. "Is There an 'Agro-Town' Model for Southern Italy? Exploring the Diverse Roots and Development of the Agro-Town Structure through a Comparative Case Study in Apulia." *Continuity and Change* 28 (2013): 377–419.

D'Angelo, Michela and Marcello Saija. "A City and Two Earthquakes: Messina 1783–1908." In *Cities and Catastrophes: Coping with Emergency in European History / Villes et catastrophes: Réaction face à l'urgence dans l'histoire européenne,* edited by Geneviève Massard-Guilbaud, Dieter Schott, and Harold L. Platt, 122–40. Frankfurt am Main, 2002.

D'Antone, Leandra. "L'interesse straordinario per il Mezzogiorno (1945–1960)." In *Alle radici dell'intervento straordinario,* edited by Leandra D'Antone, 51–109. Naples, 1996.

Davies, Timothy. "La colonizzazione feudale della Sicilia." In *Storia d'Italia, Annali 8: Insediamenti e Territorio,* edited by Cesare De Seta, 419–75. Turin, 1985.

De Lucia, Vezio. "Dalla legge del 1942 alle leggi di emergenza." In *Cinquant'anni di urbanistica in Italia 1942–1992,* edited by Giuseppe Campos-Venuti and Federico Oliva, 87–102. Rome and Bari, 1993.

De Matteis, Giuseppe. "Le trasformazioni territoriali e ambientali." In *Storia dell'Italia repubblicana.* Vol. 2, *La trasformazione dell'Italia.* Part 1, *Politica, economia società,* edited by Francesco Barbagallo, 661–709. Turin, 1994.

Dickie, John. "Stereotipi del Sud d'Italia, 1860–1900." In *Oltre il meridionalismo: Nuove prospettive sul Mezzogiorno d'Italia,* edited by Robert Lumley and Jonathan Morris, 113–43. Rome, 1999.

———. *La catastrofe patriottica: Il terremoto di Messina.* Rome and Bari, 2008.

Dickie, John, John Foot, and Frank M. Snowden, eds. *Disastro! Disasters in Italy Since 1860: Culture, Politics, Society.* New York and Basingstoke, 2002.

Di Leo, G. Laura, and Massimo Lo Curzio, eds. *Messina, una città ricostruita: Materiali per lo studio di una realtà urbana.* Bari, 1985.

Dogliani, Patrizia. "European Municipalism in the First Half of the Twentieth Century: The Socialist Network." *Contemporary European History* 11, no. 4 (2002): 573–96.

Doglioni, Carlo, Marco Ligi, Davide Scrocca, Sabina Bigi, Giovanni Bortoluzzi, Eugenio Carminati, Marco Cuffaro, Filippo D'Oriano, Filippo Muccini, and Federica Riguzzi. "The Tectonic Puzzle of the Messina Area (Southern Italy): Insights from New Seismic Reflection Data." *Scientific Reports* 2 (2012): 970.

Dosal, Paul J. "Natural Disaster, Political Earthquake: The 1972 Destruction of Managua and the Somoza Dynasty." In *Aftershocks: Earthquakes and Popular Politics in Latin*

America, edited by Jürgen Buchenau and Lyman L. Johnson, 129–55. Albuquerque, 2009.
Dufour, Liliane. "Dopo il terremoto del 1693: La ricostruzione della Val di Noto." *Storia d'Italia, Annali 8: Insediamenti e territorio*, edited by Cesare De Seta, 473–98. Turin, 1985.
Dufour, Liliane, and Henri Raymond. *1693: Catania, rinascita di una città*. Catania, 1992.
Dyl, Johanna. "The War on Rats versus the Right to Keep Chickens: Plague and the Paving of San Francisco, 1907–1908." In *The Nature of Cities*, edited by Andrew C. Isenberg, 38–61. Rochester, 2006.
Edgington, David. *Reconstructing Kobe: The Geography of Crisis and Opportunity*. Vancouver and Toronto, 2010
Edelman, Marc, and Angelique Haugerud. "Introduction." In *The Anthropology of Development and Globalization: From Classical Political Economy to Contemporary Liberalism*, edited by Marc Edelman and Angelique Haugerud, 1–74. Oxford, 2005.
Escobar, Arturo. *Encountering Development: The Making and Unmaking of the Third World*. Princeton: 1995.
Ferrari Bravo, Luciano. *Stato e sottosviluppo: Il caso del Mezzogiorno italiano*. Milan, 1972.
Ferretti, Roberto. "The Formation of a Bureaucratic Group between Center and Periphery: Engineers and Local Government in Italy from the Liberal Period to Fascism (1861–1939)." In *Municipal Services and Employees in the Modern City: New Historic Approaches*, edited by Michèle Dagenais, Pierre-Yves Saunier, and Irene Maver, 66–83. Aldershot, 2003.
Forti Messina, Annalucia. "L'Italia dell'Ottocento di fronte al colera." In *Storia d'Italia, Annali 7: Malattia e Medicina*, edited by Franco Della Peruta, 431–94. Turin, 1984.
Frioux, Stéphane. "Amélioration de l'environnement urbain et transferts de technologie entre la France et ses voisins nord-européens, années 1870-années 1910." In *Innovations, réglementations et transferts de technologie en Europe du Nord-Ouest aux XIXe et XXe siècles*, edited by Jean-François Eck and Pierre Tilly, 235–50. Berlin, 2011.
Gamba, Giuseppe, and Giuliano Martignetti. "Ambiente e territorio." In *Guida all'Italia Contemporanea 1861–1997*. Vol.1, *Risorse e strutture economiche*, edited by Massimo Firpo, Nicola Tranfaglia, and Pier Giorgio Zunino, 1–87. Milan, 1998.
Gandy, Matthew. "Rethinking Urban Metabolism: Water, Space and the Modern City." *City* 8, no. 3 (2008): 363–79.
Gasperini, Paolo, and Graziano Ferrari. "Deriving Numerical Estimates from Descriptive Information: The Computation of Earthquake Parameters." *Annali di Geofisica* 43, no. 4 (2000): 729–46.
Geschwind, Carl H. *California Earthquakes: Science, Risk, and the Politics of Hazard Mitigation*. Baltimore, 2001.
Giarrizzo, Giuseppe. "Sicilia oggi (1950–1980)." In Aymard and Giarrizzo, *Storia d'Italia*, 603–96.
———. "Lo storico e il terremoto." In *La Sicilia dei terremoti: Lunga durata e dinamiche sociali*, edited by Guiseppe Giarrizzo, 439–41. Catania, 1996.
Gigante, Amelia I. *Le città nella storia d'Italia: Messina*. Rome and Bari, 1980.
Ginsborg, Paul. *Storia d'Italia dal dopoguerra a oggi: Società e politica 1943–1988*. Turin, 1989.
Golini, Antonio, and Flavia Amato. "Uno sguardo a un secolo e mezzo di emigrazione italiana." In *Storia dell'emigrazione italiana: Partenze*, edited by Piero Bevilacqua, Andreina De Clementi, and Emilio Franzina, 45–60. Rome, 2001.

Graham, Stephen, and Simon Marvin. *Splintering Urbanism: Networked Infrastructures, Technological Mobilities and the Urban Condition.* London and New York, 2001.
Gribaudi, Gabriella, and Anna Maria Zaccaria. "Terremoti: Storia, memorie, narrazioni." Special issue, *Memoria/memorie: Materiali di storia* 5 (2012).
Guerrasi, Vincenzo, and Anna Maria La Monica. "Il Belice: trama urbana e ordito territoriale in una transizione catastrofica." In *La Sicilia dei terremoti*, edited by Giuseppe Giarrizzo, 423–38. Catania, 1997.
Guidoboni, Emanuela. "Upside-Down Landscapes: Seismicity and Seismic Disasters in Italy." In *Nature and History in Modern Italy*, edited by Marco Armiero and Marcus Hall, 33–55. Athens, OH, 2010.
Guidoboni, Emanuela, and Dante Mariotti. "Il terremoto e il maremoto del 1908: Effetti e parametri sismici." In Bertolaso et al., *Il terremoto e il maremoto del 28 dicembre 1908*, 17–136.
Guidoboni, Emanuela, Anna Muggia, Alberto Comastri, and Gianluca Valensise. "Ipotesi sul 'predecessore' del terremoto del 1908: archeologia, storia, geologia." In Bertolaso et al., *Il terremoto e il maremoto del 28 dicembre 1908*, 483–516.
Guidoboni, Emanuela, and John E. Ebel. *Earthquakes and Tsunamis in the Past: A Guide to Techniques in Historical Seismology.* Cambridge, 2009.
Guidoboni, Emanuela, and Gianluca Valensise, eds. *Il peso economico e sociale dei disastri sismici in Italia negli ultimi 150 anni.* Bologna, 2011.
Gunn, Simon, and Alastair Owens. "Nature, Technology and the Modern City: An Introduction." Special issue, *Cultural Geography* 13 (2006): 291–96.
Hall, Peter. *Cities of Tomorrow: An Intellectual History of Urban Planning and Design in the Twentieth Century.* Oxford, 1996.
Hamlin, Cristopher. *Public Health and Social Justice in the Age of Chadwick.* Cambridge, 1998.
———. *Cholera: The Biography.* Oxford and New York, 2009.
Healey, Mark. *The Ruins of the New Argentina: Peronism and the Remaking of San Juan after the 1944 Earthquake.* Durham, 2011.
Hein, Carol. "Resilient Tokyo: Disaster and Transformation in the Japanese City." In *The Resilient City: How Modern Cities Recover from Disaster*, edited by Lawrence J. Vale and Thomas J. Campanella, 213–34. Oxford and New York, 2005.
———. "Shaping Tokyo: Land Development and Planning Practice in the Early Modern Japanese Metropolis." *Journal of Urban History* 36, no. 4 (2010): 447–84.
Heynen, Nik, Maria Kaika, and Eric Swyngedouw. "Urban Political Ecology: Politicizing the Production of Urban Natures." In *In the Nature of Cities: Urban Political Ecology and the Politics of Urban Metabolism*, edited by Nik Haynen, Maria Kaika, and Eric Swyngedouw. London and New York, 2006.
Hewitt, Kenneth, ed. *Interpretations of Calamity: From the Viewpoint of Human Ecology.* Boston, 1983.
Howard-Jones, Norman. "Robert Koch and the Cholera Vibrio: A Centenary." *British Medical Journal* 288 (1984): 379–81.
Iori, Tullia, and Alessandro Marzo Magno, eds. *150 anni di storia del cemento in Italia: Le opere, gli uomini, le imprese.* Rome, 2011.
Joyce, Patrick. *The Rule of Freedom: Liberalism and the Modern City.* London, 2003.

Kausel, Edgar G. "Chilean National Centennial Report to IASPEI." In *International Handbook of Earthquake & Engineering Seismology, Part 2*, edited by William H. K. Lee, Hiroo Kanamori, Paul C. Jennings, and Carl Kisslinger, 1315. Amsterdam and Boston, 2002.
Kelman, Ari. "Boundary Issues: Clarifying New Orleans's Murky Edges." *The Journal of American History* 94 (2007): 695–703.
King, Russell, and Alan Stratchan. "Sicilian Agro-Towns." *Erdkunde: Archive for Scientific Geography* 32, no. 2 (1978): 110–23.
Lapesa, Giuliano. "Gli studi sulle città meridionali in età contemporanea: Tra storia del Mezzogiorno e storia urbana." *Meridiana: Rivista di storia e scienze sociali* 57 (2006): 169–90.
Lees, Andrew, and Lynn H. Lees. *Cities and the Making of Modern Europe, 1750–1914*. Cambridge and New York, 2007.
Lübken, Uwe, and Christof Mauch. "Uncertain Environments: Natural Hazards, Risk, and Insurance in Historical Perspective." Special issue, *Environment and History* 17, no. 1 (2011): 1–12.
Lumley, Robert, and Jonathan Morris, eds. *Oltre il meridionalismo: nuove prospettive sul Mezzogiorno d'Italia*. Rome, 1999.
Lupo, Salvatore. "L'utopia totalitaria del fascismo (1918–1942)." In Aymard and Giarrizzo, *Storia d'Italia*, 475–81
———. *Il giardino degli aranci: Il mondo degli agrumi nella storia del Mezzogiorno*. Venice, 1990.
———. *Storia della mafia: Dalle origini ai giorni nostri*. Rome, 1003.
Mamoli, Marcello, and Giorgio Trebbi. *Storia dell'urbanistica: L'Europa del secondo dopoguerra*. Rome-Bari, 2004.
Mangiameli, Rosario. "La regione in Guerra (1943–1950)." In Aymard and Giarrizzo, *Storia d'Italia*, 485–600.
Marino, Giuseppe Carlo. *Partiti e lotta di classe in Sicilia: Da Orlando a Mussolini*. Bari, 1976.
———, ed. *A cinquant'anni dalla riforma agraria in Sicilia*. Milan, 2003.
Massard-Guilbaud, Geneviève. "The Urban Catastrophe: A Challenge to the Social, Political and Cultural Order of the City." In *Cities and Catastrophes: Coping with Emergency in European History / Villes et catastrophes: Réaction face à l'urgence dans l'histoire européenne*, edited by Geneviève Massard-Guilbaud, Dieter Schott, and Harold L. Platt, 9–42. Frankfurt am Main, 2002.
Massard-Guilbaud, Geneviève, and Peter Thorsheim, eds. "Cities, Environment and European History." Special issue, *Journal of Urban History* 33, no. 5 (2007).
Mauch, Christof, and Christian Pfister, eds. *Natural Disasters, Cultural Responses: Case Studies Toward a Global Environmental History*. Lanham, 2009.
McNeill, John. *Something New Under the Sun: An Environmental History of the Twentieth Century World*. New York and London, 2000.
Meisner Rosen, Christine. *The Limits of Power: Great Fires and the Process of City Growth in America*. Cambridge, 1986.
Melosi, Martin V. *Garbage in the Cities: Refuse, Reform, and the Environment 1880–1980*. College Station and London, 1981. Revised edition 2005.

———. *The Sanitary City: Urban Infrastructure in America from Colonial Times to the Present.* Baltimore, 2000.
———. "Humans, Cities, and Nature: How Do Cities Fit in the Material World?" *Journal of Urban History* 36, no. 1 (2009): 3–21.
Mitchell, Timothy. *Rule of Experts: Egypt, Techno-Politics, Modernity.* Berkeley, 2002.
Moe, Nelson. "The Emergence of the Southern Question in Villari, Franchetti, and Sonnino." In Schneider, *Italy's Southern Question*, 51–76.
Molesky, Mark. "The Great Fire of Lisbon, 1755." In Bankoff, Lübken, and Sand, *Flammable Cities*, 147–69.
Molle, François. "River Basin Planning and Management: The Social Life of a Concept." *Geoforum* 40 (2009): 484–94.
Montalbano, Giuseppe. "La repressione del movimento contadino in Sicilia (1944–1950)." *Diacronie: Studi di Storia Contemporanea* 12, no. 4 (2002), http://www.studistorici.com/2012/12/29/montalbano_numero_12/.
Motta, Giovanna, ed. *La città ferita: Il terremoto dello Stretto e la comunità internazionale.* Milan, 2008.
Mullin, John R. "The Reconstruction of Lisbon Following the Earthquake of 1755: A Study in Despotic Planning." *Planning Perspectives: An International Journal of History, Planning, and the Environment* 7, no. 2 (1992): 157–79.
Murray Li, Tanya. *The Will to Improve: Governmentality, Development, and the Practice of Politics.* Durham and London, 2007.
Musacchio, Aldo, ed. *Stato e società nel Belice: La gestione del terremoto 1968–1976.* Milan, 1981.
Naldi, Giovanna, ed. *Terremoto calabro-messinese 1908/2008.* Rome and Florence, 2008.
Neri Serneri, Simone. *Incorporare la natura: Storie ambientali del Novecento.* Rome, 2005.
———. "The Construction of the Modern City and the Management of Water Resources in Italy, 1880–1920." *Journal of Urban History* 33 (2007): 814–15.
———. "Urbanizzazione, territorio e ambiente nell'Italia contemporanea, 1950–1970." *I Frutti di Demetra* 6 (2005): 33–39.
Nigro, Gianluigi, and Francesco Fazzio, eds. *Il territorio rinnovato: Uno sguardo urbanistico sulla ricostruzione postsismica in Umbria 1997–2007.* Perugia, 2007.
Oliver-Smith, Anthony. *The Martyred City: Death and Rebirth in the Andes.* Albuquerque, 1986.
———. "Peru's Five Hundred Years Earthquake." In *The Angry Earth: Disasters in Anthropological Perspective,* edited by Susanna Hoffman and Anthony Oliver-Smith, 74–88. New York, 1999.
———. "Theorizing Disasters: Nature, Power, and Culture." In *Catastrophe and Culture: The Anthropology of Disaster,* edited by Susanna Hoffman and Anthony Oliver-Smith, 23–47. Oxford, 2002.
Oreskes, Naomi. "From Continental Drift to Plate Tectonics." In *Plate Tectonics: An Insider's History of the Modern Theory of the Earth,* edited by Naomi Oreskes, 3–27. Boulder, 2003.
Orlando, Guido, and Salvo Vitale. *Danilo Dolci, La radio dei poveri cristi: Il progetto, la realizzazione, i testi della prima radio libera in Italia.* Marsala, 2008.
Osservatorio sul terremoto dell'Università degli Studi dell'Aquila. *Il terremoto dell'Aquila: Analisi e riflessioni sull'emergenza.* L'Aquila: 2011.

Otieri, Annunziata M. "Memorie e trasformazioni nel processo di ricostruzione di Messina." *Storia Urbana* 26, no. 106-107 (2005): 13-65.

———. "La città fantasma: Danni bellici e politiche di ricostruzione a Messina nel secondo dopoguerra (1943-1959)." *Storia Urbana* 30, no. 114-115 (2007): 63-112.

Palla, Luciana "La 'nuova città' e la sua gente: Un difficile percorso dal 1963 ad oggi." In *Il Vajont dopo il Vajont, 1963-2000*, edited by Maurizio Reberschak and Ivo Mattozzi, 51-90. Venice, 2009.

Pan, Erica Y. Z. *The Impact of the 1906 Earthquake on San Francisco's Chinatown*. New York, 1995.

Pavarin, Alessandro. *Lo sviluppo del Mezzogiorno: L'intervento dello Stato e il sistema bancario della nascita della Repubblica agli anni Sessanta*. Rome, 2011.

Pennino, Carmelo, Antonino Pennino, and Alfonsa Carbone. *Analisi demografica dei Comuni della Valle del Belice colpiti dal sisma del 1968*. Palermo, 1976.

Pereira, Alvaro S. "The Opportunity of a Disaster: The Economic Impact of the 1755 Lisbon Earthquake." *The Journal of Economic History* 69, no. 2 (2009): 466-99.

Petri, Rolf. *La frontiera industriale: Territorio, grande industria e leggi speciali prima della Cassa per il Mezzogiorno*. Milan 1990.

Petrusewicz, Marta. *Latifondo: Economia morale e vita materiale in una periferia dell'Ottocento*. Venice, 1990.

———. *Come il Meridione divenne una questione: Rappresentazioni del Sud prima e dopo il Quarantotto*. Soveria Mannelli, 1998.

———. "Il tramonto del latifondismo." In *Oltre il meridionalismo: Nuove prospettive sul Mezzogiorno d'Italia*, edited by Robert Lumley and Jonathan Morris, 1-50. Rome, 1999.

Placanica, Augusto. *Cassa sacra e beni della Chiesa nella Calabria del Settecento*. Ercolano, 1970.

———. *L'Iliade funesta: storia del terremoto calabro-messinese del 1783*. Rome, 1984.

———. *Il filosofo e la catastrophe: un terremoto del Settecento*. Turin, 1985.

Pritchard, Sarah B. "'Paris et le Désert Francais': Urban and Rural Development in Post–World War II France." In *The Nature of Cities*, edited by Andrew C. Isenberg, 175-91. Rochester, 2006.

Puelo, Thomas. "Baroque disruptions in Val di Noto, Sicily." *Geographical Review* 100 (2010): 476-93.

Quenet, Gregory. *Les tremblements de terre aux XVIIe et XVIIIe siècles: La naissance d'un risque*. Champ Vallon, 2005.

Raymond, Henri, and Liliane Dufour. *1693: Val di Noto, la rinascita dopo il disastro*. Catania, 1994.

Reitherman, Robert K. *Earthquakes and Engineers: An International History*. Reston, 2012.

Renda, Francesco. *Storia della Sicilia dalle origini ai giorni nostri*. Vol. 3, *Dall'Unità ai giorni nostri*. Palermo, 2003.

Renna, Agostino, Antonio De Bonis, and Giuseppe Gangemi, eds. *Costruzione e progetto: La valle del Belice*. Milan, 1979.

Renzoni, Cristina. "Il piano implicito: Il territorio nazionale nella programmazione economica italiana 1946-1973." *Storia Urbana* 126/127 (2010): 139-69.

Restifo, Giuseppe. "Il vortice demografico dopo la catastrofe: Morti e movimenti di popolazione a Messina fra 1908 e 1911." In Bertolaso et al., *Il terremoto e il maremoto del 28 dicembre 1908*, 295-304.

Ribeiro dos Santos, Maria Helena, and Ferran Sagarra I Trias. "Trading Properties after the Earthquake: The Rebuilding of Eighteen-Century Lisbon." *Planning Perspectives: An International Journal of History, Planning, and the Environment* 26, no. 2 (2011): 301–11.
Rigano, R., B. Antichi, L. Arena, R. Azzaro, and M. S. Barbano. "Sismicità e zonazione sismogenetica in Sicilia occidentale." In *Consiglio Nazionale delle Ricerche, Gruppo Nazionale di Geofisica della Terra Solida, Atti del 17° Convegno Nazionale*, Rome, 10–12 November 1998, http://www2.ogs.trieste.it/gngts/gngts/convegniprecedenti/1998/Contents/ordinari/12/rrigano/htm/rrigano.htm.
Rist, Gilbert. *The History of Development: From Western Origins to Global Faith*. London and New York, 2008.
Rodriguez, Havidán, Enrico L. Quarantelli, and Russell R. Dynes, eds. *Handbook of Disaster Research*. New York, 2006.
Rome, Adam. *The Bulldozer in the Countryside: Suburban Sprawl and the Rise of American Environmentalism*. Cambridge, 2001.
Rostan, Michele. *La terribile occasione: Imprenditorialità e sviluppo in una comunità del Belice*. Bologna, 1998.
Saunier, Pierre-Yves, and Shane Ewen. *Another Global City: Historical Explorations into the Transnational Municipal Moment, 1850–2000*. New York, 2008.
Schencking, Charles J. "Catastrophe, Opportunism, Contestation: The Fractured Politics of Reconstructing Tokyo Following the Great Kantô Earthquake of 1923." *Modern Asian Studies* 40, no. 4 (2006): 833–73.
Schneider, Jane, ed. *Italy's 'Southern Question': Orientalism in One Country*. Oxford and New York, 1998.
Schott, Dieter. "One City—Three Catastrophes: Hamburg from the Great Fire 1842 to the Great Flood 1962." In *Cities and Catastrophes: Coping with Emergency in European History / Villes et catastrophes: Réactions face à l'urgence dans l'histoire européenne*, edited by Geneviève Massard-Guilbaud, Harold L. Platt, and Dieter Schott, 185–204. Frankfurt am Main, 2002.
———. "Resources of the City: Toward a European Urban Environmental History." In *Resources of the City: Contributions to an Environmental History of Modern Europe*, edited by Dieter Schott, Bill Luckin, and Geneviève Massard-Guilbaud. 1–27. Aldershot, 2005.
Schubert, Dirk. 2012. "The Great Fire of Hamburg, 1842: From Catastrophe to Reform." In Bankoff, Lübken, and Sand, *Flammable Cities*, 212–34.
Scott, James C. *Seeing Like a State: How Certain Schemes to Improve the Human Condition Have Failed*. New Haven, 1998.
Seidensticker, Edward. *Tokyo Rising: The City Since the Last Earthquake*. New York, 1994.
Sica, Paolo. *Storia dell'urbanistica*. Vol. 2, *L'Ottocento*. Rome and Bari, 1985.
Sieverts, Thomas. *Cities without Cities: An Interpretation of the Zwischenstadt*. London and New York, 2003.
Slaton, Amy E. *Reinforced Concrete and the Modernization of American Building, 1900–1930*. Baltimore, 2001.
Snowden, Frank M. *Naples in the Time of Cholera, 1884–1911*. Cambridge, 1995.
Soja, Edward W. *Postmetropolis: Critical Studies of Cities and Regions*. Malden: 2000.
———. "Beyond Postmetropolis." *Urban Geography* 32, no. 4 (2011): 451–69.

Sonnino, Eugenio. "La popolazione italiana: dall'espansione al contenimento." In *Storia dell'Italia repubblicana*. Vol. 2, *La trasformazione dell'Italia*. Part 1, *Politica, economia, società*, edited by Francesco Barbagallo, 531–75. Turin, 1994.
Steinberg, Theodore. *Acts of God: The Unnatural History of Natural Disaster in America*. New York, 2006.
Susani, Carola. *L'infanzia è un terremoto*. Rome and Bari, 2008.
Sutcliffe, Anthony. *Towards the Planned City: Germany, Britain, the United States, and France, 1780–1914*. New York, 1981.
Tarr, Joel A., and Gabriel Dupuy, eds. *Technology and the Rise of the Networked City in Europe and America*. Philadelphia, 1988.
———. *The Search for the Ultimate Sink: Urban Pollution in Historical Perspective*. Akron, 1996.
———. "The City as an Artifact of Technology and the Environment." In *The Illusory Boundary: Environment and Technology in History*, edited by Martin Reuss and Stephen H. Cutcliffe, 145–70. Charlottesville, 2011.
Tobriner. Stephen. "La Casa Baraccata: Earthquake-Resistant Construction in 18th-Century Calabria." *Journal of the Society of Architectural Historians* 42, no. 2 (1983): 131–38.
Tolic, Ines. *Dopo il terremoto: La politica della ricostruzione negli anni della guerra fredda a Skopje*. Reggio Emilia, 2011.
Tranfaglia, Nicola. "La modernità squilibrata: Dalla crisi del centrismo al compromesso storico." In *Storia dell'Italia repubblicana*. Vol. 2, *La trasformazione dell'Italia*. Part 2, *Istituzioni, movimenti, culture*, edited by Francesco Barbagallo, 5–111. Turin, 1995.
Trigilia, Lucia. "Dispositivi 'antisismici' nella ricostruzione del Val di Noto dopo il terremoto del 1693." In *Presidi antisismici nell'architettura storica e monumentale*, edited by Angela Marino, 95–97. Rome, 2000.
UNESCO World Heritage Convention. *Late Baroque Towns of the Val di Noto (South-Eastern Sicily): Advisory Board Evaluation*. 2002. http://whc.unesco.org/archive/advisory_body_evaluation/1024rev.pdf.
Vai, Gian Battista. "Vajont, 1963 cinquanta anni dopo: cronaca, etica e scienza." In *L'Italia dei disastri: Dati e riflessioni sull'impatto degli eventi naturali, 1861–2013*, edited by Emanuela Guidoboni and Gianluca Valensise, 43–72. Bologna: 2013.
Valencius, Conevery Bolton. *The Lost History of the New Madrid Earthquakes*. Chicago, 2013.
Ventura, Stefano. *Non sembrava novembre quella sera: Il terremoto del 1980 tra storia e memoria*. Atripada, 2010.
———. "I ragazzi dell'Ufficio di Piano: La ricostruzione urbanistica in Irpinia." *Frutti di Demetra* 22 (2010): 37–51.
Vendramini, Ferruccio, ed. *Disastro e ricostruzione nell'area del Vajont*. Longarone, 1994.
Vicarelli, Giovanna. *Alle origini della politica sanitaria in Italia: Società e salute da Crispi al fascismo*. Bologna, 2007.
Von Kleist, Heinrich. *The Marquise of O— and Other Stories*. London, 1978.
Walker, Charles. *Shaky Colonialism: The 1746 Earthquake-Tsunami in Lima, Peru, and Its Long Aftermath*. Durham, 2008.
Ward, Stephen V. *Planning the Twentieth-Century City: The Advanced Capitalist World*. Chichester, 2002.
Winchester, Simon. *A Crack in the Edge of the World: America and the Great California Earthquake of 1906*. New York, 2005.

Winiwarter, Verena, Martin Schmid, and Gert Dressel. "Looking at Half a Millennium of Co-Existence: The Danube in Vienna as a Socio-Natural Site." Special issue, *Water History* 5, no. 2 (2013): 101–19.
Wisner, Ben, Pierce Blaikie, Terry Cannon, and Ian Davis, eds. *At Risk: Natural Hazards, People's Vulnerability and Disasters*. London, 2004.
Zucconi, Guido. *La città contesa: Dagli ingegneri sanitari agli urbanisti (1885–1942)*. Milan, 1999.

Websites

Bertrand-Krajewski, Jean Luc. "Arnold Bürkli-Ziegler," In *Short Historical Dictionary on Urban Hydrology and Drainage*, PDF. 2006. http://jlbkpro.free.fr/shduhdfromatoz/buerkli-ziegler.pdf.
Centro di Cultura Ecologica – Archivio Ambientalista, "Fabrizio Giovenale–scheda biografica." http://www.centrodiculturaecologica.it/home/node/285.
Ciavoni, Carlo. "Il sisma che ha squassato la notte: I danni, la paura, la solidarietà." *La Repubblica*, 6 April 2009, now in Archivio Storico: http://www.repubblica.it/2009/04/sezioni/cronaca/terremoto-nord-roma/terremoto-il-punto/terremoto-il-punto.html?ref=search.
Guidoboni, Emanuela, Guido Ferrari, Dante Mariotti, Alberto Comastri, Gabriele Tarabusi, and Gianluca Valensise, eds. 1997. *Catalogue of Strong Earthquakes in Italy 461 B.C.–1997 and Mediterranean Area 760 B.C.–1500*, INGV-Istituto Nazionale di Geofisica e Vulcanologia. http://storing.ingv.it/cfti4med.
Filippone, Pasquale. "Intervista a Giovanna." Cent'anni di baracche, Istituto per la formazione al giornalismo, Urbino 2008. https://www.youtube.com/watch?v=yRh-U2TDM8M&index=11&list=UUf9-qsNeUAQpLvWfYuS-igg.
Fondazione Burri, "Biografia di Alberto Burri," PDF undated. http://www.fondazioneburri.org/ita/pdf/biografia.pdf.
Il Sole 24 Ore. Interactive map based on the official data of the tax declaration IRPEF in 2007. http://www.ilsole24ore.com/art/SoleOnLine4/Italia/2008/08/italia-redditi-comuni.shtml.
Malanima, Paolo. "Italian Urban Population 1300–1861 (the database)." PDF. http://www.paolomalanima.it/default_file/Italian%20Economy/Urban_Population.pdf.
Pogliotti, Mario. TG1, 19 January 1968. https://www.youtube.com/watch?v=KD8CKSQkrj4
Regione Umbria, "Osservatorio sulla ricostruzione." http://www.osservatorioricostruzione.regione.umbria.it/.
Zavoli, Sergio, Tv7, 1968. http://www.youtube.com/watch?v=nIMFxzCoO7Y.

Index

A
Accademia dei Lincei, 36, 38, 91. See also Lincean Academy
Accardo, Nicola, 125, 128
adaptation, 4, 10, 12, 22, 35, 74, 221
    hazard, 76, 110
    seismic, 97, 107, 108, 223, 224
agrarian reform, 12, 152, 157, 158, 160, 173
    Agency for, 158, 163, 170, 171
agricultural economy, 12, 201
    cantine sociali (cellar cooperatives), 201
    cereal crop, 122, 155–156, 160, 174, 182, 199. See also cereal monoculture
    citric acid, 67, 89
    citrus, 50, 64, 67, 89
Alcantara River, 57–58
Antioci & Co, 58, 63
Apennines, the, 22
aqueduct, 65–66, 69, 76, 85, 90, 94, 158, 160, 183
    Bureau for the Aqueduct, 65
    Montescuro, 158, 173
    Niceto, 65, 90, 106
    rural, 160, 184, 187
    Ufficio acquedotto, 65. See also Bureau for the Aqueduct
    urban, 8, 9, 11, 52, 58, 60, 62, 63, 64, 65, 106
Arbuffo, Onorato, 35, 36
assistance, 25, 28, 37, 72, 125, 127, 219
autostrada, 129, 193–194, 196

B
bacteriological revolution, 53, 75
Bankoff, Greg, 4

baraccamenti, 89–91, 97, 100, 102, 106, 109, 183–184, 194, 197–198. See also provisional settlement
Baratta, Mario, 31–34, 37, 72–73, 123
Barbera, Lorenzo, 166–168, 173, 194, 196, 199
Barone, Guiseppe, 98, 154
Bechmann, George, 60–64, 75
Belice Refugees, 128, 131
Belice River, 1, 12, 122, 154–155, 159, 160, 166–168, 170–173, 181, 182, 189, 215–216
    dam on, 194, 200, 204
    Destro, 122
    Sinistro, 122
    Valley, 7–13, 111, 121–142, 150–174, 181–205, 213–218, 220–221
        Reclamation Consortium, 12, 155, 158–159, 161, 166, 170–171, 199, 200. See also Consorzio di Bonifi ca del Belice
        underdevelopment of, 11, 131–133, 142, 181, 197. See also underdevelopment of Messina.
Berardinis, Nicola De, 30
Bevilacqua, Piero, 153, 221
Bianchi, Antonio, 155
biogeophysical environment, 4, 64, 67–69, 74, 76, 109, 140
Blaikie, Pierce, 4
Blaserna, Senator Pietro, 37–39, 91
bonifica, 153, 155–156. See also land reclamation
Borzi, Luigi, 11, 67, 85, 92–97, 99, 100, 105–110

Bourbon Administration, 153, 219
British, 21, 25, 193
Bronze Age, 122
Building Association, 98, 100, 102, 103, 104, 105, 109. See also Unione Edilizia
building code, 11, 2223, 34–42, 71–76, 93–94, 141, 182, 219, 220, 224
    reinforced concrete, 1, 7, 31–32, 35, 38, 41, 73, 106–107, 129, 132, 223
building industry, 97, 102, 108, 182, 190, 215
built
    environment, 1, 4, 5, 6, 34, 39, 72, 121, 123, 126, 182, 205, 214, 216–217, 219, 220–226
    space, 50, 52, 54, 65, 74, 88, 90, 92, 97, 103, 105, 110, 214
Bureau for Hygiene, 62, 66
bureaucratic
    history, 167
    plan, 96
    procedures, 128
Burri, Alberto, 202, 203, 213

C

California, 5, 12, 40, 41, 222, 223
Cammareri, Villino, 72
Cape Peloro, 50
Cappelli, Professor Raffaele, 37
Carocci, Alberto, 163
Caronia, Salvatore, 153
Carta, Giuseppe, 190
casa baraccata, 23, 34, 71, 219. See also building code
Caselli, Leandro, 62–66
Cassa Depositi e Prestiti, 65
Cassa per il Mezzogiorno, 137, 158, 160–161, 163–164, 167, 170, 173, 182, 193, 198, 200, 215. See also Fund for the South
Catalogue of Strong Earthquakes in Italy, 23
Cavalieri, Enea, 151, 156
census, 71, 168, 173, 202
    1901 national, 25
    1911 national, 97, 102
    1921 national, 102

Center for Economic and Social Research for the South (CRESM, Centro di ricerche economiche e sociali per il Meridione), 13, 197
Center for Studies and Activities, 138, 196. See also Centro Studi e Iniziative
Centers of Research and Initiatives for Full Employment (Centri studi e iniziative per la piena occupazione) 165, 166, 168, 189
Centro Studi e Iture, 138. See also Center for Studies and Activities
cereal monoculture, 160, 174. See also agricultural economy, cereal crop
Christian Democrat, 135, 136
civilian service, 195
civil protection department, 140
Clancey, Gregory, 5
Cocco-Ortu, Francesco, 37
Coen, Deborah, 5
Colten, Craig, 4
Comitato Centrale di Soccorso (Central Relief Committee), 26, 35
comitato intercomunale (intermunicipal committee), 168
Comitato Interministeriale per lo Sviluppo Economico (CIPE, Inter-Ministerial Committee for conomic Development), 193, 194, 196
Commissione parlamentare d'inchiesta sulle condizioni dei contadini nelle provincie meridionali (parliamentary commission of enquiry on the conditions of peasants in Southern Italy), 37
common graves, 26
Communist Party, 133–136, 139, 157, 168, 224
concentration camps, 98, 185. See also campo di concentrazione
Consiglio Superiore dei Lavori Pubblici, 38, 52, 71, 94, 155, 160, 188. See also Superior Council of Public Works
consortium of damaged owners, 98
Consorzio di Bonifi ca del Belice. See Belice Reclamation Consortium

Corrao, Ludovico, 201, 202
Cronon, Bill, 6, 9

D
Das Erdbeben in Chili (The Earthquake in Chile), 2, 3
de Melo, Sebastião (Marquis de Pombal), 223, 225
development
    community-based, 12, 150
    initiatives, 136, 139, 161–162, 172, 186, 193
    local committees, 185, 189–190, 196
    post-WWII agenda, 131
    rural, 17, 174, 189–190, 215–216
    socioeconomic, 11, 121, 134–140, 181, 217, 220
Dickie, John, 26
Dolci, Danilo, 138, 162–167, 173, 194
Drago, Aurelio, 154
Duke of Camastra, 110

E
Earthquake
    1647 Chile, 2, 3, 12, 40, 41, 222
    1693 Noto Valley, 92, 110, 218–219
    1746 Lima, 5, 222–223
    1755 Lisbon, 23, 33, 92, 222–223, 225
    1783 Calabrian, 5, 23, 33, 41
    1812 New Madrid, 5
    1857 Neapolitan, 31
    1883 Casamicciola, 28, 31, 35
    1887 Ligurian, 28, 32
    1891 Mino-Owari (Nobi), 40, 41, 223
    1894 Calabrian, 31, 32, 72
    1905 Calabrian, 32, 73
    1906 San Francisco, 21, 31, 34–35, 40, 41, 223
    1907 Calabrian, 32, 73
    1915 Marsica, 42, 109
    1923 Kanto, 224
    1930 Irpinia, 42, 109
    1963 Skopje, 142
    1968 Belice, 7, 11
    1970 Peru, 142
    1972 Managua, 224
    1976 Friuli, 140, 203, 220
    1976 Tangshan, 224
    1980 Irpinia, 140, 203
    1995 Kobe, 224
    1997 Umbria and Le Marche, 220
    community response to, 26, 138, 142–143. *See also* protests
    government response to, 25, 27, 38, 41, 142
    history of, 2–6, 10, 12, 23, 28, 31, 48, 123, 174, 218, 221, 222
    impact of, 1–8, 11–12, 21, 24, 27, 31, 39–41, 140, 143, 174, 204, 221, 225
        on urban environments, 2, 10, 12, 21, 24, 28, 34, 40, 42–43, 65, 221. *See also* environments, urban
    legislation, 181, 186, 216
        1909 legislation on earthquakes, 37–39, 41, 84, 88–98, 107, 217, 220, 221
    memoryscape, 213
    prevention, 93, 110, 216
    -proof urban environment, 36–40, 85, 93, 215
    post-disaster redevelopment, 12, 35, 38, 39, 40–43, 53, 75
    resistant technology, 7, 11, 31–32, 35–37, 41, 71
    study of, 3, 4, 5, 10, 21, 22, 30–36, 41
    -tsunami, 7, 10, 22–30
    as urban hazards, 6, 12, 21, 27, 36, 42, 74
    urbanism, 36–40, 193, 214–222, 225
    voice of, 1, 2–6, 7, 10, 12, 13, 111, 203, 214, 218
    vulnerability to, 4, 11, 42, 76, 142, 217
economic activities, 72, 90, 92, 134, 172, 186, 194, 199, 217. *See also* maritime commerce
emergency
    law, 55
    response, 111
emigration, 12, 128, 161, 164, 166, 189
    Italian, 131, 152
enfiteusi (long-term rental contracts), 161

engineering, 21, 31–32, 34–35, 41, 50, 65–71, 73–76, 121, 129, 141
    civil, 31, 38, 86, 182
    construction, 141
    earthquake, 31–32, 35–36, 41, 71–73, 91–92, 215, 219, 223
    environmental, 142, 160
    Portuguese, 23, 33
Ente per la Riforma Agraria in Sicilia (Agency for Agrarian Reform in Sicily), 158
environment
    conservation, 191
    feature, 75, 221
    history, 6, 9, 222, 226
    knowledge, 186, 217
    "new", 133
    physical, 55, 67, 68
    reform, 55, 150–151, 174
    resources, 165, 216
    rural, 173, 204–205, 213
    transformation, 6, 43, 49, 65, 142, 153, 155, 163, 173, 222
epidemics
    cholera, 53–55, 58, 75
    intestinal, 52, 53, 62
    malaria, 153–155
    smallpox, 55
    typhoid, 62
    typhus, 54
    See also urban epidemics
Europe, 8, 9, 22, 42, 54, 58, 60, 74, 75, 91, 131, 157, 161, 164, 198–199, 205, 220
ex novo reconstruction, 48, 77, 84, 106, 109–110, 217–218
expropriation, 37, 50, 52, 62–63, 64, 88–89, 94, 98, 100, 157, 219

F
Fascist, 103–105, 155–158, 215
fault
    lines, 2, 6, 31, 129, 141, 204, 214, 217, 220–222, 225
    system, 123, 222
feudal
    landlords, 122, 151
    privileges, 151

feudatari, 122, 151, 156
Fiore, Giacomo, 53
Fiumedinisi River, 57, 63, 106
France, 5, 128, 150
Francese, Mario, 201
Franchetti, Leopoldo, 151–152, 156
Franchi, Secondo, 39, 40, 42, 108
Friuli Venezia Giulia 140, 220
Fulci, Ludovico, 30
Fund for the South, 137, 158, 193. *See also* Cassa per il Mezzogiorno

G
Garibaldi Street, 48, 100
Genio Civile and Genio Militare, 37, 86, 89–91, 93, 100, 104, 128, 182. *See also* Civil and Military Engineering Corps
geology, 3, 21, 121, 123, 133, 141–142, 167
General Inspectorate, 136, 139, 187, 188, 197–198. *See also* Ispettorato Generale per la ricostruzione delle zone terremotate
geophysical
    conditions, 39
    features, 4, 34, 84
    mechanisms, 31
Geshwind, Carl-Henry, 5
Giglio, Gaspare, 125, 128
Giolitti, Prime Minister Giovanni, 35, 37, 38
Giostra Valley, 88, 89
Giovannini, Alberto, 132
Giovenale, Fabrizio, 187, 190, 191, 19
Giuliano, Salvatore, 157
Goria, Giulio, 132
grassroots movements, 12, 161–166, 172, 215
Greece, 22, 122

H
hazards
    flood
        1917 flood, 100, 102
    natural hazards, 2, 12, 225, 226
Healey, Mark, 5, 224
Heinrich von Kleist, 2, 3

Hewitt, Kenneth, 4
Historical narratives, 4, 221
Homer, 22
housing
    affordable, 100, 102, 104
    huts, 11, 86, 88–91, 97, 98–109,
        183–186, 203, 213, 215
    real estate appropriations, 55, 88
    shantytown, 1, 11, 91, 97, 111, 213
    social housing, 12, 105, 108, 187, 189,
        197
    See also settlement
human intervention, 33
hydroelectric plants, 154

I
immigrants, 103, 105, 109, 202
Ionian Sea, 22
Inchiesta parlamentare sulle condizioni
   dei contadini meridionali,
   (Parliamentary Inquiry on the
   Condition of Southern Peasantry),
   154
Interdonato, Pierto, 62–66, 99, 102
International Monetary Fund, 158
industrial
    economy, 12, 193, 196, 216
    initiatives, 172
    production, 50, 161
    turn, 171
industrialization, 92, 137, 140, 161–162,
   164, 196
    capital intensive factories, 172
    of southern Italy, 137, 162, 164
    lack of, 12, 204, 216
    pre-, 158
    state-funded, 181–182, 187–188
initiatives, 26, 108, 151, 186, 173
    "productive", 187, 198
    reform, 62, 151
interventionist approach, 21, 76, 98
irrigation, 63, 64, 89, 154–155, 166, 167,
   191, 214, 216
    consortium, 58
    improvements, 138, 169, 170, 190
    large-scale, 155, 160, 168, 201
    networks, 156, 159, 165, 168, 200

ISES (Istituto per lo Sviluppo dell'Edilizia
   Sociale), 181, 187–198, 204, 216
Ispettorato Generale per la ricostruzione
   delle zone terremotate (General
   Inspectorate for the Reconstruction
   of the Earthquake-damaged Area; *See*
   General Inspectorate), 136, 139, 187,
   188, 197, 198
Istituto Nazionale Geofisica (National
   Institute for Geophysics), 42, 137, 182
Italian Economic Miracle, 161
Italy
    Camaro, 69
    Casamicciola, 28, 31
    Castelvetrano, 127, 171, 183
    Catania, 27, 38, 92, 218
    Gibellina, 7, 13, 123–127, 130, 132,
        152, 153, 158, 173, 181, 183,
        191–195, 201–203
    Menfi, 126, 166, 171, 192, 202
    Montevago, 7, 126, 132, 181,
        191–192, 195, 202, 213
    Naples, 8, 23, 27, 54–55, 57, 96, 219
    Palermo, 27, 123–128, 131, 138–141,
        150, 154–155, 162–172, 187,
        190–196
    Partanna, 126–127, 132, 138, 153,
        168, 173, 183, 192, 196
    Partinico, 162–166, 189
    Poggioreale, 7, 123–127, 153, 158,
        166, 173, 181, 183, 191–195, 202,
        213
    Reggio Calabria, 7, 21, 24, 110, 125
        Ferruzzano, 73
    Roccamena, 128, 166–168, 171, 194
    Rome, 8, 13, 25, 93, 125, 128,
        137–140, 163, 167, 185–188, 194,
        197, 220
    Salapauta, 7, 123–127, 132, 153, 158,
        166, 173, 181, 183, 191–192, 195,
        202
    Santa Margherita Belice, 171, 213
    Santa Ninfa, 126–127, 132, 153, 168,
        183, 192, 195
    Syracuse, 27, 36
    Trapani, 123–125, 127, 158, 183, 193,
        194

J

Japan, 3, 5, 12, 21, 30, 31, 35, 38, 40, 41, 222, 223, 224
    Japanese Imperial Earthquake Investigation Committee, 34, 41
Jato River, 165, 190
    Valley, 190

K

Kelman, Ari, 42
King Vittorio Emanuele III, 35
Kingdom of Italy, 49, 151, 153
Kingdom of Naples, 23, 33, 41, 71, 110
Koch, Robert, 54, 75

L

labor relations, 152, 155
land reclamation, 8, 12, 97, 102, 150–173, 199, 200, 215. *See also bonifica*
landscape
    agricultural, 109
    of deprivation, 130, 181
    physical, 100, 142
    post-earthquake, 129, 182, 224
    social, 110
Lanza, Giovanni, 218
La Santissima, 53, 57, 58, 62, 63
latifondo, 151–153, 156–157, 159, 199
legal mechanisms, 52, 58, 63, 89, 139, 196
Ligurian region, 28, 35
Lorenzoni, Gionanni, 152, 154, 156

M

Mafia
    mafiosi, 152, 170
    rural, 12, 151, 153, 157, 165, 201, 204
Maganzini, Italo, 38
Mallet, Robert, 30, 31
Mancini, Giacomo, 136, 139
Mangione, Calogero, 172
Marcelli, Liliana, 137, 191
maritime commerce, 67, 85, 87, 93, 108, 215, 217
media, 128, 131, 132
    Corriere della Sera, 126
    Epoca, 130
    Il Giorno, 132
    Il Mulino, 164
    Il Tempo, 129
    "Italy in the Mirror" newsreel, 130, 131. *See also* "Tempi Nostri" newsreel
    L'Ora, 184
    Ordini e Notizie, 30
    Paese Sera, 132
    Pianificazione Siciliana, 195
    Report from Palermo, 162, 164
    Roma, 132
    "Tempi Nostri" newsreel, 130, 131. *See also* "Italy in the Mirror" newsreel
Mediterranean, 22, 30, 70, 107, 122–123, 150, 202
Melosi, Martin, 6, 65
Mercalli, Giuseppe, 31–32, 37, 73
Mercalli scale, 31
meridionalismo, 142
Messina
    1908 earthquake, 1, 7, 10–11, 22–25, 29, 32–43, 71–76, 84, 88–99, 109, 214–215
    Amalfitani, 49
    built environment, 72. *See also* built environment
    Giudeca, 49
    rebirth of, 1, 10, 22, 29, 30, 40, 42, 87, 108
    reconstruction, 36, 40, 136
    soil, 32, 34, 36, 39, 42, 129, 159
    Strait of, 21–23
    underdevelopment of, 11, 131–133, 142, 181, 197
Mezzogiorno, 12, 129, 130, 137, 142, 158, 160–164, 167, 170–174, 181, 182, 193, 198, 200, 215
Micheli, Giuseppe, 30
Ministry
    of Agriculture, 37, 155
    of Internal Affairs, 62, 128
    of Home Affairs Taviani, 125
    of Public Works, 39, 67, 86, 88–89, 92–94, 98, 102, 104–105, 136–139, 141, 167, 183, 186–190, 193, 197, 201

for State-owned Industry (Ministero delle Partecipazioni Statali), 137, 193
Municipal Technical Bureau, 61–67, 70, 76, 85, 92, 106, 214. *See also* Ufficio Tecnico Municipale
Mussolini, Benito, 103, 104, 105, 157

N
Namazu, 3
National Institute of Geophysics and the Geological Service, 182
National Railroad Company, 93
networks
    economic, 188
    energy, 27, 85, 92, 204, 216
    transportation, 85, 97
Niceto River, 60, 62, 63, 64, 65, 75, 90, 106, 214
Nitti, Francesco Saverio, 30, 37, 154

O
obiettori di coscienza (conscientious objectors), 194, 195
Oliver-Smith, Anthony, 4
Omori, Professor, 34
Orlando, Vittorio Emanuele, 30
Orti della Mosella, 50, 52, 57, 88, 89, 91, 94, 104

P
Pancrazio De Pasquale, 134
Panfilis, Mario De, 137, 191
Parliament, 30, 37, 91, 133, 137, 152, 155, 156, 183
    communist, 134
    Italian, 152
    legislation, 37, 139, 157, 197
    protests, 137, 139, 171, 185, 194
    public appropriation, 52, 58
    regional laws, 134–135, 139
    Sicilian, 133, 138, 140, 157, 170, 172, 187–189, 193, 196, 198, 200, 202
    urban health, 54
Pasteur, Louis, 54, 75
Peloritani Mountatins, 22, 32, 58, 59, 60–61, 64, 68, 106

Pescatore, Gabriele, 200
Pizzorno, Alessandro, 134
Placanica, Augusto, 5
planning
    district plans, 170, 187, 198. *See also piano comprensoriale*
    initiatives, 139, 162
piano comprensoriale, 133–136, 140. *See also* district plans
piano di ampliamento, 52
piano di sviluppo democratico, 194
piano regolatore edilizio, 52, 92–93
Piano Territoriale di Coordinamento (PTC, territorial coordination plan), 188, 191, 195, 198
relocation, 7, 11, 23, 137, 181–182, 187–188, 191–195, 198, 204, 216–221
    permanent, 11, 188, 223
    urban, 10, 49, 50, 91–93, 135–136, 188–189, 213, 219, 223
population growth, 50, 71, 97, 99, 111, 216, 217
port renewal, 11, 67, 69, 76, 107, 110, 214
poverty
    disaster of, 128–133, 137
Prime Minister Berlusconi, 220
protests, 94, 137–139, 162–164, 167, 170, 195, 197, 216, 220
    arresting of protestors, 157, 194
    Belice, 138–139, 150, 152, 171–173, 194, 203
    biennio rosso, 152
    Fasci Siciliani, 152
    initiatives, 167, 172, 197, 216
    killing of protestors, 152, 157
    Montecitorio Square, 137, 174
    over dam, 168, 200
    outside Parliament, 139
    Palermo, 140, 194
    Rome, 138, 140, 185, 186
    sciopero alla rovescia (strike in reverse), 163
    Sicily, 165, 167
Provveditorato alle Opere Pubbliche, 183
public health, 54, 58, 65, 75, 90, 93, 106, 107, 108

Q
Quenet, Gregory, 5

R
radical redevelopment, 122, 132, 133, 142, 155, 224
rainwater
    collector, 66, 69, 96
    drainage, 11, 96, 106
    hydraulic regime, 153, 154, 159
Ranieri, Domenico, 53, 68
Reale Società Geologica (Royal Geological Society), 37
Reale Istituto d'Incoraggiamento alle Scienze di Napoli (Royal Neapolitan Institute for the Advancement of Science), 32, 34, 37
reclamation
    floodplain, 154, 157, 173
    initiatives, 157
reconstruction
    initiatives, 186
    program, 100, 102, 194, 197–198
reforestation, 11, 69, 74, 138, 154–156, 160, 165, 170
Regio Uffico Geologico (Royal Geological Bureau), 39
relief, 25, 26, 35, 123, 135, 140, 183
    aid campaign, 21, 25, 127
    donations, 21, 26, 89, 121, 183
    operations, 85, 123–131, 185, 202
    volunteers, 26, 30, 39, 85–87, 121, 127, 182
resilience, 4, 23, 85, 97
reservoir, 138, 160, 165, 166, 170, 200
    Belice River, 12, 155
    Bruca, 166
    Carboi Dam, 168, 189
    Garcia Dam, 201
    Piana degli Albanesi, 154, 155
    urban, 65
    Vajont, 134, 140, 187
Rossi-Doria, Manlio, 153
rural
    reform, 142, 150, 161, 168–169, 174, 181, 218

    South, 132
Russia, 21, 25

S
Saccà, Domenico and Roberto, 89
Saint-Just di Teulada, Edmondo, 93
Saltini, Zeno, 162
Salvemini, Gaetano, 23
Samonà, Giuseppe, 134
San Andreas Fault, 41
sanitation
    cesspools, 50, 53, 108
    framework, 75
    infrastructure, 74, 92, 97, 108, 165, 168, 204, 216, 224
    law, 63
    modernization, 84
    plan, 55, 57, 69, 70, 92, 218
    risanamento (sanitation), 8, 49–58, 65, 70, 75, 84, 214, 218
    sewage, 8, 11, 50, 66, 68–69, 184, 187
    canals, 53, 55, 66, 76, 85, 106
    system, 9, 53, 58, 65–66, 76, 94–96, 106, 163, 198
    wastewater, 66, 69, 96
    waterborne sewage system, 53, 94
Saya, Antonio Costa, 53
Sciascia, Leonardo, 185
Schirò, Borgo, 157
Schmid, Martin, 6
seismic
    hazard, 42, 73, 108, 142
    prevention, 74, 223
    risk, 22, 31, 35, 39, 41, 49, 71, 73, 74, 141, 214
    safety, 11, 73, 74, 96, 106, 108
    seismicity, 31, 34–35, 39, 40, 70, 76, 84, 107, 122–123, 214, 218, 221–223
    zone, 141
seismology, 30–35, 141
    historical, 3, 31, 123
    modern, 31, 41
Seismological Service of Chile, 41
segregation, 105, 108
Seneca, 3

settlement
    camps
        Michelopoli, 30, 39, 85, 86, 88
    dynamics, 121
    human, 4, 23, 159, 203, 216–217, 222
    hut, 11, 86, 88–91, 97, 98–109,
        183–186, 203, 213, 215
    pattern, 9, 140, 156, 189, 215–217
    provisional, 29, 72–73, 86–89, 91, 97,
        109, 111, 181–184, 215. See also
        baraccamenti
    rural, 9, 198
    temporary, 86, 88, 215
    tent camps, 39, 127–130, 138–139,
        182
Sicily
    agriculture, 89, 122, 156, 158
    Agrigento, 140
    Augusta, 172
    "backwardness," 131–132, 151–152,
        165, 198, 202
    colonizing inland, 155–156, 214
    epidemics, 55
    Gela, 172
    March for Western Sicily, 170, 190
    Milazzo, 172
    Pianificazione Siciliana (Sicilian
        Planning), 168, 186, 196
    regional government, 121, 133, 135,
        136, 138, 157
    Regione Siciliana, 133, 138, 140, 157,
        170, 172, 187–189, 193, 196, 198,
        200, 202
    separatist movement, 133
    seismic zone, 141
    Strait of, 122
Siffredi, Italo, 36
Simonini, Riccardo, 86, 87, 88
social and material effects, 121, 129, 132,
    151
social memory, 4, 73, 110
    erosion of, 71, 73, 110
socialists, 23, 60, 136, 157, 172. See also
    Fascist
Società Geografica Italiana, (Italian
    Geographical Society), 32, 37

Società degli Ingegneri e Architetti Italiani
    (Society of Italian Architects and
    Engineers), 35
socio-ecological reform, 173
socioeconomic
    conditions, 121
    development, 11, 121, 134–140, 181,
        217, 220. See also development
    engineering, 142
    growth, 129
    revolution, 182
    subdivision of the homeless, 10
socio-natural perspective, 6
Sonnino, Sidney, 151, 152, 156, 172, 199
Spadaro, Pasquale, 50, 52, 71
Steinberg, Ted, 4
subsistence garden, 122, 150, 153, 198
Superior Council of Public Works, 38, 52,
    71, 94, 155, 160, 188. See also Consiglio
    Superiore dei Lavori Pubblici

T
Tarr, Joel, 6
tectonic plates, 3, 141, 204, 222
    African, 22, 43, 122, 222
    Eurasian, 22, 43, 122, 222
Torrente
    Boccetta, 67, 68
    Portalegai, 49, 50, 66, 67, 96, 106
    Trapani, 49
    Zaera, 69
trasformazione fondiaria (rural estate
    transformation), 155
Tunisia, 122, 202
Tyrrhenian Sea, 22

U
Ufficio Tecnico Municipale, 61–67, 70,
    76, 85, 92, 106, 214. See also Municipal
    Technical Bureau
underdevelopment
    "backwardness" of the southern
        Belice Valley, 11, 129–132, 139,
        142, 152, 181, 187, 192, 197–198
    economic, 11, 132
    social, 11, 131–132

Southern, 132–133, 142, 181, 197
unions
    against *Mafiosi,* 152–153, 157, 164
    labor, 139, 153, 157, 164
    leaders, 164
Unione Edilizia, 98, 100, 102, 103, 104, 105, 109. *See also* Building Association
urban
    administration, 61, 66
    change, 10, 11, 110, 214, 224, 226
    community, 30, 39, 87
    culture, 97, 181, 189
    ecosystems, 6, 8, 64
    environments, 2, 6, 10, 12, 40, 64, 69, 75, 202, 222, 226
        historic, 111
    epidemics, 52–55, 60, 225
    expansion, 50, 52, 110, 221
    health, 53–55
    -industrial society, 29, 129, 131, 187, 191, 193, 204, 216
        network, 189
        regions, 9
    landscape, 48, 84, 104–105, 109, 213
    modernity, 11, 12, 74–75, 77, 84, 106, 108, 109–111, 131, 134
    pattern, 122, 219
    planning, 10, 49, 50, 91–93, 135–136, 188–189, 213, 219, 223. *See also* planning
    politics, 60, 103
    reform, 9, 11, 48–77, 96, 110, 214–215, 224
    renewal, 55, 75, 111, 224
    sanitation, 11, 54, 62, 93, 94. *See also* sanitation

water
    catchment area, 68–69, 75
    cycle, 11, 5354, 62, 64, 66–67, 69, 75, 107
    geography of, 74
    management, 56, 68
    supply, 27, 52–60, 75, 90, 106, 200, 214
urbanization, 1, 8–10, 12, 50, 89, 92, 102, 105, 172, 184
    as environmental transformation, 6, 222, 226
    coastal, 172
    primary, 195

V
Valencius, Conevery Bolten, 5
Vanni, Alessandro, 63, 64
Voltaire, 3

W
Walker, Charles, 5
Wilson, Tuzo, 141
Winiwarter, Verena, 6
World Bank, 158
World War I, 12, 100, 152
World War II, 11, 12, 84, 129, 131, 137, 155, 157, 173, 215, 220
    the Allies, 109
    European Recovery Plan (Marshall Plan), 157
    post-WWII development agenda, 131. *See also* development

Z
Ziegler, Arnold Bürkli-, 58, 60, 75

www.ingramcontent.com/pod-product-compliance
Lightning Source LLC
Chambersburg PA
CBHW072148100526
44589CB00015B/2135